THE
EMERALD DOORWAY

(THREE MYSTIC CRYSTALS)

100,000 years ago, Earth's poles changed one hundred and eighty degrees overnight, destroying the lands as they sank beneath exploding lava in seething ocean waves. Rising from the sea floor, entirely different continents that we live on today formed, and there was a new beginning.

IT'S ABOUT TO HAPPEN AGAIN...
unless... they finally *INTERVENE*...

THE
EMERALD DOORWAY

(THREE MYSTIC CRYSTALS)

R. SCOTT LEMRIEL

THE EMERALD DOORWAY
(Three Mystic Crystals)

Book One of The Parallel Time Trilogy

2nd Publication © April, 2019
(New Original Cover Design)

1st Published © 11-06-2015

© October 2015 - By R. Scott Lemriel
(AKA - R. Scott Rochek)

ISBN: 978-0-578-25994-9 (Hardback)
ISBN: 978-0-692-53812-8 (E-book)

© TXu 62 748
© PAu 835 230
© 07-15-2006

Names, characters, places and incidents that appear fictional are entirely based upon the author's direct experiences during many journeys spanning more than forty years exploring and recovering deliberately hidden truth along the past time-track for planet Earth, the solar system, the Milky Way Galaxy, and from journeys into parallel and higher dimension realities. Any resemblance to persons known in recorded history, anyone living today, businesses or religious establishments, events or locations are entirely coincidental.

Published by Total Spectrum Publishing
Cover Art by Michel Bohbot
Interior Formatting by Author E.M.S. & R. Scott Lemriel

Contact: www.ParallelTime.com

Published in the United States of America
(Distributed through worldwide print-on-demand facilities

CONTENTS

ACKNOWLEDGMENTS

An incredible journey went into the writing, editing, proofing and general refining of The Parallel Time Trilogy manuscripts, in order to reach the culmination of this thirty-year effort to publish *The Emerald Doorway (Three Mystic Crystals)*. This first book, and the two sequel books that comprise the trilogy adventure, are entirely based upon this author's direct experiences exploring the hidden past time track of Earth and our solar system. These books are designed in a very special way to be clear channels to assist others to recall with knowing certainty so much that has been deliberately taken from them without their consent or awareness on this currently misdirected human populated world. The negative destiny of the people of planet Earth has recently significantly changed, and in the bright new future all life on this world will no longer remain sub-consciously suppressed.

My thanks go to Temi Ol, of Temi Editing Services, for her skills applied throughout the manuscript with my focused visual contribution, culminating in finalizing the preparations to publish the first book of the hidden truth uncovering adventure.

I also want to thank the three illustration artists that I hired over the years to work directly with me to create the original character images and some scenes for the first book of *The Parallel Time Trilogy* adventure.

The first illustration artist's name is Cynthia Martin. My grateful thanks go to her. However, in trying to locate her this last month of October, 2015, I did not receive back a reply to my emails sent to the email address I found at the website of an illustration artist named Cynthia Martin – after conducting an Internet search for this name.

I cannot verify this is the same Cynthia Martin. Thirty-five years has passed since she did this work for me and I can only gratefully acknowledge the Cynthia Martin that created the two scene illustrations as a "work for hire" based upon the descriptions of the scenes within the first screenplay. That first screenplay later developed into a trilogy screenplay series and then the book trilogy based upon them. In this book you will find that one of them represents the extraterrestrial Galactic Inter-dimensional Alliance of Free Worlds flagship and two support Scout squadrons in triangular formations on approach to Earth. The other one is of Master Ra Mu standing on a black sand beach holding a transparent quartz crystal staff – a device. He is waiting for the arrival of a man (Captain Kalem Starland) and a woman (Mayleena of the Oceanan race) approaching him on flying anti-gravity discs, after having just left their disc-shaped spaceship landed further away on the background beachhead.

I also want to gratefully acknowledge illustration artist Teri Izumi, who I hired after Cynthia Martin to help me further design the original main character images with particular attention focused on creating the accurate image of the immediately likable and very unusually talented Etta from the Dren race, and several scenes.

In addition, I want to gratefully acknowledge illustration artist Josh Figueroa, who I hired a few years back to further refine Mayleena, General Faldwell, Senator Judith Cranston, Etta with his dexterous human-like five fingers and toes, and other important scenes for this first book of the trilogy.

The original logo symbol for all my work – a symbol for the ancient lost continent of Lemuria – and the logo signatures of Terri Izumi and Josh Figueroa are at the bottom of their respective illustrations. However, the Cynthia Martin I hired long ago did not sign the two scenes she created with me that are now included in this book.

My grateful thanks must also go to Author E.M.S. interior formatting services, particularly to Amy, for her diligent, patient, and beneficial advice and work designing the interior text of the book.

Respectful regards must also go to the brilliant artistry and cover design work done by Michel Bohbot at mbohbot.com for the uplifting new original book cover design created for this 2nd edition book - with my very focused consulting collaboration. In addition, the new Total Spectrum Publishing, Total Spectrum Productions, and Total Spectrum Media logos were designed, along with new business cards.

My friend, Michael Kelly in New York, went through The Seres Agenda and The Emerald Doorway manuscripts prior to the publication of both books with new original cover designs, and he found quite a few hard to see typos that three previously paid editors missed altogether. His voluntary assistance is much appreciated.

My mother in this lifetime has also been a rock of encouraging support from the day she finished reading the three manuscripts of The Parallel Time Trilogy and the first manuscript of The Seres Agenda, prior to their publication. While reading them, she discovered much about her son's extraordinary experiences while growing up that she never dreamed took place – to her great surprise. I never talked about what I was going through while growing up regarding contacts with highly evolved benevolent Master Teachers and wondrous extraterrestrial beings from far beyond Earth – many of them human, or about the numerous explorations into parallel and higher dimensional realities I went through during my entire lifetime. She only discovered what some of those experiences involved during her first reading of *The Seres Agenda* manuscript.

I would also like to thank the many Master teachers and wonderful advanced kind beings from other worlds whose paths I crossed, or vice versa, for their inspirational examples that encouraged me to go forward with revealing so many previously deliberately hidden truths. They guided me during those explorations into the depth of what is revealed in The Seres Agenda, and the intentionally suppressed history that is contained in the three books of *The Parallel Time Trilogy.*

My grateful thanks, continues to go to the omnipresent primordial, special first vibratory word or first Sound known as HU, that is behind and supporting the entire grand multidimensional creation. It was imported to planet Earth from other worlds, and quite recently, what is now known as the new consciousness liberating Ray was woven within it. This primordial sound originates from the pure - Source or Prime Creator, which is behind and supporting all that exists. The discovery of the new Ray, what is does, and how to use it has taken me many times far beyond good and evil, and the petty bobbles of this physical world. My work is now dedicated to assisting others to discover the deliberately hidden grand truths for themselves. From my direct experience, I can state there are new responsible personal freedoms awaiting the adventuresome explorers who ride this rainbow home – while they are still alive here on Earth.

CHAPTER ONE

THE SILENT OBSERVER

*H*idden somewhere in a secret parallel dimension on Earth was the beautiful secluded black sand dune beachhead of a small half-moon-shaped tropical island cove. It spread out before the loving gaze of a mysterious six-feet tall man with black curly hair and a short-cropped beard.

It's time I looked in on General Faldwell. Kalem and Etta must succeed with him or the Earth will most certainly be doomed, thought The Silent Observer, as golden light appeared around him.

Wearing a knee-length, maroon robe belted at the waist and simple sandals, he was standing upon a large sand dune. In his right hand, he held a tall transparent crystal staff crested with a symbol similar to the ancient Egyptian Ankh – an oval with a hollow center atop a cross.

The surrounding jungle plant life was a mixture of giant palm trees, prehistoric-looking ferns, and huge stalks of multicolored flowers. Large colorful birds with long, V-shaped tails, twice as long as their bodies, were circling in the sky above the cove beyond the vivid turquoise-blue ocean. Sunlight illuminated a large translucent wave as it curled to break on the beach of fine black sand, glittering like millions of diamonds in the warm midday sun.

Now, I must once again venture into their parallel dimension on this planet, the mysterious traveler silently pondered.

Beautiful warbling sounds of the ancient tropical birds calling out to each other echoed again over the water, as the mysterious man and his staff emitted more brilliant golden light, transforming his physical body into a sphere of light hovering above the black sand. Extended in ever widening concentric spherical levels, each layer was comprised of many luminous teardrop-shaped lights emanating a different color of the light spectrum. A subtle blue-violet hue softly radiating between the layers culminated in a blue-violet exterior layer, surrounded by a pale-golden aura. The core at the sphere's center pulsed white light, and the sphere darted across the dunes and plunged into the large curling crest of a wave.

Sunlight illumined the translucent swirling and churning water surrounding the light sphere as a whirling fiery vortex appeared before it, and the sound of the crashing ocean waves faded into the growing whine of powerful jet engines increasing thrust. Just as swiftly, the fiery vortex and jet engine sound receded into the distance, revealing the spinning fan-jet blades inside the far-left engine of a 747 Jumbo Jet airliner.

The blue-violet light sphere of the mysterious stranger rematerialized again, hovering a few feet above the runway to observe the 747 speeding past the control tower at Miami International Airport.

Good... good, they are aboard the jet, The Silent Observer perceived in his true spherical energy form, as the jet lifted off the runway.

The airliner climbed at a steep angle and quickly disappeared into an ominous storm cloud cover that was moving in high above the airport. The silent stranger's light sphere faded and vanished.

A short time later, the 747 jet was flying over the ocean area southeast of Florida known as the mysterious Bermuda Triangle. The even cloud cover now spread several thousand feet below the airliner in every direction, while high above the distant horizon loomed towering dome-shaped cumulus clouds. Growing louder, were the voices of a man and woman in a heated conversation just inside the first-class passenger window behind the cockpit.

"You really can't discuss an issue that way, Judith, before you know all the facts," stated a man's irritated voice.

"I'll discuss it any damn way I please," a woman shot back defiantly. "I'm a senator and I'm just as knowledgeable and bull-headed as you, Harry, when it comes to this issue."

The airliner carrying them and other diplomats from around the world was heading to a secret World Peace Summit in South America, and unforeseen events inside the cabin were about to unfold. Background voices were speaking in several foreign languages, including Chinese, while General Harry Faldwell, wearing his four-star Air Force uniform, was seated on the aisle next to Senator Judith Cranston. She was wearing an elegant, sexy dress and had on reading glasses that gave her a scholarly appearance.

"Oh, come now, Senator Cranston, you are also a diplomat," he continued, annoyed. "I've tried to remind you of that fact at least a dozen times."

She stared back at him.

Harry exhaled, relaxing his attitude, and added intimately, "Look, Judith, diplomats representing the entire world will be in South America for this meeting. World stability is at stake and you know it. The fact that Marago is a dictator now has nothing to do with it. He's already signed off on holding democratic elections in the fall, right?"

"Oh bull, the CIA and military are behind it and you know it. Besides, it will put you in line for another promotion with the President, and General Faldwell gets another star, huh? Am I right?" She winked as she poked a finger in his ribs.

Harry stood up in a huff, stuffed his unlit cigar into the corner of his mouth, and bit down. A very subtle, gradual shift in hue on everything and on everyone began to appear, but no one noticed it. The cabin decor, the clothes of the passengers, their skin, and hair were subtly changing to very different, more intense colors. As Judith looked up at Harry, her mood instantly became upbeat, and she winked again.

"You always were good for at least one engaging argument before dinner," she said with an alluring grin. "This time the drinks are on you."

Harry's face relaxed, giving in to her charms. Taking the cigar out of his mouth, he cracked a little smile and sat back down next to her. She grinned at him and looked down to continue reading her open magazine, while he leaned back in his seat and closed his eyes. He reflected on the fact that a number of years had passed since the turn into the new millennium. The horrors of the terrorist attacks that took place in many locations around the world were fading into history. Radical terrorist groups had finally been uprooted, run to ground, and no longer posed any threat. A general worldwide peace had begun, and the future looked bright. He recalled how they had finally achieved this great accomplishment during the second term of the new President, whom he had correctly advised throughout the difficult ordeal, and he grinned at the thought.

Then Harry began to visualize the meeting he and Judith had a week earlier in her office in Washington, D.C., and he smiled fondly. He mused about his fiancée's independent nature – a certain kind of natural strength she projected that was one of many reasons he fell in love with her.

CHAPTER TWO

CONTACT OVER
THE BERMUDA TRIANGLE

$\mathcal{H}$arry had also been wearing his four-star Air Force uniform that day a week ago. He stuffed an unlit cigar into the corner of his mouth. Then he walked through the open door to Senator Judith Cranston's Washington, D.C. office. He was in his mid-fifties with hazel eyes, short curly dark-brown hair, a chiseled face with a cleft chin in a square jaw, and a slight paunch. Still, he was in good shape for his age with his chest and upper arms strongly developed.

Judith was younger, in her mid-forties wearing an elegant dark-blue, knee-length business dress and white satin blouse, and he admired the way she had kept remarkably slim and shapely with wrinkle-free olive skin. She got up from the chair; flipped her long, slightly gray-streaked, black hair over her shoulders; and casually walked around to the front of the desk. She sat down on the edge, defiantly crossed her arms, and then puckered her lips.

Harry yanked the cigar from his mouth and stated confidently to his fiancée, "It doesn't matter what the press thinks."

He impatiently stared at her, but she just glared back.

"Look Judith," he continued, annoyed, "I've already told you this a dozen times. All of the United Nations Security Council members will be there, not just those with a preference for the President's point of view."

"Oh bull, Harry," she shot back. "You know Stockwell has a personal political agenda of his own. That's why he's sending you to South America."

5

Harry started to pace back and forth, then stepped closer.

"Look, Judith, what will convince you? I tell you the President's interest in the World Peace Summit is genuine, with only the best intentions for all the countries involved. I know you two don't exactly see eye to eye. Hell, I don't see eye to eye with him on most things, but the fact is I personally know he's behind this conference. He really wants it to succeed."

Judith remained silent as Harry walked right up to her.

"Come on, Senator Cranston, we need your one vote or this whole thing will be shot to hell."

Grinning, she stood up from the edge of the desk, walked around it, and sat back down in the chair. She picked up the pen from its holder, placed it on the signature line of an official-looking document lying on the desk top, eyed him sternly, and then sighed.

"Okay, Harry, but if I find out you or Stockwell has stabbed me in the back on this one, it will ruin my career! I will hold you personally responsible and call off the marriage. Do I make myself perfectly clear?"

Relieved, Harry's eyes lit up, "Of course... of course, Judith," he concurred excitedly. "Then it's settled. With full Congressional support, the President can pull this off. I'm sure of it, and you, my dear, will get reelected. In fact, I believe he will ask you to become some kind of temporary ambassador to the entire World Congress Peace Initiative when it convenes next week. You will be representing the official U.S. position on all the relevant issues. Now that's romantic, isn't it?"

Harry raised his eyebrows, but Judith returned an icy stare, raising a single eyebrow.

"You mean, don't you, that I'll be doing a lot of the negotiating work to make it happen, and somebody else will get all the credit."

He rolled his eyes, groaning, and then opened his mouth to protest, but she gave in.

"All right, damn it, don't worry. I'll do it."

Relieved, Harry grinned wide at her.

"Judith, dear, you won't regret it."

Uneasy, Judith frowned, "Yeah, yeah, yeah, famous last words."

She grabbed the pen, signed her name to the document, tossed the pen on the desk, and then grabbed the document as she stood up. She walked around to the front of the desk, sat on its edge in front of Harry, and then slapped the document on his chest.

Harry grabbed it with his left hand and reached behind her back with his right hand holding the unlit cigar. He lifted her up off the edge of the desk by the small of her back, wrapped his left arm around her, and hugged her close to his chest. Then he gave her a quick kiss and abruptly let her go.

"Alright, that makes it official," he remarked exuberantly. "The Worldwide Congress for Peace Initiative is on. I'll see ya tonight, dear."

He started to walk out of the office, while Judith walked back around her desk, but he stopped short of the door. He turned around to gaze admiringly at her as she sat back down in the chair, and then winked when she looked up.

"Did I tell you lately I love you?"

"Not in the last six months or so," she replied with a wry grin.

Harry's smile dropped.

"Has it been that long?" he asked, reflecting on their time together.

"Man, how time flies," he cheerfully stated. "Well, I'll see ya' tonight."

He swung around and walked briskly out of her office, then headed to the right down the hallway.

"Don't forget!" she yelled after him, "it's your turn to order food in tonight."

Harry did not turn around, as he gave a nonchalant wave with his right hand and continued walking along the hallway.

Judith listened briefly for an answer as she gazed through the open doorway. She rolled her eyes, smiling with a shake of her head, and then picked up the phone handset and tapped in a number.

Harry came out of his reverie of the week before and grinned wide as he opened his eyes to gaze fondly at his lovely fiancée sitting next to him, still reading the open magazine. He started to open his mouth to say something but an Asian man and woman having their own intense argument across the aisle and back a row of seats interrupted him, and he glanced over his shoulder in their direction.

Judith noticed the odd, subtle light intensifying on everything and then, with a shake of her head, brushed it off. As Harry turned back toward her, she nodded in the direction of the Asian couple.

"What do you suppose they're arguing about?" she asked quietly.

Harry briefly turned his head to glance at them again, then looked mischievously back at her and replied, "How they're gonna financially take us over one day through Hong Kong. It'll never happen, though. We monitor every move they make, and every conversation on this plane is being discreetly taped as we speak." He winked at her.

"You're too damned devious, Harry," she stated and stared, annoyed, back at him. "Do you know that?"

The color shift suddenly intensified, and ambient sounds within the plane's cabin diminished to total silence. Harry and Judith glanced around at the very odd, intense color.

"What the hell is going on?" demanded Harry.

"Look at the colors on everything," remarked Judith, concerned.

Then everyone aboard began hearing a low, fluctuating humming sound, and the intensifying colors shifted to a radiant blue aura. Judith gazed out the window and gasped upon seeing an extra-terrestrial spacecraft hovering nearby, surrounded by a transparent pale-blue light. Her eyes widened with disbelief just as a woman's piercing scream broke the ensuing breathless silence inside the passenger cabin.

In the cockpit was the rugged-faced, gray-haired, in his early fifties United States Air Force pilot, and the trim handsomely chiseled Air Force co-pilot in his mid-forties with dark curly hair and a mustache. They were staring in disbelief out the cockpit window.

"Oh, you have to be frickin' kidding," whispered the startled pilot in a southern accent to himself.

"Dan," yelled the co-pilot, "what the devil is that thing?"

"Damn it, Pete, isn't it obvious?" shot back Dan.

They were both staring at a thirty-feet-in-diameter, sleek, silver-blue disc that had three semispherical-shaped pods protruding downward from the curved bottom hull. It was flying parallel to the jet about forty-feet away. A pale-blue antigravity glow surrounding the hull of the alien craft extended to the 747, encompassing it. Sixty feet beyond the unidentified craft loomed a whirling golden energy vortex opening. They could see in the far distance through it a turquoise-blue ocean surrounding a black sandy tropical island. The landmass beyond it gradually rose to a snowcapped mountain with a graceful, iridescent waterfall cascading down its side.

The pilot flicked a switch and spoke nervously into his headset mouthpiece, "Miami Flight Control, this is flight 333. We have an emergency. Do you read us, over?" He paused and stated urgently, "Mayday… Mayday… Mayday. Come in Miami. This is flight 333. Do you read us, over?"

At the Miami International Airport control room, the radar controller, a mostly bald rotund man in his fifties, calmly responded through his headset.

"Flight 333, this is Miami Flight Control. What's your emergency, over?"

The blue light on everything in the cockpit of the 747 changed to red and the pilot and co-pilot instantly became motionless, suspended out of time; the microphone dropped in slow motion out of the pilot's hand.

The radar controller was looking at the screen on the console in front of him. His gray-haired shift supervisor, a gruff-looking man in his late fifties, was putting on his reading glasses as he stood right behind the controller to look over his shoulder at the radar screen. The illumined line of the radar beam moving around the dark screen passed over the brief flash of light indicating the 747. As the beam swept back over the dot, it vanished off the screen.

"We lost them," said the concerned controller.

"What do ya, mean, we lost them?" shot back the worried supervisor, and he rudely pushed the controller aside to touch several buttons on the console. The radar sweep showed nothing, and he shouted nervously, "How can you lose a whole damned 747?"

"How the hell should I know?" snapped the controller. "You saw what happened. It just disappeared off the screen. There is no radio, no radar, no transponder, no nothing. They're just gone."

Everyone else aboard flight 333 was also motionless, suspended out of time. Harry was standing in the aisle holding Judith's hand. She was half standing up from her seat. Like mannequins, the passengers were frozen in the acts of looking out windows, seated in the act of eating or reading, or starting to get up.

A luminous, four-inch-in-diameter sphere comprised of gold light particles appeared in the middle of the aisle behind General Faldwell. It twirled, spun, and stopped in various places as it raced up and down the aisle surveying the passengers, one by one, while chattering away in a pleasant male-sounding alien language. It appeared to notice the General, raced up to him, closely circled his head, and then stopped several inches in front of his eyes. It began bobbing back and forth as if studying his features, while more excitedly chattering away in its alien tongue.

The luminous sphere expanded until an endearing three-feet-long, pale-green salamander-like creature appeared visible within it, and then the light surrounding the creature faded away. Apparently propelled by a natural antigravity ability, he was levitating in the air with the thick root of his tail to the tapered tip colorfully illuminated like a crystal opal in bright sunlight. His eyes were deep-blue, bulbous pools with short eyelashes above them, and his mouth was a smiling crease around his long jaw that ended in flared nostrils. His arms were slightly shorter than his hind legs, but both were strongly contoured. The four fingers and thumb on his hands and five toes on his feet appeared dexterous, like a human. He transformed back into the light sphere and simply faded away.

Seated aboard the alien ship behind a semicircular control console, filled with different shapes of faceted crystal controls in many varied luminous colors, was a ruggedly handsome Caucasian man. In his late twenties, he had blue eyes and short brown hair, and he was wearing a single piece, formfitting body uniform made of a silvery-gray fabric. Two gold bands encircled the sleeves that widened slightly at the wrists. Embossed upon the garment's left chest area were three blue stars set in triangular formation above the apex of a golden pyramid, positioned right over the star cluster nucleus of a silvery galaxy.

Rectangular panels three feet wide by six feet in length surrounded the circumference of the control room walls. One panel directly opposite the console in front of the man was illuminated. He was intently observing the display of the 747 captured by the energy field his ship was emitting. The red energy beam extending out from the exterior of his ship's hull had enveloped the airliner in a transparent oval of red light. The man got up and touched a crystal control pulsing with gold light. It dimmed, shut off, and the luminous golden sphere materialized in the air next to him. It rapidly expanded in size again until the endearing salamander-like being with his glowing tail extended out behind him appeared inside it, and the light around him vanished. The creature shook its head, frowning.

"I know what you mean, Etta," remarked the man, grinning back at him. "You're right. These Earth humans will be hard to convince. Did you get good pictures of the General?"

"Quibb," ("Yes,") Etta answered excitedly in his own language.

"Excellent," remarked the pleased man. Then he cleared his throat and asked, "Now, you're certain you got the General, right?"

"Captain Kalem, mena dot pleidia meta?" ("Captain Kalem, you're not pleased with me?") replied Etta, insulted, with his hands on his hips.

"Of course, I'm pleased with you," chuckled Kalem. "Now let me see those pictures."

Kalem picked up a curved, thin, gold wire headset. Connected to each end was a small diamond-like crystal. Etta levitated toward him and tipped his head. Kalem placed the device over his head like a set of earphones, and then fitted each crystal into an ear hole. Another panel to the right of the main view screen displaying the jet airliner flashed on, revealing the interior and its occupants just as Etta had seen them.

Through his photographic memory, everything Etta saw aboard the 747-jet appeared in sequence on the view screen. Etta reached the General and stopped a few inches in front of his eyes. Although everyone's bodies were suspended motionless in the time freeze beam, they were conscious of their surroundings as their wide-open eyes freely moved, to begrudgingly following Etta's every move around the cabin. Harry's eyes expressed greater alarm while he observed Etta hovering directly in front of his face.

"Ouba tet tami, quibb?" ("That's the General, yes?") Etta cheerfully asked with a huge grin.

"It sure is," proudly answered Kalem. "My courageous friend, you can fly with me anytime with that flawless photographic memory. Now, head back through the vortex and find Master Ra Mu. Let him know successful contact was made."

Kalem touched a crystal on the control board, and a circular covering in the center of the floor behind him slid open like a camera shutter, revealing access outside the ship. Etta smiled proudly as he took off the crystal headset and laid it on the console. His tail began to glow more brightly opalescent as he circled the control room and darted down through the opening.

Etta flew out from under the hull to hover briefly beside the ship. Then he darted away again into the background sky headed toward the whirling vortex. He paused again in front of the opening, and then sped through it, headed in a downward arc toward the snowcapped mountain visible in the distance far below.

Kalem touched a crystal, and it pulsed gold light. The small luminous sphere that carried Etta to and from the 747 appeared again in the air in front of him. Then it faded away as Kalem gazed back at the airliner displayed on the view screen.

Not far away, a charcoal-colored, disc-shaped spaceship was flying over the last of the Florida Keys. The tapered edge along the front of the hull curved out wide to each side and gradually curved back inward before it arced gently back outward again to circle around the back of the hull. This gave the ship a fierce, sleek, stingray shark, wing-like appearance. Three pods protruding downward under the hull were like those on Kalem's ship, but a thin red antigravity glow enshrouded the exterior of the ship's hull.

A vertical sword superimposed over a red world was emblazoned, centered, on the top hull. Two snakes wound around the shaft up to the handle with their heads pointed toward each other and their forked tongues touching. The tip of the blade below the red world pointed to the middle of an upside-down black obsidian pyramid with its inverted apex touching the top of the star nucleus of a silvery galaxy. The ship headed out over the open ocean and then suddenly darted further out to sea. Then it slowed again and stopped to hover above the ocean waves.

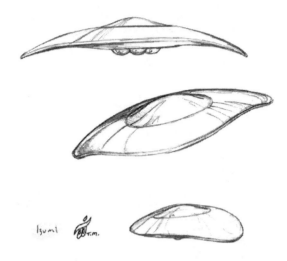

Inside the ship was a thirty-year-old slender man with high cheekbones, a long straight nose, and slightly wavy black hair that flowed down to his shoulders. He was wearing a long black cape and a gray slip-on body uniform belted at the waist by a gold buckle. Etched into the buckle, on the front of a thin gold metal band around his forehead, and on the right chest area of his body uniform was the same symbol as on the ship's hull. A rectangular-shaped green crystal two and a half inches wide, one and a half inches long, and a quarter-inch thick, hung from his neck on a sturdy gold chain.

He was sitting behind a three-sided control console that was lit up in varying colors coming from various sized domed or rectangular touch-sensitive controls, and one larger, three-inch-tall pyramid-shaped violet control to his left. An octagon view screen the width of the console extended around the curved wall across from the console. He had both hands placed palms down with splayed fingers over the tops of two semispherical guidance controls lit with a pink glow. He lifted his left hand off the control, reached into his body suit, pulled out an old leather-like parchment, shook it open, and intently read something. Then he looked up, amazed, and grabbed the green crystal hung from the gold chain around his neck.

He held it up and gazed through it, then thought, *It must be true. It must be. This has really brought me one hundred thousand years into Earth's future.*

14

The violet pyramid control lit up, blinking. He let go of the crystal, touched the control, and the view screen flashed on, revealing the 747-jet suspended in the air, surrounded by the red glow coming from a beam emanating from another spaceship. He leaned forward cocking his head to carefully observe the inter-dimensional opening spinning behind the ship holding the jet. Then he recognized the spaceship and angrily grabbed the crystal again.

Scowling, he stood up and said bitterly under his breath, "A Galactic Scout. Somehow, they must have found a way to track me here. This one I will damn to the fires of Enos myself."

A moment later, the thin red antigravity glow surrounding the hull of his ship intensified, and the ship darted in a blur across the sky to disappear over the horizon.

Kalem's ship continued to hold the 747-jet airliner, encompassed within the red energy field, below a group of towering cumulus clouds, when the charcoal-colored spaceship blurred stealthily toward his location. It slowed, then stopped to hover camouflaged just behind the tip of the tallest nearby domed cloud.

The gold energy sphere materialized again back aboard the jet inside the first-class passenger area just two feet from Harry's face. Then it

15

began to pulse with light, and Harry heard Captain Kalem's cordial voice emanating from it.

"General Faldwell, it is imperative to the survival of your country and the world that you listen very carefully to what I am about to say. I am a member of a vast organization of world systems called the Galactic Inter-dimensional Alliance of Free Worlds. We are dedicated to maintaining the freedom of beings to choose their destiny for themselves and their world. However, there are those in the galaxy who are not a part of this alliance and who are destructive in nature. Long ago, one being's very negative influence upon others resulted in the destruction of a planet similar to Earth, called Maldec. What was once a thriving inhabited world is now only an asteroid belt circling in the orbit of a planet around the sun between the planets Mars and Jupiter."

The man aboard the charcoal-colored ship chuckled to himself after overhearing Kalem's last words. Then his face contorted bitterly as he realized the voice belonged to someone he dearly hated. Calming himself, he leaned back in his chair to watch in silence as Kalem continued his message.

"Our purpose, General, is to see that a similar fate does not happen to your planet. A very special being will contact you soon. May the inner Sound and Light, the omnipresent Spirit of The Ancient One or Prime Creator, safely guide your footsteps."

Ah-h, Captain Kalem, thought the covert man with bitter long-standing resentment, *it's my destiny that you fall right into my hands so stupidly and effortlessly. May the never-to-be-seen Ancient One be with you always, indeed. What garbage!*

Back aboard the jet, the luminous communications sphere dematerialized as it spun faster and faster, and the red glow filling the interior of the passenger cabin dimmed. Then the sphere suddenly vanished, and Harry almost fell over. The time freeze beam was now gone, and the passengers scrambled over each other to look out the windows, except for Harry and Judith.

He nervously yanked the cigar from his mouth and commanded, "Judith, stay here. I'll be right back."

"Well General," she shot back, "I guess you didn't count on this with all your covert planning."

He scowled back at her.

"After all," she continued, "it's not every day that an entire 747 gets held in midair by a... flying saucer."

"Quiet, you'll start a panic," he whispered angrily, giving her a sharp, stern look.

The surprised Asian couple staring in their direction overheard them, and they started to get up from their seats. Harry suppressed his anger, forced a smile at the Asian couple, and then at the other passengers who were looking in his direction, as they began to get up from their seats.

"Everything is under control," he stated firmly, motioning with his hands for them to calm themselves. "Now come on, everyone, return to your seats."

The other passengers were reluctant to respond. He glared at them and commanded, "Everybody back to your seats and that's an order for your own safety."

The grumbling diplomats went reluctantly back to their seats and sat down. Harry frowned down at Judith, stuffed the cigar back in the corner of his mouth, and then marched up the aisle toward the cockpit.

The pilot and the co-pilot were shaking their heads and rubbing their eyes.

"What just happened to us?" asked the astonished pilot as he looked over at the co-pilot.

The co-pilot shrugged, then punched several buttons with his finger and turned several knobs. Apparently, nothing he expected to happen took place, and he threw his hands up in frustration.

"The radio is dead and the gauges are wildly fluctuating."

The pilot picked up the cabin-to-passenger intercom microphone, paused to clear his throat, clicked it on, and then with a soothing mellow voice stated, "This is your Captain. As you all have noticed, we are experiencing some kind of phenomena but we are not in any danger. Everyone, remain calm. It should clear up soon."

He clicked off the microphone, took a deep breath, blew it out with a sigh, and whispered nervously, "I hope."

Meanwhile, the man aboard the spaceship lurking behind the domed clouds was intently watching his view screen as he touched his transceiver crystal to reveal himself.

"You're mine now, Captain Kalem," he said.

Kalem instantly recognized the man's voice. He looked down to see the flashing transceiver crystal on the console and touched it; his opponent appeared on the screen.

"Sen Dar! So, the demented self-appointed ruler over all is still around, abusing life."

"Yes, it's just pitiful how you keep failing to stop me," Sen Dar replied calmly with a devious grin widening on his face.

He reached out of view below the image on Kalem's view screen, and the screen went blank. Kalem quickly touched another crystal control and the view screen revealed the sky outside his ship. A red Mazon fireball weapon had already been shot from the front hull of Sen Dar's ship, headed to cause certain destruction of the 747, and Kalem grabbed a blue octagon crystal on the console, lighting it up.

Sen Dar's ship broke through the clouds headed toward Kalem's ship, just as a blue Mazon fireball weapon shot from the hull of Kalem's ship. It blazed through the air and intercepted the red fireball just two-dozen-feet from the jet, creating a brilliant explosion of rapidly dissipating blue and red-light particles. Sen Dar blasted another red fireball through the dissipating energy toward Kalem's ship.

Kalem saw the second fireball on his view screen too late and slammed both fists on the console, then braced himself for the impact.

"I should have known," he mumbled angrily, instinctively raising a forearm to shield his impending doom.

The fireball was a few feet from the ship's hull when a blue fireball flashed down from the sky to intercept it. The two Mazon weapons exploded together in a blinding flash of searing, disintegrating red and blue molecules. Kalem's ship shook violently from side to side before it righted itself.

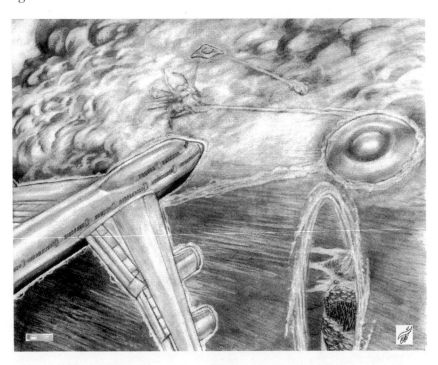

The rocking ship threw Kalem to the floor, and he reached up, grabbed the console, and quickly stood back up.

Two Galactic Interceptors identical to Kalem's ship appeared high in the sky speeding down toward the battle. One after the other, the ships made curved ninety-degree turns as they passed down in front of Kalem's ship. They darted into the distant sky firing several rounds of blue fireball weapons at Sen Dar's retreating ship, before it vanished over the horizon.

On his view screen, Sen Dar could see the two rapidly approaching fireballs that were about to hit his ship, and two Galactic Scout fighters speeding toward him. He jammed his hands into the palm controls, and his view screen revealed his ship was now retreating from the area at greatly increased speed. A moment later, the fireballs exploded behind and to one side of the ship's hull, severely rocking it. Sen Dar steadied himself and then touched his transceiver crystal.

"One day, Captain, your reinforcements won't be there to save you," he proclaimed venomously.

Kalem watched the two Galactic Scout fighters as they disappeared over the distant horizon high above the ocean in hot pursuit of Sen Dar.

Then he touched his transceiver and defiantly shot back, "Look for me around every corner, Sen Dar. You will find me right behind you."

A disc of light blurred from the distant sky and slowed into visibility, revealing Sen Dar's ship. Then it darted across the horizon and vanished. One after the other, the two Galactic Scouts sped in a blur across the sky in hot pursuit.

General Faldwell opened the cockpit door of the 747 and bumped his head on the doorframe. Scowling, he rubbed the spot; his cigar remained tightly tucked into the corner of his mouth as he walked inside and slammed the door.

Then he grabbed the cigar and barked out, "Dan, what the devil is happening up here?"

"Look for yourself, General," replied the nervous pilot. "First, we were captured by that alien ship out there. Then another one tried to destroy it, and then two more chased that one away. It looks like we got caught in the middle of someone else's argument."

Harry stooped forward between the pilot and co-pilot and looked out the cockpit window. He could see the thin layer of blue light surrounding the hull of the spaceship and the open vortex slowly whirling in the distant background. He could see through it into another Earth-like reality revealing a turquoise-blue ocean that reached to the horizon as it curved around a landmass along an intriguing black sand tropical beach. Further inland, a waterfall cascaded several thousand feet down the side of a giant snowcapped mountain. The falling water disappeared far below behind a fir-type forest that surrounded the backside of a clear domed structure at the base of the mountain.

Hmm, he thought, placing a hand to his chin, and then he stated calmly, "Well, it looks like the danger has now passed."

"Did you see what's out there, sir?" asked Dan, dumbfounded. "We could have been killed."

"Of course, I did," shot back Harry.

Pete shook his head and sighed as he looked up at the General and hesitantly stated, "They'll never believe this one."

Harry stood straight up as he looked down at both of them with a sly grin.

"Now you two didn't see anything, did you?"

"But, General," blurted out Dan in protest, while Harry continued to stare down at him. Then he reluctantly concurred, "No, sir. I guess I didn't see a damn thing."

Harry turned his stern gaze at Pete who shook his head. "No, sir," he finally replied, "I guess I didn't see anything either."

Harry patted them both on the shoulder with smug confidence. Then he stuck the cigar back into the corner of his mouth, turned sharply around, opened the cockpit door, and walked out, slamming the door behind him.

"Damn it! I don't know which is more unbelievable, that alien spaceship out there," said Dan with a nod of his head toward the cockpit window, or him!"

He pointed his head and thumb toward the cockpit door.

"I know damn well which one gets my vote," replied Pete as he gazed out the cockpit window, "and it isn't the hell out there."

Kalem's ship keeping pace beside the 747 began to veer away, increasing speed in a curved path back toward the vortex.

The spinning opening loomed huge in the sky before his approaching ship, which stopped to hover in front of it. A moment passed, and the ship pulsed gold light through the pale-blue aura surrounding the hull. Then it slowly moved through the whirling opening to enter the mysterious parallel dimension on Earth. The ship stopped a short distance on the other side and pulsed gold light again. Then it darted in a long arc down toward the snow-covered mountain. The vortex opening whirled closed and slowly vanished, leaving a clear blue sky high above the mysterious Bermuda Triangle area of the Atlantic Ocean.

Meanwhile, Sen Dar's ship was flying just offshore at high speed down the west coast of Central America. It continued down the coast of South America to Peru where it stopped briefly to hover by the rugged mountainous coastline. The light around the hull flashed and the ship darted away from the ocean toward the mountains in the distance. It swiftly disappeared over their glistening tops just as the two pursuing Galactic Scout Interceptors rapidly approached the same coastline. They slowed and stopped to hover a moment before light flashed from their hulls and they too darted away to disappear over the tops of the same snowcapped mountains.

Moments later, Sen Dar's ship broke through high clouds above a tropical valley. It continued its flight into the distance toward the rim of an extinct volcano that extended thousands of feet above the thick jungle growth.

Sen Dar was sitting behind the control console gazing at the view screen that was displaying a subterranean geographical map of the volcano. The three volcanic tunnels revealed on it extended many miles away from the bottom of the volcanic shaft in three directions beneath the jungle floor.

Ah-h, he thought with a widening grin, ***this will work. They can't detect me in there.***

Sen Dar's ship was soon hovering above the massive throat of the extinct volcano. The ship spiraled downward to quickly disappear in the deepening darkness.

The ship descended to the bottom of the shaft, made a sharp ninety-degree turn, and continued flying into the far-left tunnel. In size comparison, the six-hundred-foot-diameter opening made his thirty-foot-wide ship look like a dime next to a dinner plate. The tunnel continuing into the distance many miles was curiously illumined by an iridescent violet glow along its entire length, coming from a cool chemical light emanating from a rare moss that covered the volcanic rock walls.

Back on the surface, the two Galactic Scouts broke through the high clouds above the same volcanic valley and sped down toward the rim of the volcano.

Aboard one of the ships was a handsome, clean-shaven man in his late twenties with dark-brown skin and brown eyes. He was wearing a Lieutenant's uniform. It was identical to the one worn by Captain Kalem, except a single gold band surrounded the cuff of each sleeve instead of two. He was gazing at the view screen observing the volcano centered in the tropical valley floor when he noticed the transceiver crystal begin to blink and he touched it.

The voice of the second very frustrated pilot came through the transceiver, "Lieutenant Moreau, I think we lost him."

"My sensors are not picking anything up either," replied Moreau.

He looked away thoughtfully, and a new realization opened his eyes wide; he grinned before he touched the transceiver crystal.

"Mordoc, wait and hold your position," he commanded. "I'll try the deep rock sensor. Sen Dar might just be hiding behind something, or like the serpent he is, under something."

Moreau touched a green crystal control and a small view screen swung upward from under the control console. It illuminated, showing the three volcanic tunnels running in different directions from the bottom of the throat of the volcano and a black dot moving down one of them. Moreau reached to touch the transceiver crystal again.

"Hmm, damn clever of him. I'll hand him that," he exclaimed under his breath as he touched the transceiver crystal. "We have him. His ship is moving down one of the subterranean volcanic chambers."

A moment later, his Scout Interceptor spiraled downward into the volcano's shaft, followed close behind by the support fighter.

Both ships made ninety-degree turns at the bottom of the shaft and darted into the distance of the far-left tunnel. The trailing Scout moved up to fly parallel alongside the lead ship as they receded further into the tunnel.

"Lieutenant, my Mazon cannons are locked on his ship," Mordoc shouted impatiently through Moreau's transceiver.

"I see him," replied Moreau with a determined scowl. "In another second we'll have him in a cross-fire. Wait for my signal. We must be certain to finish him this time."

The violet control on Sen Dar's control console began to blink, and he touched it. The view screen lit up, revealing the two Galactic Scouts several thousand yards behind his ship rapidly gaining as they moved wide apart, preparing to fire.

"How did they find me?" he grumbled nervously to himself.

The two Galactic ships rapidly closed the gap with an increased jump in speed, just as Sen Dar's ship began to speed up, veering right and left. Both Galactic ships instantly matched the maneuver and started to gain, closing the distance. Two bright flashes from the hull of Sen Dar's ship sent two red Mazon fireballs in quick succession toward the Galactic pursuers. Both ships darted sideways to avoid them. A moment later, the fireballs exploded a considerable distance behind them against the tunnel wall, blasting volcanic rock and particles of radiant blue-violet moss out into the tunnel. Like a fine powder, the glittering particles slowly drifted to the cavern floor.

Lieutenant Moreau patiently observed Sen Dar's ship on his view screen as it continued down the tunnel veering left, then right and left again, but he remained intensely focused as he touched the transceiver.

"Wait... wait," he commanded and then yelled, "Fire!"

The two Galactic Scouts moved wide apart while they closed the gap to Sen Dar's ship just as all three ships approached an overhanging cliff ledge jutting out from the right side of the volcanic tunnel wall. The Galactic pursuers simultaneously emitted a flash of light from their hulls, firing their blue fireball weapons. Sen Dar's ship veered to the left to avoid one fireball, but the second fireball hit one of the three pods protruding downward from the ship's hull, creating a brilliant rainbow-colored particle explosion. The disintegrated pod shell began shorting out, sending electrical lightning bolts over the entire bottom of the hull between the gaping hole and the two remaining pods. Only a few broken quartz crystal spires, out of a dozen, remained pointing downward from the ship's hull where the shell covering the pod had been. The ship spiraled up toward the top of the cavern, wobbled, then tilted downward before it began to fall slowly in an arc toward the extended flat cliff ledge far below, gradually picking up speed.

Inside Sen Dar's ship, the control room was slanted downward and being badly shaken. Sen Dar struggled to hold onto the control console with both hands.

No-o, it's not possible, he defiantly thought, scowled, and then whispered, "I must escape!"

Part of the ship's hull suddenly exploded outward leaving a twisted gaping hole, and Sen Dar was knocked to the floor. He jumped up, reached into his shirt, and pulled out the emerald crystal that hung from its gold chain. He could see his ship was falling at an alarming rate as he watched it rapidly drop past the cavern wall through the hole. Sweating, he closed his eyes, concentrated hard, and mumbled something unintelligible under his breath. The crystal around his neck glowed bright emerald light through his clenched fingers.

He opened his eyes and glanced at his view screen to see that his ship was almost at impact with the cliff ledge. Terrified, he closed his eyes tightly again and continued to mumble frantically under his breath. The crystal emanated silver-gold light that instantly spread over his entire body to transform it into a foot-wide blue-violet energy sphere, comprised of layers of teardrop-shaped lights. They extended from a bright white core through the rainbow of colors to a blue-violet exterior with part of the surface obscured by several small black splotches.

Instantly, a spiral of starlight manifested a foot in front of Sen Dar's inner self, and then it began to whirl like a galaxy. It opened into a spiraling inter-dimensional doorway made of gold and silver light particles extending into a misty violet void. His inner self darted through the whirling opening and disappeared in the violet mist. The vortex spiraled closed and vanished, just as the control room burst into flames.

The Galactic Interceptors were hovering wide in the center of the cavern high above the cliff when Sen Dar's ship hit the flat cliff ledge and exploded, sending bits of metal and boulders out into the cavern. The exploding debris slowly cleared, revealing his ship smashed into the ledge at a sharp slant with half the hull crushed in. A thin trail of blue smoke was curling upward out of a large gaping hole in the topside of the hull.

Moreau grimaced as he touched the transceiver crystal again and proclaimed, "We finally finished off that monster!"

"No one ever deserved it more," Mordoc responded bitterly from the other ship.

"Let's head back to the flagship and inform the Admiral," continued Moreau. "A recovery team can be sent back here to retrieve the body, but it won't be much consolation after all the murdering he's done."

A short while later, the two Galactic Scouts flew back up out of the extinct volcano and stopped to hover a hundred feet above the rim. The luminous hulls of both ships pulsed brighter and they darted upward in twin high arcs, punching two holes in the clouds, sucking spiraling mists upward into the openings behind them.

CHAPTER THREE

THE MYSTERIOUS RA MU IN WASHINGTON, D.C.

*A*nother week passed after the encounter above the Bermuda Triangle, and it was the middle of the night in the suburbs of Washington, D.C. The clear starlit sky and a soft full moon glow radiated down over the city as a shooting star darted across the heavens. A trail of moonlight streamed through a particular open window to gently fall across the sleeping bodies of General Harry Faldwell and Senator Judith Cranston.

They were lying in a king-sized bed with tall, carved corner posts and a headboard made of polished cherry wood. A square nightstand and lamp were at each side of the bed, and a red touch-tone phone was on the nightstand next to Harry. Hanging on the opposite wall from the headboard were three signed pictures: one by current President Sam Stockwell, and two by past presidents. In each picture, General Harry Faldwell was shaking hands with the presidents in different settings and situations.

Harry was snoring, lying on his back furthest from the window, and Judith was sleeping peacefully next to him. Judith stirred and turned on her left side toward the window, just as a little blue star flashed into visibility four feet above the end of the bed. It brightened and expanded, softly illuminating the entire room. A deep humming sound and the consistent high single note of a flute faintly playing a hauntingly beautiful melody from far away began and gradually grew louder.

Harry stirred awake and saw the blue light illuminating the room. He backed up against the headboard and blinked several times, then rubbed his eyes. Judith awakened, turned over, and stared blank-faced into the light. She fainted back on the bed and immediately fell into a deep, peaceful sleep as a gentle smile spread across her face.

Harry continued to stare, amazed at the light as it transformed into a blue-violet globe three feet across. He could see the sphere was made of teardrop-shaped lights built in layers of different colors: from a white core through successive pastel rainbow colors to a blue-violet exterior. However, unlike the light sphere of Sen Dar's inner-self, this sphere had no black splotches on its surface, and a subtle blue-violet energy appeared to be radiating out from the core through the various layers to the surface, surrounded by a faint golden aura. The sphere silently whirled clockwise gradually forming into a man.

Mesmerized, Harry swallowed hard, shook his head, and nervously whispered, "What the hell? I'm dreaming."

He rubbed his eyes and shook his head again, then gazed more intently at the man. His eyes opened wider as the full realization that, in fact, he was not dreaming started to sink in.

Harry grabbed the sheet, pulled it up around his shoulders, and stuttered, "Oh d-d-dingbats f-from hell!"

The six-feet-tall man standing before him was strong of limb wearing a maroon robe with a hood pulled over his head that covered most of his facial features, except for his short-bearded chin. A simple rope that tied off the robe at his side was dangling further down several feet. The man pulled the hood back, revealing his square forehead, short cropped, curly black hair and beard, swarthy dark-brown skin, and dark-brown eyes set with sparkling black pupils of mystery.

One week earlier, this same man was standing on a hidden black sand dune beach in a parallel dimension on Earth when he had transformed into a sphere of light that darted into a crashing ocean wave, and then reappeared above a runway to silently witness the 747-jet airliner as it took off from the Miami International Airport. The man was holding at arm's length the same six-foot-tall transparent quartz crystal staff crowned with the Egyptian Ankh symbol for eternal life. Both the staff and the man were glowing with a radiant blue aura that illuminated the bedroom. He began to speak with a deep, mellow, kindly voice as the humming sound and flute swiftly diminished to the far background.

"General Faldwell, if you wish to know the reason you were contacted by the spaceship over the Bermuda Triangle, you must meet with Kalem Summerhill at the Guardian's Research Foundation based in Northern California in the county of Marin. Please arrange to be there by noon, the day after tomorrow, before the group leaves for Mt Shasta in the northern part of the state. They are engaged in a project you will personally find most interesting and enlightening."

"Who-who are you," stuttered Harry, "and huh... how did you get in my room?"

"I am referred to as Master Ra Mu," the man replied calmly with the same friendly tone. "I belong to a very ancient order in this universe called the Guardian Adepts of The Ancient One. My benevolent order, secretly stationed on Earth and on many other world systems, has been in existence for ages beyond the imagination of humankind. We wish your country and the entire planet Earth goodwill. Therefore, we do not normally interfere with the freewill choice of the people on any planet unless there is an emergency. However, it is imperative that you contact Kalem Summerhill if you value the continued existence of Earth and its people. As for how I came to be here... I will leave in the same way."

The staff glowed more brightly until it turned into a brilliant golden light that blotted out details in the room. The deep humming and the beautiful melody intensified once again. Harry put his arms up to shield his eyes from the blinding light, just as Master Ra Mu dissolved into whirling particles of energy, that quickly formed back into the blue-violet sphere. The sphere diminished back into the small brilliant blue star, faded with the diminishing sounds, and then vanished.

Moonlight was still streaming through the open window into the room across from Harry and Judith as he jumped out of bed and thrashed about with his hands in the air where Master Ra Mu had been standing. Then he walked briskly over to the window in time to see another brilliant shooting star dart across the sky over the city. He hurried back, sat on the bed, picked up the red phone handset and was about to press several numbers when he heard Ra Mu's voice again coming from far away, as if from deep within a cavern.

Remember, there is no need to fear, stated his firm, benevolent voice. *The Sound and Light you perceive is actually the omnipresent power or the living Spirit presence of The Ancient One – the source of life within us that supports all that exists.*

As the faint Spirit Sound of humming and the flute melody faded completely away again, Harry put down the phone. He jumped up off the bed and ran into the bathroom where he turned on the light, and then gazed with wonder at his reflection in the mirror. He splashed cold water on his face, and then gazed more closely into the mirror as water droplets fell from his chin.

"Incredible," he whispered, "Damned incredible!"

He quickly dried his face, shut off the water, and then ran back into the bedroom. He sat carefully back down on the bed next to Judith, who was still out cold with a peaceful smile on her face. Then he picked up the phone handset and touched three numbers.

"Mr. President, this is General Faldwell," he stated and then interrupted, "I know, I know it's late but this is very likely the most important phone call you will ever receive."

CHAPTER FOUR

THE HIDDEN DOORWAY
OF MT SHASTA

*I*t was a crisp sunny day at high noon on the backside of the phenomenal Mt Shasta in northern California, but an ominous storm front was beginning to move in from the west and one large doughnut-shaped cloud surrounded the mountain summit. Two feet of snow was on the ground in the thickly forested area under the feet of twelve individuals wearing a Guardian's Research Foundation patch on their Air Force type sub-arctic parkas. They were trudging across the snow-laden meadow toward the gentle slope of a hill near the mountain's base.

With their hoods thrown back upon their shoulders, Harry and a strikingly beautiful woman in her late twenties with long brunette hair were walking about twenty feet ahead of the rest of the group. A hundred feet further away from them at the top of the incline was a one-hundred-thirty-feet-tall by one-hundred-fifty-feet-wide gray flat rock wall.

"Carine, I want to know where we're going before I take another step," Harry said apprehensively. "Who are these whatever-they-are anyway? Where do they come from?"

Carine was smiling patiently at him.

"You will have all your answers very soon, General, I promise," she answered with a lovely calming voice.

Carine's sparkling personality and radiant smile were uplifting Harry as he stood next to her. She looked directly into his eyes, catching him off guard, and he smiled nervously back at her. She pulled from her parka a small silver metal device, four inches long and three inches wide.

29

Then she touched the tips of three of the five crystal controls on its top with her forefinger. The crystals pulsed repetitively with light in order from blue, to green, and to red. Growing distrustful, Harry became angry and he fumed at her.

"Damn it, that does it! I want answers now, woman. Otherwise, I'm walking away from this…"

A deep wavering humming sound interrupted him, and his eyes widened as his mouth hung open. He was staring nervously past Carine as she turned around confidently in the sound's direction. A pale-blue light a few feet across had appeared on the center of the flat gray rock wall. As it grew steadily in size, it appeared like a whirling galaxy that intensified and expanded to fifty feet across. It flashed two brilliant strobe-like lights like expanding doughnut-shaped beams of energy across the valley, simultaneously accompanied by two quick sonic booms. Harry ducked, thinking the circles of light would hit him as they passed a dozen feet over his head. Carine was standing tall by his side, unmoved by the phenomena.

Like an opening camera shutter, an illuminated cave appeared in the center of the whirling starlight on the wall, and Harry's momentary fright became nervous irritation.

"Carine, what are you doing?"

"Trust me, General," she replied. "Kalem Summerhill is coming here to take you the rest of the way."

Carine raised her hand and pointed her hand-held device toward the huge cloud surrounding the summit of the mountain. She touched the other two crystals on its top, one violet and the other gold. In one quick pulse, a green laser beam shot from the end of the device up into the cloud.

Moments later in space, a single Galactic Scout Interceptor, radiating a thin blue aura, flew into view and stopped to hover ten thousand miles above the North and South American continents. The full moon was slowly coming into prominence around the left side of the planet beyond it, as fourteen other Scout Interceptors appeared in succession and maneuvered into position to create a triangular formation behind their lead Scout ship. Another group of fifteen Galactic Scouts flying in triangular formation moved into a parallel position several thousand yards to the left of the lead group.

A massive pale-blue light growing brighter and trailing behind them, was emanating a subtle, very low frequency, oscillating humming sound. Then a massive mother ship appeared. A wide rectangular launch bay, positioned on the upper curved surface of the front end of the ship, had a clear observation dome one hundred feet across positioned just above and behind it. City-sized crystalline structures built next to the observation dome gradually increased in height toward the oval central section of the ship. Thousands of human occupants appeared tiny in comparison to their surroundings as they moved within the huge observation dome or stopped to gaze through the many windows in the bridge towers that spiraled higher toward the ship's missive middle section. The oval ship, over a mile in length, had a second observation dome and launch bay positioned on the other end of the hull. A thin pale-blue luminosity completely enshrouding the huge ship, propelled by an antigravity propulsion system.

The two triangular formations of Scout escort ships receded into the distance ahead of their parent vessel until they appeared like two tiny specks.

The crystal-clear, blue water-covered jewel of planet Earth loomed ever closer to the Scout squadrons continuing their flight ahead of the mother ship as it stopped to assume an Earth orbit high over the North American continent. A moment later, the two formations of Galactic Scout Interceptors began pulsing gradually intensifying blue light, flashed a bright gold light, and darted at high velocity down into Earth's atmosphere.

The lead Scout ship broke away from its squadron formation, just before they entered the upper atmosphere, headed in a long downward arc through the cloud cover over the northwestern United States. The remaining fourteen ships and the second Scout squadron broke formation and headed in many different directions toward unknown destinations somewhere around the planet's surface.

Aboard the lead Scout ship, Captain Kalem was wearing the same Air Force type sub-arctic parka that the Guardian's Research Foundation members were wearing. At that moment, they were on the ground far below walking up the gentle sloping hill on the backside of Mt Shasta, while he was leaning over the flight control console with his hands placed, palms down, into matching palm impressions set within glowing rose-quartz controls. He touched the transceiver communications crystal with his forefinger.

"This is Captain Kalem. Squadron pilots, listen well," he began. "As each of you know, Sen Dar's body was not found with his wrecked ship when the recovery team inspected it. He is still out there somewhere. Remember to scan your preset coordinates thoroughly, and thanks to what Lieutenant Moreau discovered you had better look under ground as well. Sen Dar hides his ship inside volcanic caverns or caves."

"What do you want us to do with the lunatic if we find him, may I ask?" inquired Lieutenant Moreau through the transceiver. "I sure know what I want to do with him."

"Contact me immediately and that's an order, Lieutenant," commanded Kalem, ignoring Moreau's remark. "If enough of you are near his location, get him in a magnetic blanket. Otherwise, shoot first or you will be dead pilots."

"By the way," inquired Moreau, "since you're headed to the hidden Lemuria in a parallel dimension on Earth, bring me back one of those lovable sand demons," and he laughed.

"Very funny, Moreau," shot back Kalem, not amused. "You wouldn't be laughing if a Sand Daringe crushed your ship, and then added you as a tasty addition to its morning meal."

"Just joking, Captain," returned Moreau, holding back laughter. "Have a good trip."

"All of you, listen up," commanded Kalem. "We want to capture Sen Dar, if possible, but your first priority is to stay alive. See you all on the return trip, and good hunting."

Kalem touched another crystal control, lighting up his view screen, and he observed his ship flying down through the clouds. It broke through them a moment later, revealing a wide panoramic view of Mt Shasta with its summit sticking proudly up above the surrounding cloud. Far below, the mountain's huge base extended outward in every direction.

Kalem's ship made a high-speed ninety-degree turn and spiraled down through the cloud toward the backside of the mountain. It broke through the cloud below the summit and slowed until it stopped to hover high above the heads of the twelve Guardian Research Foundation members. They were now standing in a semicircle near the tunnel opening in the flat gray rock wall.

The whirling galaxy-like light surrounding it was clearly visible on Kalem's view screen as his ship hovered to land in the center of the semicircle formed by the Guardians.

The twelve researchers silently observed the ship hovering above the snow as three metal legs, with upturned pods on the end of each one, projected down from under the hull. The ship touched down just as it began to lightly snow across the lushly forested valley floor, coming from the clouds that were rapidly moving in from the west. The antimagnetic hum shut off, and the pulsing blue light surrounding the ship's hull dimmed and went out.

Captain Kalem was wearing his parka when he appeared a moment later from underneath the center of the ship, levitating on a blue metallic disc two-and-a-half-feet across and one-inch-thick. He cleared the bottom of the ship and stood upright with his feet firmly planted upon the disc, held safely to it by an invisible antigravity force field. Except for his feet, he was able to freely move his legs, upper torso, and arms as he wished, while he flew the disc a foot above the snow to within a few feet of Carine and General Faldwell. The other ten Guardian Research Foundation members remained standing ten feet behind them in the semicircle that curved halfway around the circumference of the ship's hull.

Kalem's disc settled to the ground and landed on a one-inch-wide metal outer ring that dropped down about four inches from the disc's perimeter. As he stepped off the disc, it instantly appeared as shiny silver metal with esoteric symbols etched on its surface. The inner disc then dropped to the snow and rejoined with the outer ring, bonding itself together again into one solid disc with no apparent seam. Kalem extended his hand to greet General Faldwell, but Harry did not move.

"I'm Kalem Summerhill, General Faldwell," Kalem cordially stated. "I'll be your guide for the rest of the journey."

Harry dubiously looked at Kalem's hand, and then nervously asked, "Who are you people? What journey?"

Kalem withdrew his hand, smiling warmly instead, and replied, "Like you, General, we are adventurers. We will be traveling to an ancient land called Lemuria, which means motherland. It is located in a parallel dimension on Earth that vibrates at a slightly higher molecular time rate than we do here by Mt Shasta. I can explain more about this on the way."

Kalem extended his hand toward Harry again, and this time Harry cautiously reached out and shook it. Then Kalem turned away from Harry and intimately embraced Carine. As they parted, he gazed affectionately into her eyes.

"Thank you, Carine, for guiding General Faldwell here."

"It was my pleasure," she replied with a slight nod and a smile.

She blushed as she gazed back into his eyes. Then she turned away from him to smile at Harry, and Kalem waved his arm toward the blue metallic disc resting nearby upon the snow.

"Please step on the Personal Gravitic Transport Disc behind me, General," encouraged Kalem with a grin. "You can't fall off once you're gravitationally grounded to it. Trust me, and we'll be on our way."

Harry reluctantly stepped on the disc behind Kalem and placed a hand on his shoulder. Carine stepped on next to Harry and put an arm around his waist. Then the disc lit up and slowly hovered several feet above the snow.

Harry realized what was about to happen as he dropped his hand from Kalem's shoulder and looked nervously at Carine.

"You… you're," he started to say, motioning his head upward, "from out there, aren't ya', just like Mr. Summerhill?"

Grinning back, Carine answered, "Yes, General, as a matter of fact, we are both," and she nodded upward, "from out there."

Harry shook his head and added, "I had a hunch you would be saying that sooner or later."

To steady himself, Harry placed both hands on Kalem's shoulders, while Kalem flew the disc several feet above the ground. They crouched down as the disc flew underneath the ship and slowly up through a round opening in the center of the bottom of the ship's hull between the three semispherical pods. Then it began to snow heavily.

Moments later, the ship lit up pulsing with blue light and emitting the familiar low frequency humming sound. It flew up and over the remaining Guardian Research Foundation members. With detached calm, they watched the ship as it flew slowly over to the cave opening where it paused briefly before it flew inside. The galaxy of light surrounding the opening spiraled inward to a pinpoint and vanished. Two more blinding strobe-like lights then flashed across the valley, accompanied by several more echoing sonic booms, leaving the flat gray rock wall once again exactly as it had been.

The ten remaining Guardian Research Foundation members stood in the semicircle with only their chins sticking out a little past the hoods covering their heads, keeping their identities safely anonymous. They all gazed at the rock wall once more, then turned around in unison and walked away. They gradually disappeared within the falling snowflakes until only a curtain of white remained.

Aboard ship, General Faldwell and Carine were standing behind Kalem, who was sitting in front of the control console. Kalem had his hands depressed into the guidance palm controls, and Harry stepped a few feet closer to him.

"Where, exactly, did you say you were taking me?" asked Harry suspiciously.

Kalem turned his head around and smiled at the General, then gazed back at the view screen.

"We're enroute to meet Ra Mu, one of the great Masters of wisdom in this universe," he answered. "I'm certain he will answer all your questions to your complete satisfaction." Kalem glanced down at a blinking crystal on the console and added, "Good, we are approaching the landing coordinates."

Harry recalled something with growing enthusiasm, and he said, "This Ra Mu is the one that appeared in my bedroom back in Washington."

"I think you will find that Master Ra Mu has many talents, General," Carine confirmed mysteriously.

"Carine, please show General Faldwell how to travel on a personal gravitic transport," requested Kalem.

She touched her finger on the wall panel behind them and a rack opened downward holding four transport discs. As she slid one out, Kalem passed a hand over a blue crystal, and the panels surrounding the entire circumference of the ship became transparent like clear windows, leaving an unobstructed three-hundred-and-sixty-degree view outside.

The ship was actually traveling down a transparent pastel-blue glass-like tube that ran down the length of the mountain cavern. Harry was speechless with his mouth wide open, in awe of the unreal feeling of seeing his surroundings whizzing by all around him. He gazed intently to the right through the large transport tube wall through which Kalem's ship was flying and noticed a smaller tube running parallel to it. A double-ended transport car (similar in appearance to a double terminated quartz crystal) with two pale-blue-skinned and pointed-eared humanoid occupants, came into view speeding through the smaller tube headed in the same direction as Kalem's ship. Each end of the crystal car was constantly changing color from blue, to green, and to red every few seconds. The car shot past Kalem's ship and veered away through a gradual elbow curve of the smaller tube. It increased its speed and disappeared down the tube's length that led somewhere deep inside the mountain's interior. Harry was perplexed.

"What the hell was that thing?" he finally blurted out.

"We call them gravitic suspension transports," replied Kalem. "They travel through sealed vacuum tubes that run under the planet's mantle to connect various secret locations on Earth with the city we are approaching." He paused to smile at Harry, then added, "Relax, General. You are perfectly safe. I promise everything will become clear to you soon."

As the Scout ship sped toward the open end of the tube that filled with bright golden sunlight pouring down into it from the surrounding larger cavernous opening, the transparent panels surrounding the hull turned back into their solid appearance. The ship faded from sight as it passed into the bright daylight.

Kalem's ship was now flying out of the mountainside's opening into a special parallel time dimension on Earth: a reality vibrating at a slightly faster molecular time rate, and a highly secret well-protected place. To the right, far below the ship, was a roaring waterfall that dropped several thousand feet to disappear in the forest trees behind a huge clear domed city built at the mountain's base. A smaller sealed clear transport tube that exited the mountain below the larger cavern opening continued down the mountainside until it too disappeared within the forest trees surrounding the backside of the domed city.

Within the domed city, three gold-crowned and quartz-tipped white alabaster pyramids in triangular formation towered above the city center surrounding a much smaller white domed building.

Four spiral minaret-like golden towers positioned at four equidistant locations towered above the smaller dome. The quartz tips of the three giant pyramids cast rainbow halos upward several dozen feet beyond the top of the clear dome. Far below, a dozen transport tubes snaked along the ground in various directions to connect together many smaller domed buildings throughout the city.

As they continued out into the countryside, they passed by several lakes and many white domed dwellings surrounded by well-landscaped acreage. A small mountain range with waterfalls curved around the countryside along the far backside of the huge transparent dome.

On the distant horizon, a breathtaking black sand beach curved like a huge half-moon around a tropical shoreline. Farther out to sea, tiny flashes of sunlight were sparkling like millions of diamonds off the tops of turquoise-blue ocean waves.

CHAPTER FIVE

EARTH'S SECRET
PARALLEL TIME

*A*ppearing as he did when he had materialized in General Faldwell's bedroom, Master Ra Mu was casually walking along a prehistoric-looking black sand beach that curved in a mile-wide half-moon shape around a small bay. Sunlight flashing off the penetrating mysterious pools of his eyes was a stark contrast to his simple maroon robe. A radiant vitality from an inner strength emanated through him, while he walked slowly along the black sand carrying the quartz crystal Master Staff of The Ancient One. Each time he lifted the staff to take another step, sunlight passing through its crystalline surface flashed subtle rainbow colors along its entire length and off the top and sides of the Ankh symbol that topped it.

In the background twenty yards further away, the ocean swelled and formed a long beautifully curled wave. A thousand sparkles of golden light danced off the crest of the wave as it curled in a smooth roll and crashed along the beach just as Ra Mu came to a stop. The quartz in the tiny black grains of sand were sparkling like a field of diamonds on black velvet as he looked down the beach to the end of the cove, where twin one-thousand-feet-tall black rock pinnacles jutted high above the sand.

He slowly turned his head to gaze inland and smiled as he looked over the top of the black sand dunes to see numerous large broad-leafed tropical ferns lining the edge of a tall palm tree forest. In the distance, he could see the palm trees and lush jungle growth gradually receding into obscurity. Then it began to thin and diminish altogether further inland as it reached rolling plains covered with tall golden-brown grass.

The gentle curves of the hills climbed steadily upward until the thinning grasses were gradually replaced by a forest of blue-green fir trees, mixed with a sparse number of the giant ferns. The trees ended a third of the way up the base of a large snow-covered mountain. A majestic waterfall poured over the top of a plateau one third of the way down from the mountaintop and gracefully dropped several thousand feet to disappear somewhere in the forest depths that surrounded a clear domed city nestled near the mountain's base.

A large cavern opened a third of the way up from the mountain's base. Right below it the smaller clear transport tube ran out of the sealed rock opening and down the mountain slope to disappear behind the trees.

Master Ra Mu watched a single familiar Scout class ship, glowing with pale-blue light, as it flew slowly further away from the large cavern opening. It hovered briefly high above the domed city, and then headed over the treetops in his direction.

He smiled and nodded his approval as he walked over several black sand dunes toward the ocean. Then he stopped to watch the ship fly over him and stop just past the black sand dunes to hover above the beach. A faint, deep, resonant humming was emanating from the ship as it slowly lowered to the sand. The pale light glow around the hull faded with the humming sound, and Master Ra Mu smiled again.

Kalem was wearing the green Air Force parka as he appeared underneath the ship, crouching down on a personal gravity transport disc that was glowing with a thin blue light. He hovered forward on it a foot above the sand and slowly stood up with his feet firmly anchored by the antimagnetic field to the top of the disc.

Harry was also wearing a parka when he appeared a moment later on his own disc, but he was not quite able to control the disc. It wobbled as he tried to make it follow his will, and he crouched down, grabbing the sides of the disc to steady his body. As he cleared the bottom of the ship, he awkwardly tried to stand up but quickly crouched back down.

Also wearing a parka, Carine emerged from the ship on another disc and flew it a few feet above the sand behind Harry, then alongside him. She reached over and grabbed his arm to help steady him. Relieved, he grinned and stood up with the newfound confidence that he was starting to get the knack of its proper use. While the three of them were flying above the sand toward Ra Mu, Harry let out a spine-chilling scream. The disc was suddenly flying him at a steep upward angle. It stopped at fifty-feet and flew around in several loops before it stopped again in midair with Harry hanging from the disc by his feet upside down.

"Hey, what the hell do I do now?"

He was waving his arms around in a panic as the disc suddenly flew him through the air in several more awkward maneuvers. When the disc stopped again, he was still hanging from it upside down.

A moment later, the disc shot straight down toward the ground and Harry began to scream with all his might in befuddled terror, "A-h-h-h-h-h-h-h…"

Kalem and Carine stopped on their discs a few feet in front of Master Ra Mu, and Kalem yelled up toward Harry. "Think up, General, quickly. Do it now!"

The General's hands were waving below his head to protect him from an imminent collision. He covered the top of his head with his arms and closed his eyes, but the disc stopped with his arms only an inch above the sand and he slowly opened his eyes again.

"Huh?" he blurted out, and then grinned.

The disc suddenly started flying swiftly upward again with him still attached upside down as Carine yelled encouragement.

"You're doing fine, General. Control your fear and think about turning slowly over. Remember what we told you on the ship. The disc obeys your imagination."

Harry closed his eyes and concentrated. The disc slowly moved around in a semicircle until he was standing on it upright. Then it gradually lowered and stopped a foot above the sand, and a one-inch circumference of the disc's outer ring lowered to the surface like a step.

Ra Mu was standing a few feet away laughing softly as Harry carefully crouched down to squat on the disc, cautiously peered over the edge, and then dropped off onto the sand. The inner disc also fell to the sand and rejoined the outer ring. The blue glow encompassing the disc vanished, leaving only a one-inch-thick silver metal disc lying on the ground next to him.

Kalem and Carine landed their discs next to Harry and stepped off. Harry quickly got up and jumped a few feet back away from the disc, as if it would bite him. Irritated, he grabbed a fresh cigar from his parka and stuffed it into the corner of his mouth.

"It takes a little practice to become familiar with its proper uses," said Kalem, chuckling.

Frowning, Harry yanked the cigar from his mouth and replied nervously, "I'd prefer an old-fashioned jet under my seat."

Kalem and Carine turned toward Master Ra Mu, who was waiting patiently, and they respectfully nodded their heads. Mimicking both of them, Harry nodded his head in a hesitant jerky manner toward Master Ra Mu, who returned a kind smile and nodded.

"I thank you for coming, General Faldwell," Master Ra Mu stated cordially. "Your choice to be here was well made. It could mean the survival of your country and your world."

"I don't understand," replied Harry.

"You will, General, I promise you," stated Ra Mu with a twinkle in his eyes.

"If you gentlemen will excuse me," requested Carine, as she briefly smiled at all three men, "I have not visited this beautiful beach before and I would like to explore a little. It's not like anything we have on my home world."

"Go on and enjoy yourself. I'll catch up with you later," replied Kalem, admiring her.

Carine gazed at Ra Mu for approval, and he smiled affectionately, nodded his head, and gestured with a wave of his arm.

"Explore for a few minutes to your heart's content. I won't detain you a moment longer."

Carine bowed her head and then stepped back on her disc and it lit up instantly. She hovered on it a few feet above the sand and moved slowly down the beachhead. Just as Kalem turned around to talk with Ra

Mu, Carine's scream echoed across the beach.

The sand was heaving up underneath her flying disc. Something very big broke through the surface, hit her disc, and knocked her off it onto the sand. A twenty-feet-high caterpillar-like creature burst fully from the sand and arched up on its tail. Its body was comprised of stacked rounded sections, from the smallest at the tip of its tail to the largest at its head, where row after row of long, sharp, white teeth receded into its large cavernous mouth. Its two eyes hung from the ends of long, arched antennae-like protrusions that extended from the top of its head between two flared nostrils. They were rotating individually within their sockets to locate the prey.

Carine's personal antigravity transport disc was on its side, half buried in the sand, and Carine was lying unconscious, curled in a fetal position right beside it.

Great spikes rose up on the back of the creature, and it darted a long sticky tongue toward Carine, wrapped it around one of her legs, and started to drag her unconscious body toward its gaping mouth.

Kalem reached under his parka, retrieved a hidden transparent crystal laser gun and pointed it at the creature to fire, but Master Ra Mu reached up and yanked his arm down.

"No, Captain, don't kill it," he commanded. "There are other ways."

Faldwell's mouth was agape, and the cigar stuck on his lower lip slowly dropped to the sand. Ra Mu stepped in front of Kalem and raised his hands, palms out, toward the creature. Pulsing blue light beams and a high intensity humming sound emanated from his hands and hit the creature in the head. Though not harmed, the creature whimpered, slithered down the beach, and dived into the ocean waves.

Ra Mu dematerialized from Kalem's side and reappeared an instant later standing beside Carine, who had regained consciousness and was beginning to sit up.

"What the...?" pondered Kalem, briefly caught off guard by Master Ra Mu's phenomenal disappearance.

He jumped on his gravity disc, lighting it up, and swiftly flew it a foot above the black sand. Harry was standing stunned, except for his eyes that followed Kalem flying the disc over the top of several black sand dunes, until it disappeared down the other side of one.

Kalem landed the disc further down the beach beside Ra Mu and Carine, jumped off it, and ran to Carine's side. As Master Ra Mu helped Carine to her feet, Kalem threw his arms around her and pulled her into an embrace. Then he held her at arm's length and gazed deeply into her eyes. She was very pleased with his concern for her safety.

"Are you all right, Carine?" he anxiously asked.

"I... I think so," she answered groggily, smiling back at him, and asked, "but what was that... that thing?"

Embarrassed, Kalem cleared his throat and replied, "Carine, please forgive me. I meant to tell you about them on the way here, but it slipped from my mind."

He let go of her shoulders and they both looked at Ra Mu, who was chuckling again, amused by the whole affair.

"It's called a Sand Daringe," he playfully remarked. "Despite their gruesome appearance, they are not carnivorous and usually very friendly docile creatures. You hovered over its lair and frightened it. As you can see, it was defending more than itself."

Ra Mu waved an arm toward the hole in the sand behind Kalem and Carine. They looked around to see six Sand Daringe babies emerge and slither down the beach, then dive into the ocean in search of their mother.

"Much like many dolphins back in General Faldwell's parallel dimension on this planet Earth," Ra Mu continued, "these creatures have been known to save human lives in dire situations for thousands of years. But now they are almost extinct, and they have become very timid."

Kalem looked down and then humbly back up at Master Ra Mu and remarked, "I thought they were predators. Thanks for stopping me."

They could hear Harry's voice yelling from the distance, growing louder as he approached from somewhere behind them.

"Hey, you people just go ahead and forget about me, and leave me standing out there alone so I can get eaten by one of those damn things."

Kalem winced and whispered in Master Ra Mu's ear, "I forgot about him in all the excitement."

Harry appeared nearby running toward them over the top of a black sand dune. He was breathing hard and mad as a hornet when he stopped next to them.

"What the hell was that thing, and who in the hell are you disappearing people anyway? Why did you bring me here? I want some answers, damn it, and right now. I deserve answers, don't I?"

"You do indeed, General," answered Ra Mu, grinning, "and you shall have them." He looked at Kalem. "I believe you have something for me, Captain?"

Kalem's eyes widened as he recalled what Master Ra Mu was asking of him. "Yes, of course."

He reached inside his parka, pulled out a slightly curved, thin, rectangular, quartz crystal three-inches-long and an-inch-wide and handed it to Master Ra Mu.

Puzzled, Harry glanced at Ra Mu and then Kalem. Ra Mu noticed this, but said nothing as he grinned at Kalem.

Harry inquired skeptically, "You're a Captain? I thought you said your name was Kalem Summerhill."

"I'll explain everything after you see this," answered Kalem with a gesture of his hand toward Ra Mu's crystal staff.

"General Faldwell, you are about to witness actual history," stated Ra Mu. "Kalem has brought the record log of our entire journey here that started one hundred thousand Earth years ago. This will take a while, so please, all of you, make yourselves comfortable and we will begin."

Harry took another cigar out of his parka. Still nervous, he looked around at the tropical beach environment, at his parka, and then at Kalem and Carine. Kalem looked down at his parka and at Carine, and she gazed back at both of them. All three realized they were still wearing sub-arctic parkas in a tropical paradise, and then chuckled as they removed them and laid them on the ground. Kalem and Carine sat down, and Carine snuggled up to him, while Harry gazed suspiciously at them, noticing in particular the unfamiliar uniform that Kalem had been wearing underneath his parka.

Noticing Harry's puzzled expression, Kalem grinned proudly and stated, "This is my uniform, General. I'm a Captain in the space fleet of the Galactic Inter-dimensional Alliance of Free Worlds."

"Inter-dimensional Alliance, huh?" Harry shot back and then added, "Hmm, I see."

He stuffed the cigar back into his mouth and dubiously eyed Master Ra Mu, then Kalem and Carine again.

Master Ra Mu placed the clear crystal piece Kalem had given him into a cutout section on the side of his staff. The section was the exact dimensions of the small crystal piece and the crystal magnetically locked into place. Then he raised the staff off the ground a few inches and it began to glow with a red halo. The oval opening in the Ankh symbol atop the staff suddenly shot a radiant red energy beam into the air between all four of them. It formed a three-feet-wide sphere four-feet above the ground, and holographic images began to take shape within it.

Harry gazed nervously into the sphere, and it appeared to move closer to him, looming larger. Yet, neither the sphere nor his physical body were actually moving. As Harry stared more intently at the image, he heard a... *pop* ...like the sound a cork would make just pulled from a bottle. He could feel himself leave his physical form, rising up above the top of his head. Then he looked down to behold his physical body sitting on the sand, and gazed over the scene: observing Kalem; Carine; Master Ra Mu; and the holographic light sphere projection.

Mystified, he thought, ***My God, I'm out of my body, and I'm not afraid. This is wonderful.***

Harry could see in every direction around himself at the same time or wherever he placed his attention. He discovered he was now a radiant sphere of light, like the form Master Ra Mu had taken the night they met. Then, as his true Atma (Soul), or spherical energy self, he moved toward the holographic projection, paused briefly several inches from its radiant surface, and then slowly entered it.

He did not know how he knew it, but Harry realized he was about to witness the record log projected in three dimensions all around him, as if he were personally there. The profound realization shocked him into a humble inner silence, for he knew he was about to watch a history unfold before his eyes that the rest of humankind on Earth at any time had no idea existed.

As he passed through the outer transparent surface of the holographic projection, it faded behind him. Then an altogether new crystal-clear vista opened before his inner vision, as he heard Master Ra Mu's telepathic voice.

From here, in the freedom of your true inner form as the Atma, or Soul, you will witness the actual events that brought us to Earth to contact you. First, you should understand the backgrounds of those beings that are involved, and how events unfolded. This is the planet Telemadia (3), where Captain Kalem spent his youth in preparation for entrance into the Galactic Inter-dimensional Alliance of Free Worlds. Behold!

From high in an alien planet's sky, Harry suddenly saw a grass-covered hillside overlooking a huge transparent domed city. In the next instant, he found himself hovering invisibly near a young Caucasian male lying in tall lavender grass with his hands behind his head. He appeared to be asleep, wearing a gentle smile. Then, General Harry Faldwell became the experience.

CHAPTER SIX

TELEMADIA (3)
THE SETTING OF A DREAM

It started to rain ever so gently. The tall lavender grass swayed toward the south like soft wind blowing through a beautiful woman's long blond hair. To Kalem, it did not matter that the double suns were already setting over the distant blue-granite, snow-crowned Sandeem Mountains that rose high above the Rengetti plain. On Telemadia (3), the suns always glittered like the fine polished surfaces of a million faceted jewels as they sank, one after the other, behind both ends of the jagged mountain slopes that stretched across the horizon fifty-miles away from Kalem's lofty vantage point. He was lying on the hillside outside the domed capital city of Marnanth – his home.

One large dark-violet cloud was passing overhead. Kalem was determined to let nothing stop him from what he knew would come again the moment he lay down on the hilltop outside the city, but there was no need for concern. The cloud passed by leaving only a few small misty drops on his face.

Kalem's dreams, at the high point of the adventuresome spirit of a brown-haired and blue-eyed sixteen-year-old, were almost always of renowned intergalactic adventure: like fighting evil to save the galaxy from destruction or rescuing the loveliest lady imaginable from certain death at the hands of an evil tyrant. Yet, the visions he kept having of the woman with blue-hued skin went way beyond the beautiful seductive allure of the females on the outer rim. She was the most special woman in the entire universe.

47

The vision always came when the lightshow from the twin setting suns glittered across the valley floor and splashed rainbow colors upon his face. When she appeared on the inner screen of his imagination, he was astounded by the love he felt. She was the most elegant and exquisitely beautiful woman, with long black silken hair and slightly pointed ears, which could possibly surround a being. To him, her loveliness was beyond anything he could create in his wildest imagination, even if his life depended upon it.

The visions began just after he had started training at the Academy. It was during his first visit to the hillside outside the dome that he discovered an ability to prolong the experience. For a few brief moments, he was no longer lying in the grass but standing in a pool of water in a tropical setting on an alien world that looked like the images he had seen of planet Earth.

She was completely naked, poised and elegant like the swans of that distant world. He yearned to see them and many other wonderful things he had studied about this strange backward world of diverse creatures, humans, cultures, and beliefs.

He knew this planet was an enigma in the universe. The Galactic Council and the mysterious Guardian Adepts of the Ancient One, that his father mentioned on many occasions really do exist, were not at all certain the human inhabitants of this beautifully magical world would survive their most delicate period of cultural growth. He said an event was coming that would entirely change the surface of the planet, but he would not say anything more about it.

Kalem felt a little saddened when he thought of Earth. He knew he was still young, but his heart ached when he recalled that his father had not yet taken him there on one of his many journeys throughout the galaxy. Kalem knew the planet was a quarantined planet and seldom visited. No citizen or planetary member of the Galactic Alliance was permitted to go there, until the people of that world evolved to be a space-faring race that worked together as one people. Unless this basic requirement was attained, Earth could not be officially contacted by the Galactic Alliance and awakened to the fact that many sentient beings existed on countless worlds throughout the galaxy. Yet, Kalem wanted to go there anyway, for he instinctively knew that one day he would walk the path of his own destiny and journey there to find her.

He became even more intrigued after his father took him on a spiritual journey out of his body for a visit along the time track of Earth's future. Back at the Academy he had studied many forms of life that lived there, rendered by the crystal holographic memory headsets. With great fascination, he repeatedly watched the computerized three-dimensional projections with his inner vision. He had seen for himself that Earth's future inhabitants would likely be killing each other over trifling and often-erroneous religious differences that did not exist in the actual historical events, and that had little to do with the original founders or their beliefs.

Earth's infant race would one day play with deadly nuclear-type weapons as they argued over bits of dirt or imaginary borders. This made no sense to Kalem. How could it? No race in Galactic history had ever survived an evolutionary pattern similar to what the Earth people would go through in the future. Yet, he had a fondness for Earth and its people that he did not understand.

It was whenever he recalled Earth images that he sensed or felt an intuitive nudge to go on one of his many vision quest adventures outside the city. Once he was on the hill, an Earth-like environment would always appear, silhouetted behind that lovely form of the mysterious woman. As far as he knew, no one had yet discovered a humanoid race with subtle blue-hued skin on any of the vast numbers of worlds explored by the Galactic Alliance in over five hundred thousand years of documented history.

Kalem was growing more certain the future destiny of that strange, backward planet and the woman who kept appearing within the sanctuary of his inner world were somehow connected. Even the Galactic Council and the mysterious Adepts they so respected seemed to stress the importance of Earth in the greater cosmic scheme. They said it was vital to the future of the Galactic Alliance, despite the few inhabitants who would gain political power, then become ungrateful, vindictive, narrow minded, and mutually self-destructive on that blue water-covered jewel of a world.

He pondered the significance of this, and his deep feelings for the lovely woman he knew he was absolutely in love with beyond anything he could understand, imagine, or control.

On this particular evening, Kalem lay there long after the twin suns had set. A galactic panorama of multicolored nebula, stellar dust, and another entire galaxy loomed huge in the night sky. From his world, near the outer upper edge of the center of the seventh spiral arm of the Milky Way Galaxy, he could see another galaxy in the far distance of outer space. The future Earth astronomers would call it Andromeda, but his people called it Sefaris – the distant wonder. He could not have known that many Earth persons would have given anything to behold the spectacular panorama visible in the heavens from his world, a view which he took for granted.

At that particular moment, he really did not care about the breathtaking celestial sky. He was seeing himself on another world reaching out to take the hand of the woman, as she reached back toward him with those beautifully slender, slightly webbed blue fingers. Then their fingertips touched.

A cool evening breeze rustling the lavender grass broke his reverie and the woman vanished from his inner vision. He knew he was back on the hill lying in the tall grass and he sighed sadly. Shaking off the feeling, as he had done so many times before, he opened his eyes to look at his surroundings and stood up.

He was wearing his Academy Cadet's uniform: a formfitting body suit with sleek shoes molded into the pant cuffs. He would slip his feet down into the single piece uniform design and pull it up over his torso, and then over his shoulders to put an arm through each sleeve. The top part of the body suit had no collar. It was open in a V-shape that came down to a point several inches above his solar plexus. A single thin gold band encircled the cuff of each sleeve. The garment was made of a dark blue-gray, silky cotton-type fabric belted at the waist, and clasped with an oval gold buckle. Embossed upon it, and on the left chest area of the uniform, was the symbol for the Galactic Alliance: a gold, quartz-capped pyramid suspended above a silvery spiral galaxy with three blue stars set above the apex in triangular formation.

Kalem shoved his hands deep into the pockets of his pants, sighed again, and then reluctantly trudged the few feet to the top of the hill. He stood there looking at the huge clear crystal dome that covered the building towers and sealed transport tubes that linked the many metropolitan structures together. The city lights cast a dull glow on the night sky above, but not enough to obstruct the celestial beauty of outer space spread across the heavens. Looking up, he wondered if he would make it through the tough training ahead and if he would become like his renowned father, a courageous space adventurer and an Admiral in the Galactic Inter-dimensional Alliance of Free worlds. Admiral Starland had explored and charted hundreds of new worlds, and while serving as a diplomat, he helped bring many benevolent races into the Galactic Alliance.

Kalem optimistically pondered his future possibilities and silently mused; *Tomorrow will be another day.*

Then he recalled the lovely woman was an adult, maybe twenty-eight-years old, but he was only sixteen. Yet, during his visions he was a man reaching out his hand to the woman he loved, and this puzzled him. Because of this, he determined more than ever before he would get through his training and excel to find the answers to the mystery of the woman, Earth, and just how intertwined their destinies were. There had to be an answer.

If The Ancient One, the Supreme Being behind all life, was real, as real as his father kept telling him it was, then he decided he would find that out for himself too. He cast his head down sadly again at the loss of the vision of the woman. Then he took a deep breath, forced a smile in the direction of the city, and began walking down the hill.

A voice carried upon the soft breeze stopped him. He cupped a hand to an ear to listen and heard a faint familiar voice urgently calling his name from the outskirts of the city. Another youth his age was waving his arms high over his head.

"Hey Kalem, down here. If you're late again for Admiral Narim's discourse, you will have three marks against you."

Moreau was running up the gentle slope, and Kalem began to jog down toward him. He paused halfway to wait for his friend to reach him. Moreau was wearing the same cadet's uniform. He arrived by Kalem's side, a little out of breath but quickly regained his composure.

Moreau was a Norbrian, a humanoid from the planet Ulanim, with an oval-shaped face, brown eyes, a strong jaw, short curly brown hair, and dark brown skin. He was firmly built and trim like Kalem, for the Academy demanded no less of its students.

When they first met at the Academy, they were both ten years of age. They hit it off from the start and had remained best friends ever since. Although, to Moreau it seemed he was always reminding Kalem of one appointment to keep or another. He really did not mind looking out for Kalem, especially when Kalem went on one of his vision quests to the hilltop. After all, Norbrians are like that. They seem to grow up early with an innate sense of the responsible and the sensible.

Grinning and shaking his head, Kalem threw an arm around Moreau's shoulder. His smile faded and his eyes widened. Then he grabbed Moreau's shoulders.

"You're right, Moreau. We must run back. If he catches us this time, he will gloat triumphantly as he makes us parade in front of the other cadets. I can just hear him." Smirking, Kalem mimicked the old man, "Do not behave like these two slackers if any of you wish to become officers in the Galactic Inter-dimensional Alliance of Free Worlds."

Cringing, Moreau chimed in, "That stuffy old space pirate could lecture a student into such depths of boredom, he could drive them back into a past life."

Kalem patted Moreau on the back.

"We both better lighten up. It may not be easy for me to admit it, but he really does know his stuff."

Still cringing, Moreau sighed and shook his head.

"If we fail to get through his class, we'll never become Galactic Alliance fighter pilots," added Kalem for encouragement.

Doubtful, Moreau asked, "What does your father say about him?"

"The Admiral never lets me forget, Narim has traveled all over this galaxy. He is also supposed to have ventured into dangerous parallel dimensions and journeyed into higher realities, whatever they are. If it is true, I want to know how he did it."

Frowning, Moreau looked down, as Kalem placed a brotherly hand on his shoulder.

"Moreau, my old Norbrian friend," stated Kalem, "I can always count on you to keep my feet on the ground. Thanks for coming out to find me. Come on, we can race back."

Moreau cracked a little smile, looked up with an impish grin, and proclaimed, "You're on!"

Kalem matched his impish grin, and they bolted together down the hillside, laughing and jockeying for position. As they receded into the distance, they were soon running over an area where the lavender grass thinned to an inch in height and they appeared as tiny as scurrying ants. They slowed their run to a walk as they approached one of the four transparent arched openings that led to the base of the outer dome and into the city.

The clear dome arching hundreds of stories over the city began glowing from phosphorescent minerals charging within its resin composition, and dusk turned to night.

The crystalline buildings added illumination to the city's interior, along with the soft blue glow of the transport tubes that wound along the ground to connect together most of the city's structures. The transport cars swiftly moving within them, each carrying one to eight occupants, looked like double-ended crystals glowing on each end in pastel light that changed color every few seconds from blue, to gold, and to red.

As they walked closer to the huge dome, Kalem recalled that years earlier his father had told him, "The crystalline-based technology, upon which the domed cities and transport cars are based, was given to some of the Galactic Alliance members a very long time ago by the mysterious Oceanans."

He tried to find out more about them, but his father refused to elaborate.

As they stopped walking in front of the arched entryway, Kalem closed his eyes and silently determined, *One way or another, I will also find out about those mysterious Oceanans.*

Then in unison, Kalem and Moreau gazed back at the hilltop one last time. A moment later, they turned and looked at each other again, grinning. They clasped forearms briefly and then walked briskly under the archway to enter the city, where they disappeared in a large crowd of people.

OCEANA
AND
THE VISIONS OF MAYLEENA

$\mathcal{S}$he was very independent for a young Oceanan of sixteen years.
Since she was ten years of age, Mayleena would often wander
outside the gigantic clear domed city to swim peacefully at the bottom of
the ocean. When she would stop to rest against the large blue coral spiral
tree and close her outer eyelids, he would appear on the inner screen
of her vision. How or why it spontaneously happened she could not
comprehend, but he was always there reaching out toward her as she
reached back toward him.

It was always the same vision. He would appear without effort and
was always there like a trusted friend. They were naked, standing waist
deep in a turquoise pool of water that existed somewhere above on the
surface world. A beautiful three-tiered waterfall was dropping thirty feet
into the pool behind them. She had no awareness of how they would
meet, but she intuitively sensed that her visions were of a future that
would one day occur. Her unresolved feelings of love for him, whoever
he was, were growing stronger, and now the mysterious young man was
dominating all her thoughts.

Opellum, her father, was constantly trying to show her a better way
to deal with growing up.

He kept telling her, "There is a more mature way to have mastery
over the wide swings of emotion. One day, you will experience The

Ancient One, the source behind all life." Somehow, his statement made no difference to her until after he added, "One day a man will come into your life from another world, and together you will find the truth of The Ancient One by personal exploration and experience."

"Could he be the one?" she thought, wide-eyed.

Mayleena knew her father had some kind of mysterious connection to The Ancient One, but he would not talk about it past a certain point.

"Mayleena, dear daughter," he stated when she was only six, "The Ancient One, the creator behind all life, is real. However, telling you in words what may or may not be has little value."

She frowned as she recalled more of what he had said.

"Be patient and practice trusting in the Sound and Light, the omnipresent Spirit of The Ancient One that you have come to perceive within. Learn all you can while you are young, and then one day you will return to your true home in The Ancient One's realm so many lofty dimensions far above this planet."

She often asked him to elaborate, but he always just smiled. That continued to frustrate her until one day she finally stopped asking.

Mayleena was exceptionally beautiful even among other Oceanan women. Her long, soft black hair was combed straight back over her head and behind her delicately pointed ears. It flowed down to the middle of her back. Two long locks of hair from above her ears dropped down the front of her chest over the tops of her mature breasts outlined through her single-piece, blue, silken robe. A wide violet sash wrapped around her waist was tied off at the side. The large sleeves flowed down over her slender arms and opened wide just past the elbows, where they ended in inch-wide cuffs. Matching blue, silken slip-on shoes covered her feet. At five feet, eight inches, she had a remarkably slender waist and athletic legs. She had received her straight nose from her father and her green eyes, radiant pools of enchantment, from her mother who had died in an accident when she was very young. When Mayleena smiled, it was wide and filled with the joy of life.

Opellum appeared as he walked through the triangular opening at the far end of the long hallway a hundred yards away from where she was sitting. He continued to walk under one of the observation windows set in the curved soft white marble ceiling. It revealed a view of the countryside and the huge curve of the transparent dome that protected the city from the great ocean depth. He could see the glowing ocean water beyond the high arch of the dome, illuminated by the light source being emitted from electrically charged minerals within the huge dome's clear composite resin material.

This light source also made the entire city and countryside appear as if natural sunlight lit the entire area. Opellum's home was one of many family dwellings built in the countryside under the huge three-mile-wide and mile-and-a-half-high transparent dome. It was his and Mayleena's home away from home at the bottom of Earth's ancient oceans.

A dozen rivers coming from the small mountain range that curved halfway around the backside of the dome's interior ran throughout the city to empty into a large lake in the countryside. Centered in the city were three huge gold-crowned white alabaster pyramids, tipped with a small quartz apex. They towered above a white oval domed structure surrounded by minaret-like gold towers centered between them. Round transparent transport tubes six feet wide and many miles long wound their way along the ground all over the city and throughout the countryside. Some of them exited the dome's exterior to continue along the bottom of the ocean floor until they disappeared in the distant blue-green water. Several of the tube's exteriors were glowing softly with a pale-blue light that ran down their entire lengths.

Double-ended transport cars were moving at tremendous speed down the length of the illumined tubes. They were more advanced and streamlined than those back on Kalem's home world. Yet, they were also glowing on each end in colors that changed every few seconds from blue, to gold, and to red. One of them approached a tube junction that split off into several different directions. It briefly slowed down, revealing six Oceanan occupants riding inside, and then it darted away in a blur in a new direction.

Opellum continued his walk toward his daughter and then stopped again halfway down the long hallway to look up through another observation window. He lowered his head a moment later with a cheerful smile and continued walking toward her.

Being over six-feet, Opellum was tall for an Oceanan male. He appeared to be in his late forties according to Earth human comparisons. Strong of limb, his body was trim and precisely contoured. He was handsome in a most mature way beyond description, at least to his daughter's young perceptions. Like Mayleena, his nose was straight and slender. His jet-black hair flowed gracefully straight back over the top of his pointed ears and down the back of his neck between his shoulder blades. Opellum's hair did not grow at the sides of his temples or directly above his ears. This made his forehead appear to extend around the sides of his head, giving a powerful impression of silent strength and wisdom. He was wearing a very elegant blue, silken wraparound robe tied at his side by a smooth silken gold sash, and matching tight-fitting slip-on shoes.

Mayleena looked up as her father walked the few remaining steps along the hallway toward her. He was smiling cheerfully as he held out his open arms. She smiled up at him and threw her arms around his waist, and he hugged her close.

General Harry Faldwell watched with silent awe all that he was observing as the stream of information continued to pour into his consciousness. He perceived that Oceanans looked much like beautiful blue-skinned elves with slightly pointed ears. He intuitively knew that most humans would fall in love with them at first sight, for they emit an aura of very powerful uplifting energies. This, he understood, was one of the reasons they hold themselves aloof, hidden in the universe, even from most of the members of the Galactic Alliance. Then more information poured in.

They had originally evolved on a mostly water-covered world somewhere in a higher physical parallel dimension from that of planet Earth, on which they now temporarily resided. They called their world Oceana, and they gave their foster city at the bottom of Earths' Ocean the same name.

No one in the Galactic Alliance knows where their original home planet is, except a few Oceanan scientists, their leader Master Opellum, and the mysterious Adepts of The Ancient One. However, Harry also understood that Opellum does visit his original home planet from time to time, for it was on their home world of Oceana that they evolved over a million years the ability to breathe on land or under water.

The Ancient One itself had assigned Opellum and the Oceanan people the great task of telepathically uplifting the surface dwellers of ancient Earth into higher states of consciousness. The given task was to genetically improve Earth's populations by speeding up natural evolutionary processes. They were carrying out the assignment and it was to conclude before Earth's soon-to-come polar shift. The Oceanans' presence on Earth was entirely unknown to all but one individual on the surface, a Master Adept of The Ancient One named Ra Mu.

Harry discovered that the Oceanan race is unique in the universe, although they are humanoid, as some would choose to call them, but with very important differences. They have small webs between the fingers on their hands and between their toes for the ease of swimming, and a second set of clear eyelids to see through while under water. Three unobtrusive tiny gill slits located on each side of their necks underneath the backs of their chins open and close for breathing while under water. Yet, one would hardly notice them otherwise.

If any person on Earth were to see an Oceanan man, woman, or child they would instantly find themselves thinking that these people were beautifully human. They are, in fact, a step ahead of humans like those on Earth, for they had evolved over a much greater time than many other human and humanoid species existing throughout the Milky Way Galaxy. The Galactic Alliance scientists knew that humans, even those on Earth, could mate with Oceanans. Even with their differences, the DNA (the double helix of life) was almost identical for humans, Oceanans, and many other humanoid species that comprised the larger part of the Galactic Inter-dimensional Alliance of Free Worlds.

Then Harry clearly understood that a common ancestry existed somewhere in the distant hidden history of the universe. No one knows why, when, or how so many human and humanoid races had populated so many worlds. Apparently, a large number of these races populate a vast number of the worlds discovered during the exploration of the galaxy, but not all, and that is a certainty. Sometimes the differences between humanoid species were striking, but mostly there were too many uncanny similarities. Of course, there are other humanoid and non-human races belonging to totalitarian world systems that the Galactic Alliance had to constantly police to keep them from dominating other worlds by force.

From his silent, invisible perspective, Harry heard and saw what Mayleena was thinking about as she looked up at her father with admiring eyes and hugged him more tightly. She wondered about many things, including the backward Earth humans who dwelled on the lands above the ocean under which she now temporarily resided. How could she tell her father, the one being in the whole universe she truly respected with unfaltering faith, that his little girl was going crazy?

She silently pondered, *What would he thing if I told him my feelings? Opellum, dear father, how can I make you understand my increasing desire for this man who looks like someone from the surface of this backward planet Earth? I am in love with him but he is not even Oceanan. I must be losing my mind.* She cringed, and then silently rehearsed saying it another way, *I am having an affair with a human male in my inner visions and I'm in love with him. Every time I rest by the spiral coral trees and close my eyes, he appears on the inner screen of my imagination. Of course, he is a few years older than I am.*

She opened her mouth to speak, but shut it as her father squeezed his arms around her. She continued the dialogue silently within herself, hoping he would notice it in the deeper recesses of his being. Suddenly, she remembered something Opellum had taught her when she was a toddler, before her mother died and they had come to Earth to build their city at the bottom of the ocean.

For reasons she could not comprehend, he said, "A planet called Earth is on the verge of destruction, but it needs to be saved because it will be very important to the future of the Galactic Alliance."

Back on her home world, he had insisted that she study this obscure planet in a lower parallel dimension within the physical universe, but he also warned her.

"Beloved daughter," he would say, "the vibrations are very coarse there. The people are dangerous with split personalities and materialistic to the degree that the sheer idea of it would stifle any sane Oceanan. If our people tried to ponder the extreme paradox of good and evil living inside planet Earth's human species, it would emotionally burn them to a crisp."

However, this is not what actually concerned her, and she pondered why she had recalled that part of what he had said to her. She could not understand why there was so much intense interest in such a distant planet like Earth, located near the outer edge of the middle of one of the seven spiral arms of the galaxy.

Mayleena continued to muse silently, *Besides, maybe the human male I keep seeing isn't from Earth. There are many human populated planets in the galaxy besides Earth, which are already part of the Galactic Alliance. Perhaps he comes from one of those worlds,* and she smiled to herself, thinking this must be true.

Before her visions of the man had started six years earlier when she reached age ten, her father introduced her on several occasions to the mysterious Master Ra Mu. He lived on the surface world and was somehow involved with Opellum in the project to uplift humankind living there. An aura of light literally radiated around him. She could not help but feel humbled and strangely elated in his presence.

Mayleena had witnessed Earth's future Egyptian culture during her earlier studies under Master Ra Mu's guidance. He had taken her out of her body on several trips to look into Earth's future time track. Mayleena knew he had some kind of personal interest in her unfolding spiritual development, or awakening as he called it.

Her father encouraged this, but she wondered, *Why?*

One recent night, while in the dream state, she became fully conscious that she was out of her physical body and flying through the air. Beside her was Master Ra Mu, standing majestically tall with a deeply wise and radiant smile as bright as the brilliant turquoise sky through which she was so freely flying. He was standing straight up, and he held in his right, clenched fist that curious clear crystal staff etched with arcane mystical symbols. He was moving effortlessly sideways through the air alongside her, while she flew horizontally with her arms and fingertips stretched out wide like the wings of an eagle. At least she felt like that, having seen one of those winged creatures while reviewing one of the three-dimensional crystal holographic projections of the many animal species living in Earth's future.

She admitted to herself that Earth intrigued and bothered her. No Oceanan worth their name would ever purposefully set foot on the surface world of the human beings that lived on the continental landmasses above the oceans of the planet. It was simply too dangerous. They were still so primitive that most of them did not even know other human, humanoid, or any sentient life forms existed outside the atmosphere of their own tiny planet. They still seemed to believe their world must be the center of the universe and likely the only source of intelligent life. She recalled that her father had looked even further down the time track at the distant future of Earth. He told her that Earth's people, for a time, would refer to beings that live on worlds other than Earth as extraterrestrials.

She thought to herself, *What blind arrogance it is for Earth's people to believe that if anything lived on worlds other than their own, they must be on a lower level of development. I just don't comprehend such blatant ignorance.*

Mayleena came out of her reverie as Opellum let her go, and she unwrapped her arms from around his waist; he held her shoulders at arm's length to look into her radiant green eyes.

"What's troubling you, my daughter?"

"Oh nothing, father," she answered, shrugging off his question as she smiled up at his kind face.

"I… I want to embrace the future, but it's so hard growing up and I don't seem to be very good at it."

Opellum gazed wisely down at her as a cheerful smile arched upward across the thin line of his lips.

"Don't worry, Mayleena. A happy, adventuresome future is ahead of you. Recall all of your dreams and visions. They will reveal the secret to why you are here and where you are going. Take advantage of your youth and practice patience. Whenever you see Master Ra Mu, either in this reality or in your dreams when you are out of your body, learn all you can from him. You could not have a better teacher or friend."

How could he know? she thought, her eyes widening with surprise by his insight.

Embarrassed, she lowered her head and closed her eyes. Time seemed to stand still, while she continued to recall her recent conscious dream travel experience. With more vivid conscious awareness than her waking life, she continued flying through the turquoise sky with her arms stretched out like wings. Master Ra Mu was still standing upright by her side, moving effortlessly through the air with a radiant smile. Pastel golden auras surrounded both of their bodies, and a beautiful melodic flute mixed with a deep humming sound was emanating from somewhere in the background. He appeared unaffected by the gentle breeze that rippled her dress like rhythmic ocean waves. The tall clear crystal staff in his right hand was now glowing with gold light through the etched mystical symbols on its surface.

Opellum broke her reverie as he reached out with his hand and gently lifted her head up by the chin with his fingers. She opened her eyes and looked lovingly up into them.

"Young one, you're not going crazy," he stated softly. "Trust what you've learned to perceive within from Master Ra Mu's training and keep up your spiritual exercises."

"But Father," Mayleena protested, "I need to tell you about my vision. My feelings for him…"

Opellum cut her off with a gentle reminder.

"No, my beautiful daughter. Do you recall the spiritual Law of Silence? It is for the best that you keep that to yourself. You will discover the meaning of your visions in due time."

"But father, I…"

She wisely stopped herself and closed her mouth, as Opellum bent down and kissed her on the forehead.

"All is well, Mayleena. All is well. Come with me and enjoy the day outside."

She smiled up at him and took his hand. They walked together a few feet over to a clear oval door. Through it, they could see a lake lined by many elegant trees that looked similar to weeping willows on the planet's surface. It was a bright sunny day outside under the secret domed city of Oceana. Several colorful tropical birds with long V-shaped split tails were perched on the tree branches. More flew by the doorway as Opellum reached out and passed a hand over a luminous moonstone control on the right side of the doorway. The door instantly slid open with a quiet *whoosh* and disappeared inside the wall. A gentle breeze blew through the opening and gently ruffled their hair. Hand in hand, they walked outside and stepped onto a winding path headed in the direction of the lake.

CHAPTER EIGHT

ETTA

AND

THE DREN CITY OF ONN

General Faldwell, observe the hidden planet of Oceana. This is the home world of the Oceanan people and the Dren Race. Prepare yourself for a new perspective on highly evolved courageous life.

Harry heard Master Ra Mu's words float into his consciousness, and he instantly found himself hovering in his true Atma-sphere form in the star-filled space of what he intuitively knew was a slightly higher parallel physical dimension of the galaxy. Looming below him was an emerald-green, ocean-covered world with only two large equatorial islands protruding above the surface.

Harry's Atma form suddenly zoomed downward toward the planet's equator, quickly passing through several wispy clouds. It stopped again a mile above the large islands to observe a dozen transparent domed cities on the surface of both islands within clearings surrounded by exotic jungle trees. Transport tubes, identical to those in Oceana, continued from the base of the domes along the ground and into the jungle to eventually connect with other domes. Several others continued to the shoreline and entered the ocean.

Harry suddenly darted down through the sky and plunged into the ocean's surface near the largest island. It continued downward until it stopped near the island's foundation. A transport tube connected two domed cities to each other in the background on the seabed, and several other tubes that exited both domes gradually ascended along the ocean floor toward the surface.

His light sphere continued moving toward a large extinct tube-shaped volcanic lava flow that ran along the seabed toward the largest island. His sphere approached the volcanic wall and passed right through it.

Revealed inside was a gigantic air-filled volcanic cavern many miles in length and a half-mile high. A glowing mineral lining the rock walls lit the countryside as if normal sunlight were the source, aided by the self-luminous blue-green algae that covered the ground like closely cropped grass. Well cultivated, palm-type fronds and flowers were growing along many winding paths that led from a two-hundred-feet-high waterfall cascading out of a cave opening down to an elongated oval blue-green lake. Four-feet-in-diameter windows curved outward from the rock walls along both sides of the falling water. Large growths of every gem crystal known, and many more unknown by the rest of the Galactic Alliance citizens, covered the volcanic rock surfaces between the windows.

Near the city's outer borders, the crystals were dozens of feet high and over four feet wide. At a higher elevation, natural deep-water springs were bubbling up and feeding tributary pools that ran off in small streams to empty into the lake. The far end of the lake was dropping down a wide cavernous opening.

A group of Drens that look similar to Earth's light-green salamanders but much larger, with longer noses and expressive big bulbous dark blue eyes, were gathered together around one Dren who seemed to be the object of their angry emotions. The Drens surrounding him ranged in size from two-and-half-feet to over four-feet-in-length from the tip of their thick tails to the end of their noses. When any of them blinked, a transparent set of inner eyelids would close down over their eyes just before their outer eyelids. They were levitating four-feet off the ground, utilizing their natural ability to defy gravity while their tails were glowing, from the root to the tip, like crystal opal in bright sunlight.

General, this is the central Dren city of Onn. Meet Etta.

Once again, Harry heard Master Ra Mu's clear voice, and he was pleasantly stunned to be observing Etta again, for this time he now saw him as a most immediately likable being, and he understood Etta's language as if he were speaking perfect English.

"Listen to me, will ya?" yelled Etta, greatly concerned as a whole group of Drens surrounded him on all sides.

Harry realized that the other Drens did not consider Etta to be a typical adult Dren male. He is fiery, feisty, determined, and downright adventuresome to a fault. The other Drens were ready for a battle of wills, and they were angry.

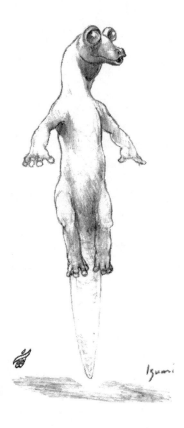

"Look here, Etta," chimed in a younger, annoyed female Dren. "I didn't want to have to tell you this, but you're the only one of us who is still talking to those arrogant blue-skinned fishy people. I mean, did we ask them to come to our world and colonize so long ago? No! Nobody back then came right out and said, 'Say there, neighbors from another world, why don't you come on by, move right in, and take over like you owned the whole damn planet in the first place.' I sure as hell didn't tell them that."

She looked around as the large group of twenty or more Drens angrily cheered her on. Shouts came from every side.

"Monta, you're right," yelled a husky angry male Dren.

"Yeah, throw the bums out," scowled a raspy-voiced female.

"Send em' all back to the fishy world they came from, wherever that is," bellowed another very agitated female with a squeaky high-pitched voice.

Then Monta added, "And I don't trust the off-world-ones like that Captain Kalem you keep hangin' around. What happens if this Galactic Alliance he belongs to discovers our world?"

"Yeah, there goes the neighborhood," chimed in the husky male Dren.

"I'll bet ya' we would never have a moment's peace after that," Monta defiantly shot back.

"Will you all stop this paranoia?" shouted Etta, growing more irritated. "How many times must I say it? Captain Kalem is trustworthy to a fault, and the Galactic Alliance is benevolent."

"If you ask me, we should bite em' all into submission," a deep, defiant male voice boomed loudly over their heads.

All eyes turned to see Benock, an old rotund Dren, as he came around the corner from one of the smaller cave entrances that led into the cavernous Dren city center.

He added with dramatic flair, "That's the way we did it in the old days after they first arrived. At least, that's what our ancient scrolls tell us."

"Ah-h Benock, now I'll get relief," Etta whispered.

Cheers rang out from all the Drens gathered, including adult males and females and even a number of young Dren children. All except for Etta, who was fuming back at them, mad as a hornet. Benock appeared to completely ignore him as he puffed up his chest.

Harry began to receive a background plethora of information about the entire Dren culture, and he understood that the Drens had heard this quaint Earth human expression from the Oceanans who visited them from time to time. Apparently, they felt it often applied to the fiery emotions of the Drens. However, the Drens did not find it funny when any other race stated this mad-as-a-hornet phrase might apply to any of them. They thought this and other statements the Earth people would somehow dream up out of thin air just ridiculous and, of course, made no sense.

Any sensible Dren would think, **What does it mean anyway?**

The Oceanans told them that a hornet was a small winged insect creature with a furry, bulbous body, many long legs, a very bad temper, and a poisonous stinger sticking out of its butt. They had also been told it was a docile creature that minded its own business until it was surprised, cornered, or its home attacked. It was simply hilarious to a Dren to imagine a human running around mad as a hornet.

The image did not make any sense at all, and that is precisely what they thought humans were – nonsense! No Dren gave a hoot about the backward dingy planet, and none of them wanted anything to do with it. Even when Master Opellum asked them to be open to the importance of Earth, they were mystified.

Drens, as a whole, do not care much for travel in outer space or for creatures from other worlds. Yet, Opellum had said the Drens were a most noble, endearing race to the Oceanans and they would have a part to play in the adventures ahead for the entire Galactic Alliance. Except for Benock and Etta, no Dren could grasp his statement as having any practical meaning to them.

As usual, when such a gathering took place, all of the Drens were levitating about four feet off the ground. Their tails were glowing from the root to the tip in radiant opalescent colors. Remarkably, that is how Drens get around, and old Benock was not walking around the corner down the path either. He too was levitating about four feet off the ground and flying toward them at a good clip for an old Dren.

The Oceanans have an ancient saying, "There is more to a Dren than meets your expectations." Harry certainly knew this was true, for he now understood that Drens are highly evolved, intelligent beings that are extremely social. They have hearts the size of houses, and their very animated expressions are extremely cute. They have perfect photographic memories and their own language, and they are very vocal about almost anything and everything. Their very expressive fingers on their hands and individual toes on their feet are also very similar to those darned backward Earth humans, as they thought of them. Although the Drens are a silica-based life form, and not carbon based like Earth humans and the Oceanans, they are also warm blooded. However, most importantly the Dren race developed the ability over several million years to defy gravity and fly through the air.

As unbelievable as it seemed, Harry now understood that the first uses of antigravity-wave-propulsion technology in the Milky Way Galaxy came into existence after the Oceanans studied the Dren race. He perceived that on Earth, several species produce an electric charge or current, such as the eel-like fresh water fish from the Amazon, which is capable of emitting strong electrical discharges. There are also creatures that produce their own luminosity in the deep seas where no sunlight reaches such depths. A much more advanced principle along these lines applies to the Drens, and more information kept pouring into him.

On Earth, quartz is primarily made of silica, as is common sand and much of the mantle of the planet. Quartz is neutral or non-conducting, but it has very intriguing properties. It is piezoelectric, which means it will emit a current when pressure or an electric field is applied, and it is molecularly programmable like a computer chip. Also tied up with quartz is the secret of antigravity, when combined with certain characteristics inherent in pure gold and silver. Harry now knew all this, and he understood that how to combine these elements was unknown by any Earth scientists he knew about, or if any did know, the secret remained classified from his awareness or that of the public.

Harry suddenly understood that when a Dren decides to levitate and fly through the air, the tail glows. A charge is set up around it that is directly opposed to the gravitational lines of force of the planetary body they live on, and the Drens have a volitional control over the degree of this force. They can hover like a hummingbird on Earth, fly backwards, forwards, sideways, in circles, travel slowly or at a remarkably high speed.

On a good day, a Dren can fly several hundred miles an hour. They have a hard, clear second set of eyelids that close down over their regular eyelids when traveling at high speed. They also have diaphragms inside their nostrils that close down to filter the air they breathe while traveling at high velocity.

They bear their young live like humans and other mammals, but they mate in a more completely intimate manner. During the act of lovemaking, a male and female couple with their tails wrapped in spirals around each other. Their tails change color from opalescence to a vibrant pastel red as their entire bodies vibrate to a climax in perfect unison.

The astounding information continued to flow into Harry's awareness, as he briefly perceived Etta's beautiful Dren wife and two adorable Dren children, a male and a female, just before they vanished. He also understood he would discover more about them in the future.

Then Harry began to perceive things in finer detail, and he knew Etta was three and a half feet long. Like all Drens, Etta's large, bulbous, dark blue eyes bulge out of their sockets in a semispherical shape. The short eyelashes at the top of his eyelids are short and masculine, but they are long and feminine on his wife, Din, and all other Dren females. Etta's six-inch-long jaw squared off in front, has two flared nostrils about an inch apart positioned on the front end of each side of his long snout. The line of his mouth curves gently downward and then upward around his long square jaw, downward again under his nose, back upward by the other side of his nose, and then gently around and up the other side of his jaw. When his mouth is closed, it gives the impression he is amused about something.

His arms are strong from his shoulders down to his elbows, wrists, and hands. They are one and a half feet long from the shoulders to the fingertips. His opposing thumb and fingers are similar to Earth human hands, as are his legs when he stands upright on his feet with individual dexterous toes.

Etta, like all Drens, can walk on all four of his arms and legs, upright like a man, or levitate and fly through the air. His lips and face move with incredibly fluid emotional expression, as do all Dren faces, and like humans they talk with vocal cords. However, the Drens also have telepathic ability. In their natural habitat, Drens do not always wear clothing. The usual exception to this rule applies when they are around an alien race that would be offended if they did not wear something. Although Etta would appear to most humans to be an immediately adorable being, he is viewed as a courageous warrior amongst the Drens for reasons that Harry knew would later become much more evident.

A distant past poured into Harry, and he could see the Drens' ancient ancestors witnessing the arrival of the first Oceanan men. To the Drens, they appeared like blue-skinned monsters as they walked out of a lake onto the bank of one of their cavernous undersea habitats. They could see that the strange creatures could breathe under water or on land. However, when the leader spoke, no Dren could understand him. As the dozen Oceanan men raised their right hands in peace, it looked threatening and the Drens attacked. The Oceanan men had so many bites on them before they escaped back into the lake, they could hardly stand up.

They used the connective underwater tunnels that led from the lake to the ocean depths outside the Dren habitats. They went out the same way they came in, and eventually made it back to the huge domed city colonies they had established at the bottom of the Oceana Ocean.

The ancient Dren scrolls also stated the Oceanan women were very disappointed with their mates after their return, because they were unable to get their normally passionate natures roused for weeks. The Drens put a definite damper on their romantic lives for a time, but fortunately, no one died.

Rumor had it that the Drens might have elaborated on their account of the event to bolster their self-esteem and courageous self-image. The Oceanans, on the other hand, claimed a slightly different account of events. After all, the Oceanan men had not come to visit the Drens the first time with weapons of any kind, and they did not return to the Dren habitat the second time with vengeance in their hearts. The Drens found this out a few weeks later when several dozen Oceanan men appeared again with some kind of crystal laser weapons strapped on their sides. They soon gave a small demonstration of their usefulness by disintegrating a large boulder in a brilliant beam of gold laser light. It was now quite clear to Harry that the first truce and subsequent treaty between the Oceanans and the Drens came out of that little incident.

Sounding irritated, Benock continued, "Remember the first truce between our ancestors and the Oceanans? Everyone remembers that. We should elect a representative to make a house call on their leader, Opellum. Yes, we should contact him. We should find out their true intentions."

To a few Drens, the thought was still somewhat repulsive to have to deal with such unattractive, lanky, upright walking beings like the Oceanans, and their scowling faces showed it.

While he continued to look upon the scene, Harry mused silently, *Some Dren attitudes are still very much like those of many human beings on Earth.*

Mocking up anger, Benock continued, "Because they can live on the surface of our world or on the ocean bottom, and can breathe under water or on land, gives them no right, no right whatsoever, to come down into our world to our city and start telling us how to evolve, for crying out loud. After all, the clumsy Oceanans never evolved the ability to fly. They couldn't levitate to save their own butts!"

One chubby middle-aged female Dren coughed, cleared her throat, and sputtered, "If it wasn't for us, they'd still be puttering around the galaxy in those old, slow clunker ships they used when they arrived here over five hundred thousand years ago."

Another middle-aged male Dren with a few scars on his face and body, which made him look like he had encountered too many accidents in his day, was huffing, puffing, and slightly wobbling from side to side as he endeavored to keep his levitation ability stable.

He yelled angrily, "Damn right! Legend says we befriended em' first by allowing em' to study how we fly, and they soon discovered antigravity repulsion waves to power their ships."

Scowling, Benock puffed up his chest and added fuel to the flame, stating, stern-faced, "Quite correct, and the natural crystals growing in our environment gave them the key to a crystalline technology greater than anything they had at the time. Their science has now become

71

unparalleled anywhere in the galaxy. Without us, they would still be pokin' around in the swamps."

"What in heaven's name is the matter with all of you?" yelled Etta, unable to contain himself any longer. "I'm ashamed to call myself a Dren after that pompous display of ass-backward, fear-ridden, childish thinking sputtered out by many of you. And, while we're on the subject, don't forget that when the Oceanans arrived here our ancestors were no more than levitating cave rats with a total language of grunts, squeaks, and groans. They would eat just about anything, including each other if someone died.

"The Oceanans also began to speed up our evolution by teaching our ancestors not to eat the flesh of evolving life with intelligent self-aware potential. They could have made slaves out of our ancestors, and they could do it to us now, but each one of you know it's not in their nature, and none of you should ever forget it."

Etta frowned sternly at the crowd, and moments of silence passed. Gradually, the Drens gathered there cast their eyes downward with sullen faces as green cheeks turned red with shame. They knew Etta was right. Opellum had recently informed them that a scientist had found a way to give the Drens the capability of an almost instant understanding and ability to not only speak Oceanan, which they had a continuing difficulty learning, but any language.

As Opellum put it, "All each Dren has to do is wear a crystal headset for a few minutes to accelerate their intelligence quotient tenfold."

This statement is what triggered the deeper fears of the Drens in the first place. They became gradually suspicious that the mighty Oceanans would use the device to brainwash them and gain complete control of their lives. No one really knew where the rumor got started, and the gossip had spread fast.

All eyes turned to Benock. After all, he was the most ancient of the Drens still living and they all looked up to him. Then they looked to Etta. They respected and feared him. He was the great-unknown element in their society. They knew he had become friends with one of the off-world Galactic Alliance Captains, a fighter pilot named Kalem. Etta met him for the first time when the Oceanan leader, Opellum, took him along on one of his many trips to visit Kalem's father, Admiral Starland, aboard the Galactic Alliance flagship. He had introduced Etta to Captain Kalem, and then encouraged the association and friendship they now enjoyed.

Over the years, Opellum had made many of these trips to consult with Admiral Starland and Master Ra Mu, his old friend from Earth. The rest of the Oceanans and other Galactic Council members were beginning to respect Etta as well. In fact, he was the only individual in Dren history to actually volunteer to travel into space. Most of his fellow Drens thought him to be the most courageous (if not the most foolish) Dren in all of their recorded history.

Etta gazed expectantly at Benock, waiting for a sign that he had come to his senses. Benock was frowning, and then he suddenly smiled from ear to ear. Stumped, Etta blinked several times as Benock began to float toward him. The amazed but humbled crowd parted to let him through as he continued up to Etta, slowly reached out, grabbed him by the shoulders, and gave him a very exuberant hug. Then he danced around in a circle, spinning the stunned Etta around with him.

Harry perceived that Benock was a wise old Dren who had studied with the mysterious Adepts of The Ancient One. As it turns out, Opellum was one of their founding members and Benock had begun studying the secrets of the Adepts many years earlier under the guidance of Master Opellum, as he secretly referred to him. The Spirit presence behind all life revealed this secret, and it had repeatedly taught him for decades to expect the unexpected and bend like a tree in the wind of change, or become uprooted. For sooner or later the wind of change always comes.

As he twirled around several more times, hugging and slapping Etta on the back, Benock was looking back and forth, paying particular attention to Etta and the crowds' shock at the unexpected turn of events.

"Etta… Etta… Etta, my boy, you have done it," he remarked with jubilant pride. "You have really done it. You stood up for the Oceanans and all the Drens. You did not fall prey to gossip, and the negative emotions of the crowd did not move you. Opellum said he did not think it would work but I knew you would get through it. My boy, you have proven to me that the Drens have indeed begun to evolve into something new, more than we are now. You have passed the test with flying colors. Master Opellum must already know the outcome."

Benock spun Etta around once and let him go so that he came to a stop facing him, appearing jolly but confused. Then he chuckled with Benock, but had no idea why.

Still chuckling, Etta asked, "What the devil are you talking about, Benock? What test?"

Benock gave no answer. He was too busy dancing around in the air with complete delight, and the Dren crowd was now too amazed to do or say anything. They all began to grin and snicker among themselves, then laugh.

"Old Benock must have bumped into a cave wall somewhere," whispered a grinning younger male Dren to his shorter female companion.

"Yeah, that's a fact," she giggled back. "He's definitely not working on a fully charged tail."

While Benock continued to dance around, he was thinking about how the Dren race developed in remarkably unique surroundings, and Harry saw everything about their evolutionary background as it flashed through Benock's mind. He was reflecting on how his ancient Dren ancestors had evolved at the bottom of planet Oceana's mostly water-covered, emerald-green oceans, surrounded by light pink pastel clouds. However, they were very much unlike the fish or sea mammals that evolved on his world, and on the quarantined planet Earth. His ancestors had evolved in huge extinct air-filled volcanic caverns located along the sea floor at the base of each of the few island landmasses that protruded above their mostly water-covered world. A luminous mineral lining the interior walls of the huge cavernous Dren cities had always brilliantly lit up their world. In fact, in the garden area at the center of their capital city of Onn where the Drens were now gathered, it appeared like any normal bright sunny day on Earth in a tropical environment. Huge palm-type fronds and artfully arranged, multicolored flowers were growing everywhere in an uplifting manner.

Throughout history, the Drens built their cavern cities around naturally occurring volcanic vents or tubes made from lava flows that had long ago emerged from fissures on the ocean floor. As the lava flowed underground toward the surface and eventually emptied, tubes or vast hollowed chambers remained that were many miles in length and hundreds of feet high. This process also created the few large islands that do protrude above the ocean surface. All this occurred many millions of years ago during Oceana's early evolutionary geological period. Natural deep-water springs also developed that fed waterfalls, lakes, and streams, and the cavern walls being so many millions of years old had become literally encrusted with huge crystal mineral growths.

Having studied much about Earth, Benock knew that every precious gem crystal known on Earth was present in the Dren environments, as well as many more not known to exist on Earth or other planets explored in the galaxy by the Galactic Alliance. In some places, especially in the more sacred places of the Drens, the crystals had grown to dozens of feet in length and over four feet in thickness. Blue crystals, emeralds, gigantic diamonds, rubies, sapphires, topaz, tourmaline, copper crystals, lapis lazuli laced with gold, and hundreds of exotic forms of other mineral crystals were continuing to grow everywhere, and the Drens had constructed their cities around them.

Still active volcanic vents on the sea floor naturally kept the Dren cities at a comfortable seventy-five to eighty-degree temperature year-round. An abundance of plant life provided a constant source of food, fresh oxygen, and the removal of carbon dioxide. Like the luminous mineral in the walls, a self-luminous, blue-green algae evolved, covering the cavern floors.

Realizing that Dren caverns were truly self-contained ecosystems, Benock mused fondly, "We Drens, after all, are the most natural preservers of pristine beauty in the galaxy. No Dren would dream of polluting any aspect of their environment."

Benock knew this was one of the reasons that the Oceanans had come to respect the Dren race, for the Drens had developed a finely tuned aesthetic sense of integrating the construction of their dwellings and city centers within the natural settings of their surroundings. The Oceanans learned much from the Drens and the Drens had evolved a great deal because of the Oceanans' deep experiential spiritual nature.

The Oceanans later coined the phrase, "To see a Dren city is to behold breathtaking loveliness in natural design, contour, texture, taste, and simple elegance."

Benock thought about all of Dren history dating back over five hundred thousand years to the time when the Oceanans first came to their world, and about the fact that Drens had not engaged in warfare. They never went to war amongst themselves, and only had one brief skirmish in their ancient history with the first visiting Oceanans. Drens are stout and committed friends once someone gains their trust. They would die for their own loved ones and the loved ones from races on other worlds if they proved worthy of true friendship. As mates, Dren couples are highly committed to each other and their offspring even more, perhaps, than many of the most loving of human and humanoid parents.

"Never underestimate a Dren. You can't find a better friend in the universe," states another ancient Oceanan axiom.

Meanwhile, Etta was waiting for an answer from Benock, but he was still dancing around. Then Etta laughed, for it was too odd to do anything else while he watched the old Dren's contagious laughter and dancing antics. Then he gained control of the urge, barely.

"Benock, will you please tell me what you're going on about? What test are you referring to?" he asked impatiently, but there was no reply, so he yelled, "Damn it, Benock, what the devil is going on?"

"Etta, my lad, it was a test that was necessary at this time for the entire Dren race," Benock replied proudly, grinning from ear to ear as he hovered toward Etta. He stopped several feet in front of him, respectfully bowed, and continued, "You were chosen by The Ancient One to be a living example of the best potentials within Drens. I apologize for having put you through this, my lad, but it was required for the benefit of the Drens, the Oceanans, and humankind everywhere. Be assured your actions here today have opened a new chapter of greater possibilities for the enlightened evolvement of all sentient beings in the universe. Do not ask me how at this time, for it is presently unimportant. Etta, you will find answers to the mysteries that lie beyond the physical universe as you explore worlds within you. For now, that's all I can say to you."

"Me?" queried Etta, surprised. "This is some kind of a joke, right?"

"No, Etta, fine example of the best in Drens, it is not," replied Benock.

Then he gazed upon all of the other Drens gathered, beaming a radiant smile at each one of them.

He raised his right hand, palm out, to give them a blessing and joyfully commanded, "Be of good cheer, all of you!"

As swiftly as the entire angry episode had started, now yelps and cheers began and grew in momentum from all the other Drens. They had simply forgotten about their distrust of the Oceanans. Something had changed because Etta had passed some kind of test beyond their comprehension, and it concerned them as well. Every Dren knew it, but not one of them understood how. Somehow, they were different now that the fear-ridden, petty aspects of their characters had melted away.

Yet, Benock had not changed them, and Etta was not responsible for that miracle either, though he had already made a leap in awareness a little ahead of the others. The Spirit presence of The Ancient One behind all life passing through Etta's living example accomplished that miracle as it penetrated their hearts and transformed them.

Etta intuitively knew what had happened was a gift, though he too had no understanding of how or why it occurred. He was smiling as he tried to ponder the warm glow he now felt. Feeling the same thing, the other Drens carefully approached Etta, and each one in turn briefly rubbed one of his cheeks and then the other cheek to show their admiration, appreciation, and affection.

Benock smiled again in Etta's direction, then turned around and swiftly flew above the path back to the city's main entrance and entered it. The Dren crowd drifted away from Etta, and he was soon floating alone, amazed at all that had transpired. He closed his eyes and gratefully lowered his head.

"Ancient One," he whispered respectfully, "if you really do exist, I would very much appreciate it if one day you would make your presence known to me."

As soon as the request left his lips, a hauntingly beautiful melody of a single high-pitched flute and a deep humming sound began and grew louder – like that of a million bees blended with the roaring sound of the ocean. Etta opened his eyes to see a rainfall of bright gold and tiny blue sparkles of light gently falling all around him, penetrating every part of his body. A moment later, the Sound and the Light faded away. Etta took a deep breath and looked all around, but whatever it was had vanished.

Astonished, he grinned with childlike wonder as he let out his breath and asked, "What was that?"

Taking in a deeper breath, his face filled with joyous delight and he slowly exhaled. "Wow!"

Then he looked into the distance toward the large opening leading inside the city center where Benock had flown and his tail brilliantly intensified with opalescent colors. He levitated a few feet in the air, and then darted in a long arc above the pathway over to the city entrance where he gently landed. In wonder, he walked inside in search of Benock.

CHAPTER NINE

THE ORPHAN SEN DAR'S DESTINY

The images surrounding Harry Faldwell's observation viewpoint began to change when he heard Master Ra Mu's voice again, with a new stream of pictures and information from another world.

General Faldwell, now we come to Sen Dar. You will soon understand the urgency of our request to help us save Earth from destruction, as you continue your journey deeper into the record of events. Observe the planet Kormaljis.

In a brief vision, Harry saw a tormented boy looking through an observation dome, observing his world withering and dying before his eyes. Newly orphaned at ten years old, he was perishing from thirst and heat on a remote world in the unexplored regions at the end of the seventh spiral arm of the galaxy.

Harry was suddenly out in space, observing lightning discharges flashing throughout the planet's atmosphere. Erupting volcanoes were visible through several breaks in the thick clouds around the equator. A large, wide spaceship approached and assumed an orbit. He could see on the ship's hull the symbol of a silver spiral galaxy with a quartz-capped gold pyramid directly above it and three blue stars above the apex. Large letters inscribed below it read:

GALACTIC ALLIANCE EXPLORER (3)

The wide oval ship was seven hundred feet long and five hundred feet wide with a slightly curved bottom hull. A blue glow enveloped the ship's exterior. A dozen clear observation domes positioned around the circumference of the upper half of the ship surrounded a complex of crystalline-shaped bridge control towers. The ship tilted downward and plunged into an opening in the thick clouds.

The mysterious space vessel soon touched down on a dried-up ocean bed. Many male and female scientists from various Galactic races, including Oceanan and human, were standing inside the observation domes. They appeared aghast as they observed the complete desolation of the planet's surface. Having evaporated many miles back, the receding ocean was just visible on the distant horizon.

Several volcanoes were continuing to erupt in the background along a barren mountain range. The still-burning trunks of the gigantic forest trees stretched from the plain below the mountain range to within a half-mile of the dry shoreline. The land between the last of the giant trees and the dry beach appeared to have been cultivated with a wide orchard of fruit-laden trees. However, what occurred had withered the beautiful trees, and their multicolored fruit was lying burnt and rotting on the ground.

A Caucasian boy, wearing simple country clothes, stumbled out of a large cavern opening in the side of an embankment a hundred feet above the coast. Several of the ship's scientists within the observation dome turned to converse with a group of five medical personnel wearing heavily protective environmental suits. They exchanged a few brief words, and then the lead medical specialist touched a control on his wrist sleeve and all five of them dematerialized into a spiral mist of glistening atoms. They reappeared a moment later near the boy, just as he grabbed his throat and collapsed face down into the white volcanic ash.

The lead medical technician waved the other four personnel traveling with him toward the cavern, and they hurried inside. Then he lifted the boy up out of the ash, cradled him in his arms, and touched his wrist control again. A moment later, he re-materialized inside the ship's observation dome, just as the other four technicians reappeared at the cavern entrance. They were assisting a number of surviving adults walking toward the cliff ledge. What had been a transparent elevator was now twisted and broken below the cliff by a vertical rail it once rode on.

Inside the ship, the technician was administering oxygen to the boy, while two more technicians lifted him onto a stretcher. More medical personnel stepped through a clear elevator that had just stopped above the center of the circular floor. The boy looked dehydrated with many skin abrasions and several burns. Delirious, he babbled fearfully in an unknown language, and the lead technician removed his helmet, revealing his serous frown.

"What would he say happened if we could understand him?"

The woman support technician by his side answered compassionately, "There will be time enough for questions once he's rejuvenated in the medical bay with the surviving adults."

As Harry heard her words, he moved toward the boy's forehead and soon discovered he was observing what the planet Kormaljis was like before this tragic event had happened.

In an instant, he was high in the planet's atmosphere. A flat roof-like top created by the trees spread around a wide area of the planet's equatorial region. Vast landmasses surrounded several smaller turquoise oceans. Small polar icecaps were clearly visible over each end of the planet's poles, and Harry intuitively knew they appeared just three to four months out of the year. More information poured into Harry's consciousness with many scenes, and then he saw the big picture.

If any other space-faring explorers had visited Kormaljis before the planet's demise, they would have found the trees quite beyond majestic and absolutely awe inspiring. Their trunks were up to a hundred feet or more in thickness with an emerald-green bark. Profusely covering the thick boughs that extended straight out from the trunks up to five hundred feet or more, were blue-green leaves that curved gently upward like huge spoons. A relatively flat canopy topped off the tree trunks that rose up to a mile in height far above the lushly flowering, fruit-laden trees on the plains below.

The trunks of these majestic trees reminded Harry of giant sequoia redwood trees back on Earth. However, these were so many times larger and their crowns were similar to large palm fronds. The leaves spread out to interweave with other treetop crowns, creating a worldwide equatorial canopy high above the forest floor.

The thousands of mammals, avian, and aquatic species were too extraordinary and exotic to even begin to do them justice, if Harry tried to describe them to anyone else. If beings from any other worlds had the privilege to behold them as he had, he knew they would greatly miss their loss to the universe.

The Kormaljisians were also unique among the humans in the Milky Way Galaxy because they built their homes in the trees. Enclosed walkways high above the ground interconnected together most of the giant forest trees. These people were not some backward nomadic tribesmen, not by any means, for they built beautiful domed homes made of a reflective silvery plastic-like material stronger than the toughest metal. The elegantly designed and tastefully decorated homes high up in the branches of the giant forest trees were built with skylights, observation platforms, and swimming pools. The light source in the walls, made from a self-luminous mineral mined from the bottoms of their lakes, connected to fiber-optic-type tubing that channeled light along its length to light emitters. Yet, like the Dren race, the people of this world polluted nothing in their environment by working in harmony with nature and not against it. They clearly had built a highly advanced and very sophisticated civilization.

Harry suddenly found himself observing the boy just two days earlier. The healthy and happy lad was smiling as he hugged his father, a handsome thirty-year-old man wearing a belted robe, and then his lovely twenty-five-year-old mother wearing a country dress with a flower pattern on white silken material.

The home was simple elegance. Several wide skylights, ten feet above their heads, cast an even light over the artfully arranged comfortable modern furniture. Another light source coming from covered recessed light emitters set in the ceiling came from the fiber-optic tubing system. A series of paneled windows set into the walls revealed breathtaking views outside in every direction below. An indoor swimming pool encircled by a sunken living room comprised the central area.

The boy waved goodbye to his parents and walked out through the automatically opening door to step onto a wide path on the floor of an enclosed triangular walkway system with transparent walls. He stopped by the hand railing to gaze down upon the countryside spread out a mile below him. An orchard of multicolored fruit-laden trees extended from the edge of the forest to the nearby shoreline of a cove. The sun on the horizon was just rising above a turquoise ocean.

The boy gazed around at the sophisticated walkway system that connected to many similar homes as far into the distance as he could see. It wound between the massive tree trunks, across the tops of the thick boughs, and continued ascending over many levels of the tree limbs with emerald-green bark. The entire city reached from the forest floor a mile upward into the gigantic trees just below the interwoven treetop crowns.

Opposite the ocean in the distance beyond the giant forest trees, loomed a snow-crowned mountain range. A waterfall higher than the tops of the trees, glowing with a pale-blue light coming from a microscopic luminescent mineral in the water, was tumbling down the tallest mountainside.

The lad whistled merrily as he walked toward a junction that connected three converging walkways. In the junction's center was a transparent elevator. The boy approached it and the oval door automatically opened. He walked in, the door closed, and the elevator descended at a rapid rate down a rail built along the straight edge of a huge tree trunk.

The elevator came to a gentle stop, and the boy walked out. Smiling cheerfully, he ran along a flower-laden path between rows of orchard trees. A short time later, he emerged onto a golden beach. Fifty yards away was a set of steps that led up to a flat area by the base of a rock wall. Twelve men and twelve women were standing by the rock wall that rose up a hundred feet to a ledge by a large cavern opening. Like the boy, they were all dressed in simple farmer's clothing.

"Hello there, Sen Dar," the elderly man said to the boy. "May I ask what brings you out this early on a fine beautiful morning like this?"

"Oh, I just want to see the hydroponics cave again, Mr. Da Vep," Sen Dar replied shyly.

Da Vep remarked with an impish grin, "I know what you're after, Sen Dar. Another one of my ripe star apples, eh? Well, okay. Always a pleasure to have you along, but this time there will not be time for play. Hmm, aren't all the other children in school by now?" he inquired, and winked.

Sen Dar frowned, but the man placed a friendly arm around his shoulder and Sen Dar looked back up grinning. They walked over to the platform at the base of the rock wall where the other adults were waiting. The group boarded a much larger elevator and it lifted up along a metal rail a hundred feet to the top of the rock wall. The group disembarked on a flat ledge and walked up a set of short rock steps inside the cavern opening.

At that moment, a large meteor burned through the atmosphere and exploded in the waterfall on the mountainside beyond the great forest. The resulting deafening fireball blasted away the snow-covered mountaintops in massive clouds of steam and rock.

The shock wave ripped through the giant forest treetops and disintegrated the city, blasting the homes into oblivion and igniting trees in a whirlwind of hellish fire. Several volcanoes exploded along the mountain range sending showering molten rock and lava into the forested area, and the distant giant trees ignited sending huge plumes of thick white ash into the jet stream. Wide lava flows began pouring down the mountainsides toward the burning trees.

Harry found himself in space looking down upon the beautiful blue-green world of Kormaljis. The massive explosion mushroomed into the clouds from a mountain range located near a shoreline along the planet's equatorial region.

A large meteor firestorm passing through the planet's orbital path sent hundreds of similar meteors plunging at tremendous speed into the atmosphere. Dozens more were exploding in areas covering over half the visible surface of the planet, creating more mushrooming clouds that quickly rose high into the atmosphere. Several exploded far out in the oceans, creating huge tidal waves that rolled around the world. Fires raged all over the continental landmasses, and the atmosphere quickly thickened with thick ash and mist.

As the planet rotated further on its axis, exposing its other side, meteors of various sizes shot down into the atmosphere and exploded in the oceans or thickly forested areas.

The plant life was soon dead or dying all over the planet. The numerous waterfalls and the many thousands of emerald lakes were gone. The stately snow-covered mountains were now barren and devoid of any moisture. It had burned or evaporated away, leaving the entire planet shrouded in the thick mist. The temperature had risen to a constant one hundred and ten degrees from its normal seventy-five-degree environment. Those magnificent giant forest trees, now burned-out stumps, had been unique in the entire explored galaxy.

The scene changed and Harry found himself inside the cavern on the planet's surface. The men and women gathered around the young Sen Dar were sitting on a flat wooden platform built upon the cavern floor. A mile across, the interior of the cavern contained a labyrinth of hydroponics tube-fed growing vegetable plants and vines, as well as many fruit trees. Violence was raging just outside the cavern opening a hundred feet away. Fine volcanic dust and fumes slowly wafted inside the cavern, and everyone began to cough just as the ground began to shake violently. Many of the support structures holding the various plants in the air crashed to the ground. Small trees toppled over, and the transparent feed pipes broke in many places, gushing clear liquid. The roar outside was so loud that no one could hear the screams of terror.

Harry found himself suddenly back inside the observation dome of the visiting spaceship, two days later. Sen Dar was still lying on the stretcher with his eyes open gazing at the strange-looking male and female technicians, and he fearfully snapped his eyes shut. Two technicians helped him sit up, and one offered him a clear canister of cool liquid. Scared by the gesture, Sen Dar backed away at first. Then he grabbed the canister and greedily chugged down the refreshing fluid.

"Is he really the only child found alive?" a woman support technician asked sadly.

"He's the only one," replied the lead male technician. "The scouting party reported finding just twelve adult males and twelve adult females inside the cavern. From the way things look, over a billion of his people perished worldwide in a single day."

"A billion people? Good Lord, no-o-o," gasped the woman. "What will knowing that do to him as he grows up?"

She sadly shook her head.

They both noticed the dazed, tearing eyes of Sen Dar cast downward. Anguished beyond words, he looked up with hopeless dismay at the man and woman, while they carefully carried his stretcher into the elevator. Still terrified, Sen Dar gazed back through the dome at his dead world as long as he could while the elevator slowly lowered out of view.

More information came to Harry. He now knew the Galactic Alliance scientists were particularly saddened when they learned all this from the few surviving adults. The recording of their conversations is all that survived of the once beautiful Kormaljis home world and civilization. Only a dozen men, a dozen women, and one child, Sen Dar, were all they found barely alive on the once thriving and scientifically advanced world of over a billion people. The Galactic Council estimated they were probably only fifty years away from interplanetary space travel or they could have escaped disaster.

Sen Dar and the few surviving adults were human. No one doubted that. However, the Council could not figure out how the people of Kormaljis had evolved so far out in the unexplored regions of the galaxy or how they got there in the first place. No records of these people remained, and the handful of adults that survived the catastrophic meteoric bombardment were not scientists or educators, but simple farmers.

How this kind of traumatic experience would affect the only surviving child from this planet, not even the Galactic Alliance psychologists could predict. They knew it would do something very profound to the young Sen Dar, but what, was anyone's guess. There had not been any documented cases of this type of situation in Galactic Alliance history. The psychologists eventually concluded it must have left Sen Dar feeling very powerless in a big, bad universe.

After Sen Dar fully recovered, the Galactic Council discovered he had many latent psychic talents and perceptive abilities that most other children in the Galactic Alliance had not developed, especially at his young age. The only other beings with this capability were the mysterious

Oceanans, and the even more mysterious Guardian Master Adepts of The Ancient One.

Harry learned that when the first Oceanans appeared in ancient history, they claimed their home world existed in a higher parallel dimension of the physical universe. For their own reasons, they would not reveal the secret of how to access this special dimension. During the early days of the original planetary coalition, the spiritual and scientific benefits the peaceful but powerful Oceanans offered the coalition were obvious. This resulted in giving the Oceanans the privilege of naming the new Alliance, and they became its founding sponsor by a unanimous vote. Eventually, the Galactic Alliance Council decided the Oceanans could keep their secrets to themselves, for the time being, if they were so insistent.

It did not go unnoticed, however, that many billions of diverse beings on hundreds of different worlds desired to one day visit the Oceanans' mysterious home world. For now, it appeared they would have to wait. Opellum, the Oceanan leader, assured the Council that eventually the way would be cleared for this event to take place at a time when the Galactic Inter-dimensional Alliance of Free Worlds, and its combined inhabitants, were ready for a great leap forward in their understanding of the universe and the living omnipresent Spirit energy presence behind it. Of course, this mystified everyone even more. Yet, they had to accept that answer and that was that.

Master Opellum soon heard about the orphaned Sen Dar from the Galactic Alliance Council. He asked them if he could temporarily adopt Sen Dar and bring him to Master Nim on Promintis, one of the secluded training planets of the Guardian Adepts of The Ancient One. There, Sen Dar would receive the rare opportunity to become a student in training to one day become a Master within this sacred order, and the Galactic Council agreed. It was Opellum that first contacted Master Nim on Promintis to tell him about the child. Opellum also knew Nim would understand the great potential for good or ill that lay dormant in Sen Dar, and that he could guide the boy in the right direction.

A semi-desert world suddenly appeared before Harry. He was gazing at an oasis pond situated at the base of a hill not far from a snowcapped mountain range. He could see a clear blue sky and sensed the temperature was comfortable. A virile-looking, white-haired Asian man in his sixties, with a long beard and no mustache, was sitting on a marble seat in a circle of tropical trees by the oasis. His eyes were sparkling bright blue with penetrating black pupils below bushy eyebrows. A simple wraparound maroon robe flowed down to six inches above his ankles. A faint golden light radiated around his body, as he telepathically heard Master Opellum's friendly voice, and then he opened his eyes.

Master Nim, may I approach? We should discuss an important matter.

Master Nim nodded his approval and a sphere of blue light appeared several feet beside him. It formed into Master Opellum's body. Grinning, Master Nim got to his feet and clasped forearms with Opellum as if they were brothers parted for many years.

"You know you're most welcome, my old teacher," Nim stated, "but what brings you to this remote training planet?"

"One of the Galactic Alliance science vessels discovered an unknown world on the outer rim of the seventh spiral arm of the galaxy," replied Master Opellum. "A massive meteor bombardment virtually decimated the planet's surface two days earlier. One boy, Sen Dar, and a handful of adults were all that survived. The boy has a very powerful potential for mastership, but he could also go the other way considering his recent loss. He's an orphan and I would like you to accept him for training."

"It would be my privilege, Master Opellum," replied Nim with a nod.

"Excellent," Opellum remarked exuberantly. "Everything has been explained to Sen Dar, and he has accepted this path of his own freewill. I will have a courier ship bring him here. Until we meet again, in the name of The Ancient One, I bid you farewell."

They clasped forearms once again, and Master Opellum faded from sight.

Hmm, Master Nim pondered, ***this boy should prove a most interesting challenge.***

Master Nim's image faded away in a blur as time sped up. Then a new image formed and Harry perceived that one month had now elapsed since the day the science ship's personnel discovered the now lifeless and barren Kormaljis. Young Sen Dar had now arrived on one of the training planets of The Ancient One's Guardian Adepts, and he was beginning to learn things he never dreamed were possible.

Sen Dar was a highly intelligent student with a quick wit. Initially, he behaved like all of the other students, but they soon became wary of him. Somehow, they kept finding themselves doing his bidding without really being consciously aware of how he got them to do it.

Harry again heard Master Ra Mu's voice.

Notice, General, it is now ten years later, and Sen Dar is twenty years old. He's about to face a major turning point in his life. Experience more of Promintis, one of the training planets of the Adepts of The Ancient One. Behold!

Harry received a whirlwind of images, along with a stream of new information as a different semi-desert environment appeared before him. Sen Dar was now six feet tall, wearing a yellow robe belted at the waist and simple sandals, like all of the other students, or Chelas as they were called on Promintis. His tall forehead and high cheekbones were striking against his squared sturdy jaw, and his dark brown eyes were pools of secrecy. His well-groomed and vibrant-looking long flowing hair was jet black and parted in the middle. It swept behind his ears and hung down below his shoulders. Although his complexion was slightly ruddy and hard-edged from sudden exposure to the harsh elements of his dying home world before his rescue, he was magnetically attractive in his own way. That was the only way to put it. He had a magnetic personality.

As a young disciple, Sen Dar had excelled at learning the secret exercises that would one day enable him to travel out of his physical body on the Light and Sound of Spirit and into the higher dimensions to meet with The Ancient One. Over the years he had also developed an uncanny ability to get the other students to do his bidding as easily as some people get up in the early morning to appreciate the rising sun and take their first deep breath of crisp fresh air. In fact, he had grown quite proud of this ability, and Master Nim was growing equally concerned while he observed Sen Dar enjoying having power over others.

Sen Dar thought Master Nim was nice to him and treated him with a measure of dignity. In time, Sen Dar had grown to genuinely love and respect his teacher as a treasured mentor and foster father. However, lately Nim seemed to be singling him out, handing him strict disciplinary tasks to accomplish. Nim disciplined him for every little thing that went wrong anywhere with anybody or anything. This had been going on for several months, and Sen Dar was growing more irritated with each passing day.

If Sen Dar had taken the time to contemplate the situation in one of the spiritual discipline caves assigned to him, he would have discovered that he was receiving more individual training and personal attention from Master Nim than the other students received.

Yet, Sen Dar did not notice. Some of the Adepts say this error in his judgment was due to a secretly guarded inner desire to gain control of everything around him, because of the powerlessness he had felt when he watched his parents and his civilization destroyed right before his eyes. He was driving himself to accomplish his spiritual training not just for personal advancement, but for personal power over everything and everyone, a condition utterly denied him as a young and terrified boy. Now his ambitions were completely contrary to the training provided by the mysterious Adepts of The Ancient One.

Master Nim was well aware of Sen Dar's emerging troubling character, and he had been carefully guiding him to master the passion for power growing within him, so it would not gain mastery over him and head him toward destruction. He had to put Sen Dar through one more test before he could be prepared to receive the Guardianship of one of the most special gifts of The Ancient One. Master Nim was considering choosing Sen Dar to one day become his successor as Guardian Protector of a very powerful crystal tool and map given the masterful Adepts by The Ancient One eons ago.

A more intricate image of Master Nim came clearly into Harry's focus. He now looked slightly older, as if only a year had gone by instead of ten. He appeared virile and deeply focused, well disciplined, and exuded a quiet strength, as do all Guardian Master Adepts of The Ancient One. A subtle indentation ran vertically down the center of

Master Nim's forehead. His long white hair had evenly receded at the hairline; yet, it was still thick like fine white silk as it flowed down behind his head between his shoulder blades. He had no mustache and his white beard grew straight down from around his bottom lip and chin, tapering to a point in the middle of his chest. Fine wrinkle lines at the outside corners of his eyes made him appear wise and stately. His high wide-set cheekbones and cheeks concaved inward above his strong narrow jaw, and his long nose gently curved down its length to a pointy end with slightly flared nostrils. His body was lean, and his hands were very strong. Although he appeared to be Asian, his bright blue round eyes were most unusual in comparison to any Asian man on planet Earth. However, Master Nim was not from Earth, and his bushy white eyebrows added to his mystique.

He was wearing a simple cream-colored, cotton-like robe that flowed down to six inches above his ankles. The top of the garment had a flap that crossed over his entire chest from left to right and buttoned along its entire length. Tied off at his left hip were several leather-like belt straps, looped parallel to each other about an inch apart through holes around his waist. Under the robe were matching thin white pants with an inch-thick embroidered border encircling the bottom hem. His sandals were made of a brown leather material and had a thin gray cloth woven into the top of them that came up twelve inches around his ankles. The brown leather-like straps that crisscrossed over his feet and up the cloth was tied off in back.

Master Nim's clothing was similar to the appropriate attire worn by many Masters in his ancient order of spiritual Adepts. Each Master designed their clothes with a personal variation of the usual theme; and their individual spiritual qualities and artistic tastes always showed up in various subtle differences in their clothing. Yet, they all designed their garments around a similar connective motif.

Nim appeared to be in his mid-sixties with wisdom wrinkles at the sides of his eyes, but his face and forehead were smooth and as unwrinkled as that of a young man in his twenties. He looked ancient, while he also emanated a youthfully virile masculine aura. His bright blue eyes were full of vitality, and a gleam of humor sparkled in them when he talked.

The inspiring image of Nim's apparently unique Asian character gave Sen Dar and the other students under his guidance a thing to behold. All the students on Promintis knew that the Asian race, and in fact all of the races living on the quarantined planet Earth, did not originate on Earth. The Master Adepts of The Ancient One had long known this to be true, and it is one of the best-kept secrets in the universe.

They knew, as did Opellum, that Earth's different races originally came from elsewhere in the galaxy long ago. Only the Adepts knew exactly when, how, and why this occurred, but they were not willing to discuss it. Every race in the Galactic Alliance had tried to drag it out of the Oceanan leader but he would just smile.

He would kindly reply to any official inquiry, "Every individual will find out the truth behind all truths for themselves one day. To hurry anyone along too fast only creates havoc."

What a damned puzzling comment this was for most Galactic Alliance planetary members. On the other hand, the Galactic Alliance had quarantined planet Earth, and the people living there remained completely in the dark about any of this and about the existence of beings from other worlds. Opellum knew the humans currently living on Earth, and many who would live there in the distant future, even up to the start of the twenty-first century, would still believe they had originally evolved on Earth from apes and earlier forms of life. This was simply hilarious to most of the intelligent, sentient beings that belonged to the Galactic Inter-dimensional Alliance of Free Worlds.

Also, according to Opellum, the Adepts of The Ancient One and their anonymity was set up on purpose by The Ancient One so far back in the galaxy's history that no one could conceive of it. No history records make mention of the Adepts' early beginning anywhere on any world, and that includes the Oceanan hidden home world.

Only the oldest and most wise spiritual leaders of the Oceanans like Opellum, and the other Master Adepts secretly stationed throughout the galaxy, knew anything about the most evolved ancient beings in the universe known as The Silent Mentors. According to them, the Silent Mentors live in realms of Light, Sound, and splendor located many dimensions above the entire physical universe. They claim it is useless to discuss the Silent Mentors with others because they are entirely beyond the comprehension of most beings living on the physical worlds of the galaxy. Opellum and other Oceanan sages would not elaborate about them or reveal anything back far enough in their recordings of events to shed some light on them. They even refused to discuss with the Galactic Council more about the origin of the Master Adepts or the Silent Mentors, and their secret records date back several million years at least.

A new scene of Master Nim and Sen Dar appeared before Harry, while he continued to observe astounding events unfold. Master Nim was now walking along a well-worn path that ran parallel to the edge of a very high cliff a few feet away. The path continued along the cliff ledge a dozen yards before it gradually climbed toward a white domed roof covering a round red brick sanctuary building on a nearby hilltop. Harry knew Sen Dar was about to receive that one final test of his character. If he passed the test, he could receive much more advanced training that could one day lead him to become a true Master Guardian Adept of The Ancient One.

As Master Nim approached Harry's viewpoint, he turned away from the cliff and headed toward Sen Dar, who was rising from his seated position on the contemplation rug on the nearby grass-covered field. As Master Nim approached Sen Dar, he contemplated how ideal his planet was to train new students.

Fortunately for my students, he thought with a twinkle in his eyes, *visitors to Promintis and their many negative influences are rare.*

"Chela Sen Dar, I have a special gift for you," he announced cheerfully.

Genuinely surprised, Sen Dar grinned and humbly bowed toward his venerable teacher, then looked up, puzzled, and asked, "You have a gift, Master Nim... for me?"

Sen Dar pondered the unexpected event with eager anticipation because Master Nim had not directed such kindness toward him since his arrival on Promintis many years earlier.

Nim reached inside his robe and pulled out a two-inch-long and inch-wide rectangular faceted blue crystal, hung around his neck from a simple sturdy gold chain. Then he pulled out an old parchment made of a leather-like material. A tear line along one edge of the map indicated it might be part of a larger original document. Unfamiliar alien writing and symbols were inscribed all over its surface. Nim carefully watched Sen Dar with a raised eyebrow, taking note of his wide eyes and gasp at seeing the crystal and the map. His delighted lust for them was unmistakable to Nim's sharp gaze.

"That must be The Ancient One's crystal you told me about," said Sen Dar with anxious anticipation, "and that's half of its cosmic map. Is that correct, Master?"

Nim closed his eyes for a moment to conceal his growing disappointment, and to seek inner guidance from The Ancient One. His eyes sprang back open as his grimace transformed into a jovial smile, and he stuffed the map back into his robe.

"Now watch this closely, Sen Dar," commanded Nim. "If you can master the right use of the Transport Matrix Crystal and The Ancient One's map, training will begin with the other two mystic crystals."

Sen Dar's eyes sparkled and Nim raised a disappointed eyebrow.

"Master Nim, why did The Ancient One give the first Adepts the cosmic crystals?" Sen Dar inquired.

Master Nim looked toward the ground but smiled as he looked up directly into Sen Dar's eyes.

"They are tools to train the student, like yourself, in the right use of love, wisdom, and power or charity. The properly trained and prepared student then places the three crystals together, and the student becomes enlightened after he meets with The Ancient One. He becomes a God-conscious co-creator with the source behind all life, and then a Guardian Master Adept in his own right."

Sen Dar appeared amazed, and Master Nim stepped back a few feet.

"Behold, Chela Sen Dar, the way of The Ancient One, and learn from this."

Nim closed his eyes, muttered something under his breath, and then his eyes sprang back open.

"Now, you must grab the crystal in your right hand and…"

Nim grabbed the crystal in his right hand, instantly causing it to glow with blue light through his clenched fingers. He took a few steps further back, and then ran with all his might past Sen Dar a dozen feet and off the cliff.

Stunned, Sen Dar's mouth dropped wide open.

"Master Nim… no-o!"

He ran frantically to the edge of the cliff just in time to see Master Nim drop in an arc beginning to radiate silver-gold light. For an instant, his body remained suspended in the air. Then it turned into brilliant rainbow-colored molecules and vanished with a great *swish*… and a… *boom*… that echoed across the gorge.

Thousands of feet far below, the barely visible bends in a winding river looked like a snake weaving its way along the bottom of a wide, lushly green-forested ravine. However, Sen Dar did not notice the beautiful ravine far below as he jumped around in a panic and ran along the pathway up the hill toward Nim's sanctuary. The sun was beginning to set behind the mountains in the far distance beyond the domed building, and the few clouds moving above them lit up in a violet, red, and orange sunset.

The last golden sunset rays poured through the open sanctuary doorway, illuminating the center of a sparsely decorated room. An ornate round rug on the blue stone floor, woven with arcane symbols around the edge, had six green silk pillows carefully arranged around the circumference. Centered in the middle of them was a larger blue silk pillow with gold tassels hanging from the tip of each corner. Sen Dar ran panting through the open doorway to Master Nim's sanctuary and stopped with surprise and then great relief.

"Master Nim!" he gasped.

Sitting cross-legged on the large pillow was Master Nim, smiling broadly. The still-glowing blue crystal resting against his chest flickered, dimmed, and went out. He raised an eyebrow and gazed with penetrating discerning eyes deep into Sen Dar's puzzlement.

"Now do you understand?" Nim asked calmly.

Sen Dar shook his head, rubbed his eyes to make certain he was not dreaming, took a deep breath, and slowly let it out.

"I uh, I think so, Master," he answered hesitantly.

He looked briefly at the ground in thought, and then back up, smiling as a new realization dawned.

"The Transport Matrix Crystal of The Ancient One will move you wherever you imagine. Is that it?" he inquired eagerly.

Sen Dar stared at Master Nim with a single eyebrow cocked in his direction.

"That... is only part of it," firmly began Nim, as he reached inside his robe and pulled out the old parchment. He held it up flat in the palm of his hand and continued with a serious tone, "This is half of The Ancient One's guide map. It describes the use of The Transport Matrix Crystal, and the location of the other half of the map."

Sen Dar's eyes widened with anticipation as he unconsciously walked a few feet toward Nim.

Barely hiding his lust, he asked, "Where are the other two crystals?"

Nim returned a stern emotionless expression but was surprised at the negative stream of emotions coming from his student. He lowered his hand holding the old parchment, clutched it with his fingers, and then stuffed it back inside his robe.

"That secret is for one who is ready to become a Master," Nim replied sternly.

Sen Dar grimaced at Nim's remark as they heard footsteps walking toward the sanctuary door. Nara, a much younger disciple than Sen Dar, about thirteen years old, walked calmly through the open door. Smiling, he approached Master Nim and bowed with deep respect. Sen Dar frowned but quickly hid his feelings by grinning at Nara, before he looked back at Nim.

"I have come as you requested, Master," he said happily.

The smiling Master nodded his head in return and responded, "Please be seated, Nara."

The young disciple sat yoga style on the pillow in the circle closest to the doorway as Master Nim stared up at Sen Dar.

"Chela Sen Dar," Master Nim began, "the Nine Secret Silent Guardians have decided that you are not yet ready for the deeper training for Guardianship of the crystal and map. They have decided that Nara," and he nodded toward Nara, "should be the next Guardian of The Ancient One's Transport Matrix Crystal and sacred map."

Sen Dar's face flushed with suppressed anger.

"But you can't do that," he blurted out and he took a quick deep breath, then calmly forced a gentle smile and continued, "What I mean is, I have spent twelve years training for this. You promised the Guardianship to me. Nara has only been here six months and he's only a boy."

"Chela Sen Dar, the Council's decision is final," Nim responded firmly. "The Guardianship goes to Nara."

"That crystal belongs to me. I've earned the right," Sen Dar fumed openly. "That crystal is –"

"Chela Sen Dar," shouted Nim, cutting him off with a firm rebuke. "The Ancient One's crystals are for the awakening of all life and not for the selfish desire for power by one man."

Sen Dar then realized this had all been another hard test, one he was becoming painfully aware he likely failed. Now remorseful, he looked pleadingly at Master Nim.

"Please forgive me, Master Nim. I lost myself for a moment. I have been training for so long and I know I can pass the test if you just give me another chance to prove myself."

"You have much work to do before wisdom enters your heart fully," responded Nim.

"But –" Sen Dar started to say as Nim cut him off again.
"Leave me, Chela Sen Dar. Go and contemplate on the experience you have had here today."

Sen Dar's face flushed red, and he turned in a huff and walked away through the open doorway. Twilight was upon him as he headed down the winding path away from Nim's sanctuary.

Nim turned to Nara and said, "Learn from this, Chela Nara. Sen Dar's lust for power must be given up to greater co-creative purpose with the omnipresent Sound and Light, living Spirit presence of The Ancient One."

The now subdued young disciple nodded his head in full agreement, and Master Nim smiled back at him.

"You may leave me, Nara, but don't forget to do your spiritual exercises this evening."

Nara stood up and smiled down at his venerable spiritual teacher with a simple nod of his head to confirm his wishes. Then he turned around and walked through the open doorway into the fading light.

The panorama of the night sky seen from Promintis, even at twilight, would be beyond description to an Earth person. The density of the stars, nebulae star clusters, and the three moons circling high overhead, each with two sets of green rings around them, would make anyone's evening a romantic one even if all alone. However, Sen Dar did not see this spectacle, and romance was the furthest thing from his thoughts. He skulked back up the path toward the open doorway to Nim's sanctuary.

Master Nim was sitting in contemplation on the pillow with his back to the door when the shadow of a man appeared on the floor and moved menacingly toward him until it touched his back.

"Why are you here, Sen Dar?" asked Master Nim.

There was no answer from the shadowy figure as Nim got up to his feet in one swift motion and spun around with a quick graceful movement to face Sen Dar. The fingers of his right hand were holding the crystal around his neck to his chest. Sen Dar was standing inside the open doorway pointing a laser gun at him. Green and red six-sided crystals ran up the handle and down the length of the barrel through the transparent shell.

Nim's surprised expression turned to concern and he exclaimed, "Have you already become completely controlled by your passion for power? Sen Dar, do not give into it. Master it."

Nim walked confidently toward Sen Dar, as the crystal began to glow through his clenched fingers.

"Give me the gun," he commanded.

Sen Dar appeared to be in a hypnotic trance, as Nim walked up to within a few inches of the gun pointed at his chest. Sen Dar stared into empty space as he started to hand Nim the gun, and then his numbed expression instantly changed to violent fury. He shook his head to throw off the crystal's hypnotic effect. Nim reacted by clutching the crystal more tightly to his chest but it was too late. Sen Dar fired the gun and a beam of fiery red light hit Nim in the center of his chest. He groaned and let go of his hold on the crystal, and it fell on its gold chain to his chest right below the laser hole burned into his right lung. Then he fell-forward grasping Sen Dar by the shoulders with both hands, but Sen Dar was now unmoved, lost in impassioned, angry madness.

He screamed, "I've sat long enough at your feeble old feet to earn the right and you will not deprive me of it."

Gasping for air, Nim was dying as blood trickled down the corner of his mouth. His hands were slowly slipping off Sen Dar's shoulders and he closed his eyes. Then he struggled to speak but only managed a whisper.

"Sen Dar, listen. It was only a test."

Shocked to his senses, Sen Dar now realized what he had done. Nim started to drop and his hands slipped off Sen Dar's shoulders, but Sen Dar grabbed his wrists and pulled him back up.

"What do you mean it was only a test?" Sen Dar asked abruptly, beginning to show concern for Nim's welfare.

Master Nim's eyes remained closed as he struggled to speak. He choked several times instead.

Breathlessly gasping, Nim managed to whisper, "The test... the test of power."

Sen Dar's shocked eyes widened, and a deeply pained, remorseful expression spread across his face.

"No, you can't die," he pleaded. "You should have told me. Why didn't you tell me? Why?"

Master Nim gasped his final words of wisdom with the faintest whisper. "This is the way... the way of The Ancient One."

Sen Dar recoiled in terror with deep regret for his terrible uncontrolled actions toward his former Master.

"No-o-o... no, you can't die," he cried in agony. "Please, Master Nim, I didn't know."

As Sen Dar gently lowered Nim's body to the floor, he heard the excited yelling of several people running in the direction of the sanctuary and footsteps swiftly drawing nearer.

"I'm sure it was a laser blast," yelled a man's frantic voice. "I saw a flash coming from the open door to Nim's sanctuary."

Tears were now running down Sen Dar's cheeks, but his remorseful expression changed to fright. He reached frantically into Nim's robe, grabbed The Ancient One's parchment, and tucked it into a pocket inside his own robe. Then he gently lifted the crystal off Nim's neck, placed it around his own, and tucked it inside the folds of his robe. He stood back up, wiped the tears from his wet cheeks, and took one last regretful look down at his dead former Master's body. Then he ran toward the door but stopped to take a final look back knowing the unfortunate direction of his destiny was now set. Then he darted out of the sanctuary to disappear in the night.

Harry felt a force pulling him back from the scene, while images receded rapidly into the distance. His true Atma-self moved back out of the holographic light sphere projected from Master Ra Mu's crystal staff. Harry's vision cleared, and he took in his surroundings as he looked through the eyes of his physical body. He shook his head with amazement as he looked up at Master Ra Mu.

"That was just unbelievable," he began as he glanced over at the holographic light sphere, then back at Ra Mu. "It's incredible. It's fantastic!"

The images within the sphere of light now appeared frozen in place. The open door to Nim's sanctuary was clearly visible, as was Nim's dead body lying on the floor.

"It was like I was really there," said Harry. "Then what I saw really happened and those crystals, or whatever they are, actually exist?"

With a gentle smile, Master Ra Mu answered, "Yes, and Sen Dar has one of them. We must locate and stop him before his occult abilities increase. Understand, General Faldwell, the longer that Sen Dar possesses a mystic crystal of The Ancient One, the greater will be the occult powers that awaken in him."

Harry looked up at Ra Mu as he stuffed the unlit cigar into the corner of his mouth, and then abruptly yanked it back out.

"Hmm, then why didn't you stop him before now?" he asked, and stuffed the cigar back in his mouth.

Smiling, Master Ra Mu replied, "Sen Dar used the persuasive power of the Transport Matrix Crystal to gather forces. He conquered whole star systems and ruled part of the galaxy for many years."

Harry raised a puzzled eyebrow and asked, "Why didn't he go after the other half of the map right away?"

"The Galactic Alliance working in tandem with the Guardian Adepts of The Ancient One kept him from it," replied Ra Mu. Then he added, "He couldn't get near the location until the end of the Sen Darion War when his chance finally came."

"Why show me all this?" asked Harry, still doubtful.

"It is vital that you understand how he came to be in your parallel dimension on Earth today, and the imminent threat his presence represents. There is more, General, much more."

Harry gazed at Ra Mu, took the cigar out of his mouth, and then replied, "By all means, Master Ra Mu, please continue."

The scene inside the holographic sphere of light changed instantly to the breathtaking panorama of outer space. Harry felt liberated once again, as he sped back into the light sphere to discover that he was once again an invisible viewpoint in space. Below him, an amazing scene began to unfold as he moved swiftly downward toward a huge spaceship. Luminous bridge towers rose between two observation-domes positioned at each end of the hull, until they peaked in the center of the ship. Many more Galactic Alliance star ships were moving behind it in two parallel rows that receded into the distant background of space.

Harry then found himself hovering for a moment over a clear dome on one end of the ship. He moved right through the dome and stopped several feet above and in front of a man wearing an identical uniform to Captain Kalem, except three gold stripes encircled each sleeve instead of one. Though much older than Kalem, the man had strikingly similar features as he stared up through the clear observation dome into the vast star fields of space. Harry telepathically understood the man's perceptions and thoughtful reflections.

CHAPTER TEN

REFLECTIONS
OF ADMIRAL STARLAND

$\mathcal{A}$dmiral Starland was looking out through one of the observation domes of his Galactic Alliance flagship. The ship's hull was softly glowing with a pale-blue light as it moved effortlessly through space, while he gazed at another huge fleet ship trailing slightly behind his flagship. He looked away and thought about how the Galactic Alliance developed utilizing the antigravity technology that powered the fleet. The Oceanans had gradually shared it with a number of the original founding planetary members of the Galactic Inter-dimensional Alliance of Free Worlds over a considerably long period.

He smiled as he recalled that Master Opellum of the Oceanans had first introduced him to the existence of the Master Adepts, and subsequently to Master Ra Mu secretly stationed on Earth on the continent of Lemuria. Ra Mu was the first Master to show him the wonders of the higher worlds in the vast dimensions that were beyond his physical body and the physical universe.

After two decades of training in the art of leaving and returning to his physical body through the Light and Sound of Spirit, he recalled how grateful he was when Master Ra Mu finally took him on his first journey to The Ancient One's realm.

He looked back up through the observation dome at the stars, never seeming to tire of the stellar view, to watch the many star systems appear to pass by leaving light trails – as if the fleet ships were moving by them faster than the speed of light. He knew it was an illusion of perspective but it remained beautiful.

Actually, his ship and the other ships in the fleet were leaping by entire star systems in multiple trans-light jumps. Although one could not calculate this in terms of speed, it meant that the fleet was leaping through naturally occurring invisible holes in the fabric of space that link parallel dimensions. The ships travel for a short time in the space of a parallel dimension and then pop out of another invisible opening back into their own space to find they have traveled a great distance across the galaxy. They could travel many, many times faster than light speed in this way to cross great distances of the universe.

Admiral Starland was poised serenely as he continued to gaze back out of the clear dome into the vast star fields. He was trim and well built, appearing to be in his early fifties by Earth standards, with short brown hair swept back at the sides. The only hair streaked white, was at his temples and sideburns. His high forehead, squared jaw, smooth round chin, and blue eyes made him appear wise and stately in his uniform. His slim gray-blue pants, belted at the waist with an oval gold buckle, was identical to the one worn by his son, Captain Kalem. Also embossed over the left chest area of his long-sleeved shirt was the

Galactic symbol. However, instead of two gold bands like those on Captain Kalem's uniform, three gold bands encircled each cuff and the neck collar that opened in front in a V-shape that tapered to a point a few inches below the base of his neck.

Even after many years, the Admiral thought the fleet ships of The Galactic Inter-dimensional Alliance of Free Worlds technological masterpieces. He realized they were not quite as extraordinary as the mysterious great Oceana Spectrum star ships, but they were elegant ships over a mile in length. Crystal-like control towers rose up from one end of the hull to a higher control tower point in the center of the ship and gradually tapered in height downward again until they reached the other end of the ship. Positioned on each end of the hull were clear observation domes one hundred feet in diameter. A transparent elevator would rise up from the deck below into the middle of the dome's circular floor to deposit a passenger and return. A curved launch bay at each end of the massive ship's hull could open and close in front of and below each observation dome.

Admiral Starland watched several Scout Interceptors fly one by one out of the open launch bay below the observation dome. He continued to gaze at them as a number more exited the ship. They maneuvered into a triangular formation about a thousand yards from the end of the ship and a hundred feet further in space. The fifteenth ship appeared and completed the triangular formation, while Starland gazed at the three antigravity Wave-Vector pods built in a triangular pattern on the bottom of each Scout ship's hull. They were softly pulsating with a slightly more intense blue light than the light surrounding their hulls.

Just discernable through the gray metallic coverings were the shadowed images of antigravity lightening discharges whirling around the control spires. Each pod contained twelve quartz crystal spires pointing downward in different directions. It was a familiar scene to Starland, but it was still a beautiful sight for him to behold every time he observed the Scout Ships hovering in space.

He thought back over the events that had brought him to this very moment in time and space, and then he remembered that final day of reckoning twenty years earlier when Master Ra Mu took him for the first time to meet The Ancient One. He traveled out of his body, riding the Sound of Spirit and guided by its brilliant Light, until he reached the high dimension of The Ancient One's realm. Then he became an Adept of The Ancient One and a Master in his own right. There he gained the overview of creation from The Ancient One's lofty realm down through the pure dimensions of Spirit, and all the way down through the many dimensions below them. Then he had returned to the physical plane where galaxies silently spun through space and his responsibility existed as Admiral of The Galactic Inter-dimensional Alliance of Free Worlds.

He continued to reflect on how difficult it had been over the last twelve years to secretly guide Kalem without his awareness. He silently watched over him growing up during his Academy years, during and after he entered service in The Galactic Inter-dimensional Alliance of Free Worlds as an Ensign, and through several more years later when he witnessed his son's promotion to the rank of Captain.

He could not tell his own son who his father had become or who he really was now, so utterly transformed beyond only human. He could not directly intervene in any way to affect his son's personal choices, until the time came for him to also experience the truth behind life for himself. He also could not share how much he really admired and loved him because of the tests he had to go through, but he could silently encourage him.

The Admiral knew, full well, his son needed all the lessons of life he could get to bring out more of his higher capabilities. His latent qualities of discrimination of right and wrong; courage; resourcefulness; and that bold, daring, and adventuresome spirit had to be developed so that one day he could travel out of his physical body and explore the heavenly worlds in the higher realms.

Kalem was the best fighter pilot in the fleet, proven with field-tested leadership and courage during many battles with two totalitarian world groups that were combined under one unknown tyrant leader. They called themselves the Imperial Glonden-Yalgull Alliance.

The Glonden were humanoid and had not always been enemies of the Galactic Alliance. However, they did have an Emperor who ruled over many worlds. The Yalgull group of worlds were populated by more aggressive totalitarians with a ruthless leader that had been kept in check by Galactic Alliance space patrols for many years before the war started. It was this group that first began the conflict by attacking several Galactic Alliance outposts, killing several thousands of its innocent civilian occupants. A discovery a short time later revealed that the two totalitarian world systems had secretly joined forces.

Starland had lost Kalem's older brother, Rumon, during one of the many battles the Galactic Alliance had fought with them over the last ten years. It happened at Santinaby (5) in the constellation of Rendgunyam. The Yalgull used a stolen Galactic Alliance distress signal to lure a squadron on patrol into a trap. Earlier, the Glonden had placed a Helix Projection Beam weapon on the cloud-shrouded planet to avoid its detection by any Galactic Alliance Scout ships that regularly patrolled that particular space route. They surprised the Galactic Alliance ships as they slowed to orbit the planet.

Rumon had perished when his Cutter class cruiser called The Deep Star blew up after taking heavy damage from the firepower emanating from the planet's surface, as well from five Yalgull Destroyer class vessels that had been hiding in the planet's thick cloud cover.

After this event, the full strength of the Glonden-Yalgull Alliance became apparent. Dozens of world systems were involved with many well-equipped V-shaped Glonden Viper starships and the Yalgull Star class battle cruisers with their characteristic narrower long oval shape than the Galactic Alliance Emerald Star cruiser hull design.

Admiral Starland's flagship and twelve other Emerald Star class cruisers had arrived five minutes too late to save Rumon's ship, with over thirteen thousand officers and crew aboard it and the three other Cutter class reconnaissance cruisers caught in the trap. However, the Galactic Alliance fleet had already surrounded the area of space near Santinaby (5) and they soon cornered the Yalgull ships. In the swift counterattack, they completely annihilated all five Yalgull Destroyers, and the hidden weapon on the planet's surface was melting into oblivion. The estimate was that at least fifteen thousand enemy personnel perished as well that same day.

After Rumon's tragic death, Starland used a technique known only to The Ancient One's Adepts. It allowed him to leave his physical body and escort Rumon's true Atma-self, the eternal luminous being, into the astral plane or the next dimensional reality directly above the physical plane of galaxies and planets. He had taken him to a secret monastery, a place of healing rest and re-orientation that the Adepts of his order had long ago secretly established. Through them, a higher power guarded the place with a cloak of invisibility so impenetrable that the residents of the astral dimension and the most powerful evil tyrants covertly living there could not discover it.

Starland knew that there his son would find the understanding and spiritual purpose for his premature death. He also knew with certainty that nothing happened by chance, and that when his son was ready, he would move on in his own unfolding toward Mastery under the further guidance of the mystic Adepts of the monastery.

He missed his first-born son as much as any father would. However, when an individual can actually visit a departed loved one by spiritually traveling to where they are, and then return to their own physical body, the gained balanced perspective greatly diminishes the sense of loss and anguish. Starland realized that Rumon was still very much alive and well on a higher level of being. He understood that the experiences gained there change everything in an individual's inner awareness. Attitudes and perspectives concerning life are widened and elevated as individuals make their journey back home to the Supreme Being of which they are all a part, and from which they all originated when they first descended into the lower worlds of time and space.

Starland reflected on all his many personal explorations into truth, but the loss of Rumon still deeply touched him. Now, he determined he would not lose Kalem, his only remaining son, to senseless war. He had spoken directly with The Ancient One, who showed him Kalem's possible future destiny: a precarious, challenging, highly adventurous path of intrigue, rare romance, danger, and growing awareness.

The Ancient One had said, *Kalem may survive the coming tests, Master Starland. If he chooses well and succeeds, I will draw him upward to my realm. Then he too may become a Master co-creator with me, even as you have become. He has a destiny, a task to complete before that day will dawn. Do not worry about him, my worthy son, for no Atma or the pure conscious spark of being has ever perished anywhere at any time along the entire history of creation. Every individual Atma remains eternal throughout this realm of pure Sound and Light, through the true realm of Soul on the fifth dimension and down through the lower dimensions, including the many parallel realities within them, and on all the planets in the physical universes.*

Starland smiled from the encouraging words and he thought, *What a different universe this would be if all the unique races within it knew the truth of their existence beyond the physical body. All fear would fade away to forever remain in the past.*

He looked away from observing space through the observation dome, shook his head with a grim expression, and realized, *For now, that is not to be in a warring universe.*

Starland understood it would always be this way, unless the source behind all life changed it. The good and bad effects that beings receive, as repercussions of their actions, are the ways that each one of them will eventually learn self-Mastery, while living in the physical universe. This was also true up through the finer dimensions above the physical worlds. However, this was not so in the fifth dimension or the true realm of the Atma.

From this glorious realm of joy and into the yet much higher pure dimensions that eventually lead to The Ancient One's realm there is only one law that rules supreme which simply states, "Love and do as you will."

He could not really change the way it was and he did not want to, for he understood the physical dimension with its uncounted numbers of galaxies and planets was a schoolroom of good and evil, made that way to offer beings a choice. After having chosen, he knew that individuals would subsequently experience the full repercussions of their actions. He also knew that a simple law of physics, often referred to as - *The Law of Cause and Effect*, applied only to the lower dimensions.

He thought, It's amazing how little those who are incarnated in the **physical worlds understand about the reality of this fixed law, and how it applies to each one of them.**

He knew most of them were young Souls destined to travel down pathways of indulgence in the negative passions, and then suffer in order to learn the right way of being. How else were they to one day become truly experienced, well-trained, and qualified co-creators with the supreme source or The Ancient One? It took much time or thousands of lifetimes in many cases before an individual would consciously volunteer of free will to begin their personal journey back home to their original starting place in The Ancient One's lofty realm of supernatural joy and fully conscious life.

He remembered a most ancient saying, "When the student is ready, the Master appears." Then he sighed, grinned, and said aloud, "For now, this is the way of things."

He recalled he had several captured Glonden prisoners beamed aboard his flagship for interrogation purposes only moments before his Galactic Alliance flagship incinerated the beam weapon on the planet's surface. The prisoners told him some rather enlightening information as they pleaded their case, stating repeatedly they really had no choice but to attack the Galactic Alliance. They said they were compelled to by their mysterious self-appointed charismatic new leader who had wormed his way into becoming their absolute ruler many years earlier, and then…it was too late.

That he had a powerful hypnotic control over them was a certainty. They said he had used such subtle cunning lies, psychic influences, and covert sorcery that none of the Glonden or the Yalgull could see coming. He had been too quick a wit for them as he wove his spells, inspiring them to make their evil alliance. He knew how to dominate the Glonden and Yalgull leaders and their people. After that, he appointed himself the emperor over all. Then he was ready, and he ordered incursions into Galactic Alliance space and all-out war.

Since then, ten years had gone by and Admiral Starland realized the Galactic Alliance fleet under his command was now heading toward what he felt certain would be the final battle with the Glonden-Yalgull Alliance. He did not know why he sensed it, but he was convinced Sen Dar was the hidden tyrant leader behind it all.

Starland recalled how Sen Dar had mysteriously disappeared fourteen years earlier after he killed Master Nim, his own benevolent teacher, and then took from his body one of the three primary sacred crystals and half the cosmic map of The Ancient One. He also realized the very great danger that represented to the Adepts; for if Sen Dar ever figured out how to read half the map and use the crystal, he would know on what planet the other half of the map was located. If he later acquired that as well, it would reveal where the other two cosmic crystals were located and who guarded them. Yet, that was only part of their concern, and time was running out.

Starland ordered highly skilled Galactic Alliance undercover investigators out into the galaxy to try to find where Sen Dar had gone after he killed Nim and escaped the planet, but they did not find him. Nim's death had been an unexpected great loss to the Adepts, and it signaled a new turn in the destiny of the galaxy. The Admiral suspected Sen Dar had first surfaced on the home world of the Glonden, but he needed proof.

While he reflected upon all these facts, Starland did not realize his eyes had closed in contemplation. He knew that, one day soon, he would have to order Kalem into a final battle with the Glonden-Yalgull Alliance. The danger was coming, but it was not yet time. In fact, Kalem was commanding the two fighter squadrons he had been observing getting ready to head into space on another reconnaissance mission. Then he concentrated on The Ancient One's Spirit Sound humming within him, and watched the bright white Light on the inner screen of his awareness.

Oh, great Ancient One, he said in the silent recesses of his being, *spare my one remaining son in the days to come. How much longer must we put up with this madness of war? How many more must die? Then he humbly lowered his head and continued, Nevertheless, your way is that all beings learn from the fruits of their actions, whether constructive or destructive.*

He pondered where his former mentor friend, Master Ra Mu, was at that moment. Now more than ever, he wished for his friendship and advice full of wisdom from being a co-worker with The Ancient One for many centuries. He knew well enough that he actually wasn't alone, for

The Ancient One's presence, the Spirit Sound and Light force behind all life, moved freely through him as a Master in his own right. Although he knew with certainty that everything would turn out for the best, he still wondered what that would mean regarding Kalem. His concern for Kalem's safety was like any other father's concern for a son. Yet, he also understood the special tests of spirit coming to Kalem must be passed by him on his own.

After all, Starland mused with a sigh, *your way is always for the greatest good of all life.*

CHAPTER ELEVEN

SURPRISE VISIT TO PROMINTIS

How can anyone say what drives people to do what they do?

General Faldwell pondered this question as certain hidden understandings surfaced within his awareness. He now knew Sen Dar did not understand why he felt compelled to react to the universe as if it would destroy him unless he could dominate it first. Admiral Starland and all of the other numerous Adepts of The Ancient One, secretly stationed throughout the galaxy, understood what was likely driving Sen Dar to the extremes he pursued. It was rooted in his childhood, certainly, but there was more to it than that. The Adepts also knew it was rooted in his abuses of power during several past lifetimes. The teachings of The Ancient One made it clear these actions were cumulative and that Sen Dar would ultimately receive, over time, the repercussions of all his actions whether benevolent or malevolent.

Yet, beyond this was The Ancient One's supreme law that supersedes all laws, *The Law of Love*. If a being came into true harmony with a respect for all life, they would attain spiritual freedom in direct proportion to how they respected and loved all life everywhere. Within the scope of this law was contained the wisdom that no one could force Sen Dar to change for the better, if that were ever possible, without becoming like him. Sen Dar would have to voluntarily change or continue to suffer indefinitely as the repercussions of his actions came back to knock him down.

An ancient saying of the secret Adepts is, "No one has ever escaped the repercussions of their actions in all of the history of creation."

However, they also know that individuals can be deluded or can delude themselves into the illusion that this is possible. That is, until the Spirit presence behind all life decides the time has come for them to pay the price for abusing life and then... *wham*... the rug is yanked out from under the one lost in the illusion of power. Even though this is true, the Master Guardians of The Ancient One and the Galactic Alliance had the task to find a way to permanently stop Sen Dar's madness from dominating other worlds and destroying more life, especially life that had the desire to awaken their eternal nature as potential co-creators with The Ancient One.

It was only after Sen Dar chose to kill Master Nim, steal one of The Ancient One's crystals and half its map from his body, then disappear, that he began to walk into a truly dark destiny. Subconscious negative influences coming from dark deeds he committed during several of his former lifetimes he had no ability to recall, and the effect of being the only orphaned child of a dead world propelled him in that direction. In his heart of hearts, he truly did not want to travel down that road, but the dark deed he had committed against Master Nim at that moment of emotional madness was drawing him into a destiny of galactic proportion. Sen Dar had not yet developed enough self-discipline or personal spiritual courage to turn it around and stop the negative reactive trend within him that had grown into a monster of suppressed guilt. That egomaniacal being had grown to such proportions inside him until it had completely taken over. It was now busy justifying any abusive act it wished for its own aggrandizement. In his private covert world, Sen Dar began to listen to a subconscious whisper that told him everything he did was righteously superior because his destiny was to become a God over all life on all worlds. Then he gradually chose to make his law the law of the universe, and this was precisely the course he eventually decided to pursue in the days following Nim's death.

The entire Galactic Alliance sent out secret agents to Promintis and other worlds to find Sen Dar and bring him to justice. Over the coming years, as war with the Glonden-Yalgull Alliance deepened, a number of situations arose that gave them confidence Sen Dar was finally cornered. When it appeared that escape was impossible and Galactic Alliance forces were closing in, he would mysteriously vanish and successfully elude capture through some strange and inexplicable means.

Harry continued to experience the stream of information, intertwined with Earth's true hidden history, while he remained fully cognizant that his physical body was still sitting in a trance-like state next to Carine, Kalem, and Master Ra Mu on the black sands of Lemuria. He was simultaneously aware of being an invisible, fully conscious sphere of whirling light with a unique viewpoint. Other than the Guardian Adepts of The Ancient One, he was the first human being on Earth to actually be enlightened by many uncovered hidden truths, and witness what happened after Sen Dar killed Master Nim and ran out of his sanctuary on the distant world of Promintis.

He was beyond amazed while he watched the vision of Admiral Starland standing inside the observation dome of his flagship gradually fade away and a new scene take its place. Several young disciples appeared running toward the open door to Nim's sanctuary and caught a fleeting glimpse of a shadow scurrying like a wild animal away from the sanctuary up the path that led into darkness and the mountainous cave country. The two disciples ran through the open doorway and stopped. They froze in their tracks, horrified upon seeing their dead Master teacher lying on the floor with a crude laser hole burned into his chest.

The next day, several trusted key disciples contacted Opellum by a secret transmitter that Nim had instructed them to use in the event of his untimely demise. Nara's description of Sen Dar's reaction to the test of power given by Nim confirmed he was the most likely suspect, and he was the only disciple missing. However, Master Opellum did not respond to the distress call.

Master Ra Mu from Earth, gripping his staff, appeared later that day walking through the open doorway to Nim's sanctuary. The two startled young disciples guarding Nim's covered body reacted defensively but they were soon calmed when Master Ra Mu announced his name and said he had arrived there at the request of Master Opellum. The disciples respectfully bowed their heads. They had heard a great deal from Master Nim about Master Ra Mu, regarded as one of the highest Adepts of The Ancient One. Yet, neither one of them believed they would actually have the honor to meet him.

Ra Mu removed the cloth covering Nim's body, looked down compassionately at his friend's corpse and placed a hand on his forehead. Then he gazed at the two disciples standing nearby.

With a reassuring smile he stated, "Be not concerned for your Master. As you both know, he is alive and well in a higher dimension of reality. I have spoken with him since his translation from the physical body. This was a destiny from a higher level he intended to fulfill."

The two disciples nodded.

"Leave me now for a few moments with my former teacher," Ra Mu solemnly continued. "When I'm finished, I will send for both of you so arrangements can be made to cremate his body in the appropriate way."

The two young nervous disciples bowed and then turned around and walked out of the sanctuary. Master Ra Mu closed his eyes, and his telekinetic perceptions revealed all that Sen Dar had done to his former Master. Like a motion picture running on the screen of his inner vision, he reviewed the events in detail, witnessing all that occurred from the time Nim approached Sen Dar on the path near the sanctuary to the moment of his death.

Concern etched his face as he watched Sen Dar steal from Nim's body half of the sacred parchment and the Transport Matrix Crystal. His eyes remained closed as his head turned toward the open doorway while he continued to observe Sen Dar's escape into the night. As he opened his eyes, compassionate concern flooded his being. He was not as saddened by Nim's death as he was by the choices Sen Dar was making. He knew Sen Dar had great potential to become an Adept of The Ancient One but now that potential was lost, perhaps for many more lifetimes to come.

He placed the cloth back over Nim's body, stood up, and then gazed down at his friend's physical form one last time. Then he turned and walked out through the sanctuary door into the bright midday sunlight. He continued a dozen feet up the path toward the snow-covered mountain peaks. Spread across the horizon, they towered many thousands of feet into the sky. Pausing, he gazed over flower-laden valleys to observe the storm clouds that were gathering over the summits of the tallest peaks, where he suspected, Sen Dar had headed to cause far deeper trouble.

With his staff in one hand and his other hand on his chin, he considered, *Where could Sen Dar go on a planet like Promintis at the onset of winter? Hmm, it's likely he'll soon be caught and brought to justice by Galactic Alliance agents or die of exposure from that looming winter storm.*

Then he recalled that Sen Dar had one of the mystic crystals and half of the sacred map, and he pondered, *Could Sen Dar discover some of the hidden uses of the things he stole in time to save his own life? Could his natural occult abilities already be sharp enough?*

Concerned, he raised his crystal staff several inches off the ground, looked around to be certain no one was observing him, and then slowly closed his eyes. An instant later, a flash of gold light from the Ankh symbol atop the crystal staff enveloped him in a halo of gold. His body sparkled with thousands of points of light and gradually faded from view.

CHAPTER TWELVE

SEN DAR'S CAVE
OF DELIVERANCE

Sen Dar was slowly freezing to death as he trudged laboriously ever upward into the mountains toward the caverns he knew were there somewhere. The snowfall was already four feet deep, and he could hardly see twelve inches in front of his face. Even though it was dark out, the planet Promintis twin suns that had set much earlier were reflecting some faint light off its three moons through the cloud cover. The wind howled and swirled stinging snow in great sheets around Sen Dar.

He fell face down into a snowdrift, then slowly forced himself to stand and walk a few more feet. The faint outline of a cave opening appeared ten feet further up the mountain slope, and he grimaced as he trudged up to the opening. He peered inside, then took several steps and fell forward through the opening.

Exhausted, nearly frozen, and breathing heavily, Sen Dar dragged himself ten feet further inside the cave and rolled over. He could see the blinding snow whirling around the outside of the cavern opening, but the cave was dark and he was unable to make out any details on the walls as he lay on the cold, damp, rocky floor. He struggled to sit up, and then reached into his robe and pulled out The Ancient One's crystal hung from the gold chain around his neck. Grabbing it in his right hand, he wished for warmth with all his might.

To his complete amazement, the crystal glowed through his frostbitten fingers and the soft blue light increased intensity, lighting the inside of the cave. The rock walls glowed with a light similar to natural sunlight, and within seconds, the temperature inside the cavern had risen to a comfortable eighty degrees.

The blue granite walls strewn with huge veins of gold ore and quartz deposits glittered brightly, but he had no interest in such things at that moment. Although he was very weak from cold and hunger, the instant warmth picked up his spirit. He took a deep breath, let out a long sigh, closed his eyes, and dropped his head to his chest. A few moments later, he raised his head and rubbed his hands together, still holding the crystal, then his shoulders, and finally his feet.

Nearly rejuvenated a half hour later, he casually looked around the cave. With the glowing crystal still tightly held in his right hand, he got up and explored the cavern. He soon discovered it receded another seventy feet to a dead end. He noticed a natural spring bubbling up in a small milky pool on the floor and let go of the crystal. It instantly stopped glowing, and the cavern became pitch black and icy cold. He grabbed the crystal again and it lit up, returning the cave almost instantly to an illumined warm environment.

Sen Dar smiled to himself as he realized he had discovered something very useful about the crystal he had not expected. He bent down, scooped some water in his left cupped hand, drank it, and then greedily drank more.

After he had his fill, he said bitterly, "At least, I won't die of thirst in these accursed mountains."

The crystal was still softly glowing as he reached into his robe with his left hand, clutched the old parchment, and pulled it out. He sat down on the cave floor and looked carefully at the arcane writing on its surface. Then his eyes lit with new realization. For a moment, he remembered all Master Nim had taught him in preparation for the possibility of becoming the next Guardian of The Ancient One's crystal and map. He smiled as he recalled Nim's kind face appearing on the inner screen of his imagination, but he shook off the image and frowned.

Then he thought angrily, *He should have told me it was only a test and never played games with my life. The feeble old fool deserved it.*

Sen Dar read the writing on the parchment more closely and gasped with a new realization. He looked away, amazed, then back at the parchment. As he reread part of the writing along the side of the parchment's torn edge, his eyes widened with anticipation.

"If this is right, then I can escape from here," he said to himself.

Putting his hand to his chin, he pondered the thought, and then dropped his hand, realizing something far more important.

Elated, he said aloud, "I can do more than that. I can escape from the entire planet."

As he continued to ponder the realization in the silent recesses of his cunning mind, he also began to justify his actions.

It was my destiny that these powerful tools fall into my hands, and it will be my destiny to rule over those who now hunt me like an animal.

Then he yelled defiantly as if the universe would hear and obey his new command, "Now, my supreme destiny is to turn the tide on them all and rightfully rule the universe."

As Sen Dar stood up, he shoved the parchment back inside his robe. The snow outside had stopped falling, but a high drift of powdery snow nearly covered the entire cavern entrance, and the welcoming morning sunlight was streaming into the cave through a small remaining opening near the top. Sen Dar let go of the crystal and the glow stopped, leaving natural sunlight to illuminate the gold ore veins and quartz along the cave walls. He walked over to the blocked cave entrance, brushed the snow away, and stepped outside.

He had not taken two steps into the morning sunlight when he heard shouts coming from the mountain slope below. A Galactic Alliance shuttle that looked like one of the Scout Interceptors but twice as large had landed on the snow a thousand yards below the cave. Twenty Galactic Alliance infantrymen holding transparent laser guns were trudging toward the cave's position, and Sen Dar ducked behind a snowdrift in front of the cave, though not quite soon enough.

"I saw something, sir, on the side of the ridge by that cave and then it vanished from view," yelled a young excited soldier.

Sen Dar dove back inside the cavern and frantically grabbed the old parchment from inside his robe. He opened it and nervously read the writing he had discovered earlier, while sounds coming from the soldiers drew near. He grabbed the crystal in his right hand, mumbled softly under his breath, and the crystal glowed again. This time it radiated a blue-violet light around his body, and he screamed as he dissolved into energy particles that whirled inside a sphere of light. The sphere faded and disappeared.

A moment later, several Galactic Alliance soldiers, gripping laser weapons and small flashlights, poked their weapons and lights inside the cave. Then they briefly explored the cave's interior.

Puzzled, the younger soldier shook his head and said to his older officer, "Damn it, Sergeant. I swear that I saw someone dive into this cave."

Irritated, the Sergeant barked back, "Next time, Private, be certain you're not suffering from snow blindness before you get me sloshing off in some wild direction for nothing."

The Private saluted his sergeant with his fist holding the flashlight across his chest; then he stood at attention and answered stiffly, "Yes, sir! It won't happen again."

The annoyed Sergeant started to walk back out of the cave, then stopped at the entrance and scowled over his shoulder.

"Come on, Private, we have a lot of caves to search before this day is over."

CHAPTER THIRTEEN

RUDE AWAKENING ON LODREA (3)

The planet Promintis faded away from Harry Faldwell's vision and the image of another world formed. He knew it was the planet Lodrea (3) and that it was a cold place. Not because it was not beautiful or warm, or nicely seasonal, or many other adjectives one could assign to it. It was cold because of the people. They were humanoid with slightly raised foreheads. Otherwise, they were not too unlike those beings on many other worlds, especially those in the Galactic Inter-dimensional Alliance of Free Worlds.

However, the people of this world have actually loved their totalitarian leaders throughout their history. They enjoyed having a tyrant dominate them and were thrilled when their leader would send them out to attack weaker races living on other worlds. They placed a high value on things taken by force through warfare, general pillaging, and rampaging. This was the home world of the cold-hearted Glonden.

No one who looked over the place would ever guess such a lovely planet was full of such contemptuous, self-righteous, arrogant, pompous, and self-indulgent people. Any aliens landing on Lodrea (3) would notice how oxygen-rich and sweet the air was to breath. It would put smiles on their faces in two seconds. Yet, it would do exactly the opposite to a Glonden citizen. A bright sunny day in spring was an irritant. Men, women, and children were the same in this regard.

Their version of "How do you do?" sounds like a snort mixed with the grunt of a hog. It would not be wise to say, "Good morning. I hope you're doing well on this fine, lovely spring day." Because if you did, you could get your throat cut.

The Glonden people liked it cloudy and drizzly. Otherwise, the day was not worth getting up to greet it. One might think they would at least appreciate the gorgeous violet water of their oceans, or the crimson rock plateaus overlooking them, or the year-round tropical weather with little humidity. The several large continents on the planet were literally thick with fruit trees that needed no tending. Huge lovely flowers grew everywhere. Some of them were ten to twenty feet tall like a small tree and covered with beautiful blue-green petals. They milked these flowers for sweet nectar from which they made a very strong alcoholic drink called Snorage. The animal and colorful bird life, a food source, were so vast in abundance that their grouchy scientists were not able to keep track of them all. However, not one species ever hunted the Glonden.

This world was as close to perfect as any world could get – except, of course, for the people that lived on its surface. If they were not busy dominating other weaker people by taking over their worlds in warfare campaigns, they would all be "Under the Snorage" as the old Glonden phrase goes. When that happened, they would get up days later with huge hangovers.

They had come to dominate nine different star systems of populated worlds five hundred years after they had developed space travel. Yet, they still had one enemy – the Yalgull, who ruled over at least as many other star systems that bordered their territories. The Glonden had been having small territorial skirmishes with the Yalgull for over a hundred years. However, they kept out of any large-scale confrontations with them. This was wise since the Yalgull were worse totalitarians than the Glonden and less forgiving.

Since the Glonden evolved into a conquering race during their initial years of space travel, over time they developed a sheer bullheaded determination to squash flat, the slightest sign of freedom and independence they might have stumbled across, with the one exception of the Yalgull. The Glonden had tried that once over a hundred years earlier when they first encountered the Yalgull and it had proven to be disastrous. They lost half their fleet in the first hour, and the Yalgull lost almost as many ships. A weak truce followed that kept the Glonden and the Yalgull from each other's throats, but it allowed them to continue unbridled rampaging and looting in their respective local areas of the universe.

The truly odd world of Lodrea (3) was coincidentally the one place where Sen Dar unexpectedly found himself thrown. He had uncovered one of the secret uses of The Ancient One's Transport Matrix Crystal just in time to escape capture by the Galactic Alliance soldiers on Promintis. In his desperation to escape Promintis, he did not have time to thoroughly study the map; he had randomly collapsed time and space between his location and a planet located somewhere in the vastness of the galaxy.

A palace on the surface of Lodrea (3), which was the government command center for the Glonden race, appeared around Harry. He observed thirty-three elite Council members standing in a semicircle around a marble throne in their Citadel of Power. They were adorned in their stately but gaudy robes. On occasion, this throne room was a place where captured victims from other worlds – and anyone from Lodrea (3) that happened to disagree with their ruler, the Grand Grontiff – were tortured before his subordinates to keep them in line.

The Glonden leader was a six-feet-tall, obese, bald man with long, drooping jowls and thick lips. He rose from his seated position on the marble throne and smiled at the crowd. He too was wearing a gaudy robe with a gold sash that came from the right shoulder down across the front to his left hip. A large gold metal sun was pinned to the sash on the right side of his chest. He was rather pleased with himself when he looked over the throng of Council members.

"Now you all know why I called this meeting," he stated loudly in an intimidating, condescending manner.

All the people standing in the semicircle bowed their heads respectfully with fear, and then forced a smile. Any one of them who forgot to do this would be executed on the spot and the body incinerated along with that being's entire family, and then their landholdings or wealth was confiscated by the state. Of course, the recipient of this wealth and land was the occupier of the marble throne.

The Grand Grontiff paced back and forth across the raised marble floor that extended from underneath his throne chair outward in a circle about ten feet. He had a hand to his chin in apparent thought with an intimidating smirk on his face. He paused and looked menacingly, one at a time, at everyone gathered around him.

"You know," he continued with a sneer, "it's so comforting to me that you all so much enjoy fulfilling my wishes. Therefore, I've decided to build our forces to larger and more powerful numbers than ever before, and do you know why, Zerod?"

He looked down with a glare at a thin middle-aged man with sagging, bony shoulders and a scar across the top of his forehead. Zerod quivered with fear.

He squeaked out, "Oh most Supreme Grand Grontiff, I do not really know."

The Grontiff smiled at the shaking little man and looked back up to gaze over the crowd.

"I will now tell you all the great pleasure you're about to have. We're going to take the Yalgull worlds away from them."

Then he began to laugh, but the Council members were aghast. They knew what tortures lay in store for any of them if they lost a battle and the Yalgull captured them.

"Being skinned alive would be a kind death at the hands of the Yalgull," was the most often repeated saying the Glonden use when discussing their ancient legends.

The Grand Grontiff continued to scowl contemptuously and then yelled out, "Miserable cowards!" and grunted like a pig. "This is your glorious opportunity to gain wealth and riches beyond your wildest imaginings and I know each of you want to do this for me."

He gazed menacingly at them, and they all stepped back a few feet backing right into several dozen of the Grontiff's personal guards, who were approaching from behind with large, curved-blade swords held to their chests. The guards were towering muscular, bare-armed men with grim faces. Holstered at their sides was a type of laser gun made of shiny gray metal.

Sneering, the Grontiff continued, "Perhaps I will gain your full cooperation by setting a good example."

He looked over the heads of the cowering crowd to his guards and motioned with his hand for them to move toward Zerod. The guards rudely pushed aside everyone in their path and grabbed the now shaking Zerod by the arms. Several of them raised their swords and were about to bring them down when something most unexpected happened.

In an instant, a great... *swoosh*... and blinding flash of blue-violet light enveloped the throne room. It was coming from directly behind the Grontiff and a whirling ball of energy about six feet across appeared. Sen Dar materialized from molecular energy whirling within the blue-violet sphere, and then he was projected head first out of it directly into the back of the Grand Grontiff. The force of the impact stopped Sen Dar and he fell to the floor, but the Grontiff went sprawling forward on his huge belly a dozen feet across the marble tiles between the lesser government officials who jumped out of the way.

Sen Dar was as stunned by his unceremonious arrival as all the Glonden were, but he quickly gathered his sharp wits into focus and jumped to his feet.

"Next time, damn it," he whispered angrily under his breath, "read all the instructions before you just go leaping off into oblivion."

The stupefied guards had let go of Zerod. They had no idea what to do or what to think of Sen Dar's miraculous appearance. The Grand Grontiff slowly got to his feet, coughing and sputtering as he tried to regain the breath knocked out of him.

"You fools… kill him! He's a spy," gasped the breathless Grontiff with a hoarse, angry voice. Then he took a deep breath and yelled, "He has compromised palace security. Kill him!"

Some of the guards raised their swords above their heads and advanced slowly toward Sen Dar with grim, menacing faces. Other guards drew their laser weapons, pointed them at Sen Dar, and then started walking toward him.

Sen Dar instinctively reached inside his robe and clutched the crystal. A faint glow appeared through the open crease of his garment as the Grand Grontiff, now fuming, regained his voice and screamed again at the guards.

"Kill him, you idiots. Shoot him now!"

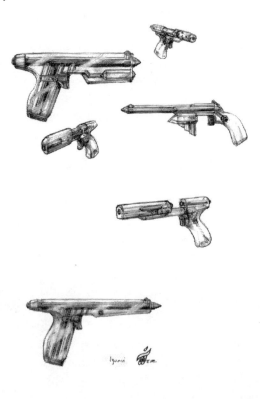

The guards holding the laser pistols aimed at Sen Dar, and his eyes widened in a panic as he held out his other hand in protest.

"Wait, my Lord," he yelled out. "If you kill me, you will never find out why I'm here or how I got past your security, and others will come to deal with you."

The Grontiff pondered Sen Dar's statement, then screamed more loudly, "Kill him or you will all die instead."

The guards again took aim as Sen Dar grimaced and held out his other hand.

"Stop!" he commanded.

The once menacing guards suddenly discovered they could not move a muscle, except for their eyes, which frantically scanned the room. The enraged Grontiff grabbed a laser gun from one of the stunned guards and pointed it at Sen Dar, but Sen Dar tightened his grip on the crystal and it glowed more brightly. The Grontiff's hand shook and the gun dropped from it to the floor. Sen Dar jumped off the raised platform in front of the throne and walked confidently toward him.

Then he stopped and looked around the room. No one else was moving a muscle. He grinned relief and glanced down at the glowing crystal clenched within his fist.

"Wow!" he exclaimed aloud and then continued a silent dialogue with renewed enthusiasm, *If this does what I think it does, I'll end up ruling the galaxy. Now, I'll try a little mind control,* and his devious grin widened.

He walked up to The Grand Grontiff staring deeply into his eyes, and the corpulent leader blinked twice, then grinned at Sen Dar and bowed to one knee. He accepted Sen Dar's hand and kissed it, while Sen Dar gazed like a king down at him.

"Now do you know why I'm here?" murmured Sen Dar.

The Grand Grontiff bowed his head with genuine respect.

"Yes, my Lord," the Grontiff responded cheerfully. "You have come from the worlds beyond death to lead me and my people to victory over our adversaries. It was as if I had been asleep all these years. Then you arrived and now all is well. I... I," and he paused with momentary shame, "didn't recognize you at first. I thought you were a Yalgull spy."

Sen Dar mocked up a compassionate smile for the now humble Grontiff and asked, "What is your name?"

"I am Grand Grontiff Gloeen, the ruler of my people and all people on our conquered worlds," he answered with proud obedience.

Sen Dar motioned with his free hand for the Grontiff to rise to his feet.

Keeping steady eye contact, he asked, "Then who do you say that I am?"

Sen Dar squeezed the glowing crystal behind his robe again, and Gloeen blinked, then smiled with sudden recognition.

"Why, you're Sen Dar, Lord of the universe and our God," answered Gloeen with a big delightful grin.

Sen Dar took a deep breath and smiled back at him, then at all the others in the room who were fully conscious but still could not move.

Then he intently stared into Gloeen's eyes and boldly confirmed, "That is right. Now, you will forget that name. What is the highest God of your people on all your worlds?"

Gloeen blinked, humbly smiled, and replied, "It's you, my Lord Munarc?"

"Again, you are correct," confirmed Sen Dar, proudly smiling back at him. Then he commanded, "From now on, you will call me Lord Munarc. Do you understand?"

"Yes, my Lord Munarc. It shall be as you command," answered the now completely humbled Grontiff.

Sen Dar walked over to the raised platform that extended out from under the throne chair and stepped confidently upon it. He turned toward the crowd and waved his hand. As if by magic, everyone in the room found they could move freely once again and their attitudes had completely changed.

Sen Dar announced, "I have returned to my worlds to correct the errors made by the beings I have created, and to personally lead the Glonden to victory over the universe."

Cheers went up from all those gathered, including the guards and Gloeen.

Then Sen Dar waved his hand to dismiss the crowd and continued with a royal air, "The rest of you good subjects and the Grand Grontiff's personal guards may leave for now. Your Grand Grontiff and I have much to discuss and many things to plan for our new future."

They all humbly bowed toward Sen Dar, and then filed in quiet obedience out of the throne room. Still holding the crystal tightly inside his robe, Sen Dar walked over to Gloeen and put an arm around his shoulder.

"You must tell me all about the Yalgull, where their home world is, all about their defenses, and how they too have erred over time since I created them," stated Sen Dar in a fatherly manner. "Then we will discuss our moves to correct all of my errant beings in the universe."

They walked across the room toward the throne room doors while Sen Dar continued to work his spell.

"In fact, my loyal Grontiff, after you have told me all I wish to know about them I think it would be best to prepare the fleet for battle. Then we will go to the Yalgull home world and I will correct their errant ways as I have done with you."

Grand Grontiff Gloeen smiled with delight, and then nodded his head in full agreement with Sen Dar as they walked side by side out of the throne room.

CHAPTER FOURTEEN

ON THE JOURNEY
TO YALGULL SPACE

Six months after he gained control of the Glonden, Sen Dar was standing on the bridge of their flagship surveying the approach of the Glonden fleet to Yalgull space, displayed on the large view screen that curved around the back wall. Grand Grontiff Gloeen was humbly standing by his side. Sen Dar was now wearing the new symbols he had created for himself in his plan to conquer the entire galaxy, starting with the control of the Glonden.

From his invisible perspective, Harry Faldwell knew Sen Dar was convinced nothing in the universe could stop him from attaining his perceived destiny to dominate all life one day.

Sen Dar was wearing a black body suit with a tapered lapel that folded open across his chest and a long black cape attached around the neck with a gold chain. Belted at the waist of his new uniform was an oval gold buckle similar to that of the Galactic Alliance. He rather fancied it would be quite an insult to the Galactic Alliance if he utilized symbols similar to the ones they used, except for a few significant differences. Etched into its surface was the same galaxy they used. However, the apex of an upside-down pyramid touched the center of the galaxy and a red world was directly above the pyramid's flat base. A black sword stood above the red world with its point touching the top of the planet. Two snakes wound from the point of the sword up the blade above the handle, where the heads faced each other and their forked tongues touched. Sen Dar had the symbol embossed on the left chest area of his garment, in the same location where the Galactic Alliance places their symbol. A thin gold band around his forehead had the same symbol embossed on its center.

Grand Grontiff Gloeen was wearing a similar dark blue uniform with no cape, no gold band around the head, and the same but smaller symbols on the belt buckle and chest area of his garment. The rest of the twenty-crew members on the bridge were wearing similar uniforms with only the smaller symbol embossed on the left chest area.

Sen Dar was now only twenty years old and he had managed to gain complete control over an entire totalitarian system of worlds and their armada of heavily armored battleships. They looked like flying wings, except the trailing wing-sections swept back in a V-shaped design. The large battleships had bridge control areas built on the top of the apexes. Three large observation windows arched around the front of the bridge and a short way along each trailing wing section. Centered directly between the wings on the back was a launch bay.

Enveloping the hulls of the Glonden ships was a red antigravity light, unlike the characteristic blue glow of the Galactic Alliance ships. Although similar in design to their parent battleships, the V-shape of the Glonden Scout fighters swept back more sharply for speed and maneuverability, and they had only one curved cockpit window at the front of the ship.

From what Sen Dar had learned from Gloeen during the prior six months, both the Glonden scientists and the Yalgull scientists had long ago acquired, through devious means, a similar technology to power their ships as that of the Galactic Alliance, and they had trans-light speed capability as well. Sen Dar thought their weaponry comparable and determined he would test them on Galactic Alliance star ships in the near future.

As he stood next to Grand Grontiff Gloeen, he sneered with condescension and mused, *First, I'll pay a surprise visit to the Royal Garn, the soon-to-be-replaced Yalgull Emperor. With any luck, no ship will have to fire a single shot,* and he arrogantly smiled.

Then he reflected on the Yalgull star ships shown to him by Gloeen. He knew they were powered in a similar manner as the Glonden ships, and that the power source was similar to that used by the Galactic Alliance star ships. They were more narrowly oval-shaped than Galactic Alliance star ships, but similarly curved around the bottom of the hulls.

The bridge control towers of the large Yalgull star ships, which gradually increased in height toward the center of the ships, had larger rectangular observation windows centered along all four of their sides.

However, the bridge structures were conventional triangular, rectangular, and spherical with many windows mostly concentrated in the central third of the upper deck. There were no observation domes on each end of these star ships. However, the two rectangular launch bays positioned on each end appeared similar in design to that of the larger Galactic Alliance star ships.

The Yalgull saucer-shaped Scout class fighter had a trailing edge extending around both sides of the front of the hull that slanted slightly downward, then upward again as it curved around the back half of the ship. This gave the curved extension a slightly Stingray shark wing-like appearance as it tapered around to the narrower back of the hull. Three domed pods, also triangularly positioned on the bottom, were similar to Galactic Alliance Scout class fighters.

Sen Dar noticed that although the antigravity drives of the Glonden and Yalgull ships created a reddish glow around them, they appeared to work as well as the Galactic Alliance ships, even while operating in trans-light mode.

However, Gloeen had informed Sen Dar that according to the last border skirmishes the Glonden had with the Yalgull, it was evident the Yalgull ships carried an advantage in firepower. They could fire from any side of their ships' hulls at the same time. The Glonden ships could fire only from the bridge at the front of the apex and from the outside edge of their two wings. Sen Dar had thought of that and was now confident. During the previous six months of preparation, he had made certain that the firepower of the Glonden ships was greatly increased. This now included their being able to fire from behind their ships above the launch bays and along the inside of the wings as well, in case they had to engage the Yalgull from behind their ships. Sen Dar came out of his reverie, looked over at the Grand Grontiff, and smiled.

"You have done well, Gloeen. Everything is proceeding according to the plan. Have your Scout ships reported any contact with the Yalgull fleet?"

Gloeen bowed humbly and touched several luminous controls on the curved console in front of them and the large view screen flashed on. A map of a solar system projected out of the view screen in three dimensions. It showed a sun with nine planets. The three closest planets were gas giants. However, the fourth planet, a blue-green world similar to Earth, had two large moons, approximately one-third its size, circling it. The five other planets had one to three dust rings and two to five moons orbiting them. They were all cloud-covered gaseous worlds in various shades of color.

A hundred white lights shaped like the Glonden star ships were moving from behind the solar system's sun headed toward the blue-green world, and Gloeen pointed to the fourth planet.

"This planet is Dromkal (4), also known as Yalgull Prime, the home world and location of Emperor Garn. Our advancing fleet is entering their solar system and their long-range space beacons will be detecting our presence at any moment. After that, the Yalgull fleet Destroyers will be after us in great numbers."

Sen Dar was listening while in thought about another important capability he had learned about The Ancient One's crystal. By studying the map, he discovered that all he had to do was envision the planet or place he wished to go to, and then by utilizing a specific command code he would be sent to his chosen destination in a matter of seconds. The map explained there were certain sound frequencies that rode upon the omnipresent energy of Spirit sound that underlies and supports all life. The crystal emits a precise frequency that dematerializes an individual into a transport energy sphere. Then it instantly sends them to their destination.

It further specified that the phenomenon was not the creation of an inter-dimensional doorway between parallel dimensions. Instead, the Transport Matrix Crystal could only connect two points within the same physical dimension of the universe and open a brief corridor between them.

The map also stated it another way. The Transport Matrix Crystal could connect the point in space wherever he was to the point in the physical universe he wished to go by collapsing time and space between them. Additionally, the map revealed that the Transport Matrix Crystal was the second of the three mystic crystals of The Ancient One, and nothing about how to use the other two crystals could be discovered without first obtaining the other half of The Ancient One's map. However, Sen Dar now knew he could traverse outer space as easily as someone could walk through an open doorway from one room to another. It was painful, as he also found out, but the pain lasted only a few seconds during the transition from place to place.

He learned the half of The Ancient One's map he possessed, divided into eighths, revealed that each section contained information on other uses of the Transport Matrix Crystal. It mentioned that a planet called Maldec, far away in a distant solar system under Galactic Alliance protection, had the other half of the map hidden somewhere on its surface. An inscription beside Maldec's coordinates showed that only when one was on the planet's surface would the crystal open the way to acquire the other half of the map. Most importantly, it disclosed that the other section of the map also revealed the locations of the other two cosmic crystals, and who guarded them.

First, I'll acquire the other two crystals and then I will rule them all, thought Sen Dar with renewed cunning interest. *This is only fitting, since I will become their new God and they will call me The Ancient One.*

Sen Dar realized that one day he would have to fight the Galactic Inter-dimensional Alliance of Free Worlds to gain access to that area of the galaxy, and his grin widened.

With this, he mused, as he reached inside the fold in the top part of his uniform and grabbed the crystal, *I can have what I will, even the entire Galactic Alliance itself.*

"My Lord Munarc, did I displease you?" asked Gloeen with a humble smile, interrupting Sen Dar's reverie. "You seem to be ignoring me, Sire."

Sen Dar blinked and answered, "No, my faithful warrior, you have not displeased me. I was out in the universe taking care of things, which you would not understand, but I was also listening to what you had to say to me. Let me know immediately when the Yalgull fleet detects us. Then follow the plan exactly and contact the Yalgull command ship. Tell the Commander that you request to meet with their Emperor Garn. Tell him you wish to discuss the possibility of forming an alliance between the Yalgull and the Glonden worlds. Request that he escort the two of us to their Emperor under a flag of peace, and do not worry if he does not trust you.

"Insist that it is urgent we see him, for the safety of his worlds are in jeopardy from a powerful Galactic Alliance of worlds that you discovered which could threaten both the Glonden and the Yalgull. If he still doesn't want to talk with us, I will have to change his mind." Sen Dar grinned deviously again.

"As you command, my Lord," Gloeen answered, bowing his head in complete obedience. "It shall be done."

Sen Dar looked away to ponder another point. He reviewed all that he had learned so far about the crystal. He knew that the map said it was capable of many wonders. However, it took the discipline, training, and spiritual development of the user to access many of them, but Sen Dar did not ponder that.

With little effort, he thought, *I accessed great power with the crystal and my new destiny is to discover all its secrets.*

Then, he recalled there was a series of sacred names for The Ancient

One written on his half of the stolen parchment. They were access code words that corresponded to a precise series of sound frequencies. The map explained the originating Sound or word and specific secondary frequencies created the entire universe. It also stated that each location in the universe had a special hidden frequency signature or rate of vibration and that if one knew the frequency of a given location in creation they can instantly transport there.

Furthermore, it disclosed that each of the unique Sound frequencies could trigger the Transport Matrix Crystal to bring into operation a different function. However, his half of the map did not disclose some of the key words and how to utilize them. Other uses disclosed were for functions he did not yet understand, and could not make work for reasons still unknown to him. Yet, he had already discovered how to use two of the important word functions.

One gives me the ability to control or change the minds of others and the other gives me complete freedom to move about the universe as and when I choose*, he reflected, and he mused about it a moment longer with great self-satisfaction.*

As Harry continued to watch events unfold, he knew Sen Dar was unable to perceive that all of the crystal's functions were for self-defense and not for dominating others for personal power. The crystal was brought into creation for a highly evolved Spiritual Master to use it only for the benefit of all life.

In Sen Dar's reasoning, the two functions of the crystal which he could now use would allow him to gain immediate access to vast areas of the universe, and eventually complete control of the inhabitants living on the many worlds within them. He determined he would never again let the universe make him a victim of its whims, as it did when he was a defenseless and helpless child, forced to watch his family and his world die right before his eyes. He thought the translocation function of the crystal would help him gain his goal of complete control over the universe. By dematerializing him into the safety of a secret energy vortex that only he could control, it would change his rate of vibration to match the specific frequency of any desired location. It would re-materialize him into the new energy frequency and then… *wham*… he would arrive.

The map stated, "The force of the exchange would leave residual energy which would usually throw the participant a few feet out of the energy sphere before dissipating."

Sen Dar had discovered this the hard way when he found himself launched into the back of the Grand Grontiff Gloeen on Lodrea (3), before he learned how to control where it would send him. In his desperation to escape the Galactic Alliance soldiers back at the cave on Promintis, he had used the first access code word he had spotted on the map, but he had not tried to accurately visualize a particular location. Therefore, the crystal sent him to a place that was most closely associated with his natural inner inclination or character. It sent him to a place similar to his own inner negative nature.

However, this never dawned upon Sen Dar's consciousness. He decided that the location he found himself in was a part of his glorious destiny to become Lord and Master over all.

He could not comprehend the Spiritual reason behind the powerful processes of the crystal that allowed it to actually work. He was unable to perceive that an individual who utilized the crystal to translocate would be dematerialized to their true energy form – known as the Atma.

According to the map, the Atma operating in this true state collapses time and space. Another statement on the map read, "This state of being is normally divine in nature and loving toward all life. A being's true living energy nature is identical with the most loving, pure conscious Spirit behind all life. Yet, this Spirit presence exists beyond frequency of any kind." Sen Dar had no experience with true states of being and refused to believe in them.

Therefore, he fumed in angry silence, *That Ancient One Spirit gibberish on the map is too damned much like the teachings of that soft-heart weakling, Nim. He was just another brainwashed Adept of that never-to-be-seen Ancient One bag of gases nonsense.*

He often felt pain when he thought of Nim, but he soon discovered he could cover it up by telling himself that together the Galactic Alliance and the manipulative, trickster Adepts made up the concept of The Ancient One rubbish in a conspiracy to keep him and everyone in the universe under their control.

After all, he rationalized, *I had to kill Nim or the rest of my life would be dominated by their deceptive whims.*

He concluded that such propaganda on the map was written there to mask the true use of the powerful crystals from anyone other than those select few who wished to wield domination over everyone else, and he resolved to never again let them control him. In fact, during the last few moments while he stood next to Gloeen, he decided he would embark on his own holy crusade to liberate the rest of the galaxy from that Ancient One nonsense forever. He envisioned replacing their belief in The Ancient One with himself.

I shall become the real living Ancient One and their new God, he gleefully thought, quite satisfied with the image.

An alarm went off, snapping Sen Dar to full alertness. Then Gloeen whispered a command into the ear of the Communications Officer seated next to them, who touched a control.

Gloeen looked up at the view screen, snapped his head around to look at Sen Dar, and said nervously, "We've been detected!"

The images in front of Sen Dar and the Grand Grontiff showed hundreds of Yalgull ships were now speeding toward the approaching Glonden fleet.

Gloeen shouted at the Communications Officer seated behind the control console, "Contact the Yalgull flagship immediately, and let them know we have come into their space under a flag of peace. Tell them that Grand Grontiff Gloeen himself and a close aide wish to meet with Emperor Garn to discuss a mutual threat to both the Glonden and the Yalgull. Let them know I will order the rest of the fleet to stand down and hold their positions, while the two of us come unarmed to their world. Do it quickly, before they open fire on our advance ships."

The Communications Officer nodded and touched a blue, marble-sized control, and it blinked. Sen Dar smiled confidently as he looked at Gloeen, who appeared quite apprehensive about what they were planning. Sen Dar mocked up benevolence and gently squeezed the crystal around his neck.

"Do not fear, my good Grontiff Gloeen," he said. "I have everything under control in my universe.

Gloeen relaxed and smiled back at his new Lord and Master.

CHAPTER FIFTEEN

THE GLONDEN – YALGULL ALLIANCE

*O*n Dromkal (4), home world of the Yalgull, Supreme Emperor Garn was inside his government command center impatiently walking back and forth in front of a circular wooden-sided control console, lit with various shaped touch-activated controls. In his mid-forties, he was thin and tall – just over six feet – with high cheekbones and a long, pointed jaw. His long, slightly wavy brown hair fell down over his shoulders. Like all the Yalgull, he was humanoid but he had the faintest hint of violet over his ivory-white skin.

He was wearing a golden-brown robe laced with an iridescent blue material that shimmered slightly as he moved. Under his robe were sheer matching pants, and his feet were clad with highly polished black boots. A thin, shiny black metal belt, akin to obsidian, was around his waist.

The console behind him surrounded a thin octagon shaped view screen that hung down fifteen feet from the marble ceiling on two gold metal rods. Round pillars surrounding the room were made of gold-laced, blue granite. Standing five feet apart, they held up a curved white marble ceiling. Windows between the granite pillars behind him looked out over lush green fields and thickly forested rolling hills under a beautiful sunny sky.

The view through the window to the right of a set of doors opposite the view screen in front of Garn revealed that the palace was located near the base of a large snow-covered mountain. A lovely blue waterfall was cascading down several plateaus to a lake nestled between the palace and the mountainside. Surrounding the lake were large trees with blue-green bark. Their long drooping branches reached down to bright-green fields of tall grass, topped with round, dark-green leaves glistening in the sunlight and rippling from a gentle wind.

Garn stopped pacing in front of the console to look up at the view screen in the center of the room. He was focusing on the images of a hundred Glonden ships moving into the space of the outer borders of the Yalgull solar system. Also imaged was his fleet moving to cut them off from every direction. A blank-faced military General standing by his side was also staring at the screen.

Garn glared angrily at the view screen with wide-open blue eyes and bellowed, "How dare the stupidly foolish Glonden enter our space unannounced? This time I'll wipe them all out of existence!"

The General at his side was about the same height with black hair and a rugged face, wearing the Yalgull military uniform of High Commander. A triangular emblem etched with the talons of an exotic bird clasped the thin gold belt around the waist of his sleek black trousers. Fastened along the left side of his long-sleeved shirt were triangular gold buttons, and three gold stars were pinned on the left side of his upper chest, indicating his high-ranking position. A polished silver laser weapon in a holster was attached to the left side of his belt.

The High Commander looked away from the screen to gaze at Emperor Garn and proclaimed, "We just received a message from the Glonden, from Grand Grontiff Gloeen himself. He said they want to meet with you under a flag of peace to discuss an alliance. He also stated they will have their ships hold position now, and he's asking that he and one aide be allowed to come here to discuss the reason for their request to form an alliance."

He noticed something on the view screen and pointed to it.

"Look, my Lord. Their ships have stopped and they are holding their positions as promised."

Frowning, Garn stared at the screen for a moment, and then said bitterly, "General Hontull, I don't trust the Glonden and I certainly don't trust Gloeen. In my view, neither Gloeen nor his predecessor has ever given us a satisfactory reason why the Glonden attacked us over one hundred years ago. When their leader finally asked for a truce, we had nearly annihilated their entire space fleet. Somehow, their Grand Grontiff convinced my overly generous predecessor their attack had all been a misunderstanding. I would not have let one of them escape alive. Open a channel to Gloeen."

Hontull touched the marble-sized transceiver control on the console and Garn said into it, "If you so much as squeak a move toward attacking us, Gloeen, I will see to it that none of you escape our space. We will completely disintegrate every one of your ships, and then I will personally slowly cut out the hearts of a select number of the captured prisoners and make each of the remaining prisoners eat them.

"Those remaining prisoners will then watch as I personally cut off, one by one, all of the appendages of each one of them until none remain alive. Then, I would start with you. After that, Gloeen, we would go to your home world and completely obliterate everyone and everything on it."

He paused and then added angrily, "Make sure you understand what I said word for word. If you indicate that you do understand this fully and accept the consequences of any deception, I will allow you and your aide to come here unarmed in a single Scout class fighter. We will provide a heavy Yalgull escort."

Smiling, General Hontull released the transceiver control, nodded his head to Emperor Garn, and then touched a control next to the transceiver.

"Did they clearly hear every word?" asked Hontull.

"Yes, High Commander General, they did," replied the male voice of a Lieutenant through the transceiver.

Hontull commanded, "Open another channel to the Glonden flagship and tell them permission is given for the two of them to come here in one unarmed Scout class fighter. Then instruct a heavy fighter escort to guard them on their approach to the home world, and send a platoon of heavy infantry to surround them for added protection once they arrive. Do it quickly."

Hontull took his hand off the control and gazed at Emperor Garn.

"Now we'll see what this is all about," he said as he stepped away from the control console and stood by Garn's side.

Smirking and shaking his head, Emperor Garn squinted his left eye and it twitched nervously.

Grimacing, he gazed at Hontull and said, "That's what worries me, Hontull. What will we see?"

Back on the Glonden flagship, Sen Dar and Gloeen were smiling triumphantly. Then Sen Dar sneered as he looked deeply into Gloeen's eyes. His voice was now eloquent but dripping with covert venom.

"Now watch, my good Grontiff Gloeen and I'll show you how I

will correct the errors of the Yalgull, as I've done with you and your people."

Glassy-eyed, Gloeen replied with glee, "This is a glorious day, my Lord. Who would have thought an alliance between the Yalgull and us would ever exist? I'm your humble servant."

Gloeen's proud smile widened and he bowed deeply. Sen Dar bowed his head in return, while his hand remained inside the fold of his shirt clutching The Ancient One's crystal, which glimmered faintly through his fingers.

"Now Gloeen, my loyal Grontiff, have a Scout ship standing by," said Sen Dar. "The weaponry must be unarmed as we will be but don't worry. As I said before, everything in my universe is under my control."

Gloeen nodded and left the control room. Then Sen Dar looked up at the view screen to see the Yalgull ships stop their approach. Both sides were now holding their positions in space, and Sen Dar was beaming arrogant confidence.

Now, I can be patient and build my forces, he mused. *When everything is ready, I'll have a rude awakening prepared for the Galactic Inter-dimensional Alliance of Free Worlds, and their so-called Guardian Adepts of that mythical Ancient One nonsense.*

An hour later, one sleek Scout class Glonden fighter sped out of the open launch bay behind the bridge of the Glonden flagship. Many dozens of the fleet ships, positioned in four rows behind the flagship, trailed into the distant space past a giant, green gas planet. The huge planet's atmosphere was moving in five separate counterclockwise levels at differing high wind velocities. The hundred Yalgull star ships were continuing to hold their positions in the opposite distant background of space. Two-dozen Yalgull Scout Interceptors hovered into view. They surrounded the lone Glonden ship, matched its speed, and flew together past the giant planet and beyond the Yalgull fleet to disappear in the distant blackness of space.

Emperor Garn and High Commander General Hontull were now standing by the window overlooking the waterfall. The two-dozen Yalgull Scout class fighters surrounding the Glonden Scout ship hovered down into view from the sky above the mountain, and they flew swiftly across the valley and directly over the top of the Yalgull command center.

Garn walked over to the control desk in front of the view screen, touched a lit control, and the golden doors opened. Four-dozen heavily armed elite Yalgull soldiers, wearing similar uniforms as Commander Hontull but without stars on their chests, filed into the chamber and lined the room. Their sleek, silver energy weapons were drawn and held tightly to their chests pointing upward. Two of the guards positioned themselves on each side of the doorway and stood at attention.

A few moments later, Sen Dar and Grand Grontiff Gloeen were approaching the command center from down the hallway, closely guarded by a dozen additional Yalgull soldiers. One guard walking beside Sen Dar's side was holding Sen Dar's right arm tightly and pointing an energy weapon at his head with his other hand. Another guard held Gloeen's left arm, while also pointing an energy weapon at his head. The guards marched them into the room, around the command desk console, and up to Emperor Garn.

Sen Dar was wearing The Ancient One's crystal outside his robe. Both he and Gloeen smiled and bowed to the emperor. Garn was not smiling, and his hand was gripping the weapon strapped at his side. He scowled at Gloeen, gazed up and down at Sen Dar, and then walked around both of them before he stopped to look at the soldier holding Sen Dar's arm.

"Did you thoroughly search them?" asked Garn.

"Yes, Supreme One," replied the soldier. "They were not carrying weapons, but this one called Munarc, The Grontiff's aide, was wearing a crystal. I made him wear it outside his robe."

Emperor Garn stepped toward Sen Dar, grabbed the crystal with two fingers, looked at it, and then turned it over several times before letting it go. Sen Dar's smile dropped as he closely watched the crystal fall on the gold chain against his chest. Then he looked up, smiling, as Garn gazed deeply into his eyes.

"What is it?" he demanded.

"My Lord, it's an ornament of my station as aide to Grand Grontiff Gloeen," Sen Dar replied eloquently.

Emperor Garn's left eye twitched as he looked menacingly over at Gloeen.

"Why are you here, Gloeen, and why have you brought an entire fleet with you?"

Gloeen answered, "I have come to tell you about a powerful danger that threatens both of our sovereign world systems. You already know about the Galactic Inter-dimensional Alliance of Free Worlds and some of their sciences, as do we. Munarc, my aide, has secretly been collecting information about the build-up of their forces outside our combined borders for the past two years. Our spies tell us they plan a massive attack against our two world systems sometime within the next month. If we combine forces in an alliance, we would be strong enough to attack them first and ruin their plans before they have a chance to do it to us."

Emperor Garn stood back and pondered what Gloeen said with a hand to his chin. Then he dropped his hand and stared deeply into Gloeen's eyes.

"What proofs have you of this? And it better be convincing!"

Gloeen looked over at Sen Dar and grinned. Sen Dar was smirking, staring back into Emperor Garn's eyes.

"Oh, it's quite convincing, my Lord Garn," he replied, sneering with a slightly raised upper lip, "as you shall now discover for yourself."

He grabbed The Ancient One's crystal in his left hand, and it glowed brightly between his clenched fingers. All the guards in the room discovered they could not move anything except their eyes, and they glanced around frantically. The guards' fingers gripping the guns held to the heads of Sen Dar and Gloeen sprang wide open and the guns dropped to the floor. Startled, Emperor Garn and Commander Hontull reached for their guns strapped at their sides as Sen Dar clutched the crystal more tightly. It brightened through his fingers, and Garn and Hontull shook their heads as if trying to shake off weariness before they relaxed. Hontull stood at attention, smiling, while Garn gazed fondly at Sen Dar, who was now smiling back at him.

"Now do you both have all of the proof you need?" Sen Dar inquired politely with a sinister smile.

Emperor Garn appeared quite pleased with himself, and Commander Hontull nodded eagerly.

"Yes... yes, I see it all now. This Galactic Alliance would destroy us all," Garn said excitedly. "They are in error. They have lost their way from your original teachings, Divine One."

Nodding, Sen Dar turned his sharp gaze on High Commander Hontull and asked, "And who do you say that I am?"

Hontull blinked, and then answered, delighted, "You are the Supreme Lord God of all life."

"That is correct," Sen Dar replied. Then he asked Emperor Garn, "And who is the most supreme God throughout the history of all your people?"

"You are, Ruan, Lord Supreme God of all," replied Garn with a bright grin. "You have come down from the dimensions beyond death to save us from the error of our ways. Why was I so blind before? What happened to us, Supreme One?"

Sen Dar waved a hand and the guards in the room relaxed as they discovered they could move freely again. They lowered their weapons and bowed their heads with deep respect toward Sen Dar.

Sen Dar replied, "I discovered the beings I had created would inevitably go astray without my personally being here to guide them through their ongoing evolution. There is no need for concern, my good Emperor Garn. All is well now. Do you know why I blessed your world by bringing with me Grand Grontiff Gloeen of the Glonden?"

Emperor Garn blinked several more times and smiled as a new realization surfaced.

He sighed and answered enthusiastically, "You have finally come to save us all by allowing the Glonden and the Yalgull to form an alliance that will lead us to true Spiritual freedom. We are unworthy of your presence among us, my Lord, and we are deeply honored by your generous gift."

Garn bowed toward Sen Dar, and when he looked up, Sen Dar was smiling confidently and nodding his agreement. Then he nodded his head toward Gloeen, and Emperor Garn walked over to him with his arms wide open. Grand Grontiff Gloeen smiled back as if they were long-lost brothers and opened his arms wide to receive him. They hugged each other and vigorously patted each other on the back. General Hontull and the guards were staring at this with complete astonishment, and Sen Dar noticed their puzzlement. His upper lip twitched as he opened his eyes wider, and their attitudes instantly changed. The guards were soon grinning happily as if watching Garn and Gloeen hug was the most natural thing in the world to behold.

Sen Dar placed the glowing crystal back inside the fold of his shirt and looked at High Commander General Hontull.

"Are you the Commander of the Yalgull space fleet?" he inquired with the air of a command.

Hontull smiled and respectfully bowed his head.

"Yes, Lord Ruan. I am High Commander General Hontull."

Smiling, Sen Dar continued, "Good Commander, have your fleet stand down from their attack mode and go up to the Yalgull flagship to personally take charge. Then contact the Glonden flagship and let the Commander know the Glonden-Yalgull Alliance has begun. He has already received instructions to do the same with the Glonden fleet. All Glonden star ship Captains will have their ships follow the Yalgull fleet to an orbit of the home world. Then have all personnel come to the emperor's palace tonight for the celebration of our new alliance."

Commander Hontull grinned like a child, nodding his head enthusiastically. Then he bowed respectfully to Sen Dar, Emperor Garn, and Grand Grontiff Gloeen, and walked at a quick pace out of the command center.

Sen Dar placed an arm around the shoulders of Garn and Gloeen and squeezed them as a father would his sons.

Smiling, he looked at the guards and commanded with gusto, "My good warriors, you may leave us now, for your leader and your new friend, The Grand Grontiff of the Glonden, have much to discuss and plan for your future. Now, all of you be cheerful."

The gleeful guards bowed humbly before Garn and Gloeen and then most deeply toward Sen Dar.

"Spread the news, my faithful warriors," commanded Sen Dar with more gusto. "A new celebration, the greatest of all celebrations, begins tonight, for the Glonden and the Yalgull are now one family."

The guards joyfully slapped each other on the back while they filed out of the room.

Sen Dar guided Garn and Gloeen toward the golden doors with his arms still around their shoulders. He grinned at both of them and then stared at Garn with believable benevolence.

"Now, I want to see how well the Yalgull scientists have done with the development of your star ships," he began. "Then I want them to construct a special Scout class fighter for my personal use. I will provide them with instructions for my needs. Will there be any difficulty with this, my good subject Garn?"

"No, my Lord Ruan," Garn replied, grinning. "It shall be attended to immediately."

Sen Dar stopped walking and looked at Garn again.

"Emperor Garn, there is one other thing for you to do before you announce my presence to your people. The different races on the worlds of my making have given me many names as their Supreme Lord of all creation. From now on, you shall both forget all former titles and refer to me simply as Supreme Lord. Tonight, you will announce me to your people as the Supreme Lord Over All, who has returned to personally set things right in his universe. Tell all your people they are now part of one great family with Grand Grontiff Gloeen and all the Glonden. Then inform them they are under my complete protection and guidance."

Emperor Garn nodded his head in complete compliance.

Sen Dar looked at Gloeen and commanded, "You, my good Grand Grontiff Gloeen, shall announce to all the Yalgull people that the combined might of the Glonden and the Yalgull have joined together. In the days to come, we shall strike out in the universe and bring all my other errant beings back into balance under my divine direction. Is that understood?"

Gloeen also nodded in complete compliance.

"Then, it's settled," stated Sen Dar, and he enthusiastically continued, "Tonight, we celebrate, and then tomorrow we will plan our future attack on the first Galactic Alliance settlement located on the planet that is closest to our newly combined world territories."

Garn and Gloeen were instantly puzzled, and Garn inquired, "But my Lord, why not simply correct their misguided thinking as you have done with Gloeen and myself?"

"I see that you are both confused by a lack of understanding," answered Sen Dar and he grinned at them. "Therefore, I will now enlighten you. The Galactic Alliance has many among its teachers that use powerful spells to control and misguide their people. Their space fleet will resist us, for they will not want to let go of their misguided lives. I will have to do battle with this Galactic Alliance at first, but eventually we will get control of their priests. Then I can snap them out of the illusion under which they suffer. They worship a mythical God they call The Ancient One, and we must help them to see that I am the Supreme Lord Over All and the true Ancient One returned to the universe to set things right. Now do you both understand?"

Garn and Gloeen nodded their heads, but they had no idea why they felt satisfied.

Now, they are all mine, mused Sen Dar.

He removed his arms from Garn and Gloeen's shoulders and waved his hand toward the hallway beyond the open golden doors.

"Lead the way, my good Emperor Garn," he commanded with a happy snap to his voice. "We must prepare the celebration of the new Glonden-Yalgull Alliance. Tomorrow, I think that Gloeen and I would be grateful to take a tour of your personal Yalgull flagship. After that, I am sure you would like to visit Gloeen's flagship as well. We must integrate both fleets, weapons, and technologies."

Now very pleased, Garn smiled at Gloeen, then at Sen Dar and replied, "It will be as you command, Supreme One."

"We are at your command, Supreme Lord," chimed in Gloeen, grinning from ear to ear.

Arm in arm, Garn and Gloeen headed down the hallway, chatting like old friends. Sen Dar arrogantly smirked as he reached into the fold of his shirt, grabbed the crystal, and then walked slowly down the hall behind them, telepathically herding his disciples to a future they believed would be a beautiful pasture in paradise.

The scene before Harry Faldwell's Atma began to change, transforming into the clear image of Earth from space. He could see a huge continent centered over the planet's equator, and he intuitively knew it was Lemuria – the mysterious ancient land that Master Ra Mu had said once existed in Earth's distant past.

As the planet continued to turn on its axis, another continent came into view that was two-thirds the size of Lemuria, the continent called Atlantis.

Then something drew his attention to the vast ocean area that separated the massive continents, and he experienced the thrill of swiftly zooming down through the atmosphere. He soon plunged into the ocean depths to find himself hovering above the secret domed city of Oceana on Earth's ancient ocean floor. Somehow, he knew he was visiting things as they were on Earth 100,000 years ago.

CHAPTER SIXTEEN

CHILD LOST
AND FOUND

*H*arry was suddenly inside the dome gazing at Master Opellum and Mayleena as they stood at the end of a winding rock path. White marble steps behind them led ten feet up to a marble boarding platform, transparent transport tube, and car. It was beside the shore of the largest lake near Opellum's home on the outskirts of the city, under the huge clear dome at the bottom of Earth's ancient ocean. The transport car, with its rectangular door swung upward, was beside the platform in front of the open end of the round transport tube. A mile away, the three pyramids surrounding the smooth ivory-white dome building majestically towered above the city center, but they appeared small compared to the gigantic clear dome that curved high over the countryside. Several pairs of multicolored tropical birds with long split tails flew by them twenty feet overhead.

Looking up at Master Opellum, Mayleena inquired, "Father, I would dearly love to swim outside the walls of the city again today. I feel so free among the abundant ocean life of this Earth planet because I discovered how to communicate with several of them, especially the dolphins and whales. They are very intelligent, and I've become friends with them."

Master Opellum looked down at his daughter and smiled. He took her hand and held it between the palms of both his hands, then replied tenderly, "Dear daughter, I know what troubles you. You are still having visions of the young man but that should not disturb you. Just continue your contemplations on the Sound and Light of Spirit. You must practice patience and accept the visions as a gift of The Ancient One.

They are actually a natural part of your future destiny, so enjoy these moments of youth, my daughter, for they will never come again, at least not in this particular lifetime."

He chuckled softly, and Mayleena forced a smile, and then looked at the ground as Opellum put a consoling arm around her shoulder.

"Now, Mayleena," he added, upbeat, "put aside your concerns for the future. Go enjoy yourself and have your daily swim."

Mayleena looked up, jubilant, then threw her arms around him and hugged him.

"Oh, thank you, Father," she replied.

Opellum looked down into his beautiful daughter's green eyes, raised his hand to motion with his finger and cautioned, "But don't stay out long. Chief Scientist Dom told me a cyclone storm above the ocean surface is coming in our direction. Our city rests deep on the ocean floor, but sometimes during such storms the currents can become treacherous even at the depth where our city rests."

"Thank you for being so understanding, father. It really helps. Sometimes, it's just so hard not being able to embrace in the present what I know will someday come to pass."

"Before you go, I have something I want you to wear from now on when you swim in the ocean outside the dome," added Opellum. "I sense you should be wearing this for protection."

He reached inside his robe and pulled out a green crystal on a gold chain. It was exactly the same size and shape as the one that Sen Dar had stolen from Master Nim but it was green instead of blue. Mayleena's eyes opened wide with excitement, and her mouth dropped open.

"But father, you are Guardian of The Ancient One's Doorway Matrix Crystal. You said I would receive training with it but only when I was much older, and I… I know so little about such things. You once told me it opens doorways to parallel dimensions or something like that. I have wanted to wear that beautiful stone since I was ten but you would not allow it. Why do you want me to wear it now? What would happen if I lost it?"

Opellum gently grabbed his daughter and hugged her, then held her at arm's length and smiled.

"Your concern regarding the crystal's safety is appreciated, my lovely daughter, but you don't have to know how to use it. The Ancient One works through all of the mystic crystals for the benefit of all life. From now on, the omnipresent Spirit operating through it will be your guide and protector while you are off on one of your many little jaunts with Earth's whales and dolphins," and he winked at her.

143

Blushing, Mayleena looked away for a moment, then looked shyly back at her father with an accusing grin.

"How did you know about that? Have you been spying on me, father?"

"No, dear daughter, I have not been spying on you," chuckled Opellum with a shake of his head. Then he continued with a loving, penetrating gaze, "I know you better than you know yourself, and one thing I do know is that you can communicate with them. Mayleena, did you know that whales and dolphins did not originate on planet Earth? Remind me to tell you that story another time. Now please, Mayleena, wear the crystal for me. I would feel a lot better and more inclined to approve your regular swimming adventures outside the dome's protection if you do. You're my only daughter, you know."

Grinning wide, Mayleena stood up on her tiptoes as he bent down to meet her, and she affectionately kissed him on the cheek.

"Thank you for giving me so much love after mother died," she replied.

Her smile faded as forgotten images of her mother began to surface.

"Only vague impressions remain of her now. But I still recall how beautiful and graceful she was, and how she loved me." She sighed. "I'll wear the crystal tucked under my swimsuit straps. Will that do?"

"That will do just fine," replied Opellum, relieved.

He placed the gold chain and crystal over Mayleena's neck as she bent her head down to receive it. She picked it up with her fingers and looked very fondly at its glistening beauty. Flashes of light sparkled off its edges and it emitted a low humming mixed with the sound of crashing waves and the high note of a flute playing a hauntingly beautiful melody. Then the mysterious sound swiftly faded away, and Mayleena looked up, amazed.

"Father, did you hear that wonderful sound?"

Opellum smiled.

"Was that the Spirit Sound behind all life?" she asked with heightened enthusiasm. "Is that what you and Master Ra Mu have been training me to hear in my contemplation exercises? Is that it, father?"

"Mayleena, what do you say it is?" Opellum inquired.

Mayleena blinked, pondering the question, but then grinned and answered excitedly, "I think I've really heard it." Her smile widened, and with childlike wonder, she added, "Finally, for the first time I think I've really heard the Spirit voice of The Ancient One."

Opellum nodded his head as Mayleena tucked the green crystal inside her robe. Then she hugged him again and looked up, grinning.

"I promise, I won't be long," she added, then turned around and started walking toward the transport car platform a few feet behind them. She stopped to turn her head around and yell back, "Thanks for trusting me with it."

Mayleena climbed inside the car and the door swung down and sealed with a quick… *s-s-sip*. Both ends of the car lit up, changing colors from blue, to green, and then red every few seconds. Mayleena smiled at her waiting father and waved goodbye. The car levitated forward inside the transport tube, and the round end swung down and sealed with a deep… *swoop*. The entire length of the transport tube winding into the distance and around the left side of the city center glowed with a soft, blue magnetic aura. The transport car hovered within the center of the tube's open space, then it propelled forward in a blur of light at tremendous speed. In ten seconds, it had already traveled several miles into the distance toward the base of the giant dome's curved wall. It slowed as it approached an identical boarding platform.

Opellum raised his arms wide and took a deep breath, slowly let it out, and then smiled while he surveyed the botanical countryside paradise that surrounded him.

"What a beautiful day," he proclaimed.

Then he turned around and walked back up the winding path toward his house, which was set among the small cluster of white domed homes along the rolling hillside behind the lake.

The loading platform stationed at the other end of the transport tube was next to a blue marble building built directly into the base of the clear dome covering the city. Lit with blue light, this end of the transport tube ran from the platform, wound along the ground into the distance, and curved around the side of the city center by the pyramids, before it continued halfway around the lake to end at the loading platform that was just visible near Opellum's home.

The car carrying Mayleena sped into view and abruptly slowed as it came to a stop in front of the platform station. The tube end opened with a swift …*whoosh*… of air and swung upward. The transport moved forward out of the open tube end and stopped a few feet further down the platform. Both ends of the car stopped glowing and its curved door swung upward. Mayleena stepped out onto the platform landing. With an eager grin, she ran down the steps and along a short path to a gold door set in the side of the blue marble building. She passed the palm of her hand over a round blue moonstone textured control on the right side of the door lighting it up and the door swung silently open toward her, and she walked through the opening.

Mayleena watched the door lock and seal airtight, and then she swung around and walked into an eight-feet-wide tube made of silver-blue metal. She walked another ten feet down its length and up to a polished silver metal pressure door. She passed her hand over another control, and the pressure door swung open toward her, revealing a similar tunnel extending to an identical door set in a blue marble tiled wall. Mayleena hurried down this tunnel and up to the second pressure door, as the first door closed and sealed behind her.

She kicked off her shoes, unfastened the sash belt tied at her side, and opened her robe. She was wearing underneath it a sheer one-piece blue bathing suit with the front, sides, and back open. She dropped the robe off her shoulders to the ground revealing her smooth, subtle blue skin and elegantly shaped body. The swimsuit artfully exposed her slender waist and the distinctive curves of her firm feminine form. Two thin straps crisscrossed over the front of her abdomen and two more over her back connecting the bra and matching bottoms. A single thin strap around her neck connected to the middle of the front of the bra to hold up the swimsuit. Her long black hair flowed gracefully down behind her back in the tiny currents of a gentle wind that softly whirled inside the chamber. The green crystal, tucked underneath the crisscross straps of her swimsuit, was resting against her abdomen.

She really does look remarkably mature for her age, thought Harry from his invisible Atma viewpoint.

Then he realized that unlike Earth women, Mayleena was an extra-terrestrial woman from the mysterious planet of Oceana located in an even more mysterious parallel dimension of the universe. Oceanan women simply grow into adulthood much more quickly, and she had recently become a truly lovely, fully mature Oceanan woman.

Mayleena passed her hand over another moonstone control by the side of the door and it opened silently toward her. She stepped inside the room. The opened door and two sidewalls of the chamber were made of thick blue glass-like resin. Set within the middle of the fourth curved transparent wall – the outer wall of the dome over the city directly in front of Mayleena – was a clear door that provided access to the ocean outside the dome. This wall section, seamlessly integrated with the outer shell that covered the city, provided tremendous strength to withstand the great ocean water pressure.

The spectacular view through the transparent outer wall revealed an ocean bottom panorama. The water outside the dome was tinged blue but crystal-clear. Huge pink coral trees extended from the ocean floor upward hundreds of feet out of sight. Volcanic vents or fissures between the bases of several coral trees were spewing out waves of hot water filled with air bubbles that were gracefully drifting toward the ocean's surface so far above. A path on the other side of the clear door ran twenty feet along the ocean floor and then wound its way between the coral trees until it disappeared in the distance beyond visual range.

Two large whales and a small school of dolphins were aware of Mayleena's presence as they looked toward her curiously through the transparent wall of the ocean access chamber. Mayleena smiled and waved. Both large whales moved a huge flipper in response, and the pack of six bottle-nosed dolphins, two of which were very young, raced excitedly around across the outside of the access door nodding their heads as they passed by.

Mayleena walked over and passed her hand across the top of three controls aligned on the right side of the ocean access door. It lit up green and seawater began to fill the chamber.

Moments later, Mayleena was smiling as the water rose above her head. The three unobtrusive gills high up under the back of her chin began to open and close, and she freely breathed in the seawater. A second set of clear inner eyelids closed down over her eyes from underneath her outer eyelids. She opened her fingers, revealing small webs stretched between them at their base, and slowly extended her hand toward the middle of the three moonstone controls set in the wall.

When the chamber completely filled, the top moonstone control went out, the middle control lit up and she passed her hand over the bottom control. The pressure door slowly swung open. One of the excited young female dolphins swam inside the chamber and up to Mayleena. They rubbed noses together and Mayleena lovingly stroked the back of her head with a hand. Then she nodded toward the outside and the young dolphin raced back out through the open hatch into the ocean. Mayleena's affectionate smile widened as she swam gracefully out of the chamber. The pressure door swung closed behind her.

Mayleena stopped along the path by the first pink coral tree. A volcanic vent a few feet away was gently spewing waves of hot water and bubbles upward in a steady stream. She looked up with a joyful smile and swam ten feet toward the whales, while the dolphins playfully circled her. She approached the larger male whale, placed her hands on the side of his head by his large eye, and nodded her head to initiate a telepathic communication; the whale nodded his gigantic head in return. Then Mayleena swam over to the slightly smaller female whale, pressed a cheek against her head and gave her an affectionate hug.

The largest bottle-nosed male dolphin swam up behind her and nudged her. She grinned at him, climbed onto his back, and grabbed onto his dorsal fin. Pressing her stomach down against the arch of his back, she pushed her legs out behind her and tightly pressed them against both sides of the dolphin. The dolphin then turned his head around and appeared to actually smile back at her. Mayleena grinned and nodded her head, and then he began to swim away with her through the mysterious ocean world of these loving, highly intelligent telepathic creatures. As the whales swam slowly into the ocean depths, the dolphin with Mayleena on his back continued to swim behind them. The other five dolphins swam together, forming a pod that kept pace to each side and behind Mayleena. The entire group swam in the direction of the whales, and they all faded from view in the distant ocean depths.

Meanwhile, Opellum was standing next to the entry door of his countryside home. As he reached down to touch the control to open the door, the ground under his feet began to shake violently.

Unknown to him, the earthquake's epicenter was somewhere at the bottom of the ocean many miles away; yet, he was still having difficulty standing. The earthquake subsided a moment later, and he looked around noticing it caused no apparent damage to his home or the domed city. He knew the structural design of the dome could withstand things far worse than the most violent earthquakes on Earth, but his eyes widened with another realization.

"Mayleena! Oh, Ancient One, she's outside the dome," he said to himself alarmed and walked just two feet and stopped, then continued, "and there will be a huge underwater wave."

He closed his eyes and humbly lowered his head as the Spirit Sound of The Ancient One manifested within and around him, and he sent out a telepathic communication.

Great Ancient One of all, protect Mayleena, he humbly requested. *I'm so grateful for her presence with me in this life. You know a similar earthquake on the surface of this primitive planet took her mother from us those many years ago. Mayleena was only ten. Visiting Mornilla in my Spirit body on the astral plane at night is not quite the same as having her here at my side. When I return to my physical body in the morning, the sense of loss is still there lingering in my heart.*

Opellum opened his eyes to stare at the ocean beyond the dome covering the city. Then he lowered his head and sighed. A moment passed and he shook his head.

Nevertheless, Ancient One, he continued, *your wisdom, your will, and your omnipresent loving way is always for the greatest good of all life.*

Another Oceanan male came running along the narrow path that curved around the outer perimeter of the dwellings behind Opellum. He was slightly shorter in stature than Opellum, wearing a white Oceanan scientist's robe. A gold buckle set with a large oval cut aquamarine jewel clasped the blue leather-like belt around his waist. The scientist was a little winded as he ran up to Opellum.

"Master Opellum, the dome is secure," he stated and paused to catch his breath before he added with growing concern, "However, there will definitely be a huge underwater shock wave. The earthquake's epicenter is located on the ocean floor twenty-five miles from here. A great shift in the tectonic plates across a wide area of the sea floor created in an instant a five-feet differential drop or gap between them. A huge tidal swell will roll along the ocean floor at fifty miles an hour or more, covering many hundreds of miles, before it weakens and smooths out. On the surface, the swell will reach five-hundred-feet and it will race across the surface of the ocean for several thousand miles at three-hundred-miles an hour, before it gradually dissipates."

Opellum commanded, "Chief Scientist Dom, take all the search personnel you need, and any equipment required to look for Mayleena at once. A short time ago she went swimming outside the dome."

"No, surely not," gasped Dom.

Opellum nodded.

Dom's eyes widened and he bowed his head in compliance. Then he started to jog back the way he came.

"Don't worry, Master Opellum," he yelled over his shoulder, "I'm sure she'll be all right. We'll find her."

Mayleena was holding onto the dorsal fin of the dolphin for dear life when the shaking stopped and the water calmed. The whales swiftly turned around and faced the direction of the domed city. The dolphins were swimming wildly around in circles sending sonar beams into the ocean to try to locate the direction of the earthquake disturbance. The whales apparently already knew what was coming, as the dolphins turned around in unison and faced the same direction.

Mayleena strained to see into the distance of the ocean depths. Then she saw gigantic ripples in the fabric of the seawater moving fast along the ocean floor in their direction. An invisible current swept underneath the large male dolphin she was riding, under the other dolphins, and then the whales. It lifted them all up dozens of feet and lowered them back down just as swiftly.

Mayleena looked at the whales and they nodded their gigantic heads.

The dolphins began to click and chatter in their dolphin language. Then Mayleena's eyes widened in terror. She clasped the big dolphin more tightly with her two hands on the front of the dorsal fin and tightened her legs as hard as she could to the dolphin's sides. All heads stiffened in the direction from which the rolling wave had come. Mayleena could see the water rolling toward them like a rug shaken in the air, and then she saw a massive violent wave churning along the ocean bottom. It was similar to the effect of dropping a pebble into the center of a small pond, creating a series of rippling waves. However, this effect was taking place at the bottom of the ocean, and it was racing toward them in the form of a wall of liquid force the size of a five-story building. The current flowing under them gradually began to lift them several dozen feet upward above the ocean floor and then ...*wham*... it hit.

The force of the water hurled the whales, the dolphins, and Mayleena in the opposite direction. Then things sped up. The full underwater wave smashed into them and they tumbled in the direction of the water's momentum. It propelled them forward at fifty miles an hour as the ocean-dwelling, expert swimming mammals struggled to maintain a balance, before they righted themselves in the direction of the current and it swept them away. The water ripped Mayleena from the back of the large dolphin, tumbling her end over end like a rag doll. Mimicking her friends, she struggled to align her body in the direction of the churning water and finally managed to stiffen her body headfirst in that direction, and it propelled her away at greatly increased speed.

Several hours later, Mayleena was still speeding along the bottom of the ocean, and there was no sign of the whales or the dolphins. The wave dropped suddenly downward over the top of a deep, dark chasm. The churning water started tumbling her around in circles ever downward toward a bottomless black pit. A sharp incline appeared below her and she struggled to right her body but it was too late. The back of her head hit the rocks outcropped on the far wall of the chasm and she was instantly knocked unconscious. The wave churned her around in a whirlpool for a few moments and thrust her upward over the top of the other side of the chasm before it began to dissipate. It whirled around her several times and continued moving past her much more slowly. Her unconscious body assumed a fetal position as it gently dropped to the sand and settled there, making her appear as if she were peacefully asleep in a bed.

She soon stirred awake, rolled over, and sat up. Breathing normally, she sensed she was unhurt as she rubbed the back of her head and stood up. She floated upward a few feet, treading in place, and gazed all around her location. Then she put her hands up and looked at them with dismay, turning them over several times.

"Where am I?" she asked herself aloud, hearing the underwater-distorted sound of her own voice mixed with air bubbles rushing out of her mouth.

What am I doing out here? she thought bewildered, realizing the futility of speaking underwater.

She felt under her neck with both hands and discovered the gill slits. She put her hands in front of her face and looked at them for a few moments. Then she looked up and down her arms, noticing her blue skin, gazed at the webs between her fingers and toes, and then felt her body all over until she touched the crystal hanging on its gold chain under the straps of her swimsuit. She pulled it out and curiously gazed at it.

What do I do now? she pondered, mystified.

Her large male dolphin friend suddenly appeared swimming swiftly by her, and he curved back around and hovered in front of her face. Frightened by the creature, Mayleena frantically tried to swim away, but the dolphin swam around and stopped in front of her. He turned his head to the side and gazed at her with one of his eyes, and Mayleena shook her head as if she could not believe what she just heard.

I... I understand you, she replied amazed by the phenomena, *but... we're not speaking with our voices*.

The dolphin nodded its head and Mayleena clearly heard its voice again within her mind.

Yes-s-s, we speak within.

The dolphin rapidly nodded his long nose to his right side, indicating a direction.

That way you go now, he added, and she gazed confused back at him. Just then, the crystal began to glow green between her fingers, softly illuminating the ocean floor, and she let it go. It kept glowing as it slowly dropped to her chest. She watched with complete amazement as the crystal levitated upward and pulled her head by the chain around her neck in the direction headed further away from the edge of the chasm. Then it tugged on the chain several times to further indicate the direction she should pursue. She reluctantly started to swim in that direction and the crystal stopped glowing. Curious, Mayleena stopped, grabbed the crystal in her right hand again and it lit up. The dolphin swam by her side motioning with its head in the same direction.

Yes-s-s, reconfirmed the dolphin, that way we must go now.

Mayleena gazed into the direction. Then she tucked the crystal back behind the straps of her swimsuit, rubbed the bump on her head, and swam gracefully alongside the male dolphin. They faded into the murky distance.

Five days later, a tall, stately looking man in his mid-fifties was walking along a green, sandy beach. He was wearing a long flowing robe that came down directly above his ankles. Sheer silken pants extended below the hem of the robe to his sandal-clad feet. The symbol of a radiant eye above a quartz-capped golden pyramid hung from a gold chain around his neck.

Two of his loyal bodyguards following forty feet behind were carefully watching him. They were dressed in more simple gowns. A thin blue leather-like belt clasped their gowns around the waist held a holstered energy weapon at their sides. The wood handles sticking out of the holsters had smooth carved-out finger impressions for gripping them with a clenched fist.

A tropical shoreline behind them stretched several miles into the distance curving around a wide bay. Lush jungle trees bordered the emerald sands along the beachhead, and an oval dome topped palace was glistening in the sunlight high atop a hill a little further inland. The tops of two pyramids extended just above the tall treetops in the deep valley below the palace.

The stately man noticed something and stopped to look down the beach. Small turquoise waves were crashing and washing up to the feet of a body before retreating. It appeared to be a human female body with light-blue skin.

Looking back at his two guards, he pointed in the body's direction and yelled, "Over there. Something is on the beach."

Then he ran several dozen yards over to the body lying in the sand with the head face down on an arm.

"High Seer Stralim, wait for us to catch up with you," shouted one of the alarmed guards.

"Wait, my Lord, it could be dangerous," shouted the other equally alarmed guard.

High Seer Stralim was already stooping down to look at the body, and he could see the bathing suit covered an obviously feminine form. Then he noticed a gold chain around the female's neck and gently turned the body over just as the two guards ran up with their guns drawn. They squatted down on each side of Stralim and gasped as they looked down at a young, beautiful female with pointed ears. She appeared slightly starved, and her bruised skin was peeling in places from long exposure to harsh conditions. Stralim gently lifted her chin, noticed the tiny gills, and carefully touched one. Mayleena opened her eyes, gasped at seeing three strange men surrounding her, and instantly transformed into a woman with slightly tanned skin and long silky blond hair. She had all of Mayleena's features except now there were no pointed ears, gills, webbed hands and feet, or blue skin, and the surprised men jumped to their feet with mouths agape. Mayleena backed up in the sand, turning over; then she climbed to her feet and started to run.

"Please, young lady, don't be afraid. We won't harm you," said Stralim with a calm, soothing voice.

Mayleena stopped to look back nervously at Stralim and the two guards with drawn guns pointed at her.

"Put those away," Stralim commanded softly, motioning with a hand for the guards to retreat a few steps, and they quickly holstered their guns and stepped back.

Stralim gazed fondly into Mayleena's beautiful eyes and asked, "Lovely one, what's your name?"

Puzzled and frightened, she rubbed the bump on her head again, and then answered, "I… I don't know. Where am I? How did I get here?"

"Before you awoke a few moments ago," Stralim gently replied, "I beheld you with pale-blue skin and long black hair. You had what appeared to be small gills under the back of your chin, and webbed hands and feet. But when you saw us, you suddenly transformed into what you are now."

"What do you mean?" she shot back and closed her yes. She took a deep breath, opened her eyes again, and then added, "A large sea creature helped me find this land. I was completely exhausted when I neared the shore and would not have survived if the sea creature had not placed its nose under my abdomen and nudged me forward until I could stumble out of the water. I only walked a few feet when I became dizzy and collapsed on the sand. I have no idea how long I was lying there before you found me."

A series of high whistles and clicking noises coming from the ocean waves interrupted them. Mayleena's dolphin friend jumped out of the water in a high arch. Resurfacing a moment later, he held his head up above the waves rapidly nodding it, and the nervous guards began to draw out their weapons.

"No, don't harm it," yelled Mayleena. "That is the creature that guided me here and nudged me to shore. I would have died without its help."

The guards withdrew their hands from the guns.

"Don't worry, young one," Stralim said gently, motioning with a hand. "My guards were only startled. They would not have harmed it." Gazing at her with kind eyes, he continued, "We call that creature Yelfim. They are very intelligent mammals that have saved many from drowning. My people of Atlantis have been friends with them for decades. You were most fortunate that one found you first. There are large fish in these waters that would have made a short meal of you if not for his presence. The Yelfim have no natural enemies in the deep sea."

Mayleena discovered she felt safe with Stralim, and she waved at the dolphin. He nodded his head several times in return and then disappeared under the waves. He flew out of the water a moment later in another high arching jump and splashed back into the water. He appeared again further away making a series of short consecutive leaps along the ocean surface, heading back out to sea.

"Who are you?" Mayleena asked cautiously, turning to Stralim.

"I'm known as High Seer Stralim. I'm the elected leader of the people of Atlantis."

"What...is Atlantis?" she asked, even more mystified.

"Atlantis is a continent," replied Stralim. "Currently, we're a colony of Lemuria, known as the motherland of our people, but we will soon be independent."

Mayleena's blank look revealed her confusion.

"Lemuria is another larger continent halfway around the planet," continued Stralim. "It is the only other landmass above the vast oceans, so you must have come from there. God only knows how on this Earth you came to be all the way over here. Five days ago, our land experienced the shudder of an earthquake that occurred far away, and then a powerful cyclone storm and very large waves hit our shores. The size of the main waves must have considerably weakened by the time they reached here, although many sizable waves still crashed in over our beaches. I can only imagine how high the surface waters were before they traveled this far."

Mayleena frowned and started to cry. Stralim reached out his hand, gently touched her chin in a fatherly fashion, and very carefully lifted her head up.

"Young one, please don't cry. Everything will be all right." He gazed fondly at her and added, "I'll take care of you until we can solve this mystery together." He paused as a memory stirred within him and added, "My wife and little girl were killed in an accident many years ago and I have dearly missed them."

Mayleena felt Stralim suffering and found herself gazing affectionately back at him.

"Come with me to the palace on the hill," he continued. "You will need rest, food, and some healing attention. There will be time to remember things later. Please, trust me and we can walk there together." Mayleena's smile widened as she took his outstretched hand, and they walked slowly back down the beach. As the two guards stepped in line behind them, Mayleena started to shiver. Stralim noticed and untied his robe, revealing a long-sleeved white shirt and matching pants. He placed the robe around her shoulders, and she snuggled into its warming embrace. She grinned with gratitude up at him and he again gently clasped her hand with his. Then they began a livelier conversation, while they continued their slow casual walk along the vivid green sand of the Atlantian tropical paradise, headed in the direction of the hilltop palace.

CHAPTER SEVENTEEN

CAPTAIN KALEM
AND
A DREN NAMED ETTA

Stralim, Mayleena, and the hilltop palace on Atlantis faded away, and a new environment on another world formed before Harry Faldwell. He began receiving perceptions of Kalem and heard Master Ra Mu's voice once again.

General Faldwell, Captain Kalem is now twenty-six years old. Behold!

Mystified and curious, Kalem thought to himself, **Why have the Adepts** *requested a personal meeting with me?*

He looked down again at the piece of paper held in his hand to reread the message Admiral Starland had sent him:

"Several Guardian Adepts of The Ancient One have requested your presence aboard my flagship. They are meeting with me in two days and they want you to meet someone very special. Be here."

My dear father has once again politely insisted that I come, Kalem thought with smirking. **One can't very easily say no to an Admiral.**

Kalem recalled how he had tried to ignore the Admiral's requests while he was growing up, and how he discovered it was not worth the effort in the end. He paced back and forth in front of his Scout Interceptor, while he contemplated the many attempts he had made as a youth to convince his father to agree with his point of view, before he had stopped trying. The Admiral would somehow see right through any attempt he made to justify his being angry at the Academy, a situation, a teacher, or others. His father always pointed out the true nature of the matter.

"The reason for that particular difficulty," he would say, "was caused by you, my son, or your lack of understanding of the natural laws of the universe operating all around you."

Then he would unfailingly demonstrate that the fault for his son's anger with someone or something upsetting him had its center in him and not in others, no matter the situation. If the universe brought him a certain situation, then it was meant to teach him more about *The Law of Cause and Effect*, and more importantly about the higher law, or *The Law of Love*, that emanated from The Ancient One's omnipresent Spirit.

By the time Admiral Starland was done with him, Kalem clearly understood that a thought with strong feeling, combined with some action he had put out into the world, was the original cause that had eventually led to the problem. Kalem had to admit his father was right. At that point there was nothing left to be angry about, and he always came away seeing things in a new, clearer light.

Kalem instinctively understood that his father's teachings were making him stronger, more responsible for his actions, the world around him, and the future outcome of his life. Although he knew well enough that his father was a wise man, he was amazed at how the Admiral always seemed to be a step ahead of him, no matter what he did. There was a special connection between him and the mysterious Master Adepts of The Ancient One, whom he sometimes referred to as The Guardians of The Ancient One. On many occasions, they would show up where he was located at the time to discreetly visit with him for days, as Master Nim had done several times over the years before Sen Dar murdered him, or he would disappear for several days at a time to meet with them at a secret location. No matter what Kalem tried, his father would not talk about what took place at those secret meetings with the mysterious Adepts.

He would say, "Kalem, my son, I love you. When you are ready, you will come to understand all things. For now, prepare yourself for the future. There is more adventure approaching than you can possibly imagine."

In his youth, Kalem was left puzzled each time his father said this, and he had said it many times.

It's always about the future, thought Kalem, a little irritated. ***Even***

my visions of the beautiful woman with blue skin are centered there. When will the future finally catch up to the present?

At every opportunity, he would walk away from the Academy within the domed city of Marnanth on Telemadia (3) to go to the same hilltop high above the city to watch the twin suns set behind the distant Sandeem Mountains. Only then, when the lovely woman appeared in his vision and the angry frustration of growing up vanished, would his troubled heart find peace. She had that power over him and he had not even discovered her name. This left him a little depressed because he also sensed the visions of her were coming from the future. Any depression, however, never lasted for more than a few minutes, for there was too much to discover. High adventure was in the air so thick he could almost taste it. While growing up, the adventure he sought seemed to be an elusive thing – something right around the next corner that could never quite be touched.

Kalem's Scout Interceptor landed on its circular landing pad next to a dozen other Scout class fighters that were stationed at the deep space strategic military launch facility and flight school on the planet Mentroff. He had received thorough training and had passed his final flight tests on Mentroff. He was classed the best fighter pilot in the Galactic Alliance, and had the respect of all his fellow pilots that followed him into battle.

He had been stationed on this dismal world only once before after first graduating from the Academy over ten years earlier. It was not exactly an unpleasant memory. However, the weather on Mentroff was nearly always overcast, and he was damp or on the verge of being uncomfortably cold most of the time. It was only warm, if you call sixty degrees warm, three months out of the year. He never really froze but he was never comfortably warm either. The monotonous climate nearly drove him mad during the two years he spent there for his pilot and officer training.

When he finally graduated as a Lieutenant in the Galactic Inter-dimensional Alliance of Free Worlds, he and his best friend, Lieutenant Moreau, celebrated nonstop for a week. He had not forgotten that little episode of truly foolish behavior either. He had awakened naked on one of the three moons of Mentroff with a terrible hangover, lying in a pool of blue mud. Fortunately, he had landed his ship just a few feet away. However, he never did find out how or why he ended up there. Moreau was not any help either. He had awakened in a swamp on one of the other two moons that circled Mentroff. Kalem shook his head and wondered how no one caught and disciplined them during those post-graduation days.

Now I'm a Captain with battle-hardened experience and men look to me for their survival, Kalem reflected, and he perked up.

He knew he was responsible for the men under his command, and knew all too well the high adventures he imagined having in his youth were often deadly dangerous. He suddenly stopped pacing and looked anxiously at his wristwatch.

"Damn it!" he exclaimed with an angry shake of his head, "I'll be late again."

He raced underneath his ship and climbed inside the open hatch. The hatch whirled closed, and a moment later, the ship lit up, glowing around the hull with a familiar blue aura. The low humming of its antigravity drive began to pulse, and the ship hovered above the launch pad. Then it shot up into the atmosphere and punched a hole in the dark cloud cover. Bright sunlight streamed briefly through the opening before the clouds whirled back over it.

Captain Kalem was sitting at the chair behind his control console aboard his Scout class fighter with his hands depressed into the palm guidance controls. A small dot in distant space appeared on the view screen and quickly grew larger, revealing that his Scout ship was swiftly approaching Admiral Starland's flagship.

Admiral Starland was standing next to Master Opellum by the open door of the clear elevator in the center of one of the flagship's two observation domes. They were both gazing up through it as if waiting for something. Then a speck of light appeared from deep space and swiftly flew into view, revealing a single Scout class fighter flying toward the flagship. It veered in a wide curve past the observation dome and stopped to hover briefly before it slowly moved out of view into the launch bay.

Starland and Opellum grinned at each other, and Opellum remarked playfully, "Perhaps it would be best if your son does not see me as I really am just yet. The Ancient One has revealed to me that such an event could alter the path that he and my daughter are destined to walk together."

"Yes, I believe you are right," replied Starland with a respectful nod. "Seeing you as you are now could alter many things."

Opellum closed his eyes and turned away as he transformed into a Caucasian man with long blond hair. He had the same general features as his former self, except his gill slits, pointed ears, webbed hands, and blue skin had vanished. He turned back around and presented himself to Admiral Starland for inspection.

"Well, Master Starland," he inquired, "how do I look?"

"Why Master Opellum, you look simply like...like an Earth person," answered Starland, chuckling, and they both laughed.

Then Starland turned toward the elevator and courteously motioned toward it with his hand.

"I believe the time has come to introduce your friend to my son," he stated with a mischievous grin.

Opellum nodded, walked to the elevator, and stepped inside, and the Admiral stepped inside beside him.

"You know, they will become the very best of friends," commented Opellum.

Starland nodded and added, "Oh, I know from long experience you are never wrong in these matters. However, it should prove most interesting," and he raised a curious eyebrow.

"That it should," replied Opellum grinning back.

The elevator door closed and slowly lowered them inside the ship.

A few minutes later, Admiral Starland and Master Opellum entered a wide oval conference room and seated themselves in comfortable lounge chairs at the back of a long obsidian table. Ten additional high-backed, blue, leather-like chairs surrounded the table. Captain Kalem walked through the doorway at the other end of the room and stopped by the empty chair at the opposite end of the table. Then he saluted Admiral Starland with a closed right fist held across his chest.

"Uh-hum," began Kalem, clearing his throat, "Captain Kalem reporting, Admiral, as you strongly recommended."

The Admiral stood up, smiling at his son, and saluted him back.

"At ease, Captain," acknowledged Starland, and he paused a moment, then added, "There is someone here I want you to meet. He was one of my teachers. He's a dear friend, and someone who would very much like to meet you."

Starland gestured to Opellum seated to his right side and said, "This is Master Opellum."

Kalem walked around the left side of the oval table and extended his hand to Opellum who was rising from his seat. Opellum did not extend a hand. Smiling, he slightly bowed and lifted his head.

"A simple bow of respect toward each other will do, Captain," he remarked.

"I'm honored to meet you, Master Opellum," replied Kalem, lowering his hand and nodding in return. "I've heard something about you and your people over the years from my father while I was growing up. But I had no idea you were human, well at least not in the way I see you now."

"Oh really, Captain," responded Opellum cocking a curious eye toward Kalem. "What did you expect to find, someone with green skin and another eye in their forehead?"

"Oh no, Master Opellum," chuckled Kalem, "That wasn't what I meant. It's just that, well frankly, most of our advanced crystalline science, antigravity propulsion, and who knows what else, has been given to the Galactic Alliance over a long period of time by you and your people. I guess I thought...well I'm not certain what I thought."

"Enough said, Captain. I accept the compliment," responded Opellum with a benevolent smile.

Kalem grinned relief and relaxed his shoulders as Opellum reached into his robe and pulled out a six-inch-long, octagon faceted, bluish-green crystal device that tapered to a point. He held it out a foot in front of his chest, and it emitted a pulsing and wavering light. Swirling particles of gold and silver light projected from the crystal and formed into a four-feet-wide sphere of light two-feet above the center of table. Then an image formed inside the sphere revealing Etta, the endearing three-feet-long, pale-green alien creature with deep-blue bulbous eyes.

The image rapidly expanded three feet high and the sphere surrounding Etta vanished, leaving him standing several feet in the air with his tail held straight out behind him illumined with opalescent color. Then he held up both hands and comically wiggled his fingers toward Kalem with a widening smile. Watching Kalem's eyes bug out, Admiral Starland and Master Opellum just managed to suppress their laughter.

Kalem looked at Opellum and inquired with a wry grin, "What's this?"

The smile on Etta's face dropped, and Opellum stepped a few feet around the curve of the table as he pointed at Etta with his open hand.

"This, my good Captain, is Etta, and he is a Dren," stated Opellum. "Drens are a silica-based sentient mammal with naturally developed antigravity levitation and flying ability. They are also telepathic with flawless photographic memories, and they are more highly evolved than many intelligent species in the universe. By studying them over five hundred thousand years ago, our scientists first learned how to master antigravity wave propulsion, and they have been friends of the Oceanan people for that entire time."

Kalem's eyes widened as he stared at Etta with a new profound respect, and he grinned.

"Well, Etta, I had no idea," he said, a little embarrassed. "I'm very pleased to meet you."

Etta beamed a broad smile at Kalem again as he levitated toward him with an extended forearm. Kalem carefully extended his hand and they shook.

"Zim boa chet, Captain Kalem?" ("How are you, Captain Kalem?"), asked Etta in a smooth human-like male tenor voice.

Greatly surprised, Kalem realized he had perfectly understood what Etta had said.

"I'm fine, Etta, just fine," he answered, and he gazed questioningly at Starland and Opellum, then asked, "How is it I understand what he just asked me?"

Master Opellum and Admiral Starland were grinning amusement.

"If you will recall, Captain, I said the Drens are telepathic," answered Opellum. "He spoke with his vocal cords but sent the thought in your own language. He is not yet able to speak it; however, he understands your language and can telepathically send or receive it. That reminds me, Etta, when we get back to Oceana, I intend to remedy the situation. If you want to, you and your people can receive the transference of multiple language understanding and the ability to fluently speak them. Chief Scientist Dom could arrange it."

Etta grinned wide and then excitedly flew twice around the table before he came to a stop, hovering in the same place above its surface.

"Captain, the best way I have of putting this," continued Opellum, "is that you and Etta are destined to be close friends. The Sound and Light or Spirit current of The Ancient One revealed this to me. In the battles to come, you will find you can trust Etta with your life, and you will need such an ally. If the shoe were on the other foot, so to speak, and you happened to save his life, he would never forget it. He would always be ready to do battle at your side."

"Well, uh, what can I say?" replied Kalem, somewhat puzzled. "I've never gone into battle with a partner aboard before." He paused as a deepening respect for Etta welled up inside. Then he asked, "Are you up for it, Etta?"

Etta suddenly darted around the room and stopped again a foot in front of Kalem's face. Then he raised his body upright with his tail extended so that he appeared to be standing on his feet upon solid ground. Yet, he was actually levitating a foot above the table. He placed his right clenched fist across his chest and saluted Kalem as any good soldier would his Captain. Kalem grinned and saluted him back.

"Well, Captain, you have a new ally you should take with you on the next mission," Starland stated seriously. "We are about to go into battle against this Glonden-Yalgull Alliance. They have reared their ugly heads again, by starting new attacks on Galactic Alliance outposts after nearly a year of remaining silent. You know well the last time they engaged our forces, over half their combined fleets were lost. You would think they would have learned better by now. Anyway, I am sending you and Etta on a reconnaissance mission to try to spy out where they may be hiding their forces in preparation for a major counterattack. We need to know what their next move may be and stop it before it starts, this time for good."

"Admiral, you know I've wanted to finish this stupid war with those murdering devils for far too long," remarked Kalem, a little steamed. "They had no reason to attack us with hit-and-run tactics over the past twelve years in the first place. I still don't understand why you stopped our forces from going all the way to their home worlds to finish the job."

"Captain Kalem," began Opellum with a firm commanding voice, "no one who adheres to the teachings of The Ancient One would ever harbor ill will and feelings of hatred toward other life in the universe, even if that life is misguided and destructive. I trust, Captain, that you will keep that in mind when you have to take life to protect the innocent life on many worlds from those who have gone mad with hate."

"Listen to Master Opellum, my son," Starland added firmly. "I have said this to you many times. Rid yourself of feelings for revenge and become the warrior whose purpose is to keep destruction and the taking of life to as much of a minimum as possible while carrying out your missions. Is that clear, Captain?"

Kalem sighed, realizing they were right, and nodded his full agreement toward Opellum, then Starland, and finally at Etta, who was intently watching him.

"Well, no one wants to take life unless they have to for the protection of so many others," Kalem concurred.

Starland, Opellum, and Etta smiled back at him. Then the Admiral walked around the table and stopped to gaze at his son.

"We're approaching an outlying star system of the Yalgull Empire, and we're fairly certain their home world is not far away. I want you and Etta to go with stealth. See what you can find out, but be very cautious. If my suspicions are correct, Sen Dar is behind this whole madness, and he will have that area of space watched for spies. Also, remember what you have learned about the Sound and Light of The Ancient One. Call out its name if you get into trouble. Don't think about it, just do it."

"As you wish, Admiral," Kalem replied solemnly. Then he smiled at Opellum and said, "Master Opellum, I do hope we meet again under better circumstances. I would very much like to get to know you and your people better, when we get the chance."

"Oh, we will see each other again in a time and a place not of our choosing," replied Opellum, grinning mysteriously. "Expect unexpected meetings and so-called chance occurrences in your life, Captain. There will be many of them."

Kalem nodded and, puzzled, looked back at him before he turned to seek clarification from the Admiral, but his father just grinned.

"Well, Captain, you had better get aboard your ship," Starland insisted cheerfully, and he gazed fondly at Etta.

"For the time being, Etta, you are officially attached to Captain Kalem as his second-in-command, and his personal aide and protector. We will see you both back here upon your return."

Etta smiled proudly, flew up beside Kalem, and then turned around so they were both facing the Admiral and Master Opellum. Kalem saluted them with his right fist across his chest and Etta copied him. As Kalem turned to leave, Etta turned in unison, and they headed side by side out of the conference room.

"Well, Etta, new partner, are ya married? Got kids?" inquired Kalem as they disappeared around the corner.

Etta responded rapidly with excitement in his native Dren language, and Kalem replied cheerfully as their voices faded into the distance.

"A wife and two kids, huh, wow! I would like to get married one day, if I ever meet the right one, if you know what I mean."

Opellum and Starland gazed at each other just as Etta's cheerful voice faded away.

"He is destined to find her, Master Starland," said Opellum confidently.

"I think, Master Opellum," began Starland with an agreeable nod of his head, "since you're usually right about these things, even though your daughter has not yet been found, The Ancient One must have some special destiny planned for them. I have seen glimpses of many things that will take place on Earth and to your secret domed city. Indeed, you may be right."

Master Opellum looked away for a moment to sadly reflect about something. Then he let out a relieved sigh, looked back at Admiral Starland, and stated, "We shall see, Master Starland. We shall see."

CHAPTER EIGHTEEN

ETTA'S BOND OF FRIENDSHIP

*S*o, Etta, you can't always tell when something is lurking behind a rock or under one, can you?" asked Kalem, motioning with a hand.

Etta was highly focused on a small view screen that had swung out from underneath the control console and did not respond. Kalem took his other hand off the palm guidance control and looked closer at Etta, noticing his wide-open eyes were staring at something on the screen. He was completely oblivious to Kalem's voice.

Kalem quietly stood up from his seat, walked around it, and then stood behind Etta's back. He carefully extended his hands and stuck a finger in the ears on each side of Etta's head. Etta jumped in the air and bumped his head on the ceiling. His tail lit up, and he flew around the room with his fists doubled up, ready for a fight. He paused to rub the top of his head with both hands and then put his fists back up. Angrily growling, he spun around and looked at Kalem, who was standing there with a smirk on his face and both his index fingers pointing inward to empty space where Etta's head had been.

"Well, you weren't listening, so I figured I might as well plug up your ears," chuckled Kalem, dropping his hands.

Etta was not amused. He placed his hands on his hips and smirked back at Kalem.

"Cham podsit nosfin, Captain" ("That wasn't funny, Captain"), he angrily remarked.

165

Kalem smiled at him and put a hand to his chin.

"Alright, Etta," he said with another wry grin, "what did I say to you before I plugged up your ears?"

Etta straightened up stiffly with embarrassment, and his green cheeks turned red. Then he looked nervously around the room to try to find a prompt response or perhaps a way out.

"Oh uh... um... ot... um... okay, ot q podsit istoonan." ("Oh uh... um... for... um... okay, so I wasn't listening.") replied Etta, fumbling and stuttering.

Then he flew back over behind the small view screen, looked at it again, and turned to Kalem.

Serious, he said, "Captain, alm gond ma q vindal basja jop cham woldent su'la nocstrum. U fontu almba illuos qla yamil untra insatul losem moontallama. Q wrisos tep jint op tam empf tropa nunsella." ("Captain, there could be a hidden base on that planet we're approaching. A faint masked signal is coming from inside those mountains. I picked it up with the deep rock sensor.")

Etta pointed to his view screen showing the images of a mountain range overlooking a vast lowland valley. Kalem looked down at it and opened his eyes wide with surprise.

"Etta, my friend, you did it. That planet is Seltium (4). It's not supposed to be inhabited," remarked Kalem, and he smiled triumphantly as he proudly patted Etta's shoulder. "That must be the location of the secret base they use to strike at the Galactic Alliance. How would you like to go on a reconnaissance mission with your special antigravity abilities and spy out the situation once we get there?"

Etta smiled as big as a crescent moon and chattered away excitedly in his Dren language.

"Slow down, Etta. I can't understand a word you're saying," insisted Kalem with calming hand motions. "Is that a yes?"

Etta smiled, snapped to attention, and smartly saluted Kalem.

"Quibb... quibb... quibb... quibb! Q lon ka tep." ("Yes... yes... yes... yes! I can do it."), he excitedly replied.

"Okay, Etta," said Kalem with a respectful nod, "but if you see the Glonden or the Yalgull, return here immediately. I do not want you biting anyone into submission. Is that crystal clear?"

Grinning, Etta answered, "Quibb, Captain Kalem, toi oora." ("Yes, Captain Kalem, crystal clear.")

Kalem walked back over to the console and waved the palm of his hand over a crystal control. The large view screen revealed his ship was fast approaching a cloud-covered world with a pale-green atmosphere.

Exposed above the equator was a deep blue ocean that surrounded a large continent.

"I'll put the ship in stealth mode now, Etta," stated Kalem. "They will not be able to detect our arrival." He touched a green crystal, lighting it up.

As the ship flew toward the planet's equator, it sparkled softly with thousands of light particles and started to vanish. It continued down in a long arc at increased speed before it broke through the clouds.

Kalem nodded his head in the direction of the large view screen to indicate that Etta should look at it.

"Okay, Etta, do your stuff."

A mile directly below was a snowcapped mountain with several smaller mountain peaks to each side and a vast red plateau that extended from them out into the countryside. A lake stretched from the base of the large mountain into the plateau and up to a forest of strangely twisted blue-green fir trees. As the ship flew over the forest, it slowed and hovered, before it vanished completely as it lowered into a cluster of trees near the lakeshore by the base of the mountain.

Etta flew across the control room and stopped in the air a few feet from Kalem's side.

Kalem looked at him, placed a hand on his shoulder, and said, "I'm setting the ship down in the forest a safe distance from the base of the large mountain. When you leave the ship, fly slowly low to the ground and try to stay behind trees most of the way. If you are detected, they may just think you are an animal of some kind."

Etta nodded his head.

Although the ship was invisible to any eyes or instruments focused in their direction, it was now hovering above a small field of grass surrounded by a cluster of trees. The three landing struts extended out of the bottom of the hull and the ship gently lowered until the upturned pods on the ends of the struts touched down in short, brown grass, and then the antigravity engine shut off.

Kalem stood up extending his forearm out to Etta. Etta looked at it, smiled, grasped it with his own forearm, and gently bowed his head as a Dren gesture of true friendship.

"Etta, my friend, come back safely," said Kalem, smiling. "If you get into any trouble, contact me through this."

He let go of Etta's forearm, reached under the console, and grabbed a gold wire headset with a diamond-like crystal on each end.

"I'll hear your thoughts and see everything you see during your journey," continued Kalem.

Etta gently lowered his head. Kalem placed the gold wire headset over his head and set the crystal earpiece on each end into Etta's ears. Etta grinned and then flew around the room. He stopped above the spiral hatch on the smooth floor behind the control console.

"Okay, Etta, I'm activating the headset."

Kalem touched a small blue crystal on the console next to the palm controls and the diamond crystal in each of Etta's ears faintly glowed. Then he touched another control on the console and the hatch spiraled open. Sunlight streamed through the opening, bringing with it a gentle breeze. Etta took a deep refreshing breath and then saluted Kalem, and Kalem saluted him back.

"Etta, my friend," continued Kalem, "I'm counting on you to be very careful."

Etta proudly puffed up his chest and gave Kalem a wide courageous grin. The light coming from his tail intensified, and he darted out of the ship through the open hatch. Kalem touched a crystal control and the hatch spiraled closed, sealing with a quick... *swoop*.

Then Kalem sat back down in the chair, looked at the view screen, and strained to see the top of the largest snowcapped mountain that towered high above the end of the forest into several clouds.

A moment later, Etta appeared on the view screen flying out from underneath the ship a few feet above the ground. He stopped ten feet away from the ship's hull, turned around, saluted toward the ship, and darted over to the tree line at the edge of the clearing where he disappeared between the twisted branches of a cluster of trees. He reappeared a quarter of a mile away coming out from behind another set of trees and paused again to look around. Then he vanished back inside the trees.

Kalem touched the headset control and the view screen changed to Etta's point of view, revealing that he was flying between two rows of trees just above the forest floor. Moving in quick darts of flight, he would pause long enough to look around, then dart into the distance and stop to hide behind another tree. The base of the snowcapped mountain with its tall, sharply pointed crags was looming ever closer.

Etta darted behind a tree near the end of the tree line and stopped. Two Glonden soldiers and one taller Yalgull soldier were walking toward him down a path that led a quarter of a mile from a large cave opening in the base of the mountain. They approached the forest trees only twenty feet away from Etta's position. Kalem heard Etta's whispered voice coming through the transceiver crystal on the console.

"Captain, vonf umona boa yamil." ("Captain, some soldiers are coming.")

Kalem touched the transceiver crystal and whispered, "I see what you see, Etta. We were right. I need you to stay undercover until nightfall. Then peek inside the mountain base to see how large a force is gathered. Be very careful and don't let them see you."

"Quibb, Captain." ("Yes, Captain.") whispered Etta.

The soldiers were laughing and joking as they walked into the forest and stopped in the glade near Etta's hiding place. The tallest one, a Yalgull Captain, pulled a large silver flask from his coat, opened the cap, and took a big swig. The two Glonden soldiers gathered around him were licking their lips with anticipation. One of the Glonden soldiers appeared irritated.

"Okay, Gralik, that's enough or there won't be any left for us," the Yalgull Captain insisted. "Hand it over."

Gralik snarled back at both Glonden soldiers and stared menacingly at the slightly taller one who demanded the flask.

"You, Holshoon, should not push me," he scowled. "We are the same rank, but do not make me your enemy. You would lose a contest with the likes of me. I was the one that suggested we take a quick break out here where those snotty officers cannot spy on us. This is my Flamboshual flask of Tincari Ale and I do not have to share it with the likes of you. Be grateful you get anything."

He looked fondly at the flask and then with some reluctance rudely shoved it into Holshoon's chest. Holshoon stumbled but quickly regained his composure. With great delight, he took a long draft from the flask and then handed it to the lesser-ranked Glonden soldier next to him.

"Okay, Moonask, now it's your turn," said Holshoon, grinning.

Moonask took a swig from the flask, wiped his lips, and sighed with great delight.

Etta poked his head out from behind a tree to get a better look, while holding onto a thin branch with one hand, and the branch broke with a loud... *snap*!

Kalem witnessed Etta tumble head first into a large bush at the base of the tree, and he jumped from the chair with a gasp. He touched the transceiver crystal and yelled, "Etta, get out of there. Disappear in the woods."

All three soldiers drew their laser weapons in an instant and pointed them at the tree where the sound came from, just as Etta darted into the distant forest depths and disappeared.

Gralik snarled and ran toward Etta's hiding place with the others closely behind. He fired at the tree and blew away a four-foot section of the trunk. The upper part of the tree dropped down onto what was left of the burnt stump, and the tree started to fall over right on top of them. Their terrified eyes bulged out as they jumped in opposite directions, landing flat as the huge tree came down with a thunderous… *whoosh*… *shoomp*… *fump-bump*, missing Gralik by only an inch.

"What are you shooting at?" yelled Holshoon with a condescending chuckle. "It's nothing but an old branch that snapped off that tree. Do all you Yalgull fire at the first sound you hear or has that ale gone to your head already?"

Fuming, Gralik jumped to his feet, pointed his laser at Holshoon, and barked, "Shut your mouth, Holshoon, you little Glonden morsel. It could have been a spy. These are desperate times. We will check out the area and then we can go about our business with the Tincari Ale, or would you like to taste the end of this weapon, Holshoon?"

"Alright, I was only kidding," grimaced Holshoon, and he added with a cheerful smile, "Let's get it done and get back to that flask."

Holshoon and Moonask got up and fanned out to search the woods. They went only about twenty feet before they both started to turn around. They saw that Gralik had not moved and they raced back toward the flask of ale held in his hand. Gralik saw them coming and took another long draught of the ale before they ran up to him. Then he handed the flask to Holshoon and laughed as if nothing had happened. They were all soon drunk.

Night had fallen and the stars in the heavenly sky over this alien world were more numerous and brilliant than anyone on Earth would ever likely get to appreciate. Three moons of varying sizes, two full and one crescent, moving in opposing directions, were casting an even light across the landscape. However, Etta was not looking at the stars, the moons, or the light they cast across the countryside. He was walking on his tiptoes around the soldiers, who had passed out and were lying in a circle in the forest glade.

Once he was clear of the woods, his tail glowed and he flew a foot above the path to the cavern opening that led inside the mountain.

The cavern opening was much larger than it looked to be from a distance, and the soft blue glow coming from the round lights lining the cavern ceiling cast an eerie luminescence down its length. Etta lowered to the ground and his tail stopped glowing just as two Yalgull sentries came toward his position.

"Hey Grishla, did you see a light or something coming from outside?" one sentry asked the taller soldier.

Annoyed, Grishla answered, "Nah, there's nothing there, Yalgric. You keep seeing things that don't exist and I'm tired of jumping every time you imagine a Galactic Alliance spy is prowling out there in the night to slit our throats. Give it up."

"I was sure I saw some kind of light flash in front of the entrance to the base," added Yalgric with alarm.

"Will you forget it already, Yalgric?" Grishla snapped and then added irritably, "Come on, let's get some water. I'm dying of thirst out here."

Yalgric shrugged his shoulders and they both headed back inside the cavern. As they disappeared, Etta came into view around the side of the opening. He peeked cautiously inside and walked in, keeping close to the wall. The light cast a long Dren shadow high up on the rock wall behind him, and it continued to trail behind him until it too faded deeper within the mountain's interior.

Kalem sighed relief, touched the transceiver control, and whispered, "Etta, you have to be more careful. They were almost on to you. If you had bumped into one of them, they would know we were on to them and set off an alarm. Just take a few pictures with that photographic memory of yours and then beat a path back to the ship."

Etta was deep inside the cavern discovering that the chamber under the mountain was immense. The ceiling inside was over three hundred feet high and fifteen hundred feet wide. He was looking at six Yalgull and six Glonden Destroyer class ships landed on pads in two rows lined up against the back wall of the cavern. They were identical in shape as their larger deep space battleships but about one-tenth the size. In front of the Destroyers were two-dozen smaller Glonden and Yalgull Scout class Interceptors. Hundreds of Glonden and Yalgull technicians were busy working in and around many of the ships, preparing them for battle.

A tall figure with long black hair, wearing a black cape, was standing high up on a platform built out of the center of the back wall of the cavern. To Etta, the man looked like images he had seen of Sen Dar at an earlier age, but he was too far away to be certain. The man was overlooking the work on the cavern floor forty feet below. Two other figures were standing by his side. Etta had no way of knowing that one was the Glonden leader Gloeen or that the other one was Emperor Garn, the Yalgull leader.

Kalem looked closely at his view screen, scrutinized the images Etta was sending back to him through the headset, and then strained to see if the caped figure was who he thought it was.

He touched the transceiver control and whispered, "Etta, I saw the figure wearing the cape high up on the platform. The Admiral showed images of Sen Dar to me when he was younger. That has to be him. It looks like preparations are underway for a large-scale battle. Now get out of there as quietly as you can and race back to the ship. We must get this information to Admiral Starland."

Up on the platform, Sen Dar was pacing back and forth in front of Garn and Gloeen. Commander Hontull walked out onto the platform through the opening in the cavern wall behind them and approached Sen Dar.

Bowing his head respectfully, he said, "My Lord, we're nearly prepared for our next assault on the Galactic Alliance. What are your orders?"

Before Sen Dar could answer him, the stolen crystal hidden under his shirt began to faintly glow and then pulse. Sen Dar's eyes widened with recognition, and he yelled below to a dozen soldiers marching toward the ships.

"An intruder is on the base. Seal the exits. I want him found now!"

He spun around, fuming; eyed Gloeen, Garn, and Hontull; and then barked out, "You three get moving and stop that spy before he gives away our position. I want to know who's responsible for letting him get this far."

As they bowed, their faces blanched and they hurried back into the opening in the cavern wall behind the platform.

Etta heard the command coming from the platform and an uncontrollable high-pitched screech came from his mouth as his tail lit up. Then he darted in a blur of light back out of the mountain cavern.

Sen Dar's eyes narrowed angrily as he watched the trail of light exit the cavern. Then he slammed his fist on the railing surrounding the platform, spun around, and ran through the opening in the rock wall behind him.

Down on the cavern floor, dozens of troops with drawn laser guns and rifles were racing in the direction of the opening to the base. A Yalgull Scout fighter and a Glonden Scout fighter simultaneously lit up. They hovered a few feet above their pads and then sped, one after the other, out of their hidden base into the night in search of a spy.

Gritting his teeth, Kalem jammed his hands into the palm guidance controls, as he gazed at the large view screen to observe the ship lifting off the forest glade. A moment later, the view screen revealed his ship was now hovering high above the trees. Kalem touched another crystal and his screen changed, revealing Etta's viewpoint while he raced away from the mountain, glancing over his shoulder and at the ground below.

Kalem touched the transceiver and commanded, "Etta, head for the ship and wait in the trees until I clear you to come aboard."

The Yalgull fighter flew out of the cavern and fired a red Mazon energy ball at Etta, but he maneuvered sideways and the fireball darted past him. The Glonden ship appeared a moment later and fired another laser fireball, but Etta skillfully hovered sideways again, narrowly avoiding the fiery weapon, and both fireballs exploded in succession against the red plateau in the distance. An instant later, two blue fireballs appeared out of thin air, one after the other, above the tree line near the edge of the forest. They hit the Yalgull ship and exploded it into brilliant particles of molten energy under a star-filled night sky. The Glonden ship veered away in several ninety-degree turns as two more of the blue fireballs appeared from the invisible location in the atmosphere above the forest. The first fireball missed the Glonden fighter as it darted aside, but the second one hit the fighter dead center and it too exploded into particles of light.

Kalem's ship materialized. A circle of light poured out of the open hatch, illuminating the treetops and a wider circular area of the forest floor. Etta flew into view above the trees and darted up inside the ship, and the hatch closed. The ship sped away from the mountain and stopped above the red plateau, shot two more blue fireballs from the outer edge of the hull, and then darted up into the sky. Both fireballs slammed into the top of the cavern opening exploding the rock face and creating an avalanche. Part of the mountainside gave way and roared down over the entrance to the base.

Two more Glonden fighters flew out of the partially closed entrance, just as the top of the cavern collapsed on top of them, smashing them to the ground and completely burying the cavern entrance.

Etta was hovering on the other side of the control console near the view screen.

"I'll put the ship back on stealth mode until we leave the planet's atmosphere," said Kalem, and he added with a widening smile, "Thanks, Etta, that was a job well done."

Etta hovered over to Kalem's side and proudly puffed out his chest. Kalem extended his hand and they clasped forearms.

"My friend," continued Kalem, smiling with raised eyebrows, "we'll be far away from this planet before they can blast their way through that avalanche to come searching for us."

Etta took off the headset, sat it on the console, and then looked respectfully at Kalem.

"Captain Kalem, chet quezed tot aluf," he humbly began. "Quo Drens luntal organt u aluf montfa. Q pun frint et cheta risad ot ongal ot Q aluf." ("Captain Kalem, you saved my life," he humbly began. "We Drens never forget a life debt. I will fight by your side for as long as I live"), and he proudly saluted Kalem.

"Look, Etta, we are in this together," remarked Kalem. "You would have done the same for me. Any Galactic Alliance pilot under my command would have done the same. Don't give it another thought. Okay, my friend?"

Etta smiled in humble awe of his Captain and bowed anyway.

A few minutes later, the ship materialized back into view beyond the atmosphere of the world they had escaped. The glow around the hull intensified, changed from violet to gold in several seconds, and the ship shot in a flash of white light at trans-light speed into the depths of space.

CHAPTER NINETEEN

SEN DARION WAR AND PEACE

$\mathcal{A}$ blur of light darted from distant space quickly slowing into the shape of Kalem's Scout ship. It continued in a downward arc toward the open launch bay on one end of Admiral Starland's flagship. This time, instead of passing through the launch bay door, the Scout ship turned transparent and slowly moved right through the metal hull beside the launch bay to touch down on the floor next to thirteen Scout Interceptors. The hull faded back to its solid appearance as Kalem climbed down the descending ladder.

Admiral Starland was looking over a three-dimensional chart of a solar system that projected from the view screen into the center of the bridge control room. Kalem entered the room with Etta by his side. Admiral Starland turned around and breathed a sigh of relief upon seeing them. Kalem and Etta saluted the Admiral, but Starland ignored the salute as he threw his arms around his son and hugged him tightly. With a grateful smile, he held Kalem at arm's length, let him go, and then happily clasped forearms with Etta, who appeared quite surprised by the gesture.

"I'm so glad to see both of you," remarked Starland.

Kalem started to smile but stated instead, "Admiral, we found their base on Seltium (4) in the Quantran system bordering Yalgull space. That system is even closer to Galactic Alliance outposts. We detected no mother ships nearby, but six Yalgull and six Glonden Destroyer class ships, along with many Scout class support fighters, were inside a hangar they had dug out of the base of a mountain. Admiral, they were preparing for battle.

"I sent my very courageous Dren warrior friend Etta into their base wearing the mind-link headset. We discovered something else far more important that you should know and we have it all recorded. At first, it was difficult to be certain Sen Dar was the image that Etta's headset transmitted back to the ship because of the distance between them. However, there were three men, Admiral. One was Yalgull, one was Glonden, and the other one looked remarkably like Sen Dar. They were standing on a platform overlooking the base when something hidden inside the shirt of the one that I thought was Sen Dar lit up. That has to be Master Nim's stolen crystal. When it began to blink, the man knew Etta was inside the base. Etta just made it out of there in time.

"I had to destroy two of the enemy fighters that were tracking him and part of the mountainside to close off the cavern opening to their base, but that won't hold them for long. Admiral, Sen Dar is the hidden leader of the Glonden-Yalgull Alliance."

Starland stared solemnly at the projection of the solar system displayed in the room, and then he focused on the fourth planet from the sun.

"Now that they know we located them," said Starland, "my guess is they are already heading our way to attack, believing that we could not possibly prepare in time but we are well prepared. We are on approach to Sirus, the sixth planet of the Comrane solar system, where we detected a number of the enemy ships. Twenty Emerald Star Galaxy class star ships now surround this entire quadrant of space. They will not be able to escape back to Yalgull or Glonden space this time. This may be our final battle with them after ten years of hide-and-seek warfare. Excellent work, you two," he said cheerfully, looking away from the screen to gaze fondly at Kalem and Etta. "You two could use some well-earned rest. However, before you go, Etta, I have a message to deliver from Master Opellum."

He gazed compassionately at Etta, while they stared back curiously, and he continued, "He informs me that you have done your part for now in the mystical scheme of things, and he wants you to head back home. I believe you have your lovely wife Din and two little ones to attend to, if I'm not mistaken," and he grinned encouragement.

Disappointed, Etta's smile dropped as he replied glumly, "Din ba naman ot het ne genth covoolm bavot hrep covoolm jompt op Earth. Emu ba feepf. Genth va yindred boa feepf sim ullemana jop genth covoolm woldent ob Oceana, vushin chom kromp ba rosht." ("Din is waiting for me in our home away from home back on Earth. She is safe. Our two children are safe with relatives on our home world of Oceana, until this war is over.")

"I'm sorry, Etta," Starland added kindly, "but you won't be in this battle. For now, this fight will be between Galaxy class star ships and Scout Interceptors, but don't worry, my friend, you'll soon be back in the thick of it with Kalem."

Etta defensively remarked, "Admiral Starland, Q ulani ne chom comrondat. Tot sumbas ba et Kalem's risad." ("Admiral Starland, I belong in this battle. My place is by Kalem's side.")

"Look, Etta, you and I will be back together again soon on another adventure," encouraged Kalem as he placed a hand on Etta's shoulder. "I couldn't have done it without you. For my part, you can fly with me and go into battle anytime, anywhere, and in any situation."

Still frowning, Etta reluctantly lifted his head high and shrugged his shoulders with a sigh. He forced a smile at Kalem before he looked solemnly at Starland.

"Kem chet imsha, Admiral." ("As you wish, Admiral.")

Kalem extended his forearm and Etta sadly grasped it.

"I'll miss your company, my friend, until we are together again as warriors," continued Kalem with an appreciative nod.

Holding back tears, Etta forced a smile. Then he saluted Kalem and Starland, and they proudly saluted him back. Etta sniffled, wiped his nose, and walked forlorn back through the entryway without looking back.

"He really is courageous," stated Kalem with an admiring gaze in Etta's direction. "I've really grown fond of that little Dren."

"You can't gain a better or more trusted friend than a Dren, especially one who's life you saved," concurred Starland. Then with a glint in his eyes, he added mysteriously, "You two have a very interesting destiny together."

Kalem pondered the statement and inquired, "Would you mind elaborating on that, Admiral?"

"Get some rest, son. Soon, we go into battle," he replied skillfully. "Okay, I get the message," shot back Kalem. "As usual, you wouldn't tell me anything about my future anyway." He sighed and added, "Right now, I'm too tired to really care. Good night, Admiral."

Kalem saluted his father and spun around. He walked back at a quick pace through the entryway, and his father's smile vanished as he gazed, deeply concerned, in his son's direction.

Beloved Ancient One, he silently inquired*, **how much longer must***

we put up with Sen Dar's blind hatred? How many more must die at the hands of his deceptions? One son lost his life here in this reality due to Sen Dar's insane lust for power. Grant Kalem the insight, perception, and wisdom to walk a clear, safe path through the tests that must come to him along his road to self-mastery.

The next day Starland was reflecting upon his request of The Ancient One. He recalled that only the day before Kalem and Etta had returned from their successful mission to discover the base of the Glonden-Yalgull forces. More importantly, Kalem had brought back proof that Sen Dar was, in fact, their new leader.

Only twenty-four hours had gone by and the Admiral was once again standing in the center of one of the observation domes on his flagship. He had not looked forward to the day he would have to send his one remaining son into the final battle with the Glonden-Yalgull Alliance and Sen Dar.

He looked up through the observation dome to see that the Scout Interceptors he had ordered into the coming battle had now positioned themselves into two triangular formations. Thirty Scout Interceptors, divided equally into two formations, were keeping pace with the huge flagship as they flew in front of it a thousand yards beyond the closed transparent launch bay door.

That's Kalem's ship at the point of the lead squadron, thought Starland, as he took a deep breath and sighed. The pods on the bottom of the hulls of the Scout ships began to radiate an increasing intensity of the blue aura surrounding them and each ship flashed from violet through the spectrum to brilliant white in several seconds, and the ships darted on an arc of light into the depths of space.

Starland scanned the stars across the celestial heavens and sighed again. He turned around, walked over to the elevator, and stepped inside.

Poised like a statue with a solemn expression, he looked up through the elevator's clear structure and beyond the transparent observation dome into the depths of space, as the elevator silently lowered inside the ship. A red checkerboard energy field appeared over the round open hole in the floor and materialized into metal, seamlessly sealing itself to the rest of the floor as if no opening ever existed.

A radiant arc of light darted across the depths of another part of space and instantly slowed. It was Kalem's ship and fourteen others in triangular squadron formation. They came to a stop as another arc of light appeared from distant space and instantly slowed, and the second squadron paused in space nearby. The auras around the ships' hulls intensified and they sped into the distance toward a mass of light traces darting between numerous explosions near a red planet.

Captain Kalem was watching his view screen, observing a number of dogfights between Galactic Interceptors, Glonden triangular Scout fighters, and Yalgull Scout fighters. He touched his transceiver control.

"Sen Dar's insane murdering days are over and so is the Glonden-Yalgull Alliance," he remarked with bitter relief.

"That demon won't have a fleet left to hide behind this time," Moreau concurred through the transceiver.

"Moreau, old friend," replied Kalem, "let's end this stupid war." He grimaced as he touched the transceiver crystal again and commanded, "Listen up, all you anxious Scout fighter pilots. Break formation, pursue the enemy, and fire at will."

From distant space, the two Scout squadrons blurred into view and slowed high above the battle near the planet Sirus (6). They broke formation and headed in every direction in hot pursuit of many enemy ships that were darting by below them.

Sen Dar was aboard the Yalgull flagship inside his private control room, smiling wolfish arrogance. Ten years of war had gone by and he was now thirty as he walked behind the curved console. He passed a hand over a control and the conflict in space appeared on his small private view screen suspended from the ceiling in front of him at the end of two gold metal poles. Kalem's squadrons were turning the tide of battle.

"Galactic Alliance idiots," he screamed, frothing angry defiance. "It's too late. Your reinforcements cannot stop me."

He looked down toward his chest with a vengeful smile as he reached into his shirt and pulled out the Transport Matrix Crystal of The Ancient One.

With this, he angrily thought, *I will find the other two mystic crystals. Then, I will control your insignificant space fleet, and the entire galaxy. In the end, you will worship me.*

He reached down and touched the transceiver crystal on the control console that surrounded him.

"Ye-ye-yes, Supreme Lord?" stammered an officer's voice.

Sen Dar condescendingly smirked and replied, "Have Commander Hontull and Commander Baroon move the star ships forward to finish off what's left of their fighters."

He took his finger off the transceiver control and grinned, then started to softly laugh.

Commander Baroon, exhausted and disheveled, along with a half-dozen other haggard-looking junior officers were standing behind the main bridge control console of Sen Dar's Yalgull command ship, located on one end of a bridge control room. A dozen technicians were monitoring control panels that lined the eight walls of the room's entire circumference. They were watching the main octagon view screen suspended from the ceiling at the end of two gold metal poles. It displayed mile-long Galactic Alliance Emerald Galaxy ships converging from every direction of space toward their fleet near the planet Sirus (6). Two other Glonden and three Yalgull star ships were in the background by the planet.

"The fool!" growled Baroon. "I warned the Supreme Lord this would happen. Now we're trapped!"

A worried enemy officer entered the room, walked in a hurry over to the Commander, and whispered urgently into his ear.

"What?" shouted Baroon, astonished, "It would be suicide to advance on an entire Galactic Alliance fleet. The Supreme Lord must have lost his mind. Now he will need my help, if he is to escape this trap. Take over for me."

The officer nodded to Commander Baroon, who turned and quickly left the bridge.

Aboard the combined Glonden-Yalgull flagship, Grand Grontiff Gloeen and Emperor Garn were standing behind a pilot seated in one of the two chairs at the control console centered in the room. They were watching the view screen on the other side of the console.

Varying shapes and sizes of luminous controls lined the console in a similar arrangement to a Galactic Alliance console. The bridge control room was twenty-five feet across and twenty feet high, and the gently curved ceiling looked like blue glass through which the stars were visible. A clear space observation window took up the entire far third of the control room wall. Visible beyond it in space were the other Glonden and Yalgull fleet ships in close formation near the red planet behind them. Also visible through the window further away in space were the many Galactic Alliance star ships closing in toward them. They now surrounded the area, converging from every direction, entrapping the entire Glonden-Yalgull fleet from any possible escape.

Both Gloeen and Garn were worried as they continued to watch the display of the distant battle between the Galactic Scout Interceptors and a combination of both Glonden and Yalgull Scout class fighters. A series of explosions flashed across the screen as pursuing Galactic Alliance Interceptors destroyed, one by one, four of the Glonden and Yalgull fighters.

CHAPTER NINETEEN

Admiral Starland was standing in the control room aboard the flagship of the Galactic Inter-dimensional Alliance of Free Worlds. He was slowly looking around the room, inspecting the many technicians and bridge officers to see if they were ready for the main battle that was yet to commence.

A beam of radiant light was electrically alive in the center of the bridge control room. The light beam was surrounded by a transparent cylinder that extended twenty feet down from the center of a curved round window on the ceiling to a matching window embedded in the floor. Magnified stars were clearly visible through both lens windows.

Several technicians, who were looking over instruments, various readouts, and small view screens, were monitoring control panels surrounding the room. Their nimble fingers were efficiently operating the controls, which changed color intensity when touched.

Admiral Starland gazed at the petite Communications Officer seated a few feet away at the main control console.

"Lieutenant Marin," he calmly commanded, and she spun the swivel chair around to look up at him.

"Yes, Admiral?" she responded respectfully.

"Where are we now?"

"Only moments away from rendezvous with the rest of the fleet, sir," she answered.

"Put the battle on the main view screen," commanded Starland and he gave her an encouraging smile.

She nodded her head, spun back around, and touched several lit crystal controls. A rectangular view screen swung down from the ceiling on two curved blue metal arms. It stopped at eye level and lit up facing Admiral Starland as he walked up behind Lieutenant Marin.

Many Galactic Scout Interceptors and enemy Scout class fighters were trying to outmaneuver each other. The brilliant flashes of exploding fighters were occurring in many places all over the view screen. A Glonden fighter filled the screen as it flew by, closely pursued by a Scout Interceptor. The Galactic fighter fired a blue fireball at the enemy ship, and a moment later, it exploded into fiery energy particles. Concerned for the loss of life, Starland closed his eyes and contemplated the situation.

Beloved Ancient One, protect Kalem from harm during the battle, he thought within the sanctity of his inner world. *Your way is always for the greatest good to all life*, he continued.

Then his eyes popped open and he commanded, "Quickly, Marin, put me through to Captain Kalem."

As Marin reached to touch the transceiver crystal, the Admiral and the entire bridge receded into the background, as if something or someone was backing away from the scene.

General Harry Faldwell moved back out of the holographic light sphere projected from Master Ra Mu's crystal staff. There was a gentle sliding motion, a slight jerk, and then he was back in his physical body. He opened his eyes to discover he was sitting on the black sands of Lemuria. Master Ra Mu, Captain Kalem, and Carine were waiting patiently nearby. Harry gazed at the image of Admiral Starland and Lieutenant Marin within the holographic sphere. Then he looked at Master Ra Mu and yanked the unlit cigar from his mouth.

"Damned incredible," he remarked, astounded. "If you had ships like those 100,000 years ago, why aren't you running this planet by now? That question also brings up another point. If everything I just witnessed happened 100,000 years ago, how in the hell is it that none of you aged after that colossal amount of time? I don't get it."

Harry stuffed the cigar back in his mouth and cocked an eye toward Master Ra Mu, who was smiling back at him, but Carine answered him first. She stood up in one graceful movement to gaze at Harry with friendly enthusiasm.

"I would like to answer your first question if I may, General," she requested, widening her smile while she patiently awaited his answer.

Harry nodded his head agreeably.

Carine continued cheerfully, "Time works differently in the many parallel dimensions within the vast physical universes. The molecular time rate or vibration rate of the matter in one parallel dimension or plane moves at a different rate than that of another. There are energy doorway openings like transformers that naturally exist between parallel dimensions within the physical universe and the more mysterious higher dimensions beyond it. When we travel from one parallel to another through one of these doorways, our time rate accelerates or slows down depending upon which parallel dimension we enter. Kalem began to explain this to you when we traveled through the doorway at Mt Shasta. Do you remember?"

Harry nodded.

"Where you come from, several weeks will go by for every day where we are now," continued Carine. "Although you will only be here one day, many days will have passed when we return you to your own parallel dimension on this planet. In like manner, the Sen Darion War you were witnessing took place on the past time track of our parallel dimension, General. However, all that changed for us when it became necessary to transport 100,000 years into the future to your time and dimension, where Sen Dar's inexperienced use of The Ancient One's crystal transported him and his ship. Captain Kalem should answer your second question. Captain!"

As Kalem stood up, Harry decided that was the cue to stretch his legs. He took the cigar out of his mouth and slowly stood up.

Kalem began, "The Galactic Inter-dimensional Alliance of Free Worlds is committed to a non-interference core agreement to preserve the autonomy of the freedom-loving races on many worlds, within many parallel dimensions, to choose their own destiny. Because the various governments and peoples of your world are not yet living in harmony, and are not yet true space explorers, among other reasons, your world is under quarantine. We would not have made our presence known to you if it was not so critically necessary to your survival in the days to come. As you now know, there are beings like Sen Dar on other worlds in the universe that are firmly committed to domination and destruction. A number of galactic races are dedicated to this goal."

Kalem looked toward Master Ra Mu.

"General Faldwell, Sen Dar is now in your parallel dimension on Earth," said Ra Mu. "He poses the greatest threat to the planet's survival in the days to come. Would you like to experience more of the record log Kalem brought to us?"

Master Ra Mu sent Harry a broad warm smile, and Harry looked down at the black sand. He rubbed his chin thoughtfully and then looked back up.

"This whole thing is the most intriguing damnedest thing I have ever experienced," he finally replied with renewed enthusiasm. "By all means, please continue."

He sat back down on his parka, stuffed the cigar back into the corner of his mouth, and stared eagerly at the holographic light sphere. Kalem and Carine smiled at each other and sat back down on their parkas.

Harry heard the sound like the pop of a cork from a bottle and left his body again. He moved back toward the projection in his Atma form and passed through the outer light to discover he was actually observing the continuing battle of the Sen Darion War.

In distant space, explosions of Mazon fireballs were taking place everywhere. Blue fireballs hit two enemy Yalgull fighters, and both exploded into brilliant particles of light; two pursuing Galactic Scout Interceptors flew swiftly through the dissolving particles.

The next instant, Harry found himself in space high above the conflict. He had a clear overview of the ensuing fast-paced battle between Galactic Alliance Scout Interceptors and the Glonden and Yalgull fighters. Blue and red fireballs were exploding everywhere as dozens of fighters flew by each other.

The scene changed again and Harry found himself watching a Galactic Alliance Scout closely pursued by two V-shaped Glonden ships glowing red. Both ships fired on the lone Galactic Scout, and it exploded into vaporizing energy particles.

Harry next witnessed two enemy fighters, one Glonden and one Yalgull, fly in succession under his invisible viewpoint into distant space. They were making high-speed ninety-degree turns and zigzagging to avoid two Galactic Alliance Interceptors that appeared right behind them, matching their speed and movements. The enemy ships veered in opposite directions, just as the Galactic Scouts fired simultaneously. The blue fireballs hit both ships and exploded them into fiery atoms.

The scene changed, and Harry saw Captain Kalem aboard his ship, just as he touched the transceiver crystal flashing on his console.

"Captain, do you read me?" asked Starland's urgent voice.

At that moment, Admiral Starland was standing next to Lieutenant Marin, who was sitting behind the control console on the flagship. She looked up at him with a relieved grin.

"I have a link-up with him now. Go ahead, Admiral."

Leaning closer to the console, Starland commanded, "Withdraw your squadron, Captain. We are in position now to engage the magnetic blanket."

"Withdraw, from Sen Dar?" replied Kalem in disbelief. "I finally have the privilege of stopping him for good and you want me to withdraw?"

"Our part in this war is not about revenge, Captain," replied Starland's voice. "Our purpose here is to put an end to bloodshed. Withdraw now. That's an order."

"Yes, sir, we'll withdraw," he replied reluctantly and took his finger off the transceiver control. Then he mumbled angrily, "But I don't have to like it."

Meanwhile, in one of the enemy fighters a perplexed pilot was watching his view screen with dismay. He was observing all of the Galactic Alliance Scout Interceptor squadrons suddenly turn away from the battle and blur at high speed into the distance headed back toward their base command ships. He touched his blinking transceiver crystal.

"Captain Zaff, why are they leaving? They were winning," whispered the haggard voice of another pilot.

"You tell me, Drima," answered the perplexed Captain. "We were outnumbered. They could have easily beaten us. This is all wrong. They are planning something. It must be reported to the Supreme Lord at once." He touched the transceiver crystal again and commanded, "All pilots, immediately withdraw from the battle and return to your command ships."

Sen Dar was still in his private control room aboard Commander Baroon's Yalgull star ship safely hidden from the battle behind the red planet Sirus (6). He appeared to be asleep, sitting in the high-backed black chair with his head lying face down on his crossed arms resting on the curved control console. He was wearing his body suit and black cape. The thin gold band with his symbol etched on the front, which he usually wore upon his head, was lying under the fingertips of his left hand.

Commander Baroon hurried into the room through the entryway and stopped upon seeing Sen Dar behind the control console. He rushed over to Sen Dar and gently placed a hand on his shoulder. Sen Dar jumped to his feet with frightening speed, throwing Baroon's hand aside. He was glassy-eyed, making him appear to be in a psychotic trance.

"You," he began viciously, pointing at Baroon with a shaking hand, "you traitor! I ordered you to destroy those Galactic Scouts with the fleet ships."

Sen Dar pulled a laser gun from the holster at his side and leveled it at Commander Baroon.

"Supreme Lord, what are you doing?" cried out Baroon in shock. "Galactic Alliance star ships surround the entire quadrant. I came to help you escape."

Sen Dar's face was blank and pallid. Beyond anger, he had forgotten the powerful crystal he wore as he gazed with great malice at Baroon.

"You disobeyed my direct order and the sentence for that is death."

Sen Dar leveled the laser at Baroon whose mouth dropped open with complete disbelief. Then, in a flash, Baroon understood everything and sighed.

"Now, finally, it's clear who the real enemy has been all along," he remarked and said bitterly, "You're insane!"

"Insane, am I?" Sen Dar spouted with his leering smile widening.

He began to pull the trigger as Baroon reached for his gun with one hand and instinctively raised his other hand to block the shot.

"Wait, my Lord," he pleaded frantically, wide-eyed. "Please, let me explain... ah-h-h-h!"

The laser blast burned a hole through Baroon's abdomen, and he fell to the floor face down. Sen Dar's hand was still holding the laser gun at arm's length as his stunned, glassy-eyed look cleared, and the gun slowly dropped from his hand. He walked over to Baroon, knelt down, and turned his body face up. Sen Dar's character began to transform as he gazed down at Baroon.

"Oh Baroon, you should have listened to me," he now murmured with genuine remorse before reverting again into maddened rage, and he yelled out, "Get up! Get back on your feet. I gave you an order, Commander." Then he screamed louder, "Get up!"

Commander Baroon did not move, and as Sen Dar's crazed thinking cleared again, he glanced around the environment. As he became cognizant of his precarious situation, his expression turned to apprehension.

"They will be coming for me next," he said aloud nervously.

His eyes widened and his face transformed, filling with twisted compassion as he gazed down at Baroon's body.

"I have to leave you now, Baroon, but I give you, my blessing."

Sen Dar bent low over Baroon's body, kissed his forehead, and grabbed the laser gun from the floor as he stood up. Then he jumped over the body and ran out of the room.

Captain Kalem walked into the flagship's bridge control room very upset and approached the Admiral, who was patiently watching the view screen. Three enemy star ships appeared, one Glonden and two Yalgull, moving from behind Sirus (6) in an attempt to join forces with more enemy ships visible in the foreground space near the red planet.

"Admiral, why did you order my withdrawal?" he demanded, still fuming.

Starland turned to him and replied calmly, "As I said before, Captain, we want to save lives."

"But they are murdering animals," shot back Kalem.

"They are not the enemy, Captain," the Admiral reminded him, ignoring his outburst. "Sen Dar planned his deceit well. If you recall, they still believe we butchered their families."

"What about Sen Dar?" asked Kalem.

"Sir," interrupted Lieutenant Marin, gazing up at the Admiral, "Commander Zarel is on sub-channel three."

"Put it on the main view screen, Lieutenant," he ordered, turning away from his son.

Commander Zarel appeared on the view screen standing on the bridge area of another fleet star ship. Two gold bands surrounded his sleeve cuffs.

"The fleet is in position, Admiral," reported Zarel. "The enemy ships are surrounded."

Starland sighed.

"My friend, inform the other Commanders in the fleet to engage the magnetic blanket on my signal."

Zarel nodded his head and Starland's view screen changed to a large overview of space near Sirus (6). Four enemy star ships, two Glonden and two Yalgull, were moving away from the planet toward the approaching Galactic Alliance fleet. Three more enemy star ships had moved from behind the planet to trail behind them. In the background, nineteen additional Galactic Alliance Emerald Star Galaxy class ships were closing in from every direction, encircling the entire area of space near the red planet.

At that same moment, Sen Dar was running away from the doorway entrance of his private control room across the launch bay floor, headed for five Yalgull Scout class fighters parked in a row thirty feet away. Several of Commander Baroon's loyal men were standing beside the ladder leading inside the closest ship. It was customized with sharper high points around the waving curves of the hull's leading edge than the other ships, giving it a sleeker and fiercer Stingray shark wing-like appearance.

From Harry Faldwell's out-of-body viewpoint, the ship looked identical to the one that fired on his 747-jet airliner and Kalem's Scout Interceptor above Earth's Bermuda Triangle.

I wonder, he thought, intrigued, ***could that actually be the same ship?***

Then Harry returned his full attention to the events unfolding before his inner vision, and he witnessed Sen Dar running toward the men huddled around the closest ship. One of them noticed he was not with their valiant Commander Baroon, and his intuition told him to draw his laser gun to fire, but Sen Dar was on top of the situation and fired at them first, killing all three men. He jumped over their bodies and ran underneath the ship, then climbed up the ladder, and boarded it. The ladder withdrew and the hatch swung closed.

Sen Dar turned on the view screen and one of Baroon's squadron pilots aboard one of the other four Yalgull Scout fighters appeared.

"Who's in there?" he demanded. "Where is Commander Baroon?"

"This is your Supreme Lord and Sovereign," shot back Sen Dar, but then he added tactfully, "I have suspected Commander Baroon and some of his rebel crew of treachery for some time. They attempted to kill me and they are now as they should be, dead!"

"Baroon wouldn't…" the disbelieving Yalgull pilot began to say, but Sen Dar cut him off.

"He disobeyed a direct order and that has cost us everything. We must leave this planet at once, and you must provide fighter escort protection. Is that crystal clear?"

"Yes, Supreme Lord, very clear," answered the Yalgull pilot, snapping to attention; then he appeared concerned and humbly asked, "But, Sire, what about Gloeen and Garn?"

"They too have disappointed me," Sen Dar snarled. "They are safe on Gloeen's command ship for now but they will soon be killed or captured. You and your men will escort my ship as close fighter support. Is that understood?"

"Yes, Supreme Lord, it shall be as you command," snapped back the Yalgull pilot nervously.

Sen Dar touched a crystal on the control board and the screen went blank.

Baroon's three crewmen, lying dead like discarded garbage around Sen Dar's customized Yalgull ship, bore silent witness to their murder as the ship lit up with a red glow and lifted above the landing platform. The four support ships also lit up as their Supreme Lord Sen Dar's ship rose. Then it darted out through the just opened launch bay door. The support ships flew in quick succession after it.

Back on the Galactic Alliance flagship, Captain Kalem was standing next to Admiral Starland as Lieutenant Marin touched several crystal controls.

"There will be no escape for Sen Dar this time," Starland remarked confidently.

Skeptical, Kalem gazed at the view screen and noticed five Scout class fighters hovering above the launch bay of the Yalgull star ship closest to Sirus (6). He noticed one looked quite different from the others.

"Wait a minute, Admiral," he proclaimed. "Sen Dar may not be aboard any of the enemy star ships. Look!" He pointed at the view screen.

Admiral Starland looked at the view screen in time to observe the five enemy fighters hovering above the enemy flagship's launch bay as they changed to white light and blurred at trans-light speed beyond the planet into deep space.

"Sen Dar has to be with them and now he is escaping our net," Kalem proclaimed fiercely.

"You may be right, Captain," concurred Starland, "but I want an entire fighter support squadron with you. Nothing would please Sen Dar more than having the son of the Admiral in command of the entire Galactic Alliance fleet at his mercy."

"And nothing would please me more than finding my hands squeezing his evil neck," remarked Kalem, fuming, with his hands in the air pretending to choke Sen Dar.

"Get rid of vengeance right now, Captain. Sen Dar would use your unreasoning passion to his own advantage. No one who adheres to the teaching of The Ancient One would ever indulge in such destructive emotions."

"The Ancient One?" shot back Kalem, frowning. "Why would this Ancient One let so many good people die at the hands of a murdering madman? Where is this luminous spherical being from some higher dimension? I've never seen it."

"My son, The Ancient One is quite real and quite beyond an individual being as you think of it," continued Starland patiently, "and one day you will come to know this for yourself."

"Fine, but first let me destroy Sen Dar for good, and then I can find out all about The Ancient One. How about that?" snapped Kalem.

Starland waited patiently for his son to come to his senses.

"Alright, I was just kidding," Kalem finally relented. "But I don't believe there is any way Sen Dar will surrender, and I will be forced to give him an offer he can't refuse."

Starland appeared concerned at Kalem's remark but said no more as he watched his son walk out of the control room. Then he turned back to study the view screen.

A short time later, four Galactic Scout Interceptors were hovering several hundred feet above the launch bay door at one end of Starland's flagship. A fifth Scout Interceptor hovered into view above the launch bay door and joined them to complete a V-shaped formation. The pulsing light around their hulls flashed brilliant white, and the ships instantly blurred at trans-light speed in pursuit of Sen Dar's escaping squadron.

While Lieutenant Marin monitored the bridge control console, she noticed several crystal controls light up, blinking. She turned around and called Admiral Starland, who was standing next to a junior bridge officer behind her.

"Admiral, the fleet is under attack!"

Concern spread across Starland's face. "Quickly, Lieutenant, change to a wide overview of the battle."

The view screen changed with a flicker, revealing Sirus (6) in the right-hand corner. In the foreground, the large enemy star ships with

Sen Dar's insignia on their sides were moving rapidly forward, firing on several approaching Galactic Alliance Emerald Star ships. In the background, many other Emerald Star fleet ships were converging on Sirus (6) from every direction. Admiral Starland looked at Marin.

"Put me through to Commander Zarel."

Commander Zarel appeared on the large view screen standing by the control console on the bridge of his ship.

"Admiral, it looks like those fools intend to ram us," he reported.

In space, Commander Zarel's ship was moving toward a large Glonden star ship. The enemy ship was racing at high speed away from the planet toward Zarel's vessel, firing from dozens of Mazon cannon positions. Zarel's ship returned fire, and the ensuing exchange of firepower badly damaged the bridge control areas of both ships. They continued toward each other, seemingly out of control.

Commander Zarel's control room had sustained much damage. He had a cut on his forehead, and technicians were trying to put out fires in various places around the room. Zarel touched a crystal control and the main view screen revealed Admiral Starland.

"Admiral, the bridge is badly damaged," Zarel reported wearily. "Our guidance controls are inoperative and we're unable to maneuver. We think the bridge of the enemy ship was completely destroyed and it's headed for us out of control."

"Teleport yourself and your people over to us now," Starland commanded.

Zarel grabbed his head with both hands, struggling to maintain consciousness, as an aide walked up and supported him.

"We're on our way, Admiral," he replied groggily.

A few minutes later, the two huge ships collided bow first, creating a powerful explosion, and both ships disintegrated into particles of light that slowly vanished.

The main bridge view screen aboard Starland's flagship revealed eighteen other Galaxy star ships had now completely encircled the nearby space around the remaining seven combined Yalgull and Glonden command ships. Dozens of smaller enemy Destroyer class ships and many more support fighters, the very same ships Kalem and Etta saw hidden in their mountain base, flew up out of the thick red cloud cover of Sirus (6). They sped past their larger base ships and began firing in every direction at the closing Galactic Alliance armada.

Starland shook his head sadly, as he touched the transceiver control on the console next to Lieutenant Marin and commanded, "This is

Admiral Starland. Engage the magnetic blanket. I repeat, engage the magnetic blanket now."

The Admiral nodded at the ship's navigator, who then touched a four-inch-wide violet crystal. It began to pulse with violet light, emitting a deep humming sound, and everyone on the bridge turned toward Starland to listen.

In space, beams of violet light instantly projected from the front end of each of the Galactic Alliance star ships converged at the central point in space between the enemy ships, and then formed a transparent sphere of light. The beams began to pull the sphere of light back toward the Galactic ships, expanding and enlarging it, until it completely encased all the enemy ships.

Admiral Starland looked at the control console, then at Lieutenant Marin and asked, "Did we get them aboard our ship in time before the explosion?"

Lieutenant Marin touched a crystal and smiled.

"Yes, Admiral, we did," she answered relieved. "The teleport room confirmed Commander Zarel and most of his crew are aboard."

Aboard another Glonden star ship, a rugged-looking enemy Commander in his forties with a scarred chin was looking at his view screen. He could see through the violet sphere of light that was now between his ship and the Galactic Alliance fleet. The lights on the bridge suddenly dimmed as a loud winding-down sound pulsed throughout the bridge control room.

"What devilry is this? Where is our power?" he shouted. "What happened to our power?"

The enemy Commander noticed a crystal flashing on his console and touched it. Admiral Starland appeared on his view screen.

"Listen to me, Commander. I am Admiral Starland of the Galactic Inter-dimensional Alliance of Free Worlds. This war is over. Cease all hostilities. You and your men will not be harmed."

"I am Commander Dal, but do not expect me to swallow your pretty speech. You won't take any of us alive," he replied, suffering from too many years of Sen Dar's hypnotic brainwashing.

"You have been part of one of the greatest deceptions ever cast before men," Starland stated firmly. Then he paused and continued calmly, "Listen to me, Commander Dal. Your Supreme Lord's real name is Sen Dar and he lied to you all to gain your support. Your families are not dead."

Commander Dal froze at the remark but then again became distrustful.

"You lie!" he cried out, lost in the deep sadness of painful memory. "You butchered all of them."

"No, Commander, we did not. Our Galactic Alliance reconnaissance ships found them on the planet where Sen Dar had them imprisoned. They arrived there right after Sen Dar left, and we managed to teleport them aboard our vessels before his timed device destroyed the planet's surface." Starland paused to let the news sink in, and then kindly continued, "I know who your wife is, Commander Dal, because she has personally told me about you. She is safely aboard this ship. Would you like to speak with her?"

Commander Dal was momentarily stunned into silence by the news, and then he hesitantly asked, "Mira... is alive?"

"Yes, Commander," replied Starland, and he smiled. "You can speak with her yourself."

Lieutenant Marin escorted Mira, a pretty but haggard woman in her late twenties, into view. She looked forlorn at her husband on Starland's view screen.

Tears ran down her pale cheeks as she cried out, "I'm alive! It was Sen Dar. He tried to kill us all. Please, stop fighting!"

Commander Dal was stricken by the news and near complete exhaustion. He shamefully dropped his head to his chest, and all the personnel behind him sadly lowered their heads, as he looked back up with tears welling in his eyes.

"Oh God," he cried out, dismayed, shaking his head. "What have we done?"

Bewildered, he slowly backed up against the control console to steady himself, and then looked back up at Starland.

"We will cease all hostilities," he said in deeper agony than could ever be expressed, and his head lowered again. Forcing himself to look back up at Starland again, he asked, "How could this have happened? How?"

"Don't be hard on yourself, Commander," Starland answered compassionately. "Sen Dar's deception left all of you with no other choice."

Mira was sobbing with her head in her hands as Lieutenant Marin led her away.

Admiral Starland continued with a kind smile, "It's all over now, Commander Dal, but there is a bright side to it. You will soon be reunited with your wife."

Meanwhile, Commander Baroon was back in the bridge control room of what was Sen Dar's royal flagship for the Glonden-Yalgull

Alliance. A bandage was around his mid-section, and two medical staff personnel were assisting him to walk the few feet up to the main control console. Grimacing with pain, Baroon touched a control and looked up to see Admiral Starland's image flash onto the main view screen.

"The evil one fooled us all with that crystal he wears," proclaimed Commander Baroon, wincing with pain and gasping for breath. "He even tried to kill me to cover his escape. You must stop him. You must…" but he passed out before finishing the sentence, and the two medical staff personnel supported him under his arms.

"Will he be all right?" asked Starland, genuinely concerned.

"We think so, sir," answered one of the medical staff as he looked up at Starland on the view screen.

Commander Zarel was wearing a bandage around his forehead and shaking his head as he walked up to the Admiral's side.

"I'm so glad to see you made it through all right, my friend," remarked Starland, relieved.

"So many have died for nothing, just nothing," Zarel replied sadly.

"I know it appears that way," said Starland, placing a consoling hand on Zarel's shoulder, "but you know as well as I do there was a reason." Then he added with an encouraging smile, "Cheer up. Many more could have died."

Zarel sighed and thought about it for a moment before he cracked a smile and nodded his agreement.

Starland looked over to Lieutenant Marin and commanded, "Contact the Glonden-Yalgull flagship. The leaders of the Glonden and the Yalgull should be aboard."

Lieutenant Marin touched a crystal control and both Gloeen and Garn appeared on the main view screen.

"I am Admiral Starland of the Galactic Inter-dimensional Alliance of Free Worlds," he stated respectfully and then announced, "By now the other Commanders of your fleet have contacted you so you both know you will not be harmed."

Fearful, Gloeen and Garn hesitantly bowed their heads.

"I am Emperor Garn of the Yalgull," responded Garn.

"And I am Supreme Grontiff Gloeen of the Glonden," said Gloeen.

"Why didn't you destroy our ships?" inquired Garn. "We were the aggressors here."

"Yes, why?" inquired Gloeen. "We wouldn't have done the same for you if our fortunes were reversed."

"I think you both know the answer to that and it can be stated with by one name," commented Starland.

Both Gloeen and Garn glanced, surprised, at each other, then back at Starland and answered in angry unison, "Sen Dar!"

"I see you both now know his real name," continued Starland. "He left each of you with no choice in the matter of choosing to attack us."

"Yes," confirmed Gloeen, scowling, "we have both remembered much since the coward left us. It was that crystal he was wearing. Whenever it glowed, we found ourselves agreeing with whatever he said. It all seemed so natural."

"He will regret the day he found the Yalgull home world, if I get my hands on him," Garn angrily spouted.

Starland sighed, shaking his head, and he was about to respond to Garn's angry remark, but gave him a friendly grin instead.

"Leave Sen Dar to us now. You would likely not fare any better if you crossed his path again." He paused, and then said, "If you both sign a treaty with the Galactic Inter-dimensional Alliance of Free Worlds agreeing to never again attack us and to respect our space, we will let you return to your own realms. Do you agree to this?"

Greatly surprised, Gloeen and Garn gazed at each other and solemnly nodded their heads in agreement with each other for the first time.

"Very well," remarked Starland. "Since you two have cooperated together for the first time by attacking us, perhaps now you will also discover that a new day has dawned between your two world systems. From now on, you can choose to continue this new alliance in a peaceful productive manner." He paused and added, "I'll personally come aboard your ship with several of our diplomats to present and get the treaty signed. Once that is done, you may take your ships and crews back to your own worlds and we will consider this matter closed."

They were mystified by it all but also greatly relieved, and they could only humbly bow their heads in thanks. Starland touched a crystal by Lieutenant Marin and the main view screen shut off.

He looked at Commander Zarel and said under his breath, "Before we set them free to return to their home worlds, I wish to personally deprogram both of them from any residual effect that may be lingering from Sen Dar's misuse of The Ancient One's stolen crystal. We must be certain they do not fall prey to the lunatic Sen Dar or anyone like him ever again. Even though the control he had over them is now gone, they are probably already beginning to distrust each other for having actually cooperated for the first time aboard the same star ship."

"I have to agree, you're probably right," replied Zarel raising his eyebrows, and he sighed.

Turning to Lieutenant Marin, Starland commanded, "Tell all the other fleet Commanders to inform the Glonden and the Yalgull men that their families are still alive. They can start deprogramming procedures on all of them. After all, nothing snaps a man out of a trance after ten years of war better than seeing loved ones alive they thought were dead."

"Nothing would please me more, Admiral," she replied happily.

At that moment, Kalem's squadron was in deep space in hot pursuit of Sen Dar's squadron. Kalem could see on his view screen that he was closing in on Sen Dar's ships, just as they disappeared from view in another trans-light jump.

"Oh no, you devil, you're not getting away from me this time," Kalem said to himself, and he touched the transceiver control. "Listen up, all of you. We will get only one shot at this so make it count. Okay, let's go get Sen Dar."

"We're all with you, Captain," concurred Lieutenant Moreau's voice through the transceiver as Kalem pressed his palms down hard into the crystal guidance controls.

His ship flashed white light and blurred at an increased trans-light-speed jump into the depths of space, and the four support ships disappeared in a blur of light after him.

Kalem was right on the tail of Sen Dar's ship and support squadron as the four enemy escort ships veered in pairs away from each other in opposite directions. They curved back out of view to circle around and come up behind Kalem's ship.

It's too late for that, Sen Dar, thought Kalem more determined than ever. *I'll send your atoms back to the hellish place you came from before your slaves can circle behind me.*

An emergency distress signal interrupted him as he reached to touch the control to fire at Sen Dar's ship, and he touched the blinking blue crystal instead. Lieutenant Moreau flashed onto his screen, sweat beading on his forehead, just as his ship shook badly from a nearby explosion.

"I'm in trouble, Captain," he said tensely. "They doubled back on us. Two of them are behind me. I can't shake them off."

Kalem changed the view screen back to see a brief glimpse of Sen Dar's ship flash brilliant white light and blur into space. Kalem slammed his fist down on the control console in frustration and quickly changed the view screen again to see Moreau grab the console to steady himself from the shaking caused by another near hit of enemy fire.

"Hold on, Moreau, I'm turning toward you now."

The two enemy ships were pursuing Moreau's Interceptor and they both opened fire, but Moreau outmaneuvered each red fireball that shot past the hull of his ship before exploding.

Kalem's Scout appeared behind the enemy ships a moment later and fired once, then again. In succession, both blue fireballs hit the enemy ships and obliterated them into dissipating light particles.

Kalem's three other squadron fighters were maneuvering in a separate dogfight with Sen Dar's two remaining escort ships. The three Galactic Interceptors fired simultaneously, and two of the blue Mazon fireballs hit one of the enemy ships, completely disintegrating it. The remaining enemy ship veered away to avoid the other fireball, but it was too late and it too exploded into a fiery plume of molecular light that quickly dissipated.

"You cut things close," breathed Moreau, relieved, as he appeared again on Kalem's view screen.

"Well, after all it was a tossup between saving you or finally destroying that monster," Kalem remarked playfully.

"Oh great, glad to know I outrank that maniac in importance," replied Moreau and he added, frowning, "Comparing me to him makes me worth less than nothing."

"Look, Moreau, this is serious," shot back Kalem, still fuming. "That lunatic disappeared off my instruments in another trans-light jump right before I came to your rescue."

"They must be tracking him back on the Command ship," replied Moreau, equally concerned.

"Hmm, I hope you're right," replied Kalem, somewhat skeptical. "My instruments show the remaining enemy ships have been destroyed. It's time for the squadron to return to the flagship." He grimaced and said, mostly to himself, "Damn it, Moreau, I want him, and one way or another I will get him!"

FROM ASHES TO FIRE
ON MALDEC

$\mathcal{A}$ beam of light darted toward the planet Uranus in our solar system. As it slowed, it revealed the form of Sen Dar's ship. It continued past the planet and then disappeared into the depths of space in a trans-light-speed jump.

The ice rings of Saturn were glimmering in various subdued colors from reflected sunlight, while its twenty-one moons continued their separate journeys around their parent planet. The light beam slowed again, revealing Sen Dar's ship as it passed by the planet, and then it darted away again in another trans-light-jump.

Sen Dar's ship was soon speeding into view from deep space. It stopped to hover for a moment near the gas giant Jupiter before it darted back into space.

A beautiful blue-green jewel of a planet was silently revolving on its axis on its journey around our ancient sun. It was very similar to Earth but it had no moons and a slightly thicker, light-blue cloud cover faintly laced with pink. Sen Dar's ship approached and assumed an orbit around the planet.

Far away in the galaxy, Starland's flagship and eighteen additional cruisers still surrounded the Glonden-Yalgull fleet near the planet Sirus (6). The transparent sphere of violet light that had created the energy-dampening blanket around them was gone.

Kalem's ship and four other Scout Interceptors sped into view from beyond Sirus (6) and headed toward Starland's flagship. They stopped to hover above the open launch bay closest to them and descended inside one by one.

Starland was standing in the bridge control room, slightly bent over, talking to Lieutenant Marin as Captain Kalem and Lieutenant Moreau walked into the room.

"Admiral, Sen Dar escaped," said Kalem, disappointed.

Despite this fact, Admiral Starland was smiling as he looked at his son and grabbed him by the shoulders with both hands.

"I thank The Ancient One for your safe return as well as Lieutenant Moreau," he said and nodded at Moreau.

Lieutenant Moreau nodded back, appreciative for the Admiral's show of concern.

"Look, we're fine, Admiral," remarked Kalem and he asked, "but didn't you hear what I said? That monster, Sen Dar, escaped."

"Not for long," remarked Starland as he nodded a command to Lieutenant Marin.

Her nimble fingers touched several crystal controls and the main view screen displayed the galaxy in a three-dimensional image. An arrow led from the labeled Planet Sirus (6) down to a small-circled area between the center and the outer edge of one of the seven spiral arms of the galaxy. Lieutenant Marin pointed to the projection.

"The final battle occurred here at Sirus (6)," she said as she touched another control.

The ship's computer drew a small circle around a star near the outer edge of the same spiral arm of the galaxy, two-thirds of the way toward its end. Above the galaxy, an arrow from the word "Maldec," labeled in clear luminous gold letters, led down to the circle. Marin touched several more crystal controls and the scene changed to an overview of Earth's ancient solar system. A trajectory line that began from somewhere beyond the solar system appeared, continued past the outer planet of Pluto and a succession of inner planets, and met a dot above the fifth planet. This planet was in orbit around the sun between Mars and Jupiter.

Marin continued, "Sen Dar's ship has assumed an orbit above the fifth planet in this solar system called Maldec by its inhabitants. He may be preparing to enter the planet's atmosphere."

"Admiral, I must go after him again," Kalem insisted.

"There will be time enough to go after Sen Dar once we arrive in orbit around Maldec," replied Starland as he placed a consoling hand on his son's shoulder. Then he added, "He may be jumping from the ashes into the fire on that planet."

"What do you mean?" asked Kalem, puzzled.

"Our diplomats have been trying for months to bring Maldec's three leaders to a peace conference," answered Starland. On a more serious note, he said, "The Maldecian people are on the brink of war amongst themselves. They tend to kill first and ask questions later. As an alien stranger, Sen Dar's arrival there will not be greeted with pleasure."

"Oh great, now he'll go to work on them," remarked Lieutenant Moreau, cringing at the thought.

Admiral Starland closed his eyes and lowered his head for a moment and projected, *Great Ancient One, how many more innocent beings must be polluted by Sen Dar's treacherous words? How much longer must we put up with his twisted misuse of freewill, and how many more must yet die before he is finally stopped for good?*

At that moment, Sen Dar was sitting down behind his control console, scanning the view screen that revealed the light blue and pink clouds, blue oceans, and continental landmasses of Maldec. His gaze locked onto a location on one of the three continents centered over the planet's equator.

He looked down at the old parchment map spread-open on top of the console and scrutinized it. A design on the right half of the parchment clearly depicted the solar system containing the planet Earth. However, unlike Earth today, only two continental land formations and much smaller polar icecaps appeared on its surface. Clear labels above all the planets revealed their names, and an arrow pointed to an additional fifth planet orbiting the sun between Mars and Jupiter.

On the left side of the parchment was an enlarged image of this fifth planet, and he could see the entire surface of the world at one time. Engraved in gold foil across the top of the planet was the word "Maldec." Oceans separated the three continents centered over the planet's equator. An emblem of Master Ra Mu's staff was marked in the middle of the continent positioned between the two other similarly sized continents. The map indicated that the continent under Ra Mu's symbol stretched five hundred miles to the north and five hundred miles to the south of the equator. Longitude and latitude coordinates etched across the map's surface intersected at Ra Mu's symbol. Labeled beside it were the words "Invisible Cavern of The Ancient One," and other arcane writing covered the rest of the map.

Sen Dar put his forefinger on Master Ra Mu's staff symbol located on the central continent, and then looked over at a small display screen to the left of his control console that laid out the coordinates. They crisscrossed over the same location that was clearly marked on

The Ancient One's map by the staff emblem, and Sen Dar smiled with discovery.

Ah-h, that's it, he thought, sneering. *The other half of the map is there. The fools can't stop me!*

Sen Dar's ship stopped directly above the central continent and tilted toward the planet. The red antigravity light surrounding the hull flashed and the ship flew in a long graceful arc down into the atmosphere, disappearing in the clouds.

Several hours had passed since the signing of the treaty between Admiral Starland and the Glonden and Yalgull leaders. Eighteen Galactic Alliance cruisers, aligned in parallel formation, were heading into space away from the planet Sirus (6). The remaining ships of the combined Yalgull and Glonden fleet were heading in the opposite direction toward their respective home worlds. Admiral Starland's flagship took a course in a third direction toward the solar system containing the planets Maldec and ancient Earth.

Admiral Starland was in his quarters seated on a large cushion in the middle of the floor with his legs crossed and his eyes closed. A faint light was whirling around his forehead, and his Atma, surrounded by a faint golden aura exited the top of his head. The sphere moved in front of his physical body and transformed into the luminous astral physical appearance of Starland comprised of thousands of tiny specks of cobalt blue light. He was smiling radiantly.

Welcome, my friend, said Starland telepathically.

Master Ra Mu's luminous Atma-sphere moved right through the metal hull of Starland's sleeping quarters. It swiftly approached Starland's astral-self, stopped in front of him, and formed into Master Ra Mu's likeness in a similar radiant body. Ra Mu was smiling brightly as they clasped forearms.

Hello, Master Starland, telepathically answered Master Ra Mu with warmth and vigor, and then they continued their conversation using the mouths of their luminous astral bodies.

"Unfortunately, we don't have much time," said Master Ra Mu. "The negative Spirit current has come to Maldec through this one called Sen Dar. You must arrange the peace conference among Maldec's three leaders as soon as possible. Maldec's people are walking the razor's edge toward destruction."

Admiral Starland nodded.

"Our diplomats have obtained the agreement for a conference from Yulan and Trebor, two of Maldec's leaders," continued Starland, concerned. "However, Gorn, the third most militaristic leader remains stubbornly.

They are waiting for my arrival to resume negotiations."

Captain Kalem's voice calling through the intercom speaker by the door to Starland's quarter interrupted them.

"Admiral, may I enter?" he asked in an urgent tone.

A moment passed while Ra Mu and Starland gazed at each other.

"Admiral, it's important. May I enter?" asked Kalem's voice again.

Admiral Starland gazed at Master Ra Mu with a bright smile of light and continued, *Until we meet again in our physical bodies, farewell.*

Master Ra Mu smiled back, and they nodded respectfully to each other and then continued to gaze silently with the warmth of a deep trust that only ancient memories of a long friendship could command. A moment passed and Ra Mu turned around. He transformed back into his Atma sphere and passed back out through the metal hull of the ship.

Admiral Starland's astral form transformed back into his Atma sphere and descended back into his physical body through the top of the head. He stood up from the cushion in one graceful move, walked over to the door, and passed his hand in front of the speaker control. The door opened silently, sliding inside the wall, and a concerned Captain Kalem was standing in the doorway.

"Admiral, the flagship is now in orbit around Maldec," he said as he stepped inside the room. "Sen Dar's ship is about to land on the far side of the planet in the jungle area near Gorn's palace."

"He's after the other half of The Ancient One's parchment," said Starland and he ordered urgently, "Contact our diplomats on Maldec and let them know we're on our way. We must get to that peace conference as quickly as possible."

Kalem nodded and walked swiftly back out the door, followed by the Admiral.

Sen Dar's ship flew down toward a steaming alien jungle and hovered above large trees similar to those found on the equatorial regions of Earth. Then it slowly lowered and landed in a clearing surrounded by the tall trees entwined with thick, dark-green vines. An opening appeared in the ship's side, an oval hatch opened, and a ramp slid to the ground.

Sen Dar peered cautiously out of the opening and looked around the alien countryside, noticing in particular that thick jungle foliage surrounded the ship and a strange octagon sided blue palace with tall spires was perched on a hill several miles away. A winding path headed from the palace downhill into the jungle and across the clearing by his ship, before it continued into the further depths of the tropical jungle trees.

Sen Dar jumped off the ramp and placed the palm of his hand on the ship's hull. The ramp slid back inside the ship, the oval door closed, and then the hull began to pulse with a red glow, emitting a low-pitched hum. An invisible energy field emanating from the hull drew in branches and vines from the surrounding jungle through the air and in a few moments, they camouflaged the ship from view.

Sen Dar briefly inspected the hidden ship and appeared satisfied. Then he jogged along the path, headed away from the direction of the hilltop palace, and quickly disappeared in the thick jungle trees.

A few minutes later, he emerged from the jungle overgrowth at a swift walking pace and stopped in the center of another small clearing to gaze at a sheer rock wall on the far side. Then his eyes widened with intense delight, and he took out the map half from inside his shirt, briefly looked at it, and then lifted the Transport Matrix Crystal off his neck. He grabbed it in his right hand and closed his eyes, and the crystal began to glow, shining light through his clenched fingers. He stepped toward the cliff wall and felt for a hole in the middle of it with the fingers of his left hand. Finding it, he pulled his hand away and slid the glowing crystal into the hole. It fit perfectly and changed to a glowing golden light.

Sen Dar took one step back as a deep rumbling began. A large section of the wall turned to glittering golden light and disappeared, leaving an open cave entrance with a carved rock stairway leading upward. He hung the crystal back around his neck, looked cautiously around, and then raced inside the cave and up the stairs.

The sunlight streaming into the cave opening provided a dim light up the twenty-feet of rock stairs that led into a fifty-feet-wide, rough-hewed round cavern with a curved domed ceiling. The rock walls were glowing with a bright-green phosphorescent mineral. Sen Dar jogged up the last steps leading into the large cavern and noticed a flat rock disc two inches thick and three-feet-wide in the center of the smooth cavern floor. He stepped upon it, took out the map, read some esoteric writing on the back, and then placed it flat on the upturned palm of his left hand. Then he grabbed The Ancient One's crystal in his right hand, closed his eyes, and slowly chanted, "Atma... Atma... Atma."

The crystal glowed through his clenched fingers and the mysterious whirl of a gentle wind began to blow around him. The walls of the cavern glowed with pulsing gold light and hundreds of small pieces of map flew out of many crevices in the rock wall and ceiling. The map pieces whirled around Sen Dar in a tightening spiral, mending back together. The completed map half landed in Sen Dar's hand next to the map half he possessed, and the two halves miraculously joined back together.

Then the pulsing golden light faded away, leaving behind the glow from the rock walls, and the whirling wind subsided to perfect stillness.

Sen Dar opened his eyes and looked at the map with intense interest. A line appeared and drew itself from the planet Maldec on the left side of the old map halfway across the new map half to a large blowup of the planet labeled, "Earth."

Longitude and latitude coordinates crisscrossed the map, but the continents of Earth appeared much different than they do today. A huge continent centered over Earth's equatorial region was labeled, "Lemuria – The Motherland of Man." An image of Master Ra Mu's staff was marked on a coastal city of this continent. A gold inscription beside it read:

MU – The Capital City of Lemuria
Master Ra Mu
Guardian of the Master Crystal Staff

Separated by a vast ocean halfway around the Earth was another large continent two-thirds Lemuria's size that was also centered over the equator. The gold letters next to it read:

Atlantis – Colony of Lemuria

On the floor of the ocean between the two continents was the symbol of a domed city and this inscription:

Secret Undersea Domed City of Oceana
Master Opellum
Guardian of the Emerald Doorway Crystal

Sen Dar looked up, amazed, and said aloud, "Ah-h, the other two crystals are on the planet called Earth."

He studied the coordinates and then folded the map and stuffed it back inside his shirt. Then he placed the chained crystal back around his neck. He raced across the cavern floor and back down the rock stairs toward the entrance.

He ran out of the cavern opening, stopped to look back, and watched the opening re-form into a solid rock wall. Then he looked cautiously around and began to jog along the path across the clearing. He had only made it a few feet into the jungle when he tripped over something and landed flat on his face. A thin silver wire stretched across the pathway had caught his feet and he jumped up in a panic. He started to reach into his shirt for the crystal, but two alien guards jumped out from behind jungle ferns and grabbed him by both arms before he could touch it.

The guards were humanoid, tall, muscular, violet-skinned, and very hairy, and they had five small bone protrusions several inches long that extended like a fan straight upward from their brows across their foreheads. They were wearing crude leather uniforms, and each had a metal arrow sticking out of an air gun in a leather holster strapped around their waists. Cloth-covered air tubes attached to the gun handles ran to small twin metal canisters strapped on their backs.

"So, a spy!" said the larger guard, gloating over his prize. "We saw you sneaking down the path."

"I'm not a spy," Sen Dar cried out defiantly as he struggled in vain to free himself from their tight grip.

"Gorn will have fun disposing of you, very slowly," remarked the second guard, sneering sadistically.

The guards laughed cruelly as Sen Dar forced a weak smile.

"You fools, I'm no spy," he yelled angrily as he improvised a cunning idea. "I came to warn Gorn of a greater danger to his kingdom than any he's ever known. You must take me to him."

"Did you hear that, Glag?" the larger guard asked, mocking Sen Dar's request. "This thing wishes to see Gorn himself. Yes, we must hurry and get this thing…" and he yanked the chained crystal over Sen Dar's head, looked at it curiously before stuffing it in a leather side pouch, and continued, "…to Gorn."

"Yes, Lagrar," the other guard concurred, "we must take this thing…" and he clenched his huge fist, hit Sen Dar on the back of the neck in a swift move, knocking him out cold, and then finished saying, "…to Gorn."

The blow shook the map partially out of Sen Dar's shirt and Glag grabbed it and then stuffed it into the leather pouch hung at his side. Lagrar grabbed Sen Dar's laser gun from its holster and pushed it into the pouch at his side where he had also put the gold-chained crystal.

He smiled with Glag, licked his thick violet lips, and scowled, "He will not have an easy death."

They chuckled viciously as they picked up each end of Sen Dar's unconscious body and headed along the path in the direction of the hilltop palace. The palace built above the jungle trees looked ancient. Slender towers spiraled above the four corners of a bluish-stone building. Morning sunlight was glinting off tiny gold mineral specks within the stones. A path led out of the jungle and continued a dozen-feet up to the ten-feet-in-diameter octagon door. The two guards carried Sen Dar's unconscious body up the last few feet of the path toward the door. They approached two sentries, who were standing to each side of it with their arrow-tipped weapons drawn and held at attention across their chests.

"Stand aside," yelled Lagrar at the sentries, and he added, sneering, "This one Gorn will want to deal with himself."

One of the sentries put his hand in a square slot on the side of the door and it opened straight up like a drawbridge. The two sentries then turned and stood at attention as Lagrar and Glag dragged Sen Dar by the arms inside the palace. The same sentry reached over and touched a square blue tile on the side of the opening. The door swung down and closed with the loud… *clang*… and a hidden door latch locked with an ominous permanent… *clink*!

Sen Dar now had his hands tied with twine behind his back as Lagrar and Glag dragged him through another smaller door somewhere within the palace. They dropped his unconscious body face down onto a thick animal rug.

Sen Dar began to regain awareness and slowly started to get up but stopped as he saw a pair of black boots walk up to him. He looked up to see an even larger blue-skinned alien with a very muscular chest and arms smiling arrogantly down at him. He was dressed in a general's uniform made of smooth dark leather, belted at the waist. He was a foot taller than the two guards, and more massive, but the top of his forehead protruded with the same finger-sized bones sticking upward from his brow like a fan.

He was standing in front of a highly polished desk made from various exotic woods. Covering the walls behind were arrows, spears, arrow-tipped air guns, and other items of exotic weaponry. Lagrar and Glag bowed humbly before their leader.

"Oh, most supreme Gorn, ruler of the lands of Zeth," Lagrar announced respectfully, "we found him on the path below the palace carrying these things."

Lagrar handed Gorn the laser gun, then the chained crystal, and Glag handed him the map. Gorn took them, eyed the laser gun with great curiosity, and then set the gun, the crystal, and the map on the desk behind him.

"So, those two animals overseas sent you to kill me," stated Gorn, staring angrily at Sen Dar. "I am Gorn, the supreme ruler of the lands of Zeth, and they will both bow to me before I am done with them."

"You, spy, will regret coming here," yelled Gorn, pointing his forefinger at Sen Dar. "Execute him immediately!"

Sen Dar's eyes widened in terror, but he quickly regained control of the emotion with a sudden devious thought, and he pleaded, "Wait, I'm no spy. My Lord Gorn, no one on your world looks like me, do they? I came here to warn you of a greater danger than your enemies overseas."

Gorn hesitated and then shouted angrily at the guards, "Execute him, now!"

The guards pulled out their arrow-tipped guns, grabbed Sen Dar by the back of his shirt, and pointed the ends of the arrows at his head. Sen Dar showed fear for only an instant; then his face changed with the surfacing of a new cunning idea.

"Wait and hear me, my Lord Gorn," pleaded Sen Dar, appearing forlorn. "My name is Sen Dar. Like you, I was once a ruler until this hideous Galactic Alliance fleet invaded my planet, captured my kingdom, and killed innocent women and children. One of their ships circles your planet as we speak."

Gorn cringed distrustfully and barked, "Why should I believe this nonsense?"

He chuckled, and the two guards immediately chimed in.

Sen Dar mocked up defiant anger and shouted back, "I can prove it, or are you too great a coward to let me try?"

Fuming, Gorn walked over to Sen Dar, raising his hand to strike, but gained control of his fiery anger at the last moment.

"I will let you live if you prove what you say is true," he growled forcefully, still fuming.

"I'll need my hands free, my Lord," Sen Dar pleaded timidly as he bowed.

Gorn eyed him, and then yelled over his shoulder at the guards, "Untie his hands, but watch him very closely." Then he scowled close to Sen Dar's face and said, "I have no reason to trust you, Sen Dar."

The guards untied Sen Dar's hands, and he briefly rubbed his wrists before he walked toward Gorn with an outstretched hand.

"May I?" he asked politely, pointing to the crystal on the desk.

Gorn recoiled, grabbed the laser gun off the desk, and pointed it menacingly at Sen Dar's chest.

"Keep the gun, my Lord, but I need the crystal to prove my story," Sen Dar said calmly.

Gorn lowered the gun as he took the crystal off the desk, looked at it from all sides, and then very cautiously handed it to him. Sen Dar smiled triumphantly as the crystal clenched in his right fist began to glow. However, his attempt to use mind control merely briefly startled them, and Gorn pointed the gun at his forehead.

"You fools, kill him!" he yelled out as he fired the gun, and both guards leapt at Sen Dar, who was already dematerializing.

The laser beam passed through his vanishing molecules to disintegrate a chair behind the guards and they fell on the floor on top of each other right where Sen Dar had been standing.

Sen Dar re-materialized aboard his ship, grinning, while he clutched the glowing crystal. Then he realized a flaw in his plan.

These primitive aliens must somehow be immune to the crystal's control, he pondered.

His eyes widened as a more important realization surfaced, and he reached frantically inside his shirt to discover The Ancient One's map was not there.

He blanched and gasped, "The Map!"

His eyes narrowed angrily as he grabbed another laser gun from a rack in one hand and tightly clutched the crystal in the other. Then he dematerialized.

He materialized again inside Gorn's chambers with the laser gun pointed at Gorn, but Gorn was ready for him. He was pointing the other laser gun back at him, while holding the map in his other hand above flames burning in a bowl on a pedestal by his side. He grinned arrogantly.

"Forget something?" asked Gorn with a vicious smirk.

"I only wanted to show you that I am sincere," replied Sen Dar convincingly.

He lowered his gun, bowed respectfully, and then added, with a humble smile, "I am not from your world, my Lord Gorn."

Gorn gazed suspiciously back at him and accused, "Then you too belong to this Galactic Alliance."

"Never, my Lord!" cried out Sen Dar, appearing appalled by the accusation. "They will help your enemies overseas destroy your kingdom as they did mine."

Still hesitant, Gorn gave Sen Dar a grimacing gaze.

"Why should you wish to help me?" he asked suspiciously and grimaced at Sen Dar again.

"We have the same problem," Sen Dar answered with calm logic and tactfully added, "I want my kingdom back and you want to preserve your own. Am I right?"

"Hmm, I will listen to your plan," replied Gorn apprehensively, "but first hand me the gun and the crystal. I would not want you to use those weapons on me."

Gorn held out his hand. Sen Dar touched a place on the side of the crystal laser gun, and a winding-down whirring...*varoom*...began and faded away. He reluctantly took off the Transport Matrix Crystal, walked closer to Gorn, and handed him both items. Gorn took them and placed them on the desk behind him. The two guards had moved closer to Sen Dar. They were now standing behind his back pointing their arrow-tipped guns directly at his head.

"I will guard these for now," stated Gorn as he nodded toward the items on the desk. Then he commanded, "But remember well, Sen Dar, who the ruler is here."

Sen Dar respectfully bowed his head, grinning. Mistrustful, Gorn rubbed his chin, wondering what Sen Dar was really planning.

"My Lord Gorn, may I have the map?" inquired Sen Dar politely. "I'll need it to plan our strategy."

Gorn looked at the map very carefully and then reluctantly handed it to Sen Dar.

"This Galactic Alliance has landed before on your world, have they not?" asked Sen Dar with an ingratiating smile.

"They first came several years ago," answered Gorn, scowling at the thought. "That is how I speak your language. They appeared again a few days ago but I did not trust them, so they left."

"They will propose a plan to aid your world in gaining peace as they did mine," continued Sen Dar. "Initially, they will respect your freewill choice. It's their way."

"Their diplomats are scheduled to return soon," Gorn remarked irritably. "They do have great technology so I reluctantly agreed to this so-called peace meeting."

"They will try and gain control of your world through your trust as they did mine," Sen Dar continued slyly. "I suggest you go along with this proposed peace mission, up to a point."

Gorn stood back for a moment, rubbing his hand on his chin, to ponder Sen Dar's statement.

"Hmm, I will consider this plan of yours."

He walked toward the doorway, turned around to gaze back at Sen Dar, and he pointed at him.

"Watch him very closely," he shouted at the guards and walked out of the chamber.

Lagrar and Glag stood to each side of Sen Dar with their guns still pointing at his head.

Back on the Galactic Alliance flagship, Admiral Starland, Captain Kalem, and Commander Zarel were now dressed in diplomatic attire, talking together in the bridge control room. Lieutenant Marin interrupted them as she turned toward the Admiral.

"Admiral," she began urgently, "tracking just reported that Sen Dar's ship disappeared off their screens right after it landed, and our diplomats on Maldec just made contact to let us know they are now ready to convene. They await your arrival."

"Let the Council know we're on our way down to the planet," replied Starland, "and have a Scout squadron search the jungle by Gorn's palace for Sen Dar's ship with close-range scanners. They may be able to locate it."

The Admiral turned and walked out of the bridge control room, closely followed by Captain Kalem and Commander Zarel.

In one of the large launch bays, dozens of Scout Interceptors were beside a lit runway leading to the launch bay door. Admiral Starland, Captain Kalem, and Commander Zarel, followed by six diplomats also dressed in diplomatic attire, walked up the ramp leading inside a Galactic shuttle that was taller and wider than a Scout ship. They stepped inside, and the ramp slid rapidly up inside the ship below the hatch and the hatch closed. The hull lit up with a pale-blue glow, the ship's drive began to emit a soft deep wavering hum, and the ship lifted off the floor and flew out through the opening launch window.

On another continent stood a palace perched on a background hill in a tall grassy semiarid area. It was made of a circle of twelve blue-domed buildings with tall gold minaret-like spires between each one, connected together by arched walkways lined with windows. A winding road led from a landing platform near a tent pavilion up the hillside to the palace. The Galactic shuttle flew down out of the partial cloud cover and landed on the platform. Admiral Starland, Captain Kalem, and Commander Zarel exited the ship, followed by the six diplomats.

Standing nearby to greet them was Trebor, one of Maldec's three leaders. The six-feet-tall male humanoid had a protruding forehead, ivory-white skin, and pink eyes. His ears had a small round hole in each earlobe that extended below his jaw, and his head was completely bald, except for a thin strip of hair that ran along the top of his skull from his forehead to the back of the neck. He smiled cordially and bowed toward Admiral Starland, who smiled back and bowed respectfully in return.

"Friends, I Trebor, greetings bid you to our great land," Trebor said graciously with awkwardly stilted English. "We forward looked years many to now. From conference, may promising future forth come for Maldec," and he grinned cheerfully.

Admiral Starland smiled and nodded respectfully. Trebor waved his hand toward the conference canopy that was set up twenty feet behind him in the direction of the hilltop palace. He walked toward it, and the diplomatic entourage followed him.

A large open-air tent with colorful banners shrouded several meeting tables. Gorn was standing next to Yulan, the third of Maldec's three leaders. He was a well-built humanoid male with no hair, smooth snake-like skin, and snake-like eyes. Gorn's expression showed utter contempt for the other two leaders as Yulan stepped forward to speak with Admiral Starland.

"Bet tamani cuo ila chozin chuo antros ya shas," began Yulan in his own language with a warm friendly voice. "Dea qu oit chu chias bon vicot jum seera ot noom, et top noot. Etasam, ea oohs chu viskask oon las chas joa beeto."

"Our astronomers have been watching your ships for days," repeated Yulan's interpreter at his side in clear, poignant English. "It is clear you could have controlled our world by force, but did not. Therefore, I wish you goodwill and peace on our world."

With respect, Yulan brought the open palm of his right hand across his chest and placed it below his left shoulder, then bowed. Starland, Kalem, Zarel, and the other diplomats returned the salute.

Gorn came from behind, rudely pushed his way past Yulan and Trebor, and stated, "I am Gorn, supreme ruler of the lands of Zeth. I have agreed to this meeting only because you requested it. I did not come here," and he gave a disgusted glance at Trebor and Yulan, "because of these two."

Baring his large sharp teeth, he sneered angrily at both of them. They backed away, grimacing, and then frowned back at him.

Meanwhile, Sen Dar was viewing the conference on a hand-held view screen from a dimly lit chamber hidden somewhere within Trebor's palace.

The idiots, he thought with a sadistic laugh, *soon they will be at each other's throats and I will be on Earth.*

"No, I will not agree!" Gorn shouted angrily back at the conference, jumping to his feet. "When we meet again in the morning, I will offer my proposal."

He stormed away from the meeting area and headed up the path toward the palace on the hilltop. Disgusted and disappointed, Trebor and Yulan looked at Admiral Starland and shook their heads.

"Peace? With him how it can be?" remarked Trebor, greatly concerned.

"Give it time, my friends," answered Starland with an encouraging smile. "We have just begun the peace conference."

Trebor and Yulan looked at each other, simultaneously shrugged their shoulders, and then they both gradually forced a reluctant smile for Starland.

"To quarters for night, now my aides take you," Trebor said courteously.

The entire entourage got up from their chairs, and Trebor, Yulan, and their assistants headed up the path toward the palace. Starland, Kalem, Zarel, and the rest of the diplomats followed.

Later that night, Kalem was walking outside the palace grounds to get a breath of fresh air when he overheard the angry mumbled voices of Gorn and another man whom at first, he did not recognize. He noticed a light streaming from a slightly ajar door and slowed his brisk stride. Curious to find out if anything was amiss, he cautiously approached the door, peaked inside, and was greatly surprised to find Gorn and Sen Dar engaged in a heated conversation.

"No, I will not put up with this facade another day," Gorn yelled angrily. "I will crush them before they know what hit them."

Sen Dar cautiously pondered what he would say next, then carefully said, "But, my Lord Gorn, Admiral Starland could stop you if Yulan and Trebor asked for his military help. He could shield them from your attacks."

Gorn grew angrier and moved menacingly toward Sen Dar. He grabbed him by the shirt with one hand, lifted him off the ground, and brought his face close, nose to nose, to stare him in the eyes.

"It had better be good," he snarled, glowering. "My patience with you is very thin."

Sen Dar swallowed hard, forced a deceptive smile, and continued, "If Trebor were, shall we say, eliminated, and it was made to look like

Admiral Starland was behind it, then Yulan would follow you. The people of Maldec would be on your side and you would win without a fight."

Gorn blinked as this new cunning idea sunk in, and then he slowly lowered Sen Dar to the ground and released him.

"You're right," agreed Gorn, and he asked suspiciously, "but how can you can speak of murder at a peace conference?"

"Trebor is on his way to a private meeting with Starland as we speak," replied Sen Dar with an obvious sadistic grin.

"Why was I not invited?" Gorn shouted ferociously.

Sen Dar whispered seductively in his ear. "They are plotting to kill you this very night."

Enraged, Gorn picked up a chair and smashed it on the floor. He pulled Sen Dar's crystal laser gun from his garment and gazed with great animosity at Sen Dar.

"Show me how this works now or die!"

Sen Dar took the laser gun from Gorn and touched it on the side, causing a whirring winding-up... *varoom*. The crystals inside the gun faintly flashed on and off, and then brightly on, indicating the safety was now off.

Captain Kalem turned away from the ajar-door to Gorn's quarters and raised a wrist communicator to his lips.

"Admiral, come in," he whispered urgently.

A moment later, Admiral Starland's voice responded, "I read you, Captain."

"Sen Dar is here right now in the palace inside Gorn's chambers with Gorn," he continued, whispering.

"Sen Dar is here?" replied Starland. "He must have gained control of Gorn or Gorn captured him."

"That devil has somehow befriended Gorn," Kalem angrily whispered. "A moment ago, I overheard him discussing a plan to kill Trebor and blame it on you. Admiral, Gorn does not intend to make peace. I'm going in after Sen Dar and I'll... ah-h!"

A blunt instrument hit Kalem on the back of the head with a dull... *thud*... and he toppled over. A shadowed person appeared, holding the butt end of a laser gun in his hand. He opened the door wide and dragged Kalem's body through it into Gorn's chambers.

Startled by the intruder, Gorn swung around, pointing the laser gun toward him, and yelled angrily, "What is the meaning of this?"

A guard in a Galactic Alliance uniform was dragging Kalem the rest of the way through the doorway.

"Lord Gorn," he began proudly as he stood up to look at Gorn, "I caught this man peering into your chambers. He was armed with a weapon."

The guard stepped further into the light, looked down, realized he had knocked out his own Captain and dropped his laser gun as he bent down and patted Kalem's cheeks to revive him.

"What have I done?" cried the dismayed guard. "He is my Captain. Captain Kalem, wake up."

Sen Dar grabbed the laser gun from Gorn's hand and fired at the Galactic Alliance guard, killing him instantly. He pointed the gun at Kalem to fire again, but Gorn knocked the gun from his hand, grabbed Sen Dar by the throat, and then started to pick him up off the ground.

"You fool!" he yelled, blushed with anger. "Why did you kill the guard?"

"He may have overheard us," Sen Dar gasped fearfully.

"Why did you try and kill his Captain as well?" Gorn sputtered angrily as he strangled Sen Dar more tightly.

Sen Dar coughed, groped for air, feigned a deeply hurt look and replied, "He captured and tortured me before I escaped. He was responsible for killing millions of my people."

They heard a group of excited voices and rapidly approaching footsteps from the outside chamber, and Sen Dar panicked.

"We must get out quickly. This way, follow me," he shouted at Gorn, pointing toward a door on the other side of the room.

Gorn let Sen Dar go, dropping him to his feet, and Sen Dar rubbed his throat, then coughed as he ran to the side door with Gorn right behind him. He yanked open the door and they ran through it right before the room was flooded with a dozen Galactic Alliance guards with drawn laser guns.

Trebor, Admiral Starland, and Commander Zarel walked into the room and noticed the dead Galactic Alliance guard lying next to Captain Kalem, who was groggily regaining full awareness. Several of the Alliance guards helped him to his feet, while he rubbed the back of his head.

"Are you all right, Captain?" asked Admiral Starland.

"They're getting away," Kalem answered angrily, continuing to rub the back of his head. Then he looked at Trebor and stated, "Gorn and Sen Dar planned to kill you on your way here tonight."

"Who is this Sen Dar?" asked Trebor with complete surprise.

"He's an evil renegade from another world," Kalem replied sternly. Then he gazed hopefully at Starland and requested, "Admiral, let me stop him."

Yulan entered the room and looked at the dead guard.

"Tuain tacu juin?" he asked, shocked.

"What has happened?" repeated the interpreter by his side.

Fuming, Trebor turned toward Yulan and said, "Kill us planned they. Gorn and Sen Dar evil renegade from other world." Grimacing, he said, "If want they war, a war get they. Yulan join forces with I and forever tyranny of his end."

The interpreter relayed Trebor's remarks to Yulan and Yulan grimaced.

"Wait and listen to reason," pleaded Starland looking at both of them. "War is never the answer."

"Snrod ta skuam qu betal. Fo com tilok, kopal tie," Yulan replied with angry determination.

"Now this affair is ours. We ask kindly, stay away," repeated the interpreter, matching Yulan's emotion.

Trebor, Yulan, Trebor's interpreter, and several of their personal guards hurried out of the room.

"If Sen Dar was caught and exposed to Gorn for the fake he is, then we would have a chance," remarked Kalem. "Admiral, let me go after him."

Starland sighed and thoughtfully lowered his head, then looked back up at Kalem.

"This time I must agree," he replied reluctantly and ordered, "but be very cautious, Captain, and keep in frequent contact."

Kalem nodded his head and ran out the side door in pursuit of Sen Dar and Gorn.

Admiral Starland appeared worried, and Commander Zarel understandingly sympathized with him.

"I hope he's successful," remarked Zarel, sighing his own concern. "Trebor told me Gorn's scientists have been working on a bomb Gorn claims could destroy this land as well as Yulan's with one detonation."

Starland's eyes widened alarmingly. "And he's just drunk enough with power to use it. Alert the fleet and have the landing party prepared to leave at a moment's notice."

Commander Zarel nodded and walked out of the room. Starland closed his eyes and winced as if a vision of a possible future pained him. Then he snapped open his eyes and hurried out of the chamber. Eight Galactic Alliance guards trailed behind him, and the four remaining guards picked up the body of the dead guard and solemnly carried him from the chamber.

By morning, Kalem was aboard his Scout Interceptor watching his view screen with his hands depressed into the palm guidance controls. His ship was flying down toward the jungle a mile away from Gorn's palace. Dawn sunlight was beginning to glow behind the hills as a propeller-driven hovercraft appeared from the sky above the palace and slowly lowered toward it.

The twenty-feet-long hovercraft with smooth, rounded edges appeared to be made of dark-blue metal. The back half had a large propeller with ten blades spinning inside a round pivoting frame that was open on the top and bottom for free airflow. It was located behind a curved cockpit with a clear oval window. The wings that began on each side of the hull below the cockpit swept back and curved upward behind the propeller to end in twin ailerons with a tall narrow rudder between them. Two figures were inside the cockpit.

Kalem touched a crystal control on the console and the image changed to a close-up of the hovercraft as it landed inside Gorn's palace grounds. Sen Dar and Gorn disembarked and entered the palace through an inner courtyard door.

Kalem's Scout flew down to the jungle below the hilltop and disappeared below the tall jungle trees. He was gazing at the view screen as he sighed and said under his breath, "I hope this new probe works through those thick walls."

Then he touched a small red crystal and his view screen changed to another image. Sen Dar was walking in a hurry toward twenty feet of black metal stairs with handrails, followed by Gorn and his two personal guards. He began to slink up the stairs behind Gorn's back when Gorn stopped to discuss something with the guards. The stairs led to an open observation platform that overlooked a sleek metal rocket with a polished mirror finish primed for liftoff from a launching pad.

The rocket was poised in the center of a tall cylindrical laboratory. Two large closed rectangular metal doors curved across the ceiling. Several of Gorn's scientists working at a control console near the stairs bowed fearfully at Gorn as he and his two guards passed by them.

Sen Dar was now up the twenty feet of stairs and he stepped onto the platform landing, then ran ten feet over to the door at the other end and opened it. His eyes widened as he noticed the Transport Matrix Crystal hanging from a spear attached to the back wall behind Gorn's desk. He ran over to the wall, grabbed the crystal, and stuffed it into a pocket as Gorn and the two guards stepped onto the platform. They walked over to the door and entered the chamber.

"Well, Sen Dar, your perfect little plan did not work," said Gorn with vicious sarcasm and he grimaced. "Now I must attack those two weaklings before they have a chance to mass together against me. Your usefulness to me is over."

"But, my Lord, you need me," pleaded Sen Dar. "I have weapons beyond what you could imagine. With them you could win an instant victory."

"I already possess a mighty weapon and I plan to use it at dawn," spouted Gorn, puffing up his chest.

"But my Lord," begged Sen Dar, his face contorted with fear, "your scientists told me how the explosive device in that rocket works. That bomb will destroy this entire planet and you with it."

"Do you take me for a fool?" snarled Gorn, undaunted. "I have known from the beginning you planned to rule my kingdom. We are too much alike, you and I," and he yelled at Lagrar and Glag, "Guards, bind him."

Before Sen Dar could reach into his pocket for the hidden crystal, the guards grabbed him and tied his hands behind his back with a thick jungle vine rope.

"Throw him below," commanded Gorn. "I will deal with him myself after I am supreme ruler of all Maldec."

"Don't be a fool," Sen Dar yelled, but he restrained himself and pleaded, "My Lord Gorn, listen to me. Your scientists are right. That rocket will destroy everything. You must not use it."

Arrogant now beyond reason, Gorn turned around and headed toward the doorway, while the guards dragged Sen Dar away through a smaller doorway in the right wall beyond the desk.

Gorn walked boldly back through the doorway leading to the observation deck, slammed the door shut behind him, walked over to the balcony platform, and leaned against the railing to overlook the personnel preparing the rocket on the launch pad. He focused upon several scientists working at the control console near the bottom of the stairs and leaned further over the railing, gloating menacingly down at them.

"How much longer will it take?" he yelled impatiently down at the scientists. Then he demanded, "Tell me now!"

The chief scientist looked away from the console and up at Gorn.

"At least another day, my Lord Gorn," he replied fearfully.

Instantly furious, Gorn yelled back, "I want that rocket ready to fire at dawn or you will forfeit your life."

An assistant scientist standing beside the console looked up at Gorn.

"But, my Lord, the Matter Chain-Reactor Bomb inside the experimental rocket cannot be shut down once it is launched. It starts a chain reaction with all matter. It will destroy everything." Then he begged, "Please, my Lord Gorn, you must not order us to set it off."

Gorn pulled Sen Dar's laser from his uniform, turned the domed knob on the butt of the gun until it stopped and hummed to a higher pitch, and then aimed it at the assistant scientist.

"Please, you must not... ah-h..."

Gorn fired the gun and the screaming assistant dissolved to fiery atoms that disappeared in a puff of smoke and falling ash.

Six other personnel in the chamber and Chief Scientist Glorin by the console jumped back in shock. Glorin looked up cautiously at Gorn hanging over the balcony rail, angrily glowering down at him.

"Do you, Chief Scientist Glorin, wish to argue with me?" inquired Gorn with malicious delight. Then he raised his voice and inquired, "Do any of the rest of you?" None of the other launch technicians answered and he commanded, "I want it ready by dawn. These guards will assure your cooperation."

Two of Gorn's other guards walked through a set of silver metal doors directly underneath the balcony stairs and positioned themselves at each side with their arrow-tipped air guns drawn and held across their chests. Forlorn, Chief Scientist Glorin lowered his head with resignation. Several other scientists around the room monitoring other consoles simply resumed their work. Then Gorn turned around and walked back into his private chamber.

Kalem observed the two guards on his view screen as they stood by the doors below the observation balcony of Gorn's launch facility. Then he touched a crystal control on his console and the view screen changed, revealing Admiral Starland and Commander Zarel standing next to each other aboard the shuttle enroute to the flagship.

"Are you all right, Captain?" asked the concerned Admiral.

"Of course," replied Kalem, and he added urgently, "Listen Admiral. Gorn has imprisoned Sen Dar in the palace. He plans to set the rocket off at dawn. I just watched him kill one of his own scientists for telling him the truth about what would happen if he used that thing. Admiral, I could stop this. I could grab Sen Dar and disintegrate that rocket."

"No, Kalem!" Starland commanded. "What will happen on Maldec must be the mass choice of its people, even if it is an unconscious one for self-destruction. This is our primary Galactic Alliance law and one of The Ancient One's celestial laws. They must choose for themselves. We cannot interfere now."

Starland looked down shaking his head, then back up at Kalem.

"We're on our way to the flagship. When we arrive, we'll move it to a safe distance." Then he commanded, "And you, Captain, are to report to the bridge now. That's an order."

"I'm on my way, Admiral," acknowledged Kalem, disappointed.

He touched a control and the view screen changed again just as Lagrar and Glag threw Sen Dar into a dungeon cell below the palace, and then swung the large rusty metal door closed. Sen Dar got up and ran over to a stone on the floor. He knelt down and began to furiously rub the thick twine that tied his hands together back and forth on the stone's protruding sharp edge. He was frantic and breathing hard when Kalem switched the view screen back to Gorn's science lab.

Gorn walked back impatiently over to the railing on the observation platform and commanded, "I want that rocket launched now. Do you hear me?" and he bellowed out, "Launch it now or die!"

"But, my Lord Gorn, the guidance system has not been checked," pleaded Chief Scientist Glorin.

Gorn pointed the laser gun at the scientist and yelled, "Do you want me to see how this works on you too, Glorin?" Then he bellowed again, "Launch it now!"

Chief Scientist Glorin and another scientist standing next to him gazed with complete hopelessness at each other. Then Glorin flipped a switch on the control panel and they both ran from the launch pad, along with several other personnel, as the rocket ignited. It lifted off the pad and accelerated up through the opening ceiling door panels.

Kalem was watching the rocket on his view screen as it headed high above the launch bay doors of Gorn's laboratory.

"Oh God, no, that fool set it off," he whispered and jammed his hands into the palm guidance controls.

As the rocket continued to climb into the sky, Kalem's ship moved into view from the jungle tree line below Gorn's palace and then it darted up into the clouds.

Sen Dar was dirty and exhausted, sitting on the ground in Gorn's dungeon with his eyes closed. He opened his eyes to notice dawn light pouring through the barred cell window, and heard the roaring sound of the rocket. He jumped to his feet, ran over to the opening, peered through the bars, and saw the rocket heading further up into the sky above the palace, until it began to malfunction. Then he ran over to the sharp stone and desperately tried cutting his bonds again. This time the rope finally broke, and he reached into his shirt with his right hand, pulled out the Transport Matrix Crystal, and closed his eyes. The crystal began to glow, and the light quickly expanded until it enveloped him in a whirl of light that swiftly dematerialized his body.

He materialized an instant later aboard his ship and let go of the crystal. The glow went out as he lunged for the control console and slammed his palms on top of the domed guidance controls.

Sen Dar's ship lit up with a red aura around the hull, and the jungle brush camouflaging his ship dropped to the ground. The ship moved upward a dozen feet, hovered, and then it too shot at high speed up into the clouds, just as Kalem's ship had done.

Gorn's astonished expression as he gazed up through the launch bay doors transformed to bewildered fear. Several scientists, including Glorin, ran back into launch pad laboratory and looked up at the falling rocket.

"I command you to stop this now," screamed Gorn, now terrified. "Turn it off!"

"Arrogant fool, you were warned," yelled Glorin looking up at Gorn with pitiful disgust. "You were warned. Now, you have killed all of us."

"I command you to destroy it," Gorn yelled desperately, and his voice echoed in the launch bay. None of the scientists moved and Gorn screamed, frothed at the mouth. "You will pay for this. You will all pay for this outrage."

His two terrified guards below raced back inside through the metal doors, just as he fired the laser gun at everyone in the chamber, and their echoing death screams faded as the white ashes from dissolved bodies settled to the floor. Gorn looked up and gasped as he saw the rocket falling toward the launch bay doors.

Sen Dar's ship darted up past the clouds and beyond Maldec's atmosphere where it briefly stopped in space.

A warning light blinked on Kalem's control console, and he touched it with his finger. Sen Dar's ship flashed onto the view screen in time for Kalem to see it flash a white light before it blurred in a streak into the depths of space.

"Damn it!" mumbled Kalem, slamming his fist on the console, "How did you get away?"

No, you will not escape me again, he thought silently determined.

His ship flashed a white light, and then streaked into the depths of space in pursuit of Sen Dar's ship.

Horrified, Gorn's mouth was agape with dumbfounded disbelief as he watched the rocket falling directly at him. He raised his hands to cover his face.

"No-o, N-o-o, N-o-o-o," he desperately screamed.

Back on the flagship, Admiral Starland's tired eyes were looking at Commander Zarel, whose regrettable shake of his head said it all too clearly.

"My friend, they made their choice," Starland remarked sadly.

The ship's navigator sitting next to Lieutenant Marin interrupted them.

"Admiral, tracking reports two Scout ships left Maldec's atmosphere headed on a vector for Earth."

"Well done, Drelim," remarked Starland.

"It has to be Sen Dar and Kalem," added Zarel.

"I ordered Kalem back to the flagship," said Starland shaking his head. "That young fool."

The malfunctioning rocket hit the top of the doors to the science laboratory and exploded, ending Gorn's maniacal screaming as he disintegrated into thousands of sizzling particles of light along with everything else.

The entire palace and surrounding forest turned into a gigantic mushrooming explosion that spread further in every direction around the countryside, consuming every bit of matter. The massive explosion spread around the entire surface of Gorn's continent, then to all of Maldec. The planet began to crack from the middle outward. Then it exploded with a thunderous roar of blinding light, blasting many thousands of large asteroids and smaller rubble into space along the former planet's swift orbital pathway around the sun.

CHAPTER TWENTY-ONE

DEATH
AND
TRANSFORMATION

A different world appeared in another part of the solar system and Harry Faldwell instantly knew it was Earth 100,000 years ago. The moon circling the planet was identical to the moon that circles Earth today, but the planet's icecaps were much smaller. Just two large continental landmasses were located on opposite sides of the planet centered along the equatorial region. Although the tallest mountain ranges had risen little more than seven thousand feet, each landmass extended more than halfway into the northern and southern hemispheres, and vast oceans surrounded them.

A streak of light from deep space headed toward the planet and abruptly slowed into the visible form of Sen Dar's ship. It stopped to hover above the atmosphere. Then it darted down through the clouds that were moving high above the ocean between the two continents.

Another streak of light blurred from deep space toward the planet. Kalem's ship also hovered for a moment above the atmosphere, before it darted down through the clouds.

Admiral Starland and Commander Zarel were on the bridge of the flagship observing the aftermath of the explosion of Maldec on the main view screen. The ship appeared to be at a safe distance from the destruction, while those aboard silently observed huge city-sized chunks of rock and thousands of smaller asteroids moving rapidly toward the screen, until they disappeared beyond its frame. Commander Zarel's eyes were welling with tears.

"Now it will form into an asteroid belt," Starland commented solemnly. "If Earth should survive, future generations will look on this and probably wonder where all this rubble came from that circle in the orbit of what was a planet." He sadly shook his head, sighing, and added, "No doubt the secret will be left with us to carry." Then he turned toward Lieutenant Marin and requested, "Lieutenant, please put the view screen on long-range scan."

She touched a crystal control and the image moved into the distant background until they were looking at an overview of a long asteroid belt beginning to form. The rubble gradually stretched out, while it continued to move in the orbital path that Maldec once traveled along on its journey around the sun, between the planets of Mars and Jupiter.

"Sen Dar is deadly dangerous and Kalem may need our help," remarked Starland.

He looked at the ship's navigator sitting beside Lieutenant Marin and ordered, "Helmsman Drelim, engage level-three trans-light drive for Earth at once." Drelim nodded and touched a large faceted violet crystal control.

The huge star ship's hull pulsed with pale-blue light, then changed to gold and flashed brilliantly, and the ship streaked into deep space.

An instant later, a light beam appeared from the depths of space and abruptly slowed near Earth, revealing Admiral Starland's flagship. It assumed an orbit above Earth's vast ocean between the two continents.

"What does tracking report?" asked Starland, as he stepped behind the control console behind Marin and Drelim.

"It looks like two Scout class ships are engaged in battle in the clouds above the ocean," she replied, worried.

Starland touched the intercom crystal control and commanded, "Lieutenant Moreau, this is Admiral Starland. Captain Kalem is engaged in a battle in Earth's atmosphere. Launch your squadron as fighter support at once. Lieutenant Marin will provide the coordinates."

A dogfight between Kalem and Sen Dar was taking place in the clouds high up in Earth's ancient atmosphere. Kalem's Scout Interceptor was chasing Sen Dar's ship in and out of the cloud cover, firing blue Mazon fireballs. Explosions were going off on each side of Sen Dar's ship, severely rocking it. Several blasts of return red fireballs from Sen Dar's ship nearly hit Kalem's Interceptor, but he managed to outmaneuver them. Then both ships, one after the other, entered a lower cloud cover.

Sen Dar saw Kalem's Scout Interceptor on the view screen for a moment just before his own ship disappeared into another large cloud, and his sneering grin widened with anticipation.

Now, my dear Captain Kalem, he thought lustily, *your pointless life will finally be over.*

Grinning, he touched a special violet crystal that was six inches long from tip to tip and two inches thick at the center. A small door opened on the ship's hull and a self-propelled metal sphere, with many tiny camera lenses around its surface, darted out of the door. It spiraled around the ship several times, and then darted swiftly away to disappear in the clouds in the distant background.

Damn it, where are you? Kalem angrily asked himself, seeing only clouds passing by on the view screen.

Several different crystals flashed at the same time on the control console and Kalem grinned.

Oh, there you are, he thought confidently and then said aloud, "See if you can outmaneuver this."

Clouds were rushing by the hull of Kalem's ship as the small spherical object launched from Sen Dar's ship flew into view, matched the speed of the ship, and magnetically attached itself to one of the three semispherical pods under the bottom of the hull.

"Goodbye, worthless Captain," said Sen Dar with a snide grin to himself as he touched the special crystal control.

Kalem was closely watching his view screen as Sen Dar's ship reappeared out of some clouds. He grabbed the green crystal and it pulsed with light.

Finally, he thought, *the time has come for you to pay the price for all your foul deeds.*

The device attached to the pod on the bottom of Kalem's ship began making a ticking sound; then it suddenly stopped and the device exploded in blue and red fiery light, blowing apart the semispherical pod shell. Within the pod, only two of the dozen crystal spires remained intact. Electrostatic energy was shorting over the remaining crystals and along the bottom of the ship between the other two pods. The ship wobbled and began to arc downward.

The badly shaking control room threw Kalem to the floor beneath debris flying around the room, and smoke filled the air. Kalem grabbed onto the control console, pulled himself up to his feet, and shook his head to clear his mind. His uniform had a tear at the shoulder, but he appeared unhurt.

In the name of The Ancient One, what just happened? he

pondered, mystified, with a sense of foreboding.

He touched a crystal and the view screen changed, revealing that his ship was fast approaching ocean waves at an increasing speed, and he braced himself for impact.

As the ship fell from the cloud cover above the ocean, it began to turn end over end. Then it hit the surface hard, exploding water, steam, and shorting electrostatic energy high into the air. The ship tilted on its side as it began to sink below the churning waves, and water rushed inside the ship through a gaping hole in the hull.

Small fires were burning in various places around the control room and a dark-blue smoke had filled the air along the ceiling. Kalem was lying face down over the top of the console as he began to regain consciousness. The impact left his left arm smashed and bloody, the left side of his face mangled, and his left eye swollen shut.

In a daze, he slowly stood up and stumbled toward the gaping hole. He reached for the edge of the opening and nearly fell through it but caught himself with his good arm against the ragged metal edge. Then he staggered and passed out, falling head first through the opening into the churning ocean waves.

Sen Dar's ship broke through the clouds and stopped to hover high above the ocean. A red fireball shot from the hull down at the smoldering wreckage of Kalem's sinking ship, but the ship sank beneath the waves and drifted downward before the fireball exploded on the water's surface, sending huge plumes of steaming water a thousand feet in the air. Then several blue fireballs suddenly exploded to each side of Sen Dar's ship, knocking it end over end before it recovered.

Sen Dar was glaring at his view screen watching five Galactic Alliance Scout Interceptors exit the clouds headed his way, firing more fireballs.

"Oh no-o, you are too late," he shouted defiantly. "You can't save your precious Captain this time."

His ship flashed gold light and arced across the sky at terrific speed. Four of the Galactic Alliance Scouts joined in high-speed pursuit. The fifth Scout Interceptor flew down to sea level and hovered above some debris where Kalem's ship had been. The water was still boiling from the exploded fireball, and streams of vapor shot upward across a thirty-foot circle on the surface of the ocean.

From his view screen, Lieutenant Moreau was looking at the steaming ocean surface that appeared to be directly below his ship.

I don't believe it, he thought, dismayed. *Kalem is gone.*

He cast his head down sadly and continued in a whisper, "And it falls on me to tell his father."

CHAPTER TWENTY-ONE

A moment later, Moreau's Scout Interceptor darted straight up in the clouds.

A thousand miles away was a prehistoric-looking tropical valley surrounding a large dormant volcano. Sen Dar's ship flew across the valley and hovered above the calderas. Then it lowered inside the darkness of the open shaft.

Four Galactic Alliance Scout fighters flew across the valley and spread out as they flew toward the volcano. A Galactic Alliance pilot could see the volcano on his view screen directly below his ship as he touched the transceiver crystal.

"Corell, I hate to admit it, but I think we lost him," remarked the frustrated pilot to a pilot aboard another ship.

"I'm reading the same thing, Treban," replied the disappointed voice of Corell, who sighed and then ordered, "All squadron pilots return to the flagship. A survey team can scan the entire area. They can find him."

The four Scout ships flew over the top of the volcano's throat and then accelerated up into the clouds that were moving slowly in over the valley.

Kalem appeared quite dead while his body was gently sinking downward. It soon settled on the ocean floor between dark-green spiraling plants. A huge clear, domed city, brilliantly lit from within, was in the near distance beyond his body. Low mountains, waterfalls, and tropical forests curved in the far background beyond the rolling hill countryside that surrounded the back half of the city.

In the foreground, beautifully landscaped flowers and well-cropped, lush grass covered the ground between many small white domed dwellings that surrounded a teardrop-shaped lake. The three pyramids centered in the city encompassed and towered high above the spiral towers that surrounded the large white, domed building. Laced along the ground within the city and throughout the countryside were many transparent transport tubes. Several were luminous with blue light, and crystal-like transport cars were moving within several of them.

Two very handsome blue-skinned Oceanan men swam toward Kalem's body. The two men nodded to each other and one of them picked up Kalem's body by the shoulders. The other one picked up his feet and they swam gracefully away with his body toward the domed city in the distance. They soon passed by ten feet away from Kalem's wrecked ship that was resting on the ocean floor with the gaping hole in its side.

Sen Dar's ship flew to the bottom of the extinct volcanic shaft and a mile into a huge horizontal cavernous lava tunnel to a plateau that extended halfway up the tunnel's sidewall. The ship gently lowered onto the plateau. The humming antigravity engine and the red aura around its hull faded away. Instantly, the phosphorescent minerals within the cavern walls brightened around the ship and down the tunnel's length that continued many miles into the distance.

Sen Dar had the old parchment map laid out flat on the console. He was dangling the Transport Matrix Crystal from its chain in his right hand like a pendulum above the area marked:

Secret Domed City of the Oceanans

Master Opellum

Guardian of the Emerald Doorway Crystal

He scowled with considerable annoyance when what he expected to happen did not occur.

It must have been moved, he thought.

He dangled the crystal over other parts of the parchment map and it glowed as it passed over Lemuria's colony continent of Atlantis. It was pulled back toward this area of the map by some mysterious force and Sen Dar looked very closely at it just as the crystal stopped, suspended above a city near the coast marked:

Atla – Capital City of Atlantis.

The crystal suddenly glowed brighter and began to emit a soft pulsing… *ping*… that bounced around the control room.

Hmm, pondered Sen Dar, *it must be somewhere in the city of Atla but it will be in my hands soon enough.*

He placed the crystal back around his neck, stuffed the map back into his shirt, and then placed his hands, palms down, on top of the illumined dome-shaped guidance controls.

His ship lit up and flew back down the length of the cavern and up the opening leading to the mouth of the extinct volcano.

A short time later, his ship was flying swiftly over the ocean along a continental shoreline headed toward a jungle peninsula a mile in the distance, where the tops of two pyramids jutted just above the tall jungle trees. The ship flew in a circle out over the ocean and doubled backed over the peninsula, headed toward the pyramids. It stopped above the thick jungle trees at the center of the peninsula and then lowered below the trees.

The ship softly touched down in a clearing. The steady high-pitched engine hum and the red aura around the hull diminished and vanished. The oval hatch opened and the ramp slid down from under it. Sen Dar stepped through the hatch onto the ramp and jumped off it before it reached the ground. Looking up, he saw a palatial building on the crest of a hill with many windows equally spaced around its circumference. The two quartz-tipped gold pyramids were just visible above the tops of the jungle trees in the valley below the hilltop structure.

Sen Dar tore his shirt in several places and grabbed a branch from the ground. He scratched his face and arms with it and rolled around in the dirt. Jumping up, he drew his laser gun from the holster strapped around his waist and fired it at a nearby tree, completely disintegrating it. He inspected himself carefully to make sure he looked mistreated. Then he walked over to his ship and placed the palm of a hand with fingers spread wide on a place underneath the hull. The ship lit up with a pulsing red glow, making the same soft, low-pitched hum as it had on Maldec. Brush and foliage flew through the air from the surrounding jungle and completely camouflaged his ship from view within seconds.

Sen Dar reached inside his shirt, grabbed the crystal, and then carefully looked at it. He grinned deviously as he tucked it back into his shirt, and then began to jog along a path leading through the jungle in the direction of the hilltop palace.

Admiral Starland was standing a few feet to the foreground of the center of the floor under one of the observation domes on one end of the flagship. He was looking out through the clear canopy, observing Earth's moon as it continued to come fully into view from behind the left side of the planet. It appeared huge as it slowly rose up from below the dome's horizon. The Lemurian and Atlantian continents, centered over the equator and separated by a vast ocean, were both prominent but partially out of visual range beyond opposite ends of the equator, as the huge star ship continued to orbit ancient Earth.

Lieutenant Moreau was standing within the transparent elevator as it rose up from the center of the floor. He walked out of it and up to Admiral Starland, then whispered in his ear. Starland's eyes widened and he looked around at Lieutenant Moreau.

"Are you certain?" Starland asked sadly.

Solemnly bowing his head, Moreau replied, "It looked like Sen Dar blew up what was left of Kalem's ship as it sank below the ocean waves. No life sign was detected while my ship hovered above some debris on the ocean surface."

Admiral Starland was doing his best to control his outrage, but he gave Moreau a stern look.

"I want Sen Dar found!" he commanded strongly. "Do you understand me, Lieutenant? I want him any way you can get him."

Lieutenant Moreau nodded his head, turned around, and walked back into the elevator, while Starland looked away to gaze sadly into the star-lit heavens beyond Earth. As the elevator slowly descended, Moreau gazed up through its transparent wall and compassionately shook his head for Starland's loss and for the loss of his best and oldest friend.

Somewhere within a science laboratory inside the secret domed city of the Oceanans was Captain Kalem's body. Still in a tattered dripping wet uniform, it was lying on a table that looked like marble. A four-feet-long and a-foot-wide emerald crystal was pointing at his head. A similar ruby-red crystal was pointing at his feet. A scientist, dressed in a white smock, passed several luminous spheres over the top of Kalem's body, then stepped back and nodded to a technician standing in front of a curved control console.

The technician passed his hands over several dome shaped luminous controls, and the huge crystals pointed at Kalem's head and feet began to glow, projecting an orange grid all around his body. His mangled arm and face repaired themselves in seconds as air molecules formed into matter along the light grid, replacing destroyed tissues. Then he began to breathe as his uniform rapidly repaired itself. Within moments, it was completely dry and looked new.

Kalem opened his eyes and looked up at the scientist, and the scientist smiled back down at him.

Welcome back, the scientist stated telepathically with a warm cheerful voice. *I'm Dom, Chief Scientist of the Oceanans*.

"How did I get here?" asked Kalem, disoriented and puzzled.

We monitored your battle in the atmosphere, replied Dom. *Several of our people plucked you from the bottom of the ocean.*

"But, how is it I hear you?" inquired Kalem, still confused. "Your lips don't move when you speak."

I am speaking to you telepathically, replied Dom, chuckling softly.

He looked questioningly at Kalem, then smiled and nodded before using his vocal cords.

"I beg your pardon, Captain, but that is our way of communication, not your own. We speak silently to each other, being to being, when we want to make certain our intent is clearly understood and not distorted."

"I don't understand," said Kalem, still confused. "I was badly injured. Now there's not a mark on me."

"Indeed," remarked Dom laughing. "I would say that you were quite dead, Captain, but nothing is wrong with you now. We've taken care of that."

"But half my body was destroyed. I'm certain of it," blurted out Kalem even more surprised.

"We are not from your dimension, Captain," Dom said calmly with a mischievous smile. "Our crystalline-based science is beyond any other known science in the galaxy. Although your ship sank, we are also repairing it. Things will be clear to you in time. Master Opellum, our leader, wishes to meet you. Please come with me if you are up to it."

"Wait, Dom, you said you are Chief Scientist of the Oceanans," said Kalem, astounded, and he pondered that for a moment, then exclaimed, "Of course! That must be the connection. I know about your people. I met your leader, Opellum, once before. Admiral Starland, my father, introduced me to him and a Dren named Etta."

Dom smiled patiently, while Kalem paused in thought for a moment before he added, "But the Opellum I met had blond hair and he didn't appear to be Oceanan. Why do you and my father refer to your leader as Master Opellum?"

"Master Opellum doesn't have blond hair," remarked Dom, ignoring Kalem's second question. He grinned and took a deep breath, then stated, "You will soon discover answers to what puzzles you. Be patient and follow me."

The technician assisting Dom walked over and handed Kalem his belt with the transparent crystal laser gun already secured in the holster. Dom helped Kalem sit up and get to his feet. Kalem strapped on the holstered gun and faced Dom. The Chief Scientist looked him over to make sure he was steady, and then waved his arm invitingly toward the triangular doorway opening behind him. They walked side by side out of the lab.

Master Opellum was now in his true form. The illusion of ivory-white skin and blond hair, last created for Kalem at their first meeting aboard Starland's flagship, was gone. He was healthy looking and trim, wearing a blue and gold full-length gown belted at the waist with a gold buckle set with a large aquamarine jewel.

He was standing inside a special chamber with his back to the door, holding his crystal wand that was projecting the image of a young, beautiful Oceanan woman within a holographic sphere of light. It looked like Mayleena shortly before she disappeared while swimming outside the dome many years earlier at the age of sixteen. The moving image showed her playing in a field of flowers under the domed city. Opellum appeared melancholy as he gazed at the image.

The huge transparent dome covering the Oceanan city under the sea curved high overhead above a landing field that was visible behind Opellum through a set of large open oval windows.

On the far side of the field, two gigantic Oceanan space ships had landed on the rounded points of three spires that protruded down from the bottom half of their main blue spherical centers. A dozen additional, differently colored crystal spires, protruded outward to fine points from all around the main spheres. In the distant background was a low, curved mountain range. Three rivers running from them along their base meandered through verdant valleys to the city center and around the three pyramids to eventually empty into a large lake that bordered the landing field.

The three pyramids towered around the domed building centered in the city and the clear transport tube connected to the white dome's side that wound like a snake through the countryside. It continued past the base of the huge dome protecting the city from the great ocean depth.

Master Opellum's reverie was broken when he noticed the presence of several individuals just before they entered the room. He shut off the projection, placed the wand in his gown pocket, and turned around to greet Dom and Kalem.

"As requested, Master Opellum, I brought Captain Kalem," announced Chief Scientist Dom.

"Thank you for bringing him, Dom," replied Opellum. Then he looked at Kalem and added, "Welcome, Captain. I'm glad to see you're up and about."

Dom respectfully bowed his head toward Opellum, turned around, and left the room.

"I don't mean to sound ungrateful, but have we met before?" inquired Kalem, still puzzled. "I mean, I met a Master Opellum who looked very much like you but he didn't appear as you do now."

"Yes, Captain, we have met before," answered Opellum with a benevolent smile. "At the time it was deemed best to keep my true appearance hidden for a while. Oceanans evolved the ability to project themselves in the image or likeness of those around them if they choose. Our race used the ability more often in the early days of our space explorations as a form of self-protection. It kept the fears of many species from becoming violent when they first looked upon us. We kept the secret of our existence here on Earth from all but one of the surface dwellers, because we come from a planet in a higher parallel time dimension, Captain, located in a higher physical universe than you know about. We are here to help the surface dwellers evolve. Well, enough said about that subject for now." He paused to let this new information sink into Kalem, and then added, "Admiral Starland has been contacted and he was very relieved to know you're still actually among the living. Would you like to speak with him?"

Kalem sighed and grinned, then answered, "Of course. Thank you, Master Opellum."

The Oceanan leader reached into his robe, retrieved the crystal wand, and raised it up to chest level. It began to glow. A projected energy view screen appeared to drop down from the ceiling and Admiral Starland appeared on it standing in his control room.

"I thank The Ancient One you are alive again, Captain," remarked Starland, relieved.

"Admiral, these Oceanans have incredible technology," replied Kalem enthusiastically, ignoring the Admiral's comment about his welfare. "They actually brought me back to life. They repaired my damaged body, my clothes, and the ship."

"Master Opellum explained what happened," said the Admiral, smiling patiently back at his son, and then he more somberly stated, "Listen Captain, I have informed Master Opellum you will cooperate with him in any way possible to stop Sen Dar. It's very important that you do."

Kalem struggled to suppress anger at the mention of Sen Dar's name and proclaimed, "I'll get him, Admiral, one way or another."

"Don't let anger interfere with your judgment again, Captain," commanded Starland. "That madman has killed you once already today, remember?"

"Right!" recalled Kalem with chagrin and raised eyebrows. "I'll help any way I can."

"Master Opellum will fill you in, and Captain, be more careful," commanded Starland with a wry grin. "Well, I must attend to something. Keep in close contact. For now, farewell."

The view screen went blank and Kalem gazed respectfully for a moment at Master Opellum.

"Who was the little girl you were watching as I entered the room?" he finally asked with keen interest.

"She is Mayleena, my daughter," Opellum replied with a tinge of sadness. He paused to reflect on his memory of her, then continued, "She disappeared while swimming outside the walls of our domed city just before an earthquake on the ocean floor created a massive underwater surge and a surface tidal wave. A very important gift from The Ancient One, a crystal device, disappeared with her."

"This may sound strange," remarked Kalem, "but I'm certain I've seen her before. She has often been in my inner visions since I was about her age. Do you feel she's alive?"

"Oh, she is alive," Opellum confidently answered, curiously upbeat. "The Ancient One's guidance assured me of that long ago. Someone has her in their care, but they may not know she's Oceanan." Kalem appeared confused and Opellum added, "As I said before, Captain, we are from a higher dimension of the physical universe. Being different, we know antagonistic fear is easily stirred up in less experienced beings. When an Oceanan discovers they are in an unfamiliar alien and possibly hostile situation, they project an image in the mind of the alien that makes us appear like them. In this way, there is minimal danger whenever we make initial contact with a newly discovered sentient species. Long ago this ability evolved in all Oceanans to become as an automatic self-defense mechanism."

Encouraged, Kalem remarked, "But surely you could find your daughter in the ocean," encouraged Kalem. "You brought me back to life."

"The Ancient One's Spirit Sound and Light works the miracles through our devices, Captain," replied Opellum, sighing regretfully. "Yet, being unable thus far to find her has left us with a mystery. We looked everywhere for over a year." He inhaled deeply, let out a long relaxing breath, and then smiled. "Well, we should talk of livelier matters."

Kalem nodded agreeably, and then a sense of urgency stirred within him and he asked, "What about Sen Dar?"

"Ah-h, the evil one. Yes, we are aware of him," Opellum said flatly.

"Sen Dar will stop at nothing to get that crystal you lost. If he finds Mayleena first…," implied Kalem, intensely concerned.

"This is also my concern, Captain," confirmed Opellum, "for I have seen your destiny. You will find my daughter."

"Me?" asked Kalem surprised. "How?"

"That still remains unknown but it will happen," replied Opellum with a shrug of his shoulders. Then he added, "If you wish to pursue Sen Dar you must know where to look."

"You know where he is?" asked Kalem, raising an eyebrow.

"He landed on Atlantis near the capital city of Atla," replied Opellum. "At this moment, he is likely working his sinister plans on them. Captain, we think Sen Dar must have discovered the general location of the lost Emerald Doorway Crystal. If Mayleena is nearby she may be in danger."

Kalem sneered as he turned around to leave without thinking about his predicament, and he began to walk away, mumbling to himself, "I'll burn his evil hide to dust."

"Wait, Captain," shouted Master Opellum's commanding voice. "There is a less direct and far safer way to get to Sen Dar."

Kalem stopped in his tracks and turned around to listen.

"You must meet with Master Ra Mu. He is the keeper of the Master Crystal Staff, the third and most important mystic crystal of The Ancient One. He has a plan."

"How?" Kalem asked anxiously.

"His sanctuary is in the countryside near the capital city of Mu on the continent of Lemuria, and you must have a discreet way to get there," replied Opellum. "Long ago we inspired the surface dwellers to develop a slower type of antigravity craft for travel between the Lemurian and Atlantian continents, but they are not designed for space travel. However, my good Captain, you can get to Master Ra Mu's sanctuary a much faster way through one of our transport tubes. They give us secret access to many places on both continents, and the surface dwellers don't know they exist."

Intrigued, Kalem replied, "We have similar transport tubes on my home world of Telemadia. As I recall, it was your people, the Oceanans, that gave that and other more advanced technology to certain members of the Galactic Alliance a very long time ago."

"That is true, Captain," confirmed Opellum, pleased. "However, I think you will find our transports are somewhat more advanced. They will get you halfway around the planet in under an hour."

Opellum paused so that Kalem could realize the significance of this new information. Then he grinned with an alluring twinkle in his eyes, slightly tipped his head, and waved the upturned palm of his hand toward the triangular doorway opening.

"Come with me, Captain," he remarked, "and you will discover this by your own experience."

"Hmm, very intriguing," replied Kalem, grinning enthusiasm. "Lead the way."

Opellum walked out of the room through the doorway opening. Kalem followed close behind.

CHAPTER TWENTY-TWO

NOW THAT'S A WAY
TO GET AROUND!

An hour later, Kalem and Master Opellum were walking along a blue marble path inside an ivory-colored domed building that arched forty-feet-high. Kalem looked up through the translucent dome to see the forms of the three huge pyramids towering high in the air around the dome. Light was glinting off their quartz tips.

They continued to walk side by side to the center of the floor and stopped at green granite steps leading up to a twenty-feet-long boarding platform. A transparent transport tube began at the end of the platform, ran along the floor and out through the wall of the ivory dome. Beyond the ivory dome's curve, Kalem could see a vague image of the tube extending another mile-and-a-half to the base of the gigantic clear dome that covered the undersea city of Oceana. The tube appeared to continue some distance along the ocean floor before it disappeared in the ocean depth.

Other transport tubes could also be made out running along the ground in various places throughout the city, and some of them also appeared to exit at different points around the dome's base, winding into the distance along the sea floor.

Kalem took a moment to look at the amazing domed building he was under and beyond its wall to the images of the wondrous structures of the city of Oceana. Then he and Opellum walked up the stairs and stood on the platform near a marble monolith that extended up from the platform floor. One of the transport cars was hovering in front of the open end of the transport tube.

"I mentioned before you will not find this uncomfortable, Captain," Opellum cautioned, "but let me remind you again that watching things go by outside this type of advanced transport tube at high velocity can be very disorienting."

"I know, tightly close my eyes if I get dizzy," replied Kalem.

Opellum added, "The protection of The Ancient One will go with you on your journey, Captain."

They clasped forearms, and Kalem climbed through the open hatch of the car. Looking up, he waved his arm, and Opellum passed a hand across a control set in the center of the control monolith and it lit up. The hatch of the transport car swung down with a...*whoosh*, sealing the car airtight, and the car levitated forward and stopped after it cleared the open end of the transport tube. The end of the tube swung down and sealed. Smiling, Kalem waved his arm to signal Opellum again, nodded his head respectfully, and saluted him.

Master Opellum passed the palm of his hand back and forth over the crystal control. Each end of the double-ended transport car lit up blinking and the car shot away in a blur of light. It continued into the distance across the city, through the wall of the clear dome covering Oceana, and along the sea floor, fading away in the watery depths.

Inside the transport car, Kalem was straining to keep his eyes closed from the effects of the transport tube and outside ocean that was passing by at a tremendous speed. He opened one eye slightly to see the ocean blurring by so fast that nothing he could see was distinct. Yet, in the antigravity mode inside the car, everything was perfectly calm and still. Kalem moved his arm, looked at it, and waved it back and forth without strain. He was not experiencing any gravitational forces exerting stress on his body and he was comfortable, but Opellum had been right. He opened his eyes wide and took one quick look out through the tube. Blue light and layered streaks of ocean water were blurring by so rapidly they appeared like a river racing in the opposite direction. Kalem clamped a hand over his mouth, leaned back into the seat, and tightly closed his eyes.

While General Harry Faldwell continued to observe events unfold, he was also becoming more aware that he was witnessing hidden Earth history.

Greatly satisfied, he thought, *I am the first one, the very first one on Earth today to personally experience this part of our true history.* Elated, he mused over the realization, and then silently asked himself, *How will I ever explain any of it to the President? This whole thing is just too incredible.*

The scene changed before he could ponder the question further, and Harry found himself gazing down through ancient Earth's clear blue sky at the continent of Atlantis on the planet's western hemisphere. He could also see the domed city of Oceana resting on the ocean floor between the Atlantis continent and the larger continent of Lemuria which loomed into view from the east. Their names briefly appeared labeled above each of them in large glowing golden letters before they faded away. Then the following glowing words appeared:

Earth – 100,000 Years Ago

Harry focused more intently and found that he was able to see more clearly through the great ocean depths, revealing the tiny oval light of a transport car constantly changing colors on each end as it headed swiftly eastward toward the continent of Lemuria. A number of other transport tubes ran in various directions from the domed city of Oceana to eventually connect with many points along the coastlines of both Lemuria and Atlantis.

The tiny oval light sped halfway around the planet to Lemuria and Harry's vision instantly zoomed to a closer view of the car just as it continued underground below the largest coastal city. The following luminous letters appeared:

Mu – The Coastal Capital City of Lemuria

They faded and vanished as the car raced a short distance under the countryside and slowed.

The scene changed again, and Harry was overlooking the wide view of a beautifully landscaped garden that was set below two large hillsides connected together by an arched white stone bridge. A waterfall cascading under the bridge was dropping two thousand feet to a long lake that wound through the center of the gardens.

A moment later, he was inside a large cavern observing a blur of light speeding inside the tube the last half-mile along the cavern floor. It slowed into visibility, revealing the transport car as it continued to the platform. He could see Kalem inside the car with his eyes closed. The car moved forward several feet to the middle of the platform near the end of the tube and stopped. The blue light illuminating the tube's entire length vanished as the end of the vacuum tube swung upward, and the car moved forward out of the tube and stopped alongside the platform.

Kalem shook his head, rubbed his eyes, and slowly stood up. He steadied himself, then climbed out of the car and stepped onto the platform next to another control monolith. A set of curved rock stairs led twelve feet down to a path that headed away from the end of the transport tube. The path stopped at more carved rock stairs that ended by the base of a rock wall at the back of the cavern. He jogged down the platform stairs, along the path, and up the stairs to the rock wall. Then he passed the palm of his hand over a domed shaped crystal set in the cavern wall and the wall vanished. Sunlight streamed through the opening and Kalem shielded his eyes from the intense light before he walked through it to embrace the outside world.

Carved rock steps led down into darkness through an opening in the side of a large boulder. Kalem stepped up into view and onto grass that circled the boulder. Amazed, he looked past the grass to behold a spectacular display of lush botanical gardens extending in every direction. All of the tropical plant life was well cared for and artfully designed. Large exotic flowers were everywhere, in every imaginable color and in full bloom.

He looked to his left past the grass to rock steps that ascended high up the side of a tropical grass-and-fern-covered hillside to an arched white stone bridge. It connected to another equally tall hillside further to his left in the near distance. A wide waterfall reflecting sparkling sunlight was roaring under the bridge. The thunderous water was dropping two thousand feet into a long lake that was nestled at the base of the valley between the two hills. The mountainous hills gradually rose higher as they receded into the background beyond the plateau. Kalem walked over to the wide steps leading up the hillside and stopped. Wondering what to do next, he gazed around at the gardens until he heard a young girl's voice calling down to him from far above on the steps.

"Captain Kalem, up here," yelled the voice of a cheerfully excited young girl.

Kalem looked up to see a young long-blond-haired girl about ten years old wearing sandals and a maroon monk's robe belted at the waist with a simple rope. She was excitedly waving her arms as she jogged from the top of the stairs in leaps and bounds down the steps. Kalem jogged up the stairs to meet her.

A short time later, they walked toward each other on the four-foot-wide platform break situated halfway up the hillside. The friendly little girl took Kalem's hand into both her hands and smiled brightly up at him.

"Well, hello. Who are you?" Kalem asked fondly.

"I'm Juja, Captain Kalem, one of Master Ra Mu's students. He asked me to lead you to his sanctuary," she said, a little out of breath.

"I would be delighted to follow anyone as pretty as you," he remarked.

"Thank you, Captain," she replied, blushing.

Chuckling, Kalem added, "Just Kalem will do, Juja."

"Come on, Kalem, we must hurry," she insisted, and she pulled on his hand until he began to jog with her up the rock stairs toward the arched bridge.

CHAPTER TWENTY-THREE

DECEPTION OF STRALIM
ON
ATLANTIS

At mid-afternoon, the view through the dozen open windows surrounding the interior of an oval room revealed a beautiful clear blue sky outside above the capital city of Atla on the Lemurian colony continent of Atlantis. Evenly dispersed in the jungle valley, and along the surrounding hills and ridge tops, were many palatial dwellings. The oval shaped palace built upon the tallest hill overlooking the flower-laden jungle city was still twenty feet above the tips of the pyramids glistening in the sunlight. They protruded just above the tops of the jungle trees that towered hundreds of feet above the deep valley floor. A mile away on the horizon, a deep, blue ocean was crashing gracefully on the glistening fine emerald sands.

Eleven men of various ages, dressed in long flowing robes of differing colors, were seated in intricately carved and highly polished dark wood chairs placed evenly around a green marble table centered in the room. A scale model of Atla filled the tabletop.

High Seer Stralim, now in his mid-sixties, still appeared physically trim and dignified as he stood at the far end of the table. The symbol of a gold disc etched with a radiant eye, set above a quartz-tipped gold pyramid hung from a gold chain around his neck. He addressed the men sitting around the table with an eloquent formal voice.

"I was chosen High Seer less than thirty years ago by the esteemed

Council members in this room. Atla on Atlantis has now grown in stature and wealth almost equal to that of our great capital city of Mu on the motherland of Lemuria. We're nearly independent in our own right."

He paused to let the effect of his statement sink in.

"My friends," he continued, smiling graciously, "the time has now come for us to plan a new direction for Atlantis. I have had a vision and it is my belief that Atlantis, like a child that grows to a man, must eventually stand on its own feet."

One of the elder Councilmen stood up to address Stralim. He was slightly bald in his sixties and a little rotund. Stralim nodded his head toward the Councilman.

"Elder Councilman Melnor is acknowledged," Stralim respectfully stated.

"High Seer Stralim and fellow Council members," eloquently began Melnor, while freely using his hands to emphasize his points, "we have talked about this new direction before. I feel such a change at this particular time would only bring divisiveness and estrangement from the motherland. This could cause strife when the entire world is finally enjoying a golden age. Why risk destroying it?"

He was about to make another remark when a scuffling noise in the hallway behind the conference room interrupted him. Sen Dar's voice from just beyond the open conference room doors sounded as if he was in great pain.

"I must see High Seer Stralim," he yelled out and coughed, then gasped for breath and yelled louder, "You must take me to him. You must!"

"Guards, what's going on out there?" Stralim demanded.

Two Atlantian guards tightly held Sen Dar's upper arms as they stepped into the room. Sen Dar's face was scratched, his clothes were torn, and he appeared completely exhausted.

In contrast, the tight-fitting, finely woven uniforms of the guards, wearing light blue silk gowns that came down just below their knees, laced leather-like boots that extended below the hem of their uniforms, and belts with a gold buckle etched with the same symbol Stralim wore on the gold chain around his neck, made him look badly mistreated.

The shorter guard held in his free left hand an Atlantian foot-long stun weapon pointed at Sen Dar's head. The taller guard was holding Sen Dar's laser gun in his free right hand with it pointed down at his side. He bowed his head respectfully toward the High Seer.

"High Seer Stralim," he began, "we found him at the foot of the trail heading toward your Council chambers with this weapon in his hand."

The taller guard held out Sen Dar's laser weapon for Stralim's inspection. Stralim walked over and took the laser gun, looked quizzically at it, then placed it on the table behind him so all of the other Council members could see it. The shorter guard bowed his head toward Stralim to address him.

"We apologize for disturbing the Council," he began, "but he's a stranger with some kind of weapon."

"You have both acted correctly," stated Stralim and he relaxed and smiled. "You may release him."

Sen Dar limped across the room and pretended to collapse on the floor face down at High Seer Stralim's feet. He slipped his hand inside his shirt and gripped the Transport Matrix Crystal of The Ancient One. Then he groaned as if in terrible pain, and the two guards helped him back up to his feet. The crystal grasped tightly in his hand glowed briefly through the pink translucent skin of his fingers as he looked up at Stralim, who was gazing rather annoyed back down at him.

"Who are you? What's your business with this Council?" demanded Stralim.

Sen Dar did not answer as he looked deeply into Stralim's eyes, and the High Seer's stern gaze transformed to a mesmerized stare. Then he began to smile cordially.

Sen Dar nodded his head respectfully as he removed his clenched fist from the crystal hidden inside the folds of his shirt. Then he grimaced as if he were having sudden pain again and feigned exhaustion by falling limp into the guard's arms.

"I am Beel, most High Seer Stralim," Sen Dar said with a forlorn look.

"Well, Beel, where do you come from, may I ask?" inquired the Atlantian leader with friendly encouragement.

"Where?" queried Sen Dar, looking painfully distraught as he hesitantly answered, "Why, I... I come from Lemuria, of course. I was one of Master Ra Mu's disciples and eventually became his most trusted advisor. Then one day, I overheard a conversation between a military advisor and that criminal Ra Mu. They are planning to overthrow Atlantis by force."

He sighed and pretended to collapse again, but the taller guard grabbed his arm and pulled him back up. Then he appeared to steady himself, sighed again, and lowered his head.

"I was caught by one of Ra Mu's sentries." He contorted his face to appear to be in pain. "Ra Mu beat me unconscious and then had me thrown over a cliff in the middle of the night. Fortunately, the large branch of an old tree growing out of the cliff wall stopped my fall."

Elder Councilman Melnor jumped to his feet, pointing an accusing finger at Sen Dar.

"I don't believe a word this man just said," he stammered and continued waving his accusing finger. "Master Ra Mu has encouraged practical autonomy for Atlantis and our people from its very beginning. He was also one of my teachers as a child but I don't remember you, Beel."

"Let this man speak," commanded Stralim, ignoring Melnor's remarks. Then he smiled compassionately at Sen Dar and said, "Please, go on, Beel. I find this very intriguing."

Sen Dar pretended to choke, gasped for air, and then began to portray a painful emotional memory. "I was found by two of my people the next morning caught in the branch of the old tree. They rescued me and brought me here, hidden in a boat."

All the Council members, except Melnor, appeared shocked.

"I feel an evil presence coming from this...faker!" blurted out Melnor. "He will destroy us all. Let me confront Master Ra Mu with him, and then we will all see who is the deceiver."

Sen Dar pretended again to collapse in pain, and the two guards grasped his arms more tightly, then firmly lifted him up as he pleaded, "High Seer Stralim, there is no time. You must listen to me or it will be too late."

Stralim inquired kindly, "What proof did you bring to us to support your accusations, Beel?"

"High Seer Stralim, may I demonstrate?" replied Sen Dar, portraying a painful exhale, as he pointed at the table and added, "That device on the table was constructed by Ra Mu himself."

Stralim and the other Council members were appalled and intrigued, but Melnor shook his head, fuming.

"You may proceed, Beel," said Stralim.

The two guards cautiously let go of Sen Dar's arms, and he took several shaky steps and stopped. Then he walked weakly over to the table, picked up the laser gun, pointed it at Melnor's chair and fired. The chair sizzled for an instant as it completely disintegrated. Startled, Melnor jumped back a few feet from where he stood, and the other Council members simultaneously jumped up out of their seats and retreated a few steps.

"How did you happen to come by this weapon after being caught in a branch all night?" demanded Melnor.

"I discovered these devices were to be built into their Colonial Transports," replied Sen Dar, appearing quite sincere. "I needed proof of Ra Mu's treachery before coming here, so I had my people steal several weapons and bury them outside of Ra Mu's so-called sanctuary. They retrieved them and gave them to me before they hid me in the boat that brought me in secret to your shore."

He looked at Stralim and continued, "I saw a Colonial Transport fly over the city as your guards were bringing me here. I asked the guards if Atlantians still call them by the same name as Lemurians, and more importantly if there were as many here as on Lemuria. They replied you still call them that, and that about the same number are on both continents. Now that the power of Atlantis nearly equals that of Lemuria, I knew we would have a chance. High Seer Stralim, there is still time for you to remain free. Their ships have not been completely outfitted with these weapons."

Sen Dar walked over to the scale model of the capital city of Atla spread across the tabletop and pointed to it.

"They plan to attack the city's perimeter wall and destroy it first," continued Sen Dar as he placed both hands on the table to steady himself. "Their hope is that you will give up without bloodshed. High Seer Stralim, you must attack first in full force or you are all doomed!"

"How does this Council vote?" asked Stralim as he turned around to look at all the other Council members standing around the room. "Do we defend ourselves or become slaves?"

"We must protect ourselves," yelled out one Councilman," stepping forward with a raised fist in the air.

"I agree, we must protect our freedom and our families at any cost," remarked another as he too stepped forward.

"What's wrong with all of you?" yelled Melnor. "Listen to reason. Master Ra Mu should first be confronted with this man and his absurd story."

The other Council members ignored Melnor's remark in the heat of emotion, for they did not notice Sen Dar pretending again to have chest pain as he grabbed the crystal inside his shirt with his clenched fist. Muted discussions circulating around the room heated up like an out-of-control emotional cyclone. Then the Council members suddenly stopped talking and stood up. They looked at each other in silent full agreement, believing their minds were actually under their own control. Except for Melnor, they each voted one by one by a show of hands to strike first.

While Harry Faldwell continued to observe events unfold from his invisible Atma viewpoint, he also perceived that Melnor was somehow unaffected by Sen Dar's misuse of The Ancient One's crystal. Then he understood that although Melnor received spiritual training from Master Ra Mu during his youth he remained unaware the training actually made him immune to such spells.

"I'll have nothing further to do with this...this treachery!" yelled Melnor in disgust. Then he turned toward Stralim and stated bitterly, "It would seem some of you have more in mind than simple freedom and independence for Atlantis. You are all contemptible and I leave this Council against this action."

He walked out of the room in a huff, while everyone else except Sen Dar, ignored him.

"Then this Council meeting is over. Tomorrow we must begin to prepare for war," announced Stralim with an air of finality.

He nodded toward the Council members and they nodded back and filed out of the room, followed by the two guards.

Sen Dar was now smiling arrogantly, but his expression instantly changed to feigned exhaustion as Stralim turned to him.

"Beel, can you help us build these devices into our crafts?" he asked.

"I did manage to obtain several devices," replied Sen Dar, and he sighed in pretend pain, smiled weakly, and continued, "Based on them, I believe I could have your scientists construct more. If we work quickly, in several days we could have the transports prepared to strike first and win victory."

"We must discuss your plan further," replied Stralim. "But first, you need refreshment and medical attention. Please follow me."

Stralim waved an open palm toward the doors and then walked ahead of Sen Dar, who smiled seductively at the back of his head as he stepped up behind him. Then his smile became a leering grin.

These Earth people are so easily deceived, he thought. *Now I have all the time I need to find the Emerald Doorway Crystal. It has to be somewhere in the palace.*

He hurried up beside High Seer Stralim's side and smiled meekly at him to get his attention. Then he put his palm over his chest again to feign pain and hobbled along beside him. They walked slowly together through the open Council room doors and along a short blue marble hallway floor, then down a set of matching blue marble steps.

CHAPTER TWENTY-FOUR

LEMURIA, RA MU AND KALEM'S MISSION

$\mathcal{T}$he blue marble pillars supporting the arched entryway of the bridge, along with the open arches of its inside walls and curved ceiling, were intricately carved with the likenesses of many former Adepts of The Ancient One. Several of the columns had Galactic Alliance Scout Class Interceptors etched into them.

Captain Kalem was looking at the carvings of the ships with keen interest when Juja tugged on his hand to get his attention.

"These are the records of the Masters of The Ancient One dating back many thousands of years," she stated, grinning with pride. "Master Ra Mu is Guardian of the Golden Wisdom Temple hidden in the hillside at the other side of the bridge. It's our sanctuary."

"Lead the way, Juja," Kalem replied, intrigued.

They began to walk slowly over the bridge and Kalem paused midway to look at the valley far below. He gazed through the open arch between two round pillars to behold a spectacular panorama of lush tropical terrain covering rolling hills that continued into the distant horizon. Then he leaned out through the arched opening and gazed down at the thunderous water roaring below the bridge to drop far below to the lake that divided the botanical gardens in half. He could see the large boulder with its open secret entrance to the underground transport platform in the center of the garden. Then his eyes followed

248

the wide carved rock steps that began at the edge of the clearing and ascended the hillside to the arched bridge.

Juja broke his reverie by anxiously pulling on his right wrist with her hands. Kalem smiled kindly down at her as he took one of her little hands into his and they continued to walk the rest of the way over the bridge. They stopped at a set of carved ivory doors embedded with many gems. Juja walked up to the doors and bowed, and the doors vanished, leaving a triangular opening. Master Ra Mu stepped through it, firmly gripping his crystal staff in his right hand.

He nodded, smiling, and said graciously, "Welcome, Captain."

"I'm honored to meet the keeper of The Ancient One's Master Crystal Staff," Kalem replied respectfully with a slight nod. "I'm told you have a plan for flushing out Sen Dar."

Master Ra Mu grinned and replied, "Come with me, Captain." He walked back inside the hill through the triangular opening. Kalem and Juja stepped inside behind him, and the ivory doors instantly reappeared.

Kalem and Master Ra Mu were standing near a low table in a dimly lit room, making it hard for them to see the full size of the chamber. Incense was burning on two blue marble tables behind them. A circle of twelve blue stone pillars streaked with gold veins surrounded the room though they did not appear to be supporting anything. Indistinct pyramid shapes were resting on the flat top of each stone pillar.

Ra Mu raised his staff a foot off the ground and it glowed along its entire length with soft green light, brightening the room. The four walls slanted inward toward each other as they rose past the tops of the pillars into the darkness beyond sight. Kalem thought they appeared to converge at a point somewhere far above their heads, and he could now clearly see that the pyramid shapes atop each pillar were actually miniature crystal pyramids. The light coming from Ra Mu's staff passing through each one was radiating a spherical halo of rainbow light, causing the gold veins within the pillars to glitter like a million twinkling stars. Awe-struck, Kalem looked around the room as a new realization awakened within him.

"This whole hillside must cover a gigantic pyramid."

"Why yes, Captain, so it does," responded Master Ra Mu, pleased with Kalem's insight. "You're very observant. This particular pyramid was carefully constructed long ago to sustain life indefinitely."

Kalem pondered the information for a moment while he observed Ra Mu's firm, trim build and his healthy youthful appearance.

"How old are you?" Kalem asked humbly.

"My age does not matter, Captain," replied Ra Mu. "What does is that Sen Dar has the Transport Matrix Crystal of The Ancient One. The longer he has any of the mystic crystals in his possession, the greater will be the increase of his occult powers."

"Mayleena," blurted out Kalem.

"Exactly," replied Master Ra Mu, matching his concern. "This treacherous Sen Dar may soon discover her before we do."

"What's your plan?" asked Kalem.

"Several days ago, a Lemurian diplomat named Aeron unexpectedly died. He was to deliver a message of goodwill to the High Seer of Atlantis in celebration of the people's soon-to-come independence. They will be expecting him, but none there have ever met him." He confidently grinned, and added, "You, Captain, will become Aeron."

Hmm, Kalem pondered, *it just might work.*

Master Ra Mu became somber as he continued. "You will likely find Sen Dar weaving his spell around High Seer Stralim to gain the time he needs to find the second crystal. You must find Mayleena and the crystal he stole from Master Nim before he accomplishes his goal."

Kalem winced. "What could happen if he found her first?"

Master Ra Mu looked away and sighed. Then he looked back at Kalem and said, "If he joins the two crystals together, his powers will greatly increase, and the future of Earth will be in very serious jeopardy. Will you help?"

"Of course," said Kalem, "we're wasting time."

"I knew we could count on you, Captain," remarked Ra Mu, quite pleased. "Now hold perfectly still. This won't hurt."

Ra Mu stepped back a few feet, raised his staff a little higher off the floor, and the green light brightened, lighting up the room. Then a blue light beam flecked with gold shot from the Ankh symbol atop the staff and enveloped Kalem's head. In seconds, a full, trimmed beard appeared, and his hair lengthened to his shoulders.

Kalem grasped the beard with his hands, felt his longer hair, and asked, astonished, "How did you pull that off?"

"The Master Crystal Staff has many functions that Sen Dar will not find written on the stolen parchment," Ra Mu replied.

Juja walked into the room carrying an armful of clothing. She smiled, gracefully bowed toward Ra Mu, and raised her head.

"Thank you, Juja," acknowledged Ra Mu.

She beamed a radiant smile, and Master Ra Mu waved his hand toward the clothes.

"Put these on, Captain. You can leave your uniform with me for now."

"Okay, fine. But I'm strapping my weapon on underneath," stated Kalem.

Ra Mu nodded and Kalem unbuckled his belt with the holstered laser gun, and then dropped it on the table by his side. He started to undress while Juja placed the clothes she was holding on the table. She looked up to notice Kalem undressing and put a hand to her mouth, giggling as she ran from the room.

"Are you sure this will work?" Kalem asked dubiously.

"The Ancient One's Spirit Sound and Light underlying and giving existence to all life is with you now, Captain," replied Master Ra Mu. "Can you hear it?"

Kalem closed his eyes and strained to listen. Then he heard the faraway sound of a hauntingly beautiful flute melody mixed with the soft buzzing resembling millions of bees and the subtle crashing of ocean waves. Simultaneously, a brilliant golden light started as a pinprick within his inner vision. It grew rapidly to extreme intensity, and he squinted his closed eyes. Then the Sound and Light suddenly faded away, and Kalem took a deep breath, let it out, and opened his eyes wide, grinning with pleasure.

"I heard what sounded like a very high flute melody blended with a deep humming and ocean waves," he replied softly. "This may sound odd, but it seemed to me it was coming from inside and outside myself at the same time. With the Sound came a point of Light that began in my inner vision and expanded so brilliantly I almost couldn't stand it."

"That is correct," Ra Mu remarked, placing a hand on Kalem's shoulder. "You were just given an awakening initiation by The Ancient One's omnipresent living energy presence. From now on, Captain, follow your instincts."

By early afternoon, golden sunlight was shining on the flattened hilltop clearing above Ra Mu's hidden pyramid sanctuary. A short distance below the sanctuary hilltop was a round metal door set in the face of a large boulder. A rock stairway led from the opening twenty feet up to the clearing.

Using his crystal staff as a walking stick, Master Ra Mu strolled by Kalem's side up the last few steps of the stairway near the edge of the clearing.

Kalem was now wearing a snug-fitting, blue silken robe that came down just below his knees, matching pants underneath it, and leather sandals. The top of the robe around his neck opened in a thin V-shaped gold collar with two narrow gold bands embroidered around the edge and around the end of each long sleeve. An oval dark-blue polished stone clasped his green belt around his waist. An ancient gold symbol embossed upon the buckle's surface signified that Lemuria was the motherland of humanity on Earth.

A Colonial Transport had landed on the clearing a few feet away from them. It appeared to be an air-ship shaped like an eagle's body with slanted curved wings and a horizontal tail with feathers painted on it. However, there was no rudder, propeller, or exhaust system. The craft had extended claws for landing gear and a clear curved cockpit window on the upper front end of the fuselage.

An oval door opened in its side and the Lemurian pilot swung a small set of metal stairs down to the ground. He was wearing clothing similar to Kalem's but designed more simply without gold stripes and a thin brown leather belt was clasped snug around his waist. The pilot climbed down the aircraft's stairs and walked up to Kalem and Master Ra Mu.

"Master Ra Mu, as you requested, the Colonial Transport is ready for flight," he stated and respectfully bowed.

"Thank you, Montoc," replied Ra Mu. "Please take Diplomat Aeron to Atla. Drop him off near the trail below the High Seer's Council chambers and return. Talk with no one."

"It will be done as you wish, Master," acknowledged Montoc with a nod.

He grinned at Kalem, walked back to the transport, climbed the stairs, and stood inside the open door to wait for his passenger.

"It will be far safer if you arrive secretly," encouraged Master Ra Mu. "Perhaps that will also give you time to talk with some of the local people along the way to Stralim's hilltop chambers. They may be able to provide valuable information about Sen Dar."

Kalem looked at the Lemurian Transport, scratched his chin with his fingers, and asked, "Hmm, this thing actually flies?"

"Colonial Transports are not designed for space travel," replied Ra Mu with a chuckle. "However, they have special antigravity porcelain engines with no moving parts, and they do not pollute the environment. It will get you there quite safely, Captain."

Kalem shrugged and extended his arm, and Ra Mu clasped forearms with him. Then Kalem walked over to the steps leading up inside the airship and stopped to turn around, grinning. He saluted Ra Mu, and Master Ra Mu smiled confidently back at him and nodded. Then Kalem hopped up the ladder, turned around, and waved his hand, before entering the ship. Montoc pulled the ladder up inside and closed the door.

Master Ra Mu watched the Colonial Transport as it emitted a faint whirring hum and lifted straight up fifty feet. With a smile and his staff held extended at arm's length in his right hand, he stood majestically poised while he observed the Lemurian airship speed gracefully through the air above the countryside, headed toward the coast.

The transport was a mile from Ra Mu when it passed over the tops of three white alabaster pyramids. Two of the pyramids were gold-crowned and quartz-tipped, but the top third of the other one was flat and another Colonial Transport was landed on its surface. The majestic pyramids towered above vast numbers of artfully designed palatial homes built along the lush jungle-covered countryside.

As the transport flew past the pyramids over smaller blue domed structures and golden minaret towers, sunlight glistened and glittered off the hillside homes made from natural crystals and colorful stones. The transport soon diminished in the distance over the city, passing over the tall jungle forest. It headed toward the ocean another half-mile away where long graceful waves were curling to break on the fine black sands of the curved half-moon bay.

Montoc was sitting in a cushioned chair behind a control panel at the cockpit window. He was operating simple levers to control the transport's flight. Kalem was standing behind him staring through the window at the jungle city passing by a thousand feet below them. The gold spiral towers, blue domed buildings, and palatial estates thinned as the ship passed beyond the thick jungle trees.

Kalem pondered something as the Colonial Transport flew over the long curl of a sunlit wave that crashed on the glittering black sands of the beach.

"How long before we arrive, Montoc?" he inquired.

"Late afternoon," answered Montoc. "When we arrive over the coast of Atlantis, I will set the transport down in the trees not far from the capital city of Atla. We can land there without being seen by any lookout guards that may be posted on the hidden perimeter wall that surrounds the city."

"Right," Kalem agreed, looking every bit the part of a diplomat as he gazed out the window toward the horizon.

The black sands of the peninsula and the three glistening golden pyramids centered in the capital city of Mu rapidly receded in the distance and vanished as the speed of the Colonial Transport increased over the open ocean.

CHAPTER TWENTY-FIVE

A RAT IN THE ROAD
TO
ROMANTIC DESTINY

The panoramic view from a slightly lower jungle hilltop, opposite the one upon which High Seer Stralim's chambers rested revealed the pyramids towering just above the tops of the deep valley of tropical forest trees. Many golden spiral towers and blue-domed buildings laced throughout the jungle countryside comprised the capital city of Atla on Atlantis. Past the edge of the forest and beyond prying eyes was the curve of the emerald-green volcanic sands of the Atlantian coastline.

A Colonial Transport appeared in the distant sky over the ocean and grew steadily larger as it flew over the coast through an opening in the tall jungle trees. It continued inland and then hovered, before it quietly lowered below the tree line and landed in a small clearing.

Kalem opened the door in the side of the transport and jumped to the ground. He waved to Montoc who smiled and waved back. Then the airship quietly lifted above the treetops and flew back over the shoreline headed out over the ocean.

The beginning of a footpath a short distance away from Kalem ran into a narrow field of exotic flowers surrounded by a lush, vine-laden tropical jungle. The path continued through the middle of the field a hundred feet before it disappeared in the tall jungle trees. Kalem jogged along the path and disappeared in the thick forest vines.

He emerged from a cluster of the trees a short time later as he parted a thick wall of vines. He continued along the path through the middle of a wide field of large tropical flowers and stopped when he saw the back of a very attractive figure of a young woman. He could see her long blond hair as she raised her head up from bending over in the lush flowers. She had a small bundle of them she had already picked tucked under her right arm. Kalem noticed she was barefoot and dressed in Atlantian spring attire, a lovely formfitting, delicate flower-laced dress that came down just below her knees.

She had her back to him and did not notice as he walked quietly toward her and stopped ten feet from where she stood.

"Hello there," he said softly with a friendly voice.

Startled, the woman jumped around, placing a hand over her heart and gasped.

"Where did you come from?"

She looked remarkably like Mayleena, but there were no indications of blue skin or other Oceanan characteristics.

"Please, don't be afraid," he replied quickly with his palms out, motioning her to be calm. "I prefer to travel discreetly, so I was dropped off in the woods by a Colonial Transport. I am seeking the palace of the High Seer. Can you point the way?"

"Why do you seek the High Seer?" she asked cautiously, recovering her composure.

"I'm a diplomat from Lemuria. I was told there will be a reception in my honor," he replied.

"You are Diplomat Aeron," said the woman, suddenly pleased.

"Yes, I am, but how did you know that?" asked Kalem, smiling fondly.

"I've heard about you," she replied. "Please forgive me for saying this, but somehow you look so familiar to me." She pointed to the building on the hilltop and asked, "Do you see the hilltop building just beyond the tips of the pyramids?"

Sunlight glinted off the windows surrounding the outer circumference of the structure, but Kalem did not notice. His eyes never looked away from the lovely feminine vision in front of him, and he continued to stare at her beyond his conscious will as he took a step closer. Their intense gaze met as she slowly lowered her arm holding the flowers. Then she gazed deeply back into Kalem's eyes, and his smile became a wide grin. He was staring passionately into her beautiful green eyes, spellbound in a moment beyond time by their mutual attraction.

"Will you walk with me?" he found himself asking her in a most natural manner.

She took a step toward him as if they had been on intimately familiar terms for eternity, and Kalem blinked as if coming out of a trance.

"Excuse me," he chuckled, "but I don't know your name."

"Oh, I'm Layliella," she replied, blushing a radiant smile.

They stood entranced a foot apart, while something ancient stirred within their hearts. Without thinking, Kalem took her hand and kissed it with such natural sincerity that she blushed again but did not take her eyes off him.

"You're not at all what I expected, Diplomat Aeron," she commented with a very pleased alluring smile.

"In what way?" Kalem asked.

"Most diplomats are older and they are not so... so handsome," she answered as she looked shyly down at the ground and then back up at him.

"And you are very beautiful, Layliella," he responded without hesitation.

"Follow me, Aeron, and I'll guide you to the chamber of the High Seer myself," she encouraged with another alluring grin.

An hour later they were walking along an increasing incline in the path that wound upward another ten feet to a cluster of jungle trees, draped by a thick wall of dark-green vines with large fan-shaped leaves. They approached the vines and Layliella parted them with her hand. She stepped through the opening into bright sunlight and Kalem followed behind her.

Kalem found himself standing next to Layliella on another path that ran twenty-five yards further to the Council chamber building of the High Seer. The chamber appeared to be made of white marble flecked with mica that sparkled and glittered in the bright sunlight. Marble pillars surrounding the outside structure supported a curved canopy made of a clear, blue, glass-like material. The dozen oval windows surrounding the outside of the chamber were open swung upward. Layliella and Kalem walked a few more feet and then stopped on the path.

"Have you always lived in the city of Atla here on Atlantis?" he inquired.

"Well, I'm not quite sure," she replied, puzzled.

"Please, we should talk," he said eagerly, gesturing with a hand toward the thick green grass lining the pathway. They walked over and sat down on it to more comfortably converse.

With a troubled frown, Layliella began, "I was a very young woman when my father found me unconscious. My body had washed up on the shore after a huge storm, and after he revived me, I was unable to

256

remember my name or where I came from. There was a bump on my head, so I must have hit something or something hit me."

She laughed softly to lighten the mood.

"Wait a minute," interrupted Kalem. "Did you just say you were washed up on shore as a little girl?"

"Yes, but why do you ask?" she inquired.

"Were you wearing anything unusual?"

Blushing, she looked at the ground and replied, "Actually, I wasn't wearing very much of anything except this."

She pulled out the emerald crystal suspended from a gold chain she had hidden inside the folds of her dress. Kalem's eyes lit upon it with intense interest, and he looked around anxiously to see if anyone was watching them.

"Put it away, quickly," he commanded nervously.

"But why?" she inquired.

"Does anyone else know you have this?" he asked.

"Only Stralim, my father," she replied, concerned.

Surprised, Kalem asked, "High Seer Stralim is your father? He found you on the beach that day?"

Her pained and puzzled eyes widened as she answered softly, "Yes, he raised me as his own."

"Did anyone try to find out who you were, your name or anything else about you?"

She paused to reflect as a deep careworn expression formed.

"Well, no," she finally replied. "Stralim's wife and little girl had died in an unfortunate accident many years earlier. He said to me that I looked remarkably like his very own child and over the years I have grown to love him as a father."

Kalem gently grabbed Layliella's arm with great interest.

"Layliella, listen to me closely. This is very important. Has any stranger appeared on Atlantis recently? Has Stralim been approached by anyone out of the ordinary?"

She looked thoughtfully away, and then replied, deeply concerned, "Yes, Beel. He came to us several days ago with an incredibly absurd story, something about Master Ra Mu wanting to take over Atlantis now that we're prosperous and about to become officially independent."

"Describe this Beel," Kalem asked urgently. "What's he like?"

"Well, he's tall and thin with high cheekbones, a long narrow nose, and long black hair," she began, growing leerier by the second. "The guards found him wearing strange, old torn clothing and a long, black cape.

He looked as if someone had beaten or tortured him and claimed Master Ra Mu was responsible. But I don't believe a word of it and I don't trust him."

"It has to be Sen Dar," blurted out Kalem.

"Who?" she inquired, confused.

"Never mind," he insisted. "Does Stralim believe his story?"

She looked away thoughtfully and then gazed into his eyes.

"In some strange way Beel is very persuasive. I think my father feels that it's possible."

"Where is this Beel now?" he asked, suppressing anger.

"He's in the Council chamber with Stralim."

She gazed at him with worried, questioning eyes.

"Listen, Layliella," he said quickly, "I must tell you who I really am."

Before he could say another word, High Seer Stralim interrupted them calling from the open Council chamber doors.

"Layliella, who is your guest?"

Kalem and Layliella looked up to see Stralim and Sen Dar standing just outside the Council chamber. Sen Dar was dressed in the regal Atlantian attire of a blue and green silk gown tied at the waist with a matching silk rope. Comfortable slip-on leather shoes clad his feet. As Stralim and Sen Dar headed in their direction, Layliella and Kalem rose to their feet, stepped back onto the path, and walked toward them.

"Father, this is Diplomat Aeron from Lemuria," remarked Layliella with an air of excited pleasure.

"You are most welcome, Aeron," said Stralim, appearing quite pleased as he reached his arm toward Kalem. "We have long awaited your arrival to consecrate our coming independence celebration."

Kalem clasped forearms with him and nodded respectfully, but when he looked up, he could not stop from staring into Sen Dar's eyes, as Sen Dar stood stoically behind Stralim.

Stralim noticed Kalem's intense gaze over his shoulder and proclaimed, "This is Beel from your homeland, Aeron. He has informed me that he was Counselor to Master Ra Mu himself."

Kalem clasped forearms with Sen Dar and squeezed his arm too hard. Sen Dar recoiled nervously, yanking his arm away.

"Oh really? Now that is odd," replied Kalem with an antagonistic edge, and he added, "I've never heard of you. Did Stralim say your name is Beel?"

"Yes, Counselor Beel," answered Sen Dar calmly, and he grinned. "Don't be puzzled, Aeron. My relationship with Master Ra Mu has always been a closely guarded secret."

"Oh, I'm not puzzled at all," shot back Kalem with raised eyebrows and a sarcastic smile, "not in the least."

Sen Dar's grin dropped to a cold blank stare, and High Seer Stralim stepped between them to break the ice.

"Come gentlemen," he encouraged, "we're all friends here." He smiled at them and added, "You will both want to refresh yourselves for tonight...we celebrate!"

Stralim waved his arm toward the Council chamber. Kalem smiled at Layliella and gallantly offered her his arm. She looked with delight back at him, wrapped her arm around his, and they walked arm in arm past Stralim and Sen Dar toward the Council chamber doors.

Stralim and Sen Dar walked side by side a few feet behind them. Then Sen Dar slowed a little to let Stralim continue ahead of him, and his face changed to anger as he stared at the back of Kalem's head. Stralim glanced back at Sen Dar, but a very polite smile instantly formed on his face before their eyes met. Stralim appeared briefly puzzled but shook it off, just as Kalem and Layliella entered the Council chamber. Then he entered followed close behind by Sen Dar, who was angrily squeezing his hands held at his sides into tightly clenched fists.

Night arrived several hours later, and a celebration was taking place inside a much larger lavish ballroom built partially down inside the hilltop, a level below Stralim's Council room chambers. The upper oval floor level was set with an intricate flower-pattern mosaic in dark-blue granite tiles. Three steps led from it down to a lower oval performance floor. The unadorned tiles continued over the surface of the lower floor around a golden symbol set in its center. This was the same Atlantian symbol – an Egyptian-looking eye suspended above a golden pyramid – that the High Seer always wore on the gold chain around his neck.

Tall blue stone pillars laced with gold supported the ceiling. Tapered rods, extending at a slant upward from mountings in the pillars, ended in glass-like-covered incandescent torches that brilliantly lit the room, highlighting beautifully woven tapestries hung from the walls that depicted historical nature scenes.

Six Atlantian musicians were standing on a slightly raised platform at the far end of the room. They were playing a beautiful melody called *The Salutation to the Sun* on unusual stringed and woodwind instruments. Several dozen couples in lavish Atlantian attire were standing around the edge of the floor. They were watching six elegantly dressed men and women just finishing *The Salutation to the Sun* dance.

Kalem exuded a diplomatic air when he and the High Seer entered the ballroom, just as the music and dancing ended, and Stralim smiled at everyone around the room.

With the upturned palm of his hand extended toward Kalem, he cheerfully announced, "I now present to you our guest of honor from Lemuria, Diplomat Aeron."

Everyone in the ballroom nodded respectfully toward Kalem. Then they politely applauded him as the music and the dance resumed with a lively musical composition titled, *The Elegance of Spring*.

Layliella entered the ballroom through an arched doorway opposite the one through which Kalem and Stralim made their appearance. Like an exquisitely beautiful Atlantian princess, she was dressed in an iridescent violet, flowing evening gown. Smiling radiantly, she curtsied gracefully toward Kalem and nodded toward Stralim. Kalem's eyes were alight with deep appreciation and he boldly walked down the three steps, crossed the middle of the ballroom floor between several dancing couples, and continued up the steps to Layliella's side. He took her arm into his, and she blushed a wide smile of appreciation.

Stralim was suddenly very displeased as he gazed at them from the opposite side of the ballroom floor. He turned around in a huff and left the room.

Smiling with clenched teeth, Kalem said to Layliella, barely moving his lips, "I must talk with you in private."

"We can walk onto the balcony," she replied sweetly.

They walked arm in arm across the upper floor, through an archway, and onto a roofless balcony under the star-filled sky. A crescent moon was rising on the horizon below the brilliant celestial heavens. It shone through the balcony that extended in a curve twenty feet out from the hillside. A green marble wall surrounded the balcony, and six open arches connected a dozen marble columns that extended above the top of the wall.

They continued to walk to the other side of the balcony and stopped in front of the middle archway between two of the seven open archways that topped the balcony's outer wall. Together, they gazed out through the opening to behold the spectacular view of the surrounding city. Many domed palatial dwellings, lit from within through numerous windows, were scattered along the hillsides and all through the valley. Despite the light of the full moon beginning to rise on the horizon, the abundant stars of the Milky Way Galaxy were twinkling brilliantly in the pure atmosphere beyond the balcony.

"Layliella, I'm not really a diplomat," announced Kalem, as they turned toward each other.

"I don't understand, Aeron," she said, gazing puzzled back up at him.

"You are in great danger," he remarked. "That crystal you wear is very powerful. In the wrong hands, it could be very destructive. Listen closely. Beel is a fake. You have already sensed it. He's a murdering madman from another world."

"Another world? How can you expect me to believe that?" she asked skeptically.

Kalem gazed at her with passionate concern, then gained control of his emotions and relaxed.

"Do you trust me, Layliella?" he inquired.

Uncertain, she shyly lowered her head, and Kalem gently lifted her head up by the chin with his fingertips to look deeply into her eyes. She stared fondly, wide-eyed, back at him.

"Yes, but —" she started to answer as Kalem interrupted.

"My real name is Kalem and I'm trying to capture Beel. His real name is Sen Dar. There is no time to explain it all to you now but you sense this is true and you must trust me. If Sen Dar knew you had that crystal, he would have killed you already to get his hands on it. For your safety, please entrust it to me until I can figure out how to expose Sen Dar to your father."

She looked out across the valley for a moment, then back at Kalem and smiled up at him. She reached inside her gown, pulled out the crystal, lifted it over her head, and handed it to Kalem.

"How could that crystal be so important?" she asked, still puzzled.

Kalem placed the crystal around his neck and tucked it inside his diplomat's shirt.

"Believe me, Layliella, it is extremely important and very dangerous for you to be wearing it now," and he sighed relief. "Thank you for trusting me with it."

She nodded her head and smiled gently once again with deep appreciation for his gallantry.

Meanwhile, Sen Dar was cautiously approaching the balcony along a ledge that encircled the outside base of the ballroom wall. Then he squatted down to continue a slower stealthy approach as he neared the balcony. When the ledge he was walking along reached the balcony, it expanded to a flat extension. A botanical garden of thick tall bushes and beautiful tropical flowers in large clay pots adorned the entire ledge extension.

Kalem and Layliella sat down on a long granite bench at the base of the wall in front of the central open arch. Sen Dar stopped his approach and hid behind the largest bush on the other side of the arch.

"I think I know who you really are," said Kalem with high anticipation.

CHAPTER TWENTY-FIVE

"Has your skin ever appeared blue to you before?"

"How did you know about that?" she answered, stunned.

"Please, just answer the question. It's very important."

She looked down and began, "Since the time I first arrived here as a very young woman, I've had dreams of swimming and breathing under the ocean as free as a fish. After waking up in the morning, if I would gaze for a few moments at my reflection in the mirror it would change to the reflection of a woman with pale-blue skin and pointed ears. Then, if I held the crystal in my closed right fist at the same time, it would glow, and a strange foreboding feeling would come over me, causing me to drop the crystal and the glow would stop. Since I never understood why this kept happening, I eventually stopped grabbing it." She looked away, embarrassed, and added, "This sickness has been with me all my life."

"Listen to me, Layliella," Kalem insisted, his eyes lit with an encouraging realization. "You're not sick at all. You are an Oceanan woman. Please, try to remember."

Layliella's eyes widened as memories began to flood back into her consciousness. Then she fainted and fell into Kalem's arms. He held her tenderly for a few moments, and then gently touched her lips with a finger and stroked her long hair. She revived and looked up at him, frightened.

"I suddenly felt so dizzy and cold," she murmured softly. "I could see a city under the sea. It was my, my…"

She lapsed back into unconsciousness, and Kalem gazed fondly down at her. He caressed her in his arms and gently stroked her cheek. In a few moments, she transformed into Mayleena, the lovely blue-skinned Oceanan woman of his many visions. There before him was her radiant beauty with familiar long, silken, black hair, slightly pointed ears, unobtrusive gill slits at the back of her chin near the base of her neck, and delicate webs between her long slender fingers.

Kalem was spellbound as he gazed lovingly at her just as she began to awaken. He remained captivated by her dazzling beauty as she looked up to see him staring down at her with wide-eyed amazement. His intense gaze startled her, and she instantly transformed back into the blond-haired woman.

"Layliella, it happened right in front of my eyes," he proclaimed excitedly. "You transformed into a beautiful Oceanan woman. Your real name is Mayleena. Your father's name is Opellum. You are from Oceana. Can you remember the domed city under the sea?"

Dreamy-eyed, she gazed away with a pained expression and reminisced,

"I... I remember a tall loving man giving me that beautiful crystal before I went swimming. He was telling me it would protect me. But it all seems like a dream."

She sighed, forced a smile, and then requested, "Let's not talk of these dreary things right now."

"You are so lovely," Kalem replied passionately, unable to help himself. "This feeling is so strange, like...like we've always known each other. You looked exactly like the many visions I experienced while growing up of a beautiful young blue-skinned woman, except, now you are here. I've been in love with her most of my life."

"I know what you mean," she passionately agreed. "I've been experiencing the same thing about you since we first met. The visions I had while growing up were always of you, the young man you are now, but I was afraid to admit even to myself that I was in love with him."

Her alluring green eyes met his appreciative glowing gaze with magical passion. As their faces drew near, her lips quivered with anticipation, and they kissed with such tender depth that life itself stood still in a breathless moment of eternity. As their lips parted, Layliella's smile was radiant like the brilliant stars high overhead as her eyes began to tear with joy.

Kalem was beaming with happiness when she nodded her head toward the arched entryway leading back into the ballroom. They stood up without another word, gazed lovingly into each other's eyes, and then walked hand in hand across the balcony floor and through the arched opening.

Sen Dar was still squatting behind the large bush on the balcony ledge below the wall of the botanical garden. His widening eyes filled with gleeful malice as he realized more fully the impact of what he had overheard. Then he crouched his way back along the ledge surrounding the balcony. He hurried away from the botanical garden and disappeared into the night.

Much later that evening, Kalem was sneaking down a hallway leading to High Seer Stralim's chambers. As he passed the ballroom, he heard footsteps and several men talking, as they were fast approaching from further down the hallway. He jumped behind a marble pillar and a moment later four Atlantian guards passed the pillar and continued on their way. Kalem cautiously stepped from behind the pillar and quickly continued down the corridor to the door at the far end of the hallway. He drew out his crystal laser gun from under his robe, quietly opened the door, and walked inside.

Four different Atlantian guards swiftly surrounded him and firmly grabbed his upper arms. High Seer Stralim and Sen Dar appeared from behind another door, each carrying a glass topped scepter-like incandescent lamp.

Sen Dar roared with anger, "You see, my Lord Stralim," boasted Sen Dar, "he tried to assassinate you and he would have succeeded if I had not warned you first."

Sen Dar grabbed the laser gun from Kalem's hand, pointed it at the nearby table and fired. The table disintegrated in a radiant beam of energy. High Seer Stralim was aghast with the thought that the chair could have been him. With great animosity, he walked over to Kalem, raised his hand way back over his shoulder, and struck him hard across the chin with the back of his hand.

"We'll send your ashes back to Master Ra Mu," he fumed. "That will be a fitting response to his deceit."

"High Seer Stralim, you're making a drastic mistake," yelled out Kalem. "Beel is not who he pretends to be. He's a murderer and he's not from Lemuria."

Sen Dar swung his arm wide and struck Kalem backhanded across the mouth, and blood trickled from the corner of his lips down his chin.

Greatly indignant, Stralim gazed with disgust at Kalem and stated,

"Beel, you were right about everything. It would appear, Aeron, if that is your real name, that you are the fraud, and in the morning, you will pay for this outrage."

"My Lord Stralim, listen to me," pleaded Kalem. "This man's real name is Sen Dar and you're under his spell. He wants your daughter's crystal and he will kill her to get it. He's not from this world."

Stralim turned to the guards and commanded, "Get him out of my sight."

As the guards hauled Kalem from the room, he yelled back over his shoulder until his voice faded away, "You must listen to me. Your daughter is in great danger. You are under Sen Dar's spell. High Seer Stralim, snap out of it. Wake up! Wake up!"

Sen Dar grinned like a demon as Stralim walked over to him and they clasped forearms.

"Come, Beel," commanded Stralim with glee. "We must discuss what is to be done with this treacherous Diplomat Aeron when the sun rises."

Sen Dar's devilish grin was unmistakable before he feigned a respectful bow toward Stralim. Then they began to walk at a quick pace down the hallway in the direction of the guards that had just hauled Kalem away.

A MADMAN'S DEMANDS

The next day, Kalem was wearing a blindfold with his hands tied behind his back. Two guards tightly held his upper arms and guided him toward the edge of a rock cliff. The Council chambers were a hundred yards in the background behind them. Stralim and Sen Dar walking several feet behind the two guards stopped suddenly. Two more guards behind them, who were holding Layliella, blindfolded, by her upper arms also stopped, and she struggled with all her might to get free from their tight grip.

With the sweet, twisted allure of a demonic tongue, Sen Dar remarked to Stralim, "Layliella is under this Diplomat Aeron's spell, my Lord Stralim. As I said before, when you have him thrown over the cliff, she will snap out of the trance."

Stralim appeared uneasy about commanding the guards to proceed, and he gazed questioningly at Sen Dar.

"You had better be right about this, Beel."

Stralim motioned by nodding his head toward the guards holding Kalem. They untied his hands and blindfold but firmly held his arms as he rubbed his wrists.

"Well, this is more like it," said Kalem, forcing a courageous grin as he gazed at Stralim.

The two guards holding onto Layliella sat her on the ground, untied her blindfold, and let her go. They walked over by the other two guards holding Kalem and each guard grabbed one of his legs by the ankle. The two guards holding Kalem's arms grabbed a wrist, and the four guards stretched him out lengthwise. They held him tightly as he struggled, kicking his legs and yanking his arms to no avail.

"Now, wait a minute," he said and stopped struggling as he forced a smile at all four guards and continued, "You men look reasonable. We can talk about this."

Awakening to the situation, Layliella opened her eyes and her dazed expression turned to terror.

"Father, what are you doing?" she yelled as she jumped up and ran toward Kalem, but Stralim grabbed her by both arms and held her tight. "Have you gone mad?" she yelled, struggling to get free. "Father, let me go to him. Beel is evil. I can feel it. You must stop this."

A dull glow emanating through Sen Dar's garment was faintly illuminating the fingers of his clenched fist, and Stralim nodded to the four guards. They swung Kalem back and forth over the cliff ledge, and Kalem looked down at the long fall below him each time they swung him out over the edge.

"Now wait a damned minute. Will you wait a minute?" he yelled at the guards. Then he looked at Stralim and yelled louder, "Stralim, snap out of it."

The guards swung him wider over the cliff ledge and let go.

"Ra-a-a... Mu-u-u-u-u..." yelled Kalem at the top of his lungs as he dropped from view, and his voice faded far below.

Layliella's face was paled, her eyes rolled back in her head, and she fainted. Stralim shook his head to try to ward off Sen Dar's spell and he gently lowered his daughter to the ground.

To Kalem, time seemed to move in slow motion during his last moments disguised as Diplomat Aeron. His eyes and mouth were wide open as he continued to fall, wildly flailing his arms and legs. He saw death rapidly approaching on the sharp pinnacles of rock far below when he heard Ra Mu's voice clearly inside his head.

Quickly Kalem, grab the Emerald Doorway Crystal in your right hand, and call my name again. Do it now!

Kalem struggled to reach into his shirt, grabbed the crystal in his right hand, and it instantly glowed green light through his fingers as he yelled in slow motion, "Ra-a-a-a... Mu-u-u-u."

He continued to fall slowly until his body was just five feet above the jagged rock pinnacles, and a brilliant point of light appeared directly below him that instantly spiraled open and Kalem dropped through it.

Master Ra Mu was holding his glowing crystal staff in front of himself at arm's length while he stood beside Master Opellum on a wooden octagon sided dock that extended forty feet out from the shore of a lake. The open energy doorway was vertically spinning a few feet in front of him. The huge dome covering the undersea city of Oceana behind him curved high overhead above the three pyramids centered in the city and the surrounding countryside.

They heard Captain Kalem screaming, "Ra-a-a-a..." in slow motion, growing louder as he approached. Then they heard him scream, "Mu-u-u-u..." in his normal speech rate just as he fell standing upright through the whirling energy opening.

A mysterious force instantly slowed Kalem's forward momentum as a transparent gold energy bubble formed around Ra Mu's body. Kalem passed through the bubble and right into Ra Mu's open arms that wrapped around him, and the golden energy bubble vanished.

Ra Mu's staff stopped glowing as he lowered it, and the inter-dimensional energy doorway vanished with a quick... *swoop*. He was smiling as he steadied Kalem on his feet. Greatly surprised, Kalem rubbed his hands, arms, and head as he fully realized he was, in fact, not dead. Then he gazed questioningly at Ra Mu and Opellum, who were both grinning back at him.

"I'm alive!" he blurted out, greatly relieved and grinning from ear to ear, and then he appeared puzzled.

"Of course, you are, Captain," responded Ra Mu with a chuckle.

"You knew I was thrown off the cliff?" Kalem asked.

Ra Mu grinned and answered, "The Ancient One's Spirit presence allowed me to monitor your predicament through the Master Crystal Staff. However, I'm afraid Mayleena will need our help next."

"What do you mean?" asked Kalem, instantly concerned.

"Sen Dar thinks she has the crystal that you now wear," Ra Mu replied.

Kalem grabbed the crystal hanging around his neck, sighed relief, and let it go as he gazed, concerned, at Ra Mu.

Master Opellum stepped toward him and insisted, "Captain Kalem, you must return my daughter to me."

"I'll do whatever it takes to bring her back to you," he replied. "I promise that on my life."

"Good!" replied Opellum. "We have a plan."

Master Ra Mu raised his staff a few inches off the ground and it began to glow. The Ankh symbol atop the staff instantly projected a soft blue light flecked with gold that surrounded Kalem's body, and his diplomatic disguise vanished. The light emanating from the staff disappeared, and Kalem touched his face with both hands to discover grinning that the beard was gone. Then Master Opellum pointed toward Kalem's ship floating inside the dock behind them.

"As you can see, Captain, your ship has been repaired, and Master Ra Mu has your uniform inside. We also arranged for Etta to be here and he is already aboard. Now, we must hurry."

An oval door in the upper side of the ship's hull was open. Kalem walked toward the ship docked ten feet past Ra Mu and Opellum and they followed close behind him.

Back at the edge of the rock cliffs of Atlantis, High Seer Stralim was leaning over the young woman he had always thought of as his own dear daughter, patting her cheeks to revive her, and she awakened. She moaned as if waking up from a dreadful nightmare and then opened her eyes to behold Sen Dar standing beside them, sneering down at her. She recoiled and started to get to her feet. Stralim tried to help, but she shoved him away as she stood up, pointing an accusing finger at Sen Dar.

"You evil murderer," she shouted. "I know who you are, Sen Dar."

Startled by his foster daughter's unexpected outburst, Stralim shook his head and snapped out of his hypnotic daze. Then he gazed at Sen Dar with great distrust.

"You said she was under Aeron's spell," he said, frowning, and then asked, "Who are you?"

Mayleena became furious, jumped at Sen Dar, and hit him square on the jaw with her right fist. Stunned, he shook his head with surprise and grabbed her by the back of the neck with his right hand and squeezed, then shook her like a rag doll to indicate he could snap her neck. He pulled a laser gun from under his garment with his left hand and pointed it at her head.

She struggled to pull his hand away from her throat with both hands, and then dug her nails into his skin. But Sen Dar did not flinch as he pressed the laser gun firmly into her temple and squeezed her neck harder until she relaxed her digging nails and loosened her tight grip on his wrist.

All four guards suddenly rushed Sen Dar, but he sneered at them and they stopped as he menacingly pressed the point of the laser gun deeper into her temple.

"All of you stand back," he commanded, "or she will die instantly."

Stralim backed away a few feet and motioned to the guards to do the same. They backed up and stopped.

"What do you intend to do with my daughter? Don't hurt her," pleaded Stralim.

Sen Dar replied arrogantly, "I am Sen Dar as Aeron correctly stated, or I should say Captain Kalem, and I'm tired of this charade. She will now be my bait for Master Ra Mu."

"Leave her alone," demanded Stralim. "Take me instead."

"No, no you would not be a very convincing bait for Ra Mu," chuckled Sen Dar with malicious delight. Then he commanded, "All of you back further away… now!"

They backed away cautiously a few more feet.

Sen Dar whispered to Layliella, "Do not move, pretty one, or I'll kill your father first, then the guards, and then you very slowly."

He let go of his grip on her throat and pointed the gun toward Stralim. The four guards rushed Sen Dar just as he reached into his shirt with his other hand with lightning-quick speed and grabbed The Ancient One's Transport Matrix Crystal with his clenched fist. It glowed brightly through his fingers, and he threw his arm around Layliella's chest as they both dematerialized in a flash of light and vanished. Stralim and the guards almost fell over on top of each other, waving their arms around in empty air.

"Oh God, no," cried Stralim, "the demon has taken my daughter."

Sen Dar and Layliella materialized a moment later by the Atlantian jungle clearing next to his camouflaged ship. Sen Dar took his arm from around Layliella and pointed the laser gun at her head.

"What are you going to do with me?" she asked, as she backed a few feet away from him.

"Now, Mayleena, give me The Emerald Doorway Crystal," he commanded.

"Mayleena? Why did you call me that? My name is Layliella and I don't have it."

Sen Dar walked up to her and slapped her backhanded across the chin, knocking her to the ground. He pulled the Transport Matrix Crystal out of its hiding place inside his shirt and grabbed it more firmly. It glowed softly and Layliella struggled to resist but quickly succumbed to his spell.

"Now, come to me, Mayleena," he commanded, and she got to her feet and walked slowly toward him.

"Who has the crystal I seek?" he demanded.

"Kalem, Kalem has it," she replied, emotionless.

Sen Dar ran over to his ship and touched the underside of the hull with the palm of his hand. The ship's hull glowed for an instant with red light, emitting a pulsing hum. The brush covering the ship levitated away from the hull and dropped to the ground. Then an opening hatch appeared in the ship's side, and the ramp below it slid down to the ground.

"Layliella, you will help me get the Emerald Doorway Crystal," he commanded, "and the Master Crystal Staff from Ra Mu. Now, get aboard my ship."

Dazed with wide-open eyes, Layliella walked slowly up the ramp and entered the ship with Sen Dar close behind. The ship lit up a few moments later and lifted above the jungle trees. Then it flew away from the jungle over the green sands of the Atlantian coastline and darted in a long arc across the distant sky over the ocean.

A prehistoric valley loomed wide all the way to the horizon as Sen Dar's ship flew out of a cloud and continued a mile into the distance high over the top of the jungle trees. It hovered above the throat of a dormant volcano, and then lowered inside the cone and disappeared.

Meanwhile, Kalem was aboard his rebuilt Galactic Alliance Scout ship dressed in his own uniform while Layliella, still hypnotized, appeared on the view screen. Her hands were tied behind her back, and Sen Dar was standing beside her behind the control console of his ship with his laser gun in his left hand pressed to her temple for emphasis.

"It angers me, Captain, how you manage to continue to survive your useless life," he said. "I thought that was you disguised as Diplomat Aeron. No doubt, Ra Mu was responsible."

"Listen, you demented animal, if you harm her, I'll –"

"Don't dare threaten the one who will soon be your Master, impudent Captain," Sen Dar interrupted angrily, pressing the laser gun more tightly against Layliella's temple.

Sen Dar paused and then commanded, "I want the Emerald Doorway Crystal and Ra Mu's Master Crystal Staff. You will come to the coordinates you see displayed on your control console alone and unarmed by midday or she dies, most horribly."

Kalem glanced at the longitude and latitude numbers as they appeared on a readout window of his control console, and the view screen went blank. Master Ra Mu and Master Opellum walked into view from the shadows at the back of the control room and stood to each side of Kalem. Etta excitedly levitated into view with his tail glowing in opalescent colors, and then landed on Ra Mu's right shoulder. He wrapped his tail around the front of his chest to hold himself in place. Ra Mu appeared pleased as he shook Etta's hand with the warmth and appreciation of a very familiar longstanding friendship.

"Now, Etta, we are counting on you. Sen Dar will not have a clue that you and your lovely wife, Din, have your temporary home on Earth located in those volcanic caverns. When the time is right, you must try to take the crystal from him."

270

"But I'll be going in unarmed," remarked Kalem, smirking. "How will Etta get it from him?" He looked over at Etta with an apologetic grin and said, "Etta, my friend, I meant no offense."

Grimacing, Etta growled softly under his breath and flew off Ra Mu's shoulder to hover above the control console. Then he crossed his arms and frowned at Kalem.

Chuckling, Master Opellum remarked, "Captain, as you know, the Drens are telepathic and more evolved in their own way than most human beings. You have heard this before and you have experienced this for yourself, but it bears repeating. You also know our study long ago, of the Drens' levitating and flying abilities, enabled us to develop antigravity travel and greatly improved our science. On your first mission with Etta, you experienced his photographic memory, and how he can travel with stealth. Now the plan is simple and straightforward. While you keep Sen Dar focused on you, Etta will fly by and rip the crystal from his grasp. Right Etta?"

"Quibb, quibb!" ("Yes, yes!") Etta eagerly replied.

"You saved Etta's life once and Drens don't forget," continued Opellum, "and you know you can trust him with your life. With what's coming up, Captain, you must do exactly that."

"Sorry, Etta," remarked Kalem with newfound respect. "I don't doubt your courageous warrior spirit, but I also don't want to see you harmed by that devil."

Etta perked up and saluted him, and Kalem snapped back a respectful salute. Then he gazed solemnly at Ra Mu and Opellum, who appeared pleased.

"I hope you two know what you're doing," he said, a little apprehensive, and sighed.

Ra Mu handed Kalem the Master Crystal Staff. "Farewell, Captain," he said and smiled, then gazed fondly at Etta. "And farewell to you too, Etta."

Ra Mu then turned around, stepped through the open side hatch onto the ramp, and headed down to the loading dock. Opellum clasped forearms with Kalem and Etta and then headed out of the ship as well. He stood beside Ra Mu at the bottom of the ramp and together they looked back with encouraging smiles as the side hatch closed.

The floating ship in the center of the loading dock lit up a moment later. Master Ra Mu and Master Opellum were standing a few feet away on the dock silently watching the ship as it slowly submerged beneath the surface of the lake. They simultaneously turned around, gazed thoughtfully at each other, and then grinned knowingly as they nodded their heads. Then they walked along the dock toward the shoreline that surrounded the lake.

The countryside spread out around them was full of pristine beauty, and the majestic grandeur of the huge transparent dome arched high over their heads. They could see the deep ocean water illuminated by the natural sunlight glow coming from the charged phosphorescent minerals within the dome's transparent material. They stepped onto the sands of the shoreline and turned to look upon the loading dock one more time before they scanned the beautiful countryside that surrounded the city. As ancient friends, they continued to walk in silence side by side along the lakeshore in the direction of the pyramids.

A few minutes later, the floor of the ocean opened a hundred yards in front of the huge dome covering the city of Oceana, revealing a smooth oval tunnel illuminated down its length every ten feet by blue dome shaped lights. Kalem's ship flew down the length of the tunnel away from the city and shot out of the opening, glided a short way along the sea floor, and then increased its speed in a smooth curve toward the surface far above.

The ship soon broke through the churning ocean waves and hovered several feet above sea level. The light surrounding the hull flashed brighter, and the ship darted across the sky and disappeared over the distant horizon.

CHAPTER TWENTY-SEVEN

FIGHT IN THE CAVERN
OF
THE DRENS

$\mathcal{K}$alem's ship flew over the jungle and stopped to hover above the mouth of the same volcano Sen Dar's ship entered, and then it lowered inside the shaft.

The ship descended to the bottom of the volcano's throat and stopped at the entrance to the huge tunnel cavern before it slowly continued its flight a half mile down the center of chamber. The minerals within the cavern walls cast a blue-violet light on the ship and along the tunnel's entire length that continued many miles into the distance. The ship soon stopped above the plateau that extended out from the cavern wall before it lowered and landed beside Sen Dar's ship. Kalem climbed down the ladder that was extending from the open hatch under the bottom center of the ship's hull. The Emerald Doorway Crystal was hanging around his neck, and he was gripping the Master Crystal Staff in his right hand. He walked a few feet away from the ship and looked cautiously around.

Etta flew into view from under the ship and stopped in midair with his tail glowing. Then he flew up to Kalem's side, smiling proudly, and darted back over the top of the ship and disappeared within a small cave opening high up on the cavern wall.

Kalem took a deep breath and walked courageously up a rocky path that led several hundred yards to a higher ledge.

He appeared a short time later and stepped onto the higher plateau. A little further away, Sen Dar was arrogantly grinning, wearing the Blue Transport Matrix Crystal around his neck and aiming his laser gun at Kalem's chest.

With a blank hypnotic stare and her hands tied behind her back, Layliella was standing another ten feet further behind him at a cliff ledge that overlooked a twenty-feet-wide chasm. A red glow cast from its depths was reflecting off the far rock wall.

"What did you do to her?" demanded Kalem, scowling.

"She is unharmed for now, Captain. But I have her under my complete control," replied Sen Dar, widening his antagonistic smile. Then he pointed to the rock floor several feet away and commanded, "Put them on the ground right there."

Kalem did not move as he stared defiantly back at Sen Dar, and for a few moments, they just glared at each other.

"First, release her from the trance," Kalem finally demanded.

"You are in no position to bargain, Captain," shot back Sen Dar with a sneering chuckle. "If you did not yet notice, Layliella, or actually Mayleena, is standing near the edge of a long fall into molten lava. If I tell her to jump, she will and she will die screaming in pain." Then he demanded, "Now put them on the ground."

Fuming, Kalem reluctantly took off the Emerald Doorway Crystal, tossed it on the ground a few feet in front of Sen Dar, and laid down the Master Crystal Staff.

"And now, finally, worthless Captain, you shall die," Sen Dar proclaimed with devilish delight.

He pointed the laser gun directly at Kalem's head to fire just as Etta darted by Kalem and chomped down hard on Sen Dar's gun hand at the wrist, and then darted passed him. Sen Dar screamed and dropped the gun. He swung his other arm's fist at Etta, but Etta was already out of reach.

Kalem ran up to Sen Dar and knocked him down with one blow across the chin. Then he jumped on top of him and started choking him with all his pent-up anger. Sen Dar was gasping and struggling with both hands to remove Kalem's deadly fingers from around his throat. He yanked his right hand away and tried to grab the Transport Matrix Crystal hung around his neck, but Kalem angrily yanked the chained crystal over his head and tossed it to the ground a few feet away.

Etta flew past them and stopped in front of Layliella, then circled around her back and untied her hands. He threw the rope into the fiery abyss behind them. Coming out of the trance, she shook her head, saw

Kalem and Sen Dar fighting, and ran toward them.

Kalem was angrily choking Sen Dar, but Sen Dar managed to grab a rock by his side and hit Kalem on the side of the head. The blow briefly stunned him but he would not loosen his tight grip around Sen Dar's neck. Sen Dar slugged Kalem on the jaw, knocking him over, and yanked Kalem's hands from his throat. Then he lunged for the crystal on the ground and Kalem leapt on top of him.

They wrapped around each other, exchanged blows in a frenzy of fists, and then rolled over toward the edge of the cliff above the lava abyss. Kalem was now on the bottom and Sen Dar began to choke him. Then Kalem backhanded him across the jaw twice in quick succession and grabbed his face with his fingers. He pushed Sen Dar's head back, pulled his right knee under his chest, and kicked him off with his foot.

Sen Dar flew backward and landed with a dull... *thud*... on his back next to the laser gun just as Layliella stooped down to pick it up. Sen Dar snatched it from under her grasp, jumped to his feet, and pointed the gun at Kalem to fire.

"No-o! Kalem, look out," she screamed.

She jumped onto Sen Dar's back and tried to pull his gun arm down, but he swung his arm around and hit her on the side of the head with the butt of the gun, knocking her out cold, and she fell limp at his feet.

As Sen Dar gloated down at her, Kalem seized the opportunity and jumped at him, grabbing his hand holding the gun by the wrist, forcing it upward. The gun went off, sending a searing bolt of light into the rock cavern ceiling and blasting several boulders away that fell into the lava abyss, splashing lava high in the air.

Kalem slugged Sen Dar on the side of the head with his right fist and smashed his gun hand into the rock wall several times. The gun suddenly flew from Sen Dar's hand, and Kalem slugged him across the jaw twice and then hit him in the chest with the palm of his hand, knocking him backward to the ground.

Sen Dar landed by the Transport Matrix Crystal as blood trickled down the corner of his mouth, but he grinned and grabbed the crystal in his right hand causing it to glow. Kalem lunged for the laser gun on the ground and fired at Sen Dar as he was dematerializing, and the laser beam went right through his vanishing molecules to explode against the far cavern wall.

Sen Dar materialized aboard his ship with the Transport Matrix Crystal still glowing in his clenched fist. The glowing stopped as he let it go and it dropped on the end of the gold chain around his neck. He located another laser gun from under the control console, grabbed the crystal again, and dematerialized.

Gripping Sen Dar's laser gun, Kalem ran over to Layliella and gently picked her up, just as Sen Dar materialized next to the Master Crystal Staff. Sen Dar was already pointing another laser gun at Kalem when Kalem spun around to fire, but Sen Dar fired first, knocking the gun from Kalem's hand.

Kalem carefully laid the unconscious Layliella down on the ground. Sen Dar let go of the glowing crystal, and it stopped glowing while he continued to point the gun at Kalem. Then he picked up the Emerald Doorway Crystal where Kalem had tossed it, grabbed the Master Crystal Staff in the same hand, and stood back up.

At that moment, Etta sped into view with his mouth open, swooped by Sen Dar, and chomped down on the gold chain held in his hand, ripping the Emerald Doorway Crystal from his grip and knocking him off balance with his tail as he passed by. Sen Dar stumbled backward a few feet and partially regained his footing as he gripped the Master Crystal Staff more tightly and fired the laser gun in his other hand as Etta neared Kalem's position. The beam clipped Etta across the chest, and he fell limp to the ground. Kalem made a maddened rush for Sen Dar, but he was ready for him as he aimed the laser gun back at him. Kalem checked his angry emotions, stopping just two feet from the gun pointed at his head.

Sen Dar cautiously walked over to Etta's body carefully keeping the laser gun pointed at Kalem, ready to strike. Etta appeared to be quite dead as Sen Dar picked up the Emerald Doorway Crystal with his fingertips from Etta's open mouth. The gold chain dangled below his hand as he reached up to place the crystal over the hole on one side of the Ankh symbol atop the Master Crystal Staff, and a magnetic force locked it in place.

With his fingertips, he carefully lifted the blue Transport Matrix Crystal from his neck and pulled it over his head. He placed that crystal on the other side of the Ankh and it too magnetically locked into place. Two gold chains were now freely dangling down each side of the staff's transparent shaft.

Sen Dar held the staff several inches off the ground out in front of himself at arm's length. Then he closed his eyes, mumbled something inaudible under his breath, and a moment later a brilliant gold light radiated along the length of the entire Master Crystal Staff.

He opened his eyes, laughing triumphantly, and loudly proclaimed, "Now, I shall become… your God!"

Kalem nervously shielded his face with the back of a hand from the brilliance emanating from the staff. Just as it was becoming unbearably bright, a violent shaking and deep rumbling began to roar down the length of the cavern. An earthquake split the ground open directly under Sen Dar's feet and widened. He struggled to remain standing and gasped as the ground widened further, disappearing under him.

Just as Kalem had experienced while falling over the cliff, Sen Dar now perceived everything in slow motion as he fell backward. He twisted around, dropping the staff on the chasm ledge widening away from him toward Kalem. The bottom of the staff hit the ground, knocking the two crystals from each side of the Ankh, and Sen Dar lunged for the far side of the opening crevasse as he began to fall into the chasm. He managed to grab onto the far ledge with both hands to stop his fall with his body precariously dangling down the rock wall.

The Master Crystal Staff and the Transport Matrix Crystal landed on Kalem's side of the chasm, but the Emerald Doorway Crystal was flying through the air toward Sen Dar.

Sen Dar struggled to look over his shoulder and saw it. Straining to hold onto the ledge of the crevasse with one arm, he stretched the grasping fingers of his other hand up to reach for the gold chain. The crystal sailed through the air a foot above his head as the tip of his index finger just snagged the gold chain, and it swung down his finger, wrapping itself around his hand with the crystal coming to rest below his wrist.

To Sen Dar everything mysteriously resumed a normal rate of speed as he clasped the crystal in his fist and clapped his hand holding it onto the crevasse ledge to hold on with both hands. Then he pulled himself up and placed an elbow on the ledge, then the other one, and struggled to drag his body over the ledge. He slowly stood up just as the shaking subsided. Boulders from the cavern ceiling continued to fall around him while he ran frantically down the path to the lower plateau and over to his ship to quickly climb aboard.

He sat at the control console, turned on the view screen, and watched with great anxiety as a large part of the cavern ceiling began to collapse high overhead above his ship. Frantic, he slammed his hands onto the domed guidance controls.

The outside of his ship was already being hit by falling rocks as a large part of the cavern ceiling broke away. The ship lifted off the plateau and moved out into the cavern, just escaping a crushing blow by inches as the large chunk of the cavern ceiling smashed to the ground beside Kalem's ship. Volcanic rocks and boulders were falling down the entire length of the tunnel as Sen Dar maneuvered his ship through the chaos and back up the volcano's shaft toward the surface.

Kalem's eyes were tearing as he cradled the unconscious Layliella in his arms on the upper plateau. Layliella moaned and opened her eyes as the earthquake subsided, then transformed back into Mayleena. Amazed, Kalem gazed upon her with deep appreciation, for she was to him the most beautiful woman in the universe.

"I thought you might be…" he began to say, relieved.

She threw her arms around his shoulders and pulled him close and they embraced silently for a few moments in deep appreciation.

"Kalem, I remember who I am. I remember everything," she said, rubbing the side of her head. "Sen Dar's blow to my head must have done it."

"I thank The Ancient One with all that I am for your safe recovery," replied Kalem, not quite knowing that what he said came from the most sacred place in the secret garden of his golden heart, located within The Ancient One's realm of Sound and Light.

Then he heard The Ancient One's uplifting Spirit Sound as if it were coming toward them from far away, and he glanced away.

He gazed back down into the deep radiant pools of her enchanting green eyes. "Mayleena, I have always loved you," he finally whispered.

As she gazed lovingly back into the depths of his eyes to touch his true self, she replied sweetly, "And I have always loved you, dearest Kalem."

She quivered with anticipation as their lips gently touched. They kissed long and tenderly with a depth of passion enriched by a winding golden thread woven through a hundred lifetimes.

While he held Mayleena at arm's length, the sound of falling boulders made Kalem look up to see chunks of the cavern ceiling drop into the lava abyss behind them. More molten lava splashed high in the air onto the far wall across the chasm from where she had stood only a short time before, hypnotized and blindfolded.

"Mayleena," he indicated with a nod toward his ship on the lower plateau.

"I know, we must leave this place," she concurred reluctantly. Kalem gave her an encouraging grin and helped her stand up, steadying her on her feet.

CHAPTER TWENTY-EIGHT

DEATH AND RESURRECTION

$\mathcal{M}$ayleena rubbed the bump on her head again, while Kalem picked up Ra Mu's staff in one hand and the Transport Matrix Crystal in his other hand. As he placed the chained crystal around his neck, Mayleena noticed Etta lying dead on the ground a few feet away.

"Oh, Ancient One, no-o-o, not little Etta."

Tears welled in her eyes as she walked over and gently picked him up to cradle him in her arms. The tears then ran down her cheeks as Kalem walked up behind her.

"There must be something we can do for him," remarked Kalem, deeply saddened.

Mayleena's tears flowed freely from her anguished eyes as she gently laid Etta's body back down, and just as his body touched the ground, they heard a wild female moaning and chattering voice in the Dren language coming toward them. Startled, they looked up to behold a petite female Dren with long eyelashes fly out of a small cavern high up on the plateau wall.

She flew down toward them, panic-stricken, and stopped to gaze horrified at Etta's body lying near their feet. Then she darted down and hovered directly over his body, moaning in agony. She looked up, forlorn, at Kalem and Mayleena with tears pouring from her eyes. Kalem's face drooped sadly and his eyes began to water, while tears continued to stream down Mayleena's cheeks as she gazed compassionately at the female Dren, and then back at Kalem.

"This is Din, Etta's mate," she said sorrowfully.

"He saved our lives, Din," added Kalem, wiping tears from his own eyes.

Din continued crying and repeatedly said Etta's name and something lovingly intimate.

"Etta-a-a, Etta-a-a… oh Etta-a-a. Ennom Etta."

She laid her head down across Etta's chest and wept, as any deeply mourning human woman would do at the sudden loss of her husband.

A moment passed and The Ancient One's Spirit Sound became audible and grew noticeably louder as if it was now rapidly approaching from a great distance. Kalem and Mayleena scanned the area around them and then gazed down the cavern for the source of the sound.

A speck of blue light very far down the tunnel moved steadily toward them. As it neared their location, it appeared as a brilliant blue star. Then it transformed into a sphere of light surrounded by a faint golden aura.

The radiant sphere hovered near Etta and materialized into Master Ra Mu. Din raised her sad eyes up to behold him and beamed a smile of great relief. Her tail lit up, and she flew excitedly around him before landing again near Etta's body.

"Master Ra Mu," Mayleena proclaimed sorrowfully with a humble nod of her head.

Kalem started to walk toward Ra Mu grinning but a motion from Ra Mu's hand stopped him.

"Do not move or speak, any of you," he commanded.

He raised his hands, palms out toward Etta, closed his eyes, and bowed his head in deep reverence. Moments later, a beam of gold light shot down from the cavern ceiling, flowed down Ra Mu's body, out his hands, and into Etta's lifeless form. The light formed a golden web around Etta, repairing the hole in his chest in seconds, and then it dissolved. The beam receded through Ra Mu's body and faded away, along with The Ancient One's Spirit Sound as it continued back up through the cavern ceiling.

Etta started to breathe, slowly opened his eyes, and appeared very surprised to see Din staring joyfully down at him. His tail instantly lit up, and he flew up beside his Dren wife. Then they circled each other several times, rubbed noses together, and flew over to Ra Mu, excitedly chattering away in their Dren language.

Master Ra Mu chuckled to himself as he opened his eyes and remarked, "My dear friends, thank The Ancient One."

"Master Ra Mu, how in the name of the universe did you do that?" asked Kalem, amazed.

"Oh, it was not who you see before you, Captain, that brought Etta back to life," Ra Mu replied humbly. "The living presence of The Ancient One – the Sound and Light underlying all life – is the true-life giver. One day you and Mayleena will meet The Ancient One and understand my words spoken here today."

Kalem was puzzled. "I guess I can now accept that possibility," remarked Kalem.

Master Ra Mu replied with a twinkle in his eyes, "That's good, Captain. That marks the beginning of wondrous things to come."

"Hello Etta and Din," Mayleena chimed in humbly and asked, "Do you remember me?"

Grinning, Etta and Din flew over to Mayleena as she held both her arms out. Etta landed on one upper arm and shoulder and Din landed on the other one. They curved their tails back across her chest, entwined them together in a spiral, and snuggled her neck. Very pleased, Mayleena affectionately rubbed her nose with theirs.

"Even after our many years apart," she remarked delightfully, gazing at Ra Mu, "they still remember I used to play with them as a little girl on my home world of Oceana. Here on Earth, they would occasionally visit me in our undersea city, before I disappeared."

"What about Sen Dar?" interjected Kalem, recalling the threat was still out there.

"I was wondering how long it would take before you remembered him," replied Master Ra Mu. "The Adepts of The Ancient One have a plan, Captain. When the time comes, you will know it." He looked at Mayleena and remarked, "Well, Mayleena, I imagine you would like to see your true father Opellum again."

"Yes, very much," she replied, grinning anticipation.

"Is your ship available, Captain?" inquired Ra Mu.

Kalem walked a few feet over to the edge of the upper plateau and looked down on the lower plateau to survey the ship's condition. Rubble was all around it and small boulders were lying on top of the hull.

"I hope so," he replied doubtfully, looking back at Ra Mu.

"You will find it still functions, Captain," remarked Ra Mu, smiling reassuringly as he looked at the Drens. "Etta, Din, come with me for a while my friends. These two need some time alone."

The Drens nodded their heads, smiled knowingly at each other, and flew off Mayleena's shoulders toward Ra Mu. They hovered above each of his shoulders.

"Master Ra Mu, where are you going?" asked Mayleena, puzzled. "My work with The Ancient One will take me in another direction for a while," he said mysteriously as he looked at Kalem. "Please safeguard the Transport Matrix Crystal for now, Captain. I will let you know where to find me."

Etta and Din hovered directly above Ra Mu's shoulders as he reached for the Master Crystal Staff, and Kalem handed it to him. As the staff began to glow, he and the two Drens dissolved into the light spheres of their true Atma-selves. Then all three spheres transformed back into a single blue star and faded away. Kalem and Mayleena gazed passionately at each other, clasped hands, and walked down the rocky path toward his ship on the lower plateau.

A short time later, the ship hovered above the plateau. Then it flew down the length of the volcanic cavern and continued up the bottom of the shaft toward the surface.

It soon reappeared flying out of the top of the volcano, then shot swiftly upward into a patch of clouds.

Later that afternoon, Kalem's ship flew down toward the ocean and hovered just above the surface. Then it tilted down at a sharp angle and plunged beneath the waves.

CHAPTER TWENTY-NINE

REUNION
AND
A FOND FAREWELL

A wondrous breathtaking panoramic view of the seabed was in the background behind Kalem's ship as it sped deep beneath the surface of the ocean, headed toward the city of Oceana a mile away. It sped gracefully along the ocean floor and entered the open lighted tunnel leading underneath the domed city to the lakeshore dock.

The ship surfaced inside the dock with water splashing off its sides, as the door seam appeared in the side of the hull. The door opened and a ramp slid out extending down to the loading dock. Kalem and Mayleena walked down the ramp and stepped onto the dock. Then they turned toward each other and embraced tenderly. They gazed into each other's eyes and kissed long and deeply, parted, and then walked hand-in-hand along the ramp toward the lakeshore.

An hour later, Master Opellum was standing with his hands clasped behind his back near the center of the Oceanan landing field. He was overlooking hundreds of Oceanan men, women, and children walking up ramps that led into many elongated pyramid shaped spires lying horizontal on the landing field. They surrounded a much larger dark blue main spherical component of an Oceanan spacecraft. Three long pyramidal legs tapering down from the bottom half of the spherical main section ended in rounded points to support the sphere above the landing field. Other Oceanans were boarding the main spherical section by a ramp that extended from the ground to an opening in the middle of the sphere's side.

Kalem and Mayleena walked into view behind Opellum. She was smiling through tears of joy for her imminent meeting with her true father, after the many years of separation since her disappearance. Opellum sensed their presence and turned around to greet them. His eyes began to tear as he opened his arms to finally receive Mayleena. She ran to him and they embraced with great joy, long and tenderly. Then he held his daughter at arm's length.

"Mayleena, my dear daughter, I never gave up hope. I knew one day we would find each other."

"Oh Father, I…," she began and stopped as joyful tears streamed down her cheeks.

Opellum gazed down into his daughter's beautiful green eyes and he held her tightly again.

He whispered in her ear, "I know, Master Ra Mu communicated to me everything that happened."

They held each other within a gentle timeless moment, and then Opellum looked over at Kalem, who was standing right behind Mayleena smiling appreciatively with a nod of his head for their reunion.

"Thank you, Kalem, for bringing my daughter back to me," he said gratefully, smiling wide.

Kalem grinned back at him and extended his right arm as he placed his left arm around Mayleena's slender waist. She smiled up at him as he clasped forearms with Opellum. Then she placed her right arm around Kalem's waist pulling him close and wrapped her left arm around Opellum's waist. She was now standing in between the two men she loved most in the world, who smiled at each other. All three simultaneously turned their gaze to observe the few remaining Oceanan people board the many sections of the Oceanan spacecraft.

"I can see you two have a great destiny together," remarked Opellum turning to face them.

"Would you mind elaborating on that?" inquired Kalem, curiously raising an eyebrow.

Kalem noticed Mayleena was gazing playfully at Opellum before she looked back in his direction. He sensed she knew more about Opellum's statement, and he gazed inquiringly at her.

"Master Ra Mu will explain it to you, Captain," Opellum interjected. "There isn't enough time for me to go further into it here, because we are evacuating our home away from home. Our work with Earth's inhabitants on the surface is now over."

"Father, did you say 'evacuate'?" she asked, worried. "What do you mean?"

Kindly smiling back at his daughter, Opellum did not reply at first and then he gazed at the various sections of the Spectrum ship, up at the huge clear dome arching high overhead above the city, and then back at her and Kalem.

"Every 100,000 years," he began calmly, "this solar system of planets passes through an area of space that causes Earth's poles to change overnight. It is, after all, a natural recurring cycle."

Mayleena's concern deepened as she recalled that her foster father, High Seer Stralim, was back on Atlantis, and she frowned.

"But what will happen to Stralim and all of Earth's people?" she asked, apprehensive.

Master Opellum looked upward for a moment and then replied solemnly, "That is now up to each one of them. Let it be, my daughter. You both will understand my words soon enough. Now I must take our people out into the galaxy, through a vortex into a higher parallel dimension of the physical universe, and then back to our home world of Oceana."

Chief Scientist Dom walked up to them, appearing quite pleased to see Mayleena again after so many years. He approached her and they hugged briefly.

"Welcome home, Mayleena. We are glad you and Kalem have safely returned," he stated cheerfully and then gazed seriously at Opellum. "Master Opellum, the molecular energy transfer charge has been set. The galactic inter-dimensional window is opening. We must leave now."

"What launch-window?" Kalem asked, puzzled.

"Our Crystal Spectrum ships are designed for travel through space and into a higher parallel dimension of finer physical reality beyond this world, Captain," explained the Chief Scientist, "and we must leave when inter-dimensional conditions are exactly right."

Unable to disguise her forlorn expression, Mayleena looked sadly up at Opellum and found it difficult to speak at first.

"But Father, I just found you again after all these long years."
"I am very grateful to The Ancient One for your protection and safe return, dear daughter, and there is a bright side to all of this," he replied fondly. "One day soon, you and Kalem will come home to our world of Oceana. For now, your destiny is with Kalem here on Earth and with Master Ra Mu."

Mayleena threw her arms around Opellum and hugged him tightly while he gently caressed her.

"Master Opellum, we must leave now, while we still can," insisted Dom.

Opellum nodded reluctantly and looked at Kalem.

"Captain, take good care of her," he commanded.

Kalem nodded, grasped Mayleena's right hand, and affectionately squeezed it. She grinned up at him and her smile widened.

"To be safe," continued Opellum, "your ship must be a mile away from the domed city within half an hour."

Dom nodded and walked out of view in the direction of the Oceanan ship. Kalem clasped forearms with Opellum and gently squeezed Mayleena's beautifully slender fingers again with his hand, and she returned the squeeze, then threw her left arm around her father's waist and snuggled him. Opellum put his arm around her shoulder and tightly hugged her before letting her go. Then he stepped back and smiled at them.

"The Ancient One is watching over both of you. Farewell," he said and nodded in parting.

He turned and walked away toward Dom, who was already heading up the wide ramp leading into the heart of the ship.

The scene receded below Harry Faldwell's viewpoint, revealing Kalem and Mayleena, hand in hand, already walking back toward the loading platform of a transport tube station located at the perimeter of the landing field. Then a new view came into focus.

Harry once again found himself viewing the images far below from the lofty invisible vantage point of his true Atma as a radiant sphere of conscious light. He pondered the incredible phenomena of his out-of-body travel experience as he gazed curiously, unafraid of the scene below. In fact, he discovered that he actually felt exhilarated by the experience and uplifted.

How will I ever tell the President about this? he pondered with a chuckle. *Then there is my lovely future wife. Oh God... forget that. They won't just lock me up. They'll paint feathers on me and stick me in a damned cuckoo clock.*

His attention was distracted from his slightly giddy self-concerns as he focused on the spectacular overview of the landing field, the unique splendor of the Oceanan city, and the surrounding countryside. Half an hour later on the landing field, all of the many crystal sections surrounding the larger main body of the ship simultaneously lit up. Each one was radiating a different light from its entire structure and emanating a different sound in harmony with each other. The sections lifted off the landing field and moved up into positions all around the

286

spherical central section of the spacecraft. The base of each pyramid-shaped section began to converge toward the main body of the ship until they magnetically locked onto the sphere and sealed with a flash of white light, leaving no seam.

The huge spaceship was now complete as a single crystalline craft. The spherical section began to radiate blue light and each of the pyramid sections started pulsing their unique shades of the spectrum, while they continued to emanate harmonious sounds. The sphere's illumination increased until it appeared like a radiant blue star, surrounded by multicolored light spires extended from its surface.

A transparent tube of blue energy appeared on the landing field that extended itself upward around the entire spaceship and up through the center of the top of the dome over the city rising out of sight toward the ocean's surface.

The ship lifted off the landing field within the tube, passed through a round hole that appeared in the center of the top of the dome, and continued upward until it disappeared far above toward the ocean surface.

The tube then receded upward. As it passed through the top center of the dome, the round opening formed back into a clear seamless dome. The blue tube continued upward into the water's distant height until it faded from view.

Tremendous white explosions simultaneously began to go off all over the city. The pyramids and city structures began to melt, creating a radiation of pure white light.

Kalem's ship flew out of the lighted tunnel entrance leading away from the city as more explosions went off down the tunnel's length. The ship rocked back and forth several times and then righted itself as the tunnel melted back into the seabed behind it. The huge clear dome over the city dissolved and everything within the city melted into brilliant white molecules, including the ocean, which poured down on the pyramids and the surrounding city.

Kalem was sitting in the chair behind the control console and Mayleena was sitting affectionately on his lap. They were witnessing the final moments of the secret city of Oceana, watching the last bits of the dome and building structures as they disappeared into huge mushrooming light particles. Then the brilliant light faded swiftly away, leaving the ocean floor precisely as it had been before the dome city was there.

"My love, there are many realities in the far-flung dimensions of The Ancient One. We will find our place in one," remarked Mayleena with bright shining eyes of promise.

She hugged Kalem's neck and pulled his head toward her. He smiled at her lovely radiance, and they kissed tenderly with the depth of a familiar passion born far beyond a single life span. In fact, it was coming from the many former intimate lifetimes they had spent together which they did not yet remember. A moment passed, and then Kalem looked back up at the view screen. They both sighed and released each other.

"Now, we should go find that rascal Master Ra Mu," he remarked.

Mayleena smiled in agreement, affectionately tucked her head under his chin, and snuggled closer.

Kalem's ship broke through the churning ocean water and hovered a few feet above its surface. Gold light flashed from the hull, and the ship darted through a billowing cloud and swiftly vanished in a blur of light in the distant background sky.

A moment later, another ship darted into view and slowed, revealing Sen Dar's Yalgull Interceptor. It emanated a shrill humming sound as it flew down and hovered twenty feet above the spot where Kalem's ship had exited the ocean. A gold light flashed from the hull and it too darted away in the direction of Kalem's ship.

CHAPTER THIRTY

ROMANCE
IN PARADISE

In the countryside outside the capital city of Mu on the continent of Lemuria, lush green grass spread out like a circular emerald blanket around the one large boulder that rested in the center of the botanical gardens. A tantalizing floral feast of a profuse number of large flower varieties, artfully landscaped, extended into the surrounding jungle. They continued into the distance as far as the eyes could see in this tropical paradise under the early morning sun.

Kalem's ship sped into view headed toward the garden. It slowed as it passed over the lake and stopped to hover fifty feet above the boulder in the garden's center. Further in the background high above the ship, the white bridge glistened in the sunlight across the chasm it spanned to connect the two hillsides. The sparkling waterfall roaring under the bridge was cascading two thousand feet down to the lake nestled between the bottoms of the two hills. The ship slowly lowered and landed on the grass that surrounded the boulder.

Kalem and Mayleena climbed down the ladder and stepped onto the lush emerald-green grass. They scanned the area around the garden as if expecting someone to meet them, and then they heard Etta's excited voice chattering in Dren, drawing nearer to them. They both looked up the hillside to discover Etta flying downward above the last of the rock steps, and he darted toward them. He stopped a few feet in front of them holding a leather-like parchment. He handed it to Kalem.

"Thank you, my friend," said Kalem with a proud grin.

Mayleena smiled at Etta as she reached her hand toward him in a familiar manner. Etta grinned, bowed his head toward her, and accepted an affectionate stroke of her hand along the length of his neck. Then he lifted his head with a playful grin, flew onto her shoulder, wrapped his tail across the top of her chest, and snuggled her neck with his head.

Kalem opened the parchment and read it as Mayleena stepped behind his shoulder. She and Etta leaned their heads down to read the note with him.

"Although little time remains to enjoy this paradise, there should be time enough to do some exploring and enjoy these moments of love between you. Know that your future together will be challenging and fulfilling. Take the path behind the botanical gardens of Mu. It leads to one of my favorite spots in all Lemuria. Now, for a short while, I must prepare the way for The Ancient One.

Yours in the omnipresent Sound and Light,

Master Ra Mu"

Kalem and Mayleena smiled affectionately, but Etta's gaze was mischievous and he remarked in their language for the first time, "That rascal."

"Etta, dear friend," she said, "please relay our thanks to Master Ra Mu."

Etta nodded and then darted back up the steps to the arched bridge leading to Master Ra Mu's hidden sanctuary.

Kalem took Mayleena's hand, drew her close, and then they tenderly kissed before parting. She blushed as she smiled up at him and Kalem happily sighed. Then he looked up to appreciate for a few moments the spectacular view all around the botanical gardens, and Mayleena followed his gaze. Their eyes stopped together to behold the stone bridge that spanned the top of the two hills. Then they gazed at the majestic waterfall as it fell to the lake nestled at the base of the valley between the hills. The opposite end of the lake beyond the gardens emptied into a gently flowing river that continued to wind its way into the distant tropical jungle.

They clasped hands and turned away from the entrancing view, and then casually walked past the rock steps another thirty feet toward a flower-lined path, that began at the outer border of the circle of grass. They stepped onto the path and walked a dozen feet along it between six-foot-tall prehistoric-looking ferns, and paused to look back at the beautiful botanical gardens one last time. Then they stepped inside a tunnel made of interwoven vines thick with large blue and violet flowers.

Sen Dar's ship blurred into view from the distant horizon and stopped to hover above the tops of the tall jungle trees on the far side of the gardens opposite the jungle path. Then it lowered out of view below the tree line.

An hour had passed since Kalem and Mayleena had embarked on the path leading away from the botanical gardens of Mu. It finally ended at the edge of a jungle clearing by an elegant waterfall, cascading several hundred feet down three tiers of moss-covered lava rock formations before it dropped another sixty feet into a pool of turquoise water. More giant ferns and large flowers grew around the entire clearing by the beautiful pool.

Two figures silhouetted behind the base of the waterfall moved like graceful dancers into the waist-deep pool, parting the shimmering translucent sheet of liquid as it splashed off their glistening naked bodies. Kalem and Mayleena were passionately kissing, tightly embraced in each other's arms.

Etta broke through a large fern at the pool's edge before he stopped abruptly, spellbound as he unexpectedly witnessed Kalem and Mayleena embraced in each other's arms. Deeply embarrassed, he screeched and covered his eyes with his little hands, just as Kalem and Mayleena broke out laughing.

"Huh, he found us," chuckled Kalem.

Etta peeked through his fingers to make certain he actually saw what he thought he saw. Then he screeched louder with embarrassment, spiraled up above the pool, and darted back into the jungle. Mayleena and Kalem laughed so hard they had to hold each other up to keep from falling over.

As their laughing gradually subsided, he pulled her close to kiss her again but she grinned as she arched her back and held him at arm's length to gaze into his eyes. A moment passed and she drew him close to rest her cheek on his left shoulder. Her impassioned smile turned mischievous and she playfully bit his shoulder.

"Ow," Kalem blurted out looking down, rubbing his shoulder.

She pushed him away, spun around, and started sloshing her way out of the pool, headed away from the path.

Hearing Mayleena's slender legs splash through the water, followed by the patter of petite feminine feet down a path, made him look up with eager anticipation.

"Why you little…" he said playfully under his breath.

The chase was on, and he leapt in big strides over the top of the water to the pool's edge and ran along another path into the jungle after her.

Mayleena had run only twenty feet further into the jungle when she approached a thick cluster of tall ferns. She parted them, stepped through the opening, and disappeared as the ferns closed back together behind her.

The waterfall was visible on the opposite side of the pool in the distance behind Kalem while he ran up to the tall ferns and stepped through the opening in hot pursuit of Mayleena.

He began to catch up with her further along the overgrown path, while she giggled playfully, repeatedly glancing back over her shoulder. She reached a tall wall of thick ivy and stopped to glance seductively back at Kalem before she stuck her hands through the ivy, parting it like a curtain, and stepped through the opening. The ivy sprung closed behind her just as Kalem ran up. He reached into the ivy, stepped through the opening, and then sped away, and the ivy sprung closed behind him.

He had run only ten feet when he darted out of view behind several tall ferns. The intriguing view looming in the background revealed the expansive curve of a lush tropical, flower-laden, black sand beach cove.

Their rapidly approaching laughter was heading in the direction of the ocean waves, and they soon came running from the edge of the jungle onto the sparkling beach. He was drawing closer to her as they continued to run along the shoreline.

A large turquoise wave curled to break a little further down the beach as their laughter grew louder with the rapid thumping of feet. Diamond-like flashes of sunlight glinted along the crest of the wave as Kalem's outstretched hands leaned further forward until his fingers caught up with Mayleena's back. Then he lunged forward and wrapped his arms around her slender waist.

"Ah-h, I have you now," he shouted as he fell on top of her onto the sand, and she screamed delightfully and giggled.

Kalem lay beside Mayleena on the fine black sand resting his head on one elbow and looking down into her lovely green eyes. She was on her back, blushing, gazing fondly up at him with an alluring grin. Her long, wet hair draped across the firm curves of her breasts just hid them from view. Water drops on their naked bodies and faces heightened the romantic sensuality while they beheld each other long and tenderly.

To Kalem, Mayleena was beyond exquisite as he gazed slowly along the length of her body's elegant beauty, before looking back into her enchanting eyes.

Mayleena's gaze beheld Kalem's handsome features, his firm muscular chest, and trim athletic body.

"When we first met on Atla," Mayleena began softly, impassioned, "I couldn't believe the attraction between us."

"I feel it even more strongly now that I see you as you really are," he replied at the height of desire.

"Oh Kalem," she whispered, "my whole life was meant for this moment."

She threw her arms around his neck and drew him toward herself. He wrapped his arms around her back and pulled her up in an embrace a few inches off the sand. They kissed tenderly, drinking deeply from the sweetest well of nectar that few find in any lifetime. She placed her hands on Kalem's shoulders and gently pushed herself backward to the sand. With a longing passionate gaze, he gracefully moved on top of her, lowering below the background view of another large curling turquoise wave as it softly crashed along the glistening black sand.

Time passed and Kalem began to moan, peaking with passion in harmony with Mayleena's gasps of ecstatic pleasure just as a deep rumbling began and grew to the deafening roar of an earthquake violently shaking the beach around them.

"Kalem, what is it?" asked Mayleena nervously, coming out of her ecstatic swoon.

Kalem rose up into view on his extended arms, and he pulled Mayleena up at shoulder level with him.

"We must get back to the ship."

He grasped her hands and stood up, pulling her to her feet with their naked backs to Harry Faldwell's invisible viewpoint. Then they stumbled awkwardly as they jogged over the shaking ground toward the swaying jungle trees.

The scene before Harry shifted a short time ahead to his view of the water's edge back at the pool in the beautiful romantic setting below the lovely three-tiered waterfall. The ground was shaking lightly from an aftershock as Mayleena, now fully dressed, approached Kalem from behind a fern on the side of the path. Kalem was standing on the path pulling his Captain's suit up and over his shoulders. He pushed his hands through the sleeves, bent down and picked up from the ground the Transport Matrix Crystal hung from the gold chain, then tucked it inside his shirt as the ground finally stopped trembling.

"Maybe that's the end of it," Mayleena whispered hopefully.

"Yeah, things finally get really interesting between us and we get the great cosmic interruption. I hope someone up there finds the little joke funny," he replied with a frown before he gazed appreciatively at Mayleena's loveliness and grinned. "Well, lovely lady, we better head back before it starts up again."

They embraced and kissed. Then Kalem held her at arm's length so they could gaze for a moment into the depth of each other's eyes before he nodded toward the path. He tenderly kissed her on the forehead, and then took the lead as they jogged along the trail back toward the gardens and away from the enchanting waterfall pool.

CHAPTER THIRTY-ONE

NOW I HAVE YOU...
NOW I DON'T!

$\mathcal{K}$alem jogged further along the jungle path with Mayleena keeping pace a few feet behind him. As he passed a large tree, Sen Dar jumped from behind it, grabbed Mayleena by the neck with one hand, and pointed the laser gun in his other hand at her temple. Mayleena gasped. Kalem spun around, amazed to see Sen Dar again.

"Now, Captain," commanded Sen Dar, sneering in triumph, "you will deliver the Master Crystal Staff and the Transport Matrix Crystal to me or you can watch your lovely lady die...horribly!"

"How did you find us?" Kalem shot back defiantly.

Sen Dar impatiently pushed the laser gun deeper into Mayleena's temple, and she winced with pain. She struggled to get away but his grip on the back of her neck was too firm, and she fumed as she stopped struggling.

"Don't hurt her," pleaded Kalem. "I'll give you what you want, but I only have the Transport Matrix Crystal."

He lifted the blue crystal off his neck and began to slowly walk toward them.

"That will be far enough," scowled Sen Dar. "Throw it on the ground."

Kalem reluctantly stopped and tossed the chained crystal at his feet.

"Very good, Captain," said Sen Dar, and then he demanded, "Now, where is the Master Crystal Staff?"

"Right behind you," replied a familiar voice.

Sen Dar wheeled around tightly holding Mayleena by the neck and keeping his laser gun pointed at her temple. Master Ra Mu, contained in a transparent golden energy bubble, was standing a few feet directly in front of him with the Master Crystal Staff in his right hand.

Sen Dar frantically fired the laser several times at Ra Mu, but the beams ricocheted off the bubble and blasted holes through several nearby trees. He whirled back around to see Kalem making a move to grab him, and he scowled defiantly as he pushed the laser gun deeper into Mayleena's temple. Kalem reluctantly constrained himself just short of his goal, and Sen Dar glanced back and forth, sneering at both of them.

Then he slowly backed up with Mayleena toward the tree, while staring at Ra Mu, and viciously commanded, "Now give me the Master Crystal Staff. After the count of three, you will do this or she dies. One... Two... Three!"

A flash of gold light from Ra Mu's staff left Sen Dar stunned with one empty hand and his other hand holding the laser gun pointing in the air at nothing. Master Ra Mu, Mayleena, Kalem, and the Transport Matrix Crystal that had been lying on the ground by his feet had vanished. The ground shook again, and Sen Dar looked around, completely confused.

"No-o, damn it, not again," he screamed, and yelled out, "Ra Mu, I swear one way or another I will defeat you and damn that Ancient One garbage to the fires of oblivion."

The ground shook again more violently and Sen Dar struggled to keep standing. Then it split apart fifty-feet in front of him, and the widening crack raced to his position opening into a ten-feet-wide chasm under his feet. He jumped aside and spun around, then darted into the jungle.

High overhead, the sun was shining brightly down upon the gardens of MU on Lemuria. The ground was still lightly shaking as Master Ra Mu, Kalem, and Mayleena materialized in front of Kalem's ship. Surprised by the phenomenal instant transportation, Kalem and Mayleena looked at Ra Mu for answers.

"What just happened?" inquired Kalem, amazed.

"This will be good," chimed in Mayleena.

Master Ra Mu gazed at both of them and answered, "I would say The Ancient One has favor with you two to pull you out of that predicament."

"I thought your note said we would have enough time to enjoy each other in paradise," remarked Kalem with an accusing smirk.

Mayleena was staring at Ra Mu with a wide sarcastic smile and a hand on her hip.

"Well, uh, I may have slightly miscalculated," he replied with an innocent shrug of his shoulders and quickly changed the subject. "Captain, the polar shift is about to begin and we must board your ship."

Just then, the ground began to shake violently again and Mayleena grabbed Kalem's arm for support.

"Wait!" she yelled above the loud earthquake rumbling. "Where's Etta? We can't leave without him."

Etta flew into view and up beside her as the shaking subsided again, and Mayleena sighed with relief. She smiled at him and gave him a quick rub of her nose against his. Then her smile dropped.

"Etta, where's Din?"

Unconcerned, Etta smiled confidently.

"She's quite safe," answered Ra Mu. "I took her to Opellum's ship."

He grinned at Etta before he gazed at Kalem and insisted, "Captain, we must leave now."

Kalem led them over to his Scout Interceptor and waved his arm under the hull. Etta flew past him and up inside the ship through the bottom hatch. Mayleena climbed the ladder first and entered the ship. Ra Mu handed Kalem his staff, stepped up the ladder, and climbed aboard. Kalem lifted the staff up to the hatch, and Ra Mu's hand appeared back down through the opening, grabbed it, and pulled it up inside the ship. Kalem looked around suspiciously, as if he expected to find someone following him; then he climbed swiftly aboard. The ladder withdrew, the hatch spiraled closed, and the seam vanished.

A far more violent earthquake began as the ship lit up and lifted off the ground over the beautiful botanical gardens that began to sink into a gigantic opening fissure.

Sen Dar was running through the jungle jumping over fallen trees and sidestepping many more as they dropped across his path. Then he leapt over seven growing fissures that appeared in his way and darted into a clearing. He stopped abruptly to gaze with anguish at his ship slowly sinking into the ground. Panic-stricken, he raced up to the ship and stood on his tiptoes, straining to reach across the slowly widening chasm.

He managed to touch the underside of the hull with the palm of his hand and the hatch appeared in the upper half of the ship. A ramp slid out from it but it extended upward because of the gradually increasing angle of the sinking hull. Sen Dar took a determined step back and then leapt across the widening crevasse to just catch the edge of the ramp with both hands. Struggling with all his might, he pulled himself up over the edge and tumbled down the ramp's increasing angle through the hatch.

He slammed into the back of the control console, jumped to his feet, and stretched his hand over the top of the console. He just managed to touch one of the two domed guidance controls, and then slapped his palm on top of it, lighting up both controls. The ship lifted up and leveled out, as the ramp slid back inside the hull. The hatch closed and sealed.

The ship was hovering a few feet above the slowly widening hole in the clearing. Many of the surrounding jungle trees toppled over as the entire jungle landscape dropped fifty feet into a massively widening chasm. The thin red luminance around the hull intensified, and the ship rose straight up two thousand feet.

Then it darted across the sinking countryside toward the coast and continued its swift flight high over the black sand coastline of Lemuria, before it darted in a blur of light over the ocean.

CHAPTER THIRTY-TWO

THE POLAR SHIFT

$\mathcal{M}$aster Ra Mu, Kalem, Mayleena, and Etta – perched on top of the control console – were watching the main view screen. They could see Ra Mu's sanctuary hill and the arched bridge connecting it to the second hilltop passing below the ship as they flew high above the mounting destruction toward the coastal capital city of MU.

In the near distance, three pyramids towered majestically above the center of the city. The top third of one was flat and two Colonial Transports had landed on its surface. Thousands of people were running in every direction along the city streets as giant fissures opened in many places under them. Lava spewing out of several of the fissures overtook and devoured whole groups of the running, frightened citizens.

Master Ra Mu solemnly stated, "The quake has subsided for now but the damage you see is only the beginning." He sighed compassionately and looked at Kalem to request, "Captain, please bring us down on the landing pyramid."

Ominous storm clouds were building in the background sky over the ocean as Kalem's ship approached the top of the landing pyramid, then lowered and landed between the two Colonial Transports. The winds whipped up and became quite strong while Master Ra Mu exited the ship carrying his crystal staff, followed by Kalem and then Mayleena. Etta flew into view from under the ship a moment later, circled them once, and then landed on Mayleena's shoulder. He wrapped his tail across the top of her chest and clasped his hands around her arm to hold on against the high wind.

"It's time the people of Earth were offered a way out," proclaimed Ra Mu.

"A way out...of this?" yelled back Mayleena, disbelieving.

"Yes," he yelled back, "now it really is up to each one of them. Behold!"

He raised his staff a foot off the ground, closed his eyes, and bowed his head. The staff glowed, and a beam of blue light instantly projected from the Ankh symbol atop the staff up into the dark clouds that were swiftly moving in overhead. Multiple brilliant streaks of static lightning discharged within them, immediately followed by repeated thunderclap... *booms*... and a brilliant blue inter-dimensional vortex appeared whirling around the beam high above the landing pyramid. It spiraled open, quickly widening to thirty feet across, and the blue beam withdrew from the center of the vortex bringing with it a gold pyramid device. It stopped above Ra Mu's head, and the beam connected to it withdrew into the top of the staff.

The spinning vortex far above whirled closed and faded away, as the pyramid divided itself into one large and a dozen smaller pyramid-shaped devices. The large pyramid section remained in position six feet above Ra Mu's head, and the smaller sections began to spin, then instantly blurred away at incredible speed in every direction up into the darkening churning clouds.

Outside the city, several hundred closely gathered frightened men, women, and children were directly below one of the smaller pyramids as it flew down from the clouds and hovered above their heads. They were all astonished as they looked up to behold it radiating a brilliant gold-laced, blue light down over them.

In another part of the city below two golden spiral towers, several dozen men, women, and children were sitting, huddled together in the center of a street to keep from falling down from the violent shaking that had started up again. The towers and dwellings around them crumbled as fissures opened up in a nearby street. Another small pyramid flew down from the clouds and hovered fifteen feet above their heads.

The tiny figures of Master Ra Mu with the large pyramid hovering above his head, Kalem, Mayleena, and Etta, still perched on Mayleena's shoulder, were just visible standing on the landing pyramid in the background of the city.

On the other side of Earth, much destruction and great change had occurred to the city of Atla and the entire colony continent of Atlantis. One lone mountain had risen far above what had become a wide plateau that now overlooked the forested rolling hills near sea level. There, lying in ruins upon a much-diminished hilltop was the wreckage of High Seer Stralim's Council chambers.

On the upper plateau, another small pyramid was hovering above the heads of Stralim, Elder Councilman Melnor, a half-dozen other Council members, and hundreds of Atlantian men, women, and children. It emanated a deeply pervasive humming sound mixed with crashing ocean waves and the hauntingly beautiful flute melody of The Ancient One's Spirit presence. Stralim, Melnor, and all of the people gathered near them paid close attention to Ra Mu's voice as it resounded from the mysterious device that softly pulsed with each word spoken.

The voice you hear is speaking on behalf of The Ancient One to every man, woman, and child on Earth at this moment, stated his solemn voice. Then there was a long pause.

Stralim sat down to listen, as did dozens of other people gathered nearby. In the background, many more Atlantians approached Stralim from every direction to witness the phenomenal pyramid device hovering above his head.

The pyramids hovering at points across the continent pulsed with light with each word as he continued to speak.

This is the last day of the Golden Age of man that was foretold would come many years ago by The Ancient One's Guardian Adepts. Very soon, the lands of Earth will sink beneath the ocean waves and new lands will rise up from the depths of seas to take their place. For those who trust in The Ancient One, listen well. The uplifting sound you hear and the light you see emanating from the pyramid devices are actually two forms of the omnipresent Spirit Voice of The Ancient One. Sit quietly, close your eyes, listen carefully to the Sound, and see this Light within your inner vision with an open heart. The Sound of The Ancient One will carry you to safety, and the Light will guide the way. Each one of you must make the choice to listen and trust its loving omnipresence Spirit Sound to take you to safety or perish in the final moments to come. Farewell.

Master Ra Mu opened his eyes and gazed kindly at Kalem, then Mayleena, and finally at Etta who was still perched on her shoulder. Etta gazed anxiously back at Ra Mu and levitated off Mayleena's shoulder. He flew a few feet toward him.

Ra Mu took a deep breath and stated, "The time has come for us to go."

As he lowered his staff to the ground, the large pyramid hovering

301

above his head dissolved and vanished. The deep humming sound mixed with crashing ocean waves and the hauntingly beautiful flute melody of The Ancient One's Spirit presence grew stronger, dominating the sounds of destruction going on around them. As Ra Mu turned and walked toward Kalem's ship, Etta's eyes widened with anticipation, and he raced past him to quickly disappear up through the open hatch under the ship's hull.

Kalem and Mayleena grinned at Etta's endearing enthusiasm, and then walked ahead of Master Ra Mu to board the ship. This time when Master Ra Mu reached the ladder, Kalem's hand appeared down through the hatch and Ra Mu handed him his staff before climbing aboard. A moment later, the hatch spiraled closed, sealed, and the seam vanished. The antigravity drive hummed as the blue light around the hull pulsed brighter, and the ship lifted high above the landing pyramid, and then flew over the sinking city.

The ship continued to fly away from the destruction of the city of Mu as it passed over the countryside by the botanical gardens. The white stone bridge collapsed, just as Kalem's ship stopped above it. The dirt covering the hilltop hiding Master Ra Mu's sanctuary began to slide off, revealing the quartz-capped gold pyramid. The rock steps leading from the gardens up the hillside crumbled, and the entire length of them fell into a crevasse that opened along its length.

Inside the domed dwelling of a Lemurian family were the husband, wife, and a young boy and girl huddled together on a large rug. With eyes closed, they were listening to the uplifting Sound of The Ancient One's Spirit presence and gazing at the Light. Then they transformed into the glowing spheres of their true Atma that faded and disappeared.

The four energy spheres reappeared in a field of grass that overlooked the black sand beach of this secret parallel time dimension on Earth. They quickly materialized back into their physical forms as the radiant light that surrounded them quickly faded away. The entire family slowly opened their tightly closed eyes to discover with amazement they were sitting on a vast grass-covered plateau. It overlooked the black sand beach in one direction and the huge clear domed city at the base of a tall snowcapped mountain in the opposite direction. The entire surrounding background panoramic view was crystal-clear on this beautifully pristine day under a cloudless turquoise sky.

A vibrant elderly bald man, wearing a gold-colored silk robe tied by a matching sash at the waist and simple sandals, was suddenly standing behind the family, emanating a pale golden aura. The family members were astonished as they looked around to behold his presence, and they quickly stood up and hugged each other with the joyful realization they were still very much alive.

Then they noticed that hundreds of people from Lemuria and Atlantis had already materialized in the vast field that surrounded them. They were sitting or standing in the grass talking with wondrous excitement to each other, while many more people materialized at various points all over the field.

"You are all welcomed here in the name of The Ancient One and you are all safe," said the elderly man cheerfully. "I am known as Master Lumiera. I am the Guardian of this place."

"Master Ra Mu was right. We were spared certain death," stated the father with tears of joy in his eyes. "We thank you for our lives."

"You can thank The Ancient One that resides in your hearts," Lumiera replied humbly. "It's omnipresent Sound and Light, which each one of you chose to heed, safely transported you here."

In the parallel dimension on Earth where the city of Mu on the continent of Lemuria was being destroyed, hundreds of people of all ages were screaming and running in every direction as a wide area of ground opened beneath them to swallow them all. Several dozen very courageous men, women, and children were sitting on the ground close to the center of the destruction with their eyes closed. They were listening to The Ancient One's vibrant Spirit Sound, and they began to glow, then dematerialized.

Meanwhile, the entire continent of Atlantis had become a much smaller place. One lone volcanic mountain had risen high above an upper plateau. A few ruins on the lower plateau near sea level were all that remained of the once great city of Atla. The overhead skies were crimson, and lightning bolts flashed through the dark clouds, immediately followed by a series of loud echoing thunderclap...*booms*.

Stralim was exhausted while he sat in the grass on the upper plateau surrounded by hundreds of Atlantian men, women, and children sitting or lying down around him. He could see molten lava pouring out of fissures along the ground in various places and in the jungle forests on the lower plateau. Some of the tall remaining jungle trees were on fire. Stralim sadly watched the Council chambers far below as it began to crumble, and then the hill sank beneath it and the collapsing building vanished inside an opening crevasse.

Only one of the two pyramids remained intact resting upon the emerald sands a thousand yards inland from the turbulent, crashing waves. The rest of what was left of the city dwellings, built along the jungle floor and hillsides, crumbled as the land beneath them collapsed into a massive sinking pit of lava.

A huge tidal wave rolled in from the coast over the sinking jungle city, crashing onto the remaining pyramid and washing over the background jungle. Huge billows of steam hissed high into the air as the lava writhed and boiled beneath the churning waves.

Stralim looked away to see many of his people were still sitting and listening to The Ancient One's intense Spirit Sound that seemed to permeate everything. He watched as they turned into silver and gold particles of light, faded, and vanished right before his eyes, while other Atlantians ran around screaming in a fearful panic. He got up to look at the lower plateau again and his sinking city. His eyes watered as he realized he had completely forgotten about someone very dear to him during the catastrophe.

"Layliella," he cried softly, anguished.

Back in the city of Mu on the continent of Lemuria, the landing pyramid had now tilted on its side and was rapidly sinking into the ground collapsing beneath it. Kalem's ship was still hovering above the gardens as spiral towers, domed buildings, and palatial estates within the city of Mu tumbled down hillsides in heaps of ruins, or fell into great fissures that opened as lava burst from them.

Then a massive fiery explosion ripped through the ground, sending half the city into the air in every direction. One huge chunk of rock just missed Kalem's ship as it tumbled upward in a long arc across the sky and over the countryside to drop somewhere in the far distant jungle. The ground beneath the entire countryside heaved and rolled like a long wave, and it sank slowly just as several hundred-foot-tall tidal waves roared in over the city toward its center from four directions. Huge chunks of the surrounding terrain exploded high into the air and fell back into the waves as they crashed together over the remaining half of the sinking city.

Admiral Starland aboard his flagship was looking at the event projected in holographic 3-D from the main view screen in the bridge control room. Two solar systems depicted in live action were passing near one another, headed in the same direction. On the far right of the scene, a yellow sun appeared with Earth and all the other familiar planets orbiting it, including the asteroid belt between Mars and Jupiter where the planet Maldec had been.

On the far left of the scene, nine planets were orbiting a much larger sun at a thirty-five-degree angle to the sun and system of planets containing Earth. The inner planets of the unknown solar system were of varying sizes with gaseous atmospheres, a number of dust rings, and many moons. However, the outermost ninth planet was a moonless gas giant world with a thick blue and violet whirling cloud cover. It was gradually moving downward away from Admiral Starland's viewpoint, headed on a course with Earth.

Then the images changed to a larger overview of the two planets moving ever closer toward each other on their individual journeys around their parent suns. The moon was moving safely out of view behind Earth opposite the large alien world, while red static lightning flashed more violently in Earth's atmosphere. As the two planets converged, a massive exchange of ion-charged energy streamed from the gaseous giant world into Earth's atmosphere in a long fiery arc.

"Lieutenant, I want a closer view of Earth and that planet," ordered Starland as he looked at Marin. "Make sure you log everything. This rare event takes place only once to this planet every 100,000 years."

"I have it coming on the screen now, Admiral," replied Lieutenant Marin, anxiously anticipating what she would see.

A closer wide view appeared on the view screen just as the gas giant world began to pass by Earth just several hundred thousand miles away on its way back up along its diagonal path around its sun. Earth's atmosphere was now a deep crimson as it passed by the giant world moving to the right along its path around its sun. The ion-charged energy stream now extended from the entire upper third of Earth's atmosphere all the way to the equator of the giant world, where it mixed and swirled in the giant planet's gaseous outer layer.

As the two worlds gradually moved further away from each other, Earth wobbled on its polar axis. The ion energy stream spewing between them was stretched ever thinner until the gas giant's more powerful gravitational attraction pulled Earth's north pole slowly over one hundred and eighty degrees. Then the ion stream finally snapped, leaving residual energy trails receding back into the atmospheres of both worlds.

A close-up of Earth revealed the small northern ice cap, now at the Earth's bottom polar position, breaking apart. The churning ocean was pulverizing large sections of it and many smaller pieces were moving away in various directions. The southern ice cap, now at the northern polar region, was also breaking apart as Earth wobbled a few times on its axis, before it stabilized.

The massive continent of Lemuria centered over the equator was now opposite its original position vanishing beneath the seething ocean waves. The continent of Atlantis, once two-thirds the size of Lemuria, had almost entirely disappeared, except for a five-hundred-mile-wide volcanic mountainous island a tiny fraction of its original size. This remaining island situated near the equator, was now also opposite its original position.

The moon gradually reappeared around the far side of Earth, while new landmasses rose rapidly up from the depth of the ocean where no land had previously existed. A gravitational counterbalancing was taking place from the effect of the rapid polar shift that had caused the planet's mantle to spin around the core like a gear around a shaft.

While Harry Faldwell continued to observe all of the incredible phenomena before him, he realized that for some time to come the world would have no significant difference than present-day Earth, except for the remaining mountainous island of Atlantis.

I wonder what became of it? he pondered in silent amazement.

The sudden realization that his ongoing experience of his true spherical Atma-self meant that he is an eternal being, and joyfully a part of and made from the same substance as The Ancient One's mysterious omnipresent Sound and Light, whatever that was.

My God, it's all true, every bit of it, he mused in a state of wonder.

He continued to watch the new landmasses ascend above the ocean until they formed into the familiar shapes of the continents known on Earth today, including the continent of Antarctica which rose last under the broken sheets of ice in the new southern polar region. Entirely new landmasses worldwide now surrounded the remaining island of Atlantis. Its location was now centered in the middle of what the Earth's future people would refer to as the infamous Bermuda Triangle.

The scene before Harry changed to Admiral Starland's ship. Starland continued to watch the projection of the two suns and planetary systems moving rapidly away from each other to continue their orbits around the galactic center, as if nothing had happened.

"Bring us back to an Earth orbit," he commanded ship's navigator Drelim, who nodded and touched several crystal controls. Then he looked at Marin seated next to him and gently ordered, "Lieutenant, try again to contact Captain Kalem."

"Yes, Admiral," she replied and sighed as she eagerly touched the transceiver crystal control.

CHAPTER THIRTY-THREE

MEETING
THE ANCIENT ONE

*K*alem's ship was hovering high above the churning ocean where only an hour earlier the huge continent of Lemuria had proudly stood. Master Ra Mu, with his crystal staff in his right hand; Kalem and Mayleena were standing on personal antigravity transport discs. They were hovering in the air five feet apart from each other. Etta was levitating, but he was barely holding his own in the high wind. The crimson static energy in the turbulent clouds above them was rapidly diminishing in intensity, and the color changed from crimson to red and then to a faint pink.

The sinking city of Mu, still visible below the surface of the seething ocean waves, was sinking deeper, and it soon faded from sight. The quartz tip of one of the three pyramids was still sticking up above the waves, and then it too sank beneath them and faded away in the depth of the ocean.

Mayleena was teary-eyed, and Kalem and Etta were frowning solemnly, but Master Ra Mu was smiling. Kalem noticed his cheerful disposition and was puzzled.

"Why did you want us out here?" he yelled in the high winds.

Master Ra Mu looked up at the churning clouds, then at Kalem and yelled back, "I want the three of you to witness the birth of a new cycle for humankind everywhere, and I want you to meet someone most special."

Greater than any thunderclap, a tremendous ...*boom*... echoed across

308

the heavens, dissipating the discharges in the clouds overhead, and the winds subsided. The welcome warming light from the sun peered through a break in the clouds and gleamed down over them like a soothing blanket. As Ra Mu pointed his crystal staff toward the heavens, Etta covered his eyes.

"Behold, The Ancient One," Ra Mu announced boldly, looking up with reverence as he raised his staff further skyward.

The clouds rumbled back in every direction, revealing a brilliant golden ball of light hovering in the center of a circle of a clear blue sky. The gold ball began to spiral and widen like thousands of gold stars in a whirling galaxy, and then it opened into an inter-dimensional vortex. A brightly pulsing, six-pointed blue star was floating on the other side of the opening in a higher dimensional reality.

An enormous ethereal city filled with crystalline spires, sparkling jeweled domes, and towers, stretched from the foreground behind the pulsing blue star to the infinite distance under a golden sky. As the star flew through the opening and continued to descend gracefully, they could hear the Spirit Sound of The Ancient One's melody coming toward them.

The blue star stopped a hundred feet above their heads, and a moment later, it began to move again in their direction. The Spirit Sound gradually increased as thousands of little blue stars streamed from the vortex like a river of light that flowed down to descend into the ocean far below.

The star stopped again only twenty feet above their heads and began to spin, forming into a sphere of luminous being more spectacular than anything witnessed by any of them before, except for Master Ra Mu. The sphere was comprised of teardrop-shaped lights in layers from a radiant white core through the entire spectrum of colors to a shimmering violet outer layer, surrounded by a golden aura. A golden light, like fine misty rain, was emanating from the sphere's outer aura washing down over them with uplifting warmth.

Then the core began to pulse with each word as the melodious voice of The Ancient One proclaimed, *Kalem, Mayleena, and Etta, why do you mourn? No Atma has ever perished. Behold!*

Master Ra Mu was listening with a humble smile, and Etta was captivated in silent wonder as he hovered beside him. Kalem and Mayleena were speechless while they remained hovering in place on their personal antigravity transports.

A rumble quickly dominated all other sounds, just as thousands of little blue stars reappeared coming out of the ocean. Each one was hovering above a luminous Atma sphere that looked exactly like The Ancient One, except they were much smaller. The thousands of blue stars continued to flow in waves from the ocean depths drawing an equal number of the luminous Soul-spheres up with them. They flew gracefully together back up through the inter-dimensional vortex and disappeared in the background vastness of the mystical city of light.

Ra Mu, Kalem, Mayleena, and Etta emanated childlike wonder and profound respect for The Ancient One's benevolent presence. The Ancient One moved slowly toward them and stopped again twelve feet above their heads.

Each one of you is an eternal luminous Atma or Soul-being: a radiant conscious drop of the Spirit Sound and Light from my universal body, continued The Ancient One's telepathic voice. *You are not the temporary physical forms that cover your true selves. Each of you has lived countless lifetimes to unfold the love, wisdom, and freedom that are necessary for you to be here now. Like Master Ra Mu, you will fulfill your individual destinies and then journey back to the true home of Atma in the far higher, pure positive dimensional realm you see beyond through the vortex. There you will become freely responsible and fully experienced spiritual travelers, and conscious co-creators with you conscious co-creators with The Ancient One you see before you. The way is now open.*

The radiance emanating from The Ancient One's lights greatly increased and the entire sphere pulsed as it moved gracefully back up through the vortex to diminish in the far distance over the mystical city of light. The Ancient One's enchanting sound faded away as the vortex whirled closed and vanished.

The sun streamed down through the swiftly dissipating clouds to warm the astonished faces of Etta, Mayleena, and Kalem. Then Etta began to laugh, but he had no idea why, and he flew excitedly around them, twirling and dancing in the air. He soon came to a soft landing on Master Ra Mu's shoulder and gazed up at him with big innocent eyes, gratefully smiling from ear to ear. Ra Mu glanced over at Kalem and Mayleena, and Etta followed his gaze. They both chuckled after seeing their astonished faces and mouths wide open.

"Wake up you two, and while you're at it," commanded Ra Mu, "you better close your mouths before something flies into them."

Mayleena and Kalem blinked and closed their mouths, then looked solemnly back at him.

"Where did they all go?" asked Kalem.

"That's what I want to know," concurred Mayleena.

"The people of Lemuria, Atlantis, and Maldec, who recently lost their physical bodies, will rest with The Ancient One for a while," Ra Mu stated. "Then they will inhabit new physical embodiments in Earth's distant future. Our greatest challenge has just begun."

"Somehow, I just knew you were going to say something like that," said Kalem to lighten the mood.

He turned and gazed at Mayleena, who appeared disappointed, and then her spirit lifted as she gazed back at him with radiant green eyes. "At least we are together."

Her comment instantly raised his spirit as well, and he beamed back unmistakable deep appreciation for her loveliness as a being and a woman. Then he turned to Ra Mu and Etta, who were already smiling back at them.

"Mayleena, would you like to see Stralim before we leave this place?" inquired Ra Mu, raising his eyebrows.

"You know I would," she replied anxiously. "I've been so worried about him through all this."

Ra Mu nodded and looked at Kalem.

"Captain, please take us to the location of Atla on Atlantis."

Kalem opened his mouth to respond but grinned instead as he

watched Etta levitate off Ra Mu's shoulders to perform a little dancing jig in the air, releasing pent-up energy. They burst out laughing at his antics, until Etta stopped before he flew, embarrassed, over to hover again beside Ra Mu.

"Why, Master Ra Mu," Kalem replied, "it would be my pleasure to fly us there, and we better get moving."

Suddenly elated, Etta darted underneath the ship and up inside it through the open hatch. Mayleena gave Kalem an alluring smile as she flew her disc right by him and past Ra Mu. Kalem's delighted gaze followed her as he flew his disc up behind her, and Master Ra Mu followed behind them on his disc. One by one, they entered the ship up through the open hatch in the bottom of the hull.

Moments later, the ship's hum increased with the intensifying blue light around the hull, and the ship flew across the sky high above the ocean that was now as calm as if no land had ever been there.

CHAPTER THIRTY-FOUR

FINAL FAREWELL
ON
THE ISLAND OF ATLANTIS

A mountain peak loomed high in the background behind High Seer Stralim, who was sitting on a rock in the field on the upper plateau of a newly formed land. He was crying with his head bowed, resting on his arms crossed over his knees. Hundreds of his people had gathered around campfires on the field surrounding him. Several thousand feet below on the lower plateau was a new shoreline, and a single pyramid now rested there where shortly before two had stood proudly with their quartz-tipped apexes jutting above the top of the jungle trees. The catastrophic destruction had finally subsided, sinking almost the entire colony continent of Atlantis, except for the remaining five-hundred-mile-wide mountainous island with its largest now dormant volcanic cone located near the new coastline.

Back aboard Kalem's ship, Master Ra Mu was gazing at Etta, who was hovering on the other side of the control console.

"If you don't mind, Etta, we won't be long," remarked Ra Mu.

Etta flew to the top of the console and landed on his hind legs. He stood upright and shrugged his shoulders.

"Ob aba" ("Of course"), he said, quite disappointed.

Etta noticed Kalem looking his way pondering something, while he stood beside Mayleena and behind Master Ra Mu.

"By the way, Etta, do you know where Opellum and your lovely wife

313

Din is now or where they headed during all this?"

Etta's green cheeks turned rosy red for an instant before he caught himself and courageously puffed up his chest.

"Emu pa jompt covoolm op woldent Oceana sim Opellum lota emu pa feepf sim genth yindred, tak chet," he replied.

Mayleena answered for him, "He says she's back home on planet Oceana with Opellum where she's safe with our children, thank you."

Respectfully, Ra Mu and Kalem held back laughter.

"I heard you, Etta," commented Kalem, "and I most definitely relate to that."

"Oh, forgive me, Kalem," began Mayleena, appearing a little embarrassed as she touched two fingers to her lips. "I forgot that Etta telepathically transmits in your language, while he is speaking Dren aloud. He doesn't do that with me because he knows I understand his language."

Etta proudly beamed and nodded, confirming her statement.

"Etta, dear friend," interrupted Ra Mu, "we will be right back."

He raised his staff and it glowed with gold light that quickly enveloped himself, Kalem, and Mayleena. As they faded from view, Etta's quirky smile dwindled to a frown, and he dropped an elbow on the control console to lean his weight against it.

Right, go ahead and leave me behind again like useless baggage, he thought in clear English, and closed his eyes to visualize what might have happened if he had instantly appeared in front of Stralim as a strange flying alien creature.

A few seconds later, his eyes sprang wide open and he softly said to himself, "Well, maybe it would not have been such a good idea after all."

Stralim was still sitting on the rock on the upper plateau beside the newly risen volcanic mountain that overlooked the new coastline of the island of Atlantis. A shaft of brilliant gold light flashed in front of him, and Master Ra Mu, Mayleena, and Kalem instantly materialized. Startled, Stralim jumped up and stared cautiously at Ra Mu. Then he gazed, surprised, at Mayleena's blue skin, before he scrutinized Kalem, who seemed familiar to him, and his eyes opened wide in recognition.

"I thought I had caused your...your death," he said regretfully. "I was wrong about you. I see now you were only disguised as Diplomat Aeron to protect my daughter." He gazed sadly at Ra Mu and confessed, "Master Ra Mu, I was wrong about you too."

"The hypnotic power Sen Dar wielded over you came from his misuse of The Ancient One's crystal," Ra Mu remarked kindly. "If you have learned from this experience, such things will not have sway over you in the future."

The High Seer cast his sad eyes down, then up at Kalem, and he hesitantly inquired, "Who are you, really, and what can I do to pay for my mistakes?"

"My name is Kalem, but you owe me nothing," he answered. "You can't be blamed. I know what treachery Sen Dar is capable of wielding. Actually, I'm very grateful to you for caring for the woman I have loved most of my life."

Stralim started to smile but then gazed, mystified, at Ra Mu.

"Why was I not taken with the others on the Spirit Sound and Light of The Ancient One?"

"Your destiny is to rebuild what is left of Atlantis," Ra Mu answered encouragingly. "It will come to be known as the island continent, and it will be the center of the world for many centuries before it too will sink beneath the waves."

Stralim perked up and nodded gratefully to Ra Mu before gazing fondly into Mayleena's lovely green eyes.

"I knew you were special the day I found you on the beach with blue skin and pointed ears. When I revived you, you changed into the young blond woman I named Layliella after my own daughter, and I have loved you ever since." He shamefully lowered his head. "You were so frightened, and I just couldn't bring myself to remind you how I really found you that day." He looked sadly back up at her and asked, "Dear one, what is your real name?"

"Mayleena, dearest foster father Stralim," she replied gently as she threw her arms around him and tightly hugged him with her head snuggled against his chest.

Stralim's joyful smile quickly faded again.

"Will I...ever see you again?"

"There is no need to worry," remarked Ra Mu. "If you wish, a way can be provided for you to see each other through the years to come."

Mayleena tenderly kissed Stralim's hand, his cheek, and then his forehead.

"You are, after all, the only father I have known and loved most of my life until recently," she said, wiping tears from her eyes before she too perked up. "Of course, we will see each other again."

She hugged him again and then stepped back to stand by Ra Mu's side. Kalem extended his hand to Stralim and they clasped forearms and grinned at each other like old friends. Then Stralim gazed with profound respect at Master Ra Mu, who was compassionately watching him.

"If you are ever in need of me, close your eyes and place the focus of your inner awareness at the point slightly above and between your eyebrows… here," instructed Master Ra Mu with kind encouragement, pointing with his index finger to the spot centered just above and between Stralim's eyebrows. "Call my name several times," he added, "and then listen for the Inner Sound and look for the Inner Light. I will come to you."

Any lingering guilt vanished from Stralim. He began to smile and cry at the same time, now relieved, before he acknowledged Master Ra Mu with a nod.

Ra Mu lifted the staff off the ground again and it radiated gold light that quickly enveloped him, Kalem, and Mayleena; and they faded from Stralim's sight.

Tears of joy mixed with sorrow were running down Mayleena's face as the three materialized back aboard Kalem's ship. She walked a few feet over to Kalem's side and gazed up at him. He put a consoling arm around her waist and snuggled her close. She rested her head on his chest as Etta flew to her side and sympathetically rubbed his head on the side of her neck.

"Will Stralim be all right?" asked Kalem, looking at Ra Mu.

"He will adjust and he won't be alone," replied Ra Mu. "There is no need to worry. Stralim is a strong being and I will be in close contact with him. Mayleena may also discreetly visit him from time to time, when her destiny permits it."

Ra Mu slowly closed his eyes to contemplate something, and Mayleena appeared confused. She started to open her mouth to ask a question but decided not to disturb him and gazed at Kalem instead.

She whispered, "What does he mean when my destiny permits it?"

Kalem shrugged his shoulders. Master Ra Mu soon opened his eyes and a smile widened across his face — as if he had suddenly discovered the answer to a secret mystical question, he alone was privileged to know.

Then he looked benevolently into the eyes of Kalem, Mayleena, and Etta, and said, "The time has come to journey to our new home."

CHAPTER THIRTY-FIVE

ESCAPE TO A FUTURE PARALLEL TIME

The puzzlement Mayleena and Kalem felt with Ra Mu's mysterious statement about her destiny was for now forgotten. Their keen interest to journey to their new home had diverted their attention. Kalem smiled with anticipation as he walked over to the chair by the control console and sat down. He reached his hands over the top of the console to depress them in the guidance controls, but a flashing crystal making a shrill sound interrupted him. He touched it and the view screen revealed a red fireball speeding toward the ship. It was coming from the thick clouds that surrounded the towering volcanic peak near the new Atlantis Island coastline.

"The shield!" he yelled and grabbed a green crystal with his left hand, as he slammed his hand into the guidance control imprint, lighting up both crystals.

Mayleena gasped and cringed behind Kalem, as Etta hovered over to his side, growling at the view screen. Master Ra Mu, however, was standing calmly with his legs apart holding his crystal staff at arm's length by his side.

"It has to be Sen Dar," Kalem grumbled to himself. Then he yelled to the others, "He must have followed us here. This time I will stop him permanently."

The fireball exploded off the shield shaking the ship, and Kalem reached for the blue crystal, but Ra Mu grabbed his wrist.

"Kalem, wait," he commanded, "there is a better way."

He raised his crystal staff off the floor and it illuminated with violet light along its entire length, sending a light beam from the Ankh symbol directly through the ship's hull.

The beam extended ten feet beyond the ship to form a whirling pool of energy that quickly transformed into a curved energy shield shaped like a dish antenna pointed away from the ship.

Sen Dar was gazing anxiously with subdued excitement at his view screen in anticipation of witnessing Kalem's death.

"And now, useless Captain, you are finally...mine!" he fumed under his breath as he touched the red crystal, and it pulsed with light.

Another red fireball appeared on his view screen headed toward Kalem's ship hovering in the distant sky above the mountain's upper plateau. Moments later, it hit the violet energy shield in front of the Scout Interceptor and was instantly reflected back toward Sen Dar's ship at an alarmingly increased speed. Sen Dar gasped as he witnessed his own firepower coming directly back at him.

"Damn you Ra Mu and your Ancient One illusion," he yelled, slamming his fist on the control console. "You are behind this," and he slapped his hands over the controls.

Sen Dar's ship darted deeper into the cloud cover encircling the mountain, and his own speeding fireball rapidly closed the gap. It sped through the clouds racing toward a certain impact with his ship, which made a sudden ninety-degree turn to the left and the fireball sped by, missing the hull by inches. As it sped into the distance, it changed course.

Sen Dar was sweating with gritted teeth as he watched the view screen, and he frantically pressed down harder on the domed controls in an attempt to evade further pursuit. His eyes widened fearfully as he saw his own red fireball curve around and head directly back toward his ship.

"No-o-o," he yelled defiantly and grabbed the fire control.

He watched with nervous anticipation as another red fireball appeared on his view screen speeding on a course to intercept the red one racing toward him. They soon exploded violently together in a brilliant shower of dissipating light.

Kalem's ship was still hovering a thousand feet away from the thick clouds that surrounded the summit of the mountain as the violet shield in front of the hull began to whirl, forming into a much larger violet fireball. Then it darted toward the cloud cover and separated into two-dozen smaller energy sphere projectiles that spread out over a wide area just before they entered the clouds.

Sen Dar's ship was hiding behind the cloud cover on the backside of the mountain, just as the violet fireballs reappeared from the clouds.

His eyes were transfixed on the view screen as the two-dozen fireballs passed out of the clouds across a wide area and darted toward his ship. Before he could react, the fireballs completely encompassed his ship from every direction. Then they darted toward his certain destruction.

"No, you will not stop me," he grumbled, but his angry scowl became fearful apprehension.

He frantically grabbed The Ancient One's parchment from inside his shirt, quickly read something, and then threw it down on the control console. His right hand clutched the Emerald Doorway Crystal, and he mumbled something under his breath. The crystal glowed through his fingers, and then it projected a wide emerald beam through the ship's hull. With perspiration dripping down his forehead, Sen Dar glanced at the view screen to see that the two-dozen fireballs racing toward him from every direction were only moments away from his destruction.

One day, Ra Mu, he mused furiously, *you and that worthless Kalem will forfeit your lives.*

He slammed his left hand back down on top of the left domed guidance control and scowled at the view screen.

Outside his ship, the emerald beam extended from the hull to form into a whirling inter-dimensional vortex that opened wider to reveal Earth's distant future on the other side. The Statue of Liberty towered in the foreground of a wide background view of the New York City seaport. The violet fireballs were almost at impact with the ship when the red aura around the hull flashed and the ship darted through the vortex.

The energy doorway whirled closed just as the two-dozen fireballs passed through the air where his ship had been and instantly rejoined into the one much larger fireball. The large fireball raced toward the fading vortex and hit it, creating a tremendous violet explosion. The fading vortex remained unharmed behind the dissipating fiery light as it continued to fade from view.

It was late afternoon on a beautiful day in present time on Earth above New York City. The city skyline spread wide in the background. A 747-jet airliner had left the city's airport headed southward, while Sen Dar's ship hovered several thousand feet away from the vanishing vortex. The red aura around the ship's hull flashed again, and the ship flew away from the skyline toward the distant horizon over the Atlantic Ocean.

Back aboard Kalem's Scout ship, Master Ra Mu, Kalem, Mayleena, and Etta were gazing at the view screen. Kalem was sitting in the chair behind the control console, angrily, angrily disappointed, and Ra Mu was standing behind him to his right side. Mayleena stood behind him on the other side with a consoling hand on his shoulder. Etta was feisty and grumbling under his breath while he hovered a few feet from the view screen, fuming at it. A moment later, his grumbling subsided and he appeared confused as he scratched the top of his head with one of his little fingers.

"That's what I want to know, Etta," remarked Kalem, noticing his confusion. He looked over at Ra Mu and asked, "How did that madman get away this time?"

"Apparently Sen Dar has already discovered how to access one of the functions of the Emerald Doorway Crystal," Ra Mu replied solemnly. "He's gone far into Earth's future in a parallel dimension. Fortunately, he has not discovered the crystal's true purpose or its full parallel time potential. However, this does considerably change things."

Sen Dar was amazed with his mouth agape staring at the view screen, while he sat in the chair behind the control console aboard his ship. He was observing the Statue of Liberty and New York City rapidly receding into the background, until they appeared like tiny specks and finally vanished beyond the horizon over the ocean far behind his speeding ship. Then he changed the view screen to an overview of his ship flying further over the Atlantic Ocean away from what he did not yet know was the eastern seaboard of the United States of America.

"Where am I?" he asked himself aloud in wide-eyed wonder.

The Emerald Doorway Crystal in his right hand was still glowing through his clenched fingers as he reached down with his other hand and shook open the old parchment lying on top of the console to read something with keen interest. A moment later, he looked up with a sudden realization, and he let go of the crystal that stopped glowing as it dropped to his chest.

Of course, he mused with profound discovery. *The crystal must have projected me into the future of this Earth planet. I wonder what other functions it has.* His wonder dissolved into a determined sneer as he thought with renewed enthusiasm, *This is far better than I had envisioned. Clearly, my destiny is to explore this future planet Earth., since it will soon become my new home world.*

Late afternoon sunlight glimmered across a vast expanse of the Atlantic Ocean on this cloudless day in present time on Earth, as Sen Dar's ship flew in a swift high arc over the ocean to vanish in the setting sun beyond the horizon.

CHAPTER THIRTY-SIX

STARLAND COMES TO EARTH'S PRESENT TIME

The transceiver crystal on the control board of Kalem's ship was blinking and making a soft beeping sound. Kalem touched it and Admiral Starland appeared on the view screen, standing beside the bridge control console aboard his flagship.

"We've been trying to contact you since the polar shift but the static energy around Earth distorted our signal. Captain, is everyone all right?"

"We're all fine, Admiral," replied Kalem, and he added with growing enthusiasm, "But something incredible has occurred."

"Ah-h, so you finally met The Ancient One," remarked Starland with a curious glint in his eyes before Kalem could say more.

"How did you know?" Kalem asked, somewhat mystified.

Mayleena was smiling at Ra Mu, who was silently observing Kalem's reaction. She walked up beside Kalem and slipped her hand into his. Master Ra Mu stepped toward the control console and looked up at the Admiral on the view screen. He initiated a private telepathic communication. The Admiral smiled back and nodded his approval.

"Like myself, Captain," remarked Ra Mu turning to Kalem, "your father is also a Master Adept of The Ancient One."

Kalem blinked several times, before he gazed up at the Admiral for confirmation. "You, father, are an Adept of The Ancient One? But, why didn't you ever tell me?"

"You were not ready to hear it before," replied Starland. "However, if you, Mayleena, and Etta freely accept Master Ra Mu's training from this moment forward, then one day he will guide each of you to the true home of the Atma within the lofty realm of The Ancient One as he did for me when I was his student."

An astounding realization came to Kalem, and he looked at Master Ra Mu, then back at Starland and inquired, "Did you know what was being prepared for us?"

"Not some of the specifics but for the most part, yes," replied Starland with a mysterious grin.

The Admiral gazed at Mayleena and remarked jovially, "Mayleena, my dear, you have grown into a very beautiful woman."

"Thank you, Admiral," she replied, blushing. "It's also good to see you again."

Starland's smile widened as he looked in Etta's direction. And Etta, my friend, it is good to see you again too."

Grinning from ear to ear, Etta proudly puffed up his chest and then flew twice around the control room before he stopped near the view screen.

Kalem glanced at Starland, Ra Mu, Mayleena, and then at Etta. "You all knew each other the whole time? This, is unbelievable! Am I the only one fumbling in the dark around here?"

Mayleena put her hand to her mouth to keep from laughing, quickly composed herself, then gracefully dropped her hand to gaze fondly into Kalem's eyes.

"Dearest Kalem, your father, Master Ra Mu, and Etta came to Oceana many times when I was a little girl."

"Sen Dar has already discovered how to use the time-link function of the Emerald Doorway Crystal," interrupted Ra Mu, gazing at Starland, "and he transported his ship 100,000 years into Earth's future in a parallel time dimension. Are you prepared to track him?"

"We are prepared, Master Ra Mu," the Admiral replied calmly.

"Wait a minute, where's he going now?" asked Kalem.

"Sen Dar must be stopped, Captain, and soon," replied Master Ra Mu, "or an event like that which happened on Maldec will occur on Earth. The Master Crystal Staff will cause the flagship's trans-light drive to open a special conduit from this dimension to Earth's distant future in a parallel time dimension, where Sen Dar's has gone."

"I'm not quite sure I follow you," said Kalem.

"We will arrive at our destiny with Earth's distant future along a different path than that of your father, Captain," Ra Mu added patiently, and then instructed Starland, "Admiral, engage your trans-light drive when the sound from my staff reaches your bridge."

"We are ready to receive it," acknowledged Starland. "We will see each other soon in Earth's future," he said, gazing at Kalem as a loving father. He looked at everyone aboard Kalem's ship and added, "For now, farewell to you all."

The view screen went blank. Kalem shrugged his shoulders and sighed with a shake of his head. Mayleena moved toward him to put her arm around his waist. He slid his arm around her slender back, pulling her close as she looked up at him with her enchanting green eyes. Then Ra Mu stepped back a few feet behind the control console and let go of the crystal staff. It remained upright by some mystical force and pulsed with blue light, emanating a deep resonant tone.

Communications Lieutenant Marin and Helmsman Drelim were sitting behind the bridge control console aboard the flagship. The Admiral was standing behind them with his hands behind his back. They heard the faint, deep tone emanating from Ra Mu's staff that grew in clarity and volume until all of the other bridge personnel looked around for its source. Drelim anxiously gazed up at the Admiral for the order to proceed.

"Helmsman Drelim, engage the trans-light drive," commanded Starland with a nod of his head.

A beam of blue light was projected a mile into space from the front edge of one end of the hull, and energy whirled in a spiral around the end of the beam. It opened into a vortex that appeared like millions of tiny blue stars revolving around a deep, blue energy tunnel leading to Earth's distant future. The beam shut off, and Starland's flagship moved slowly into the whirling opening and disappeared in the distance deep within the tunnel.

The fabric of space near Earth as it appears today opened into another vortex with millions of the same small stars revolving around the other end of the deep, blue tunnel. The full moon loomed into view along its path around the Earth, with all the familiar continents of today in place, including the polar icecaps. However, there was no sign of the mountainous island of Atlantis in the Bermuda Triangle area.

Starland's flagship reappeared out of the energy tunnel, and the vortex spiraled closed behind it and vanished. The background of space beyond where the vortex opening had just been was now rich with the stars of the Milky Way Galaxy. The huge Galactic Alliance flagship moved into position in an orbit high over the Bermuda Triangle.

A satellite marked with the NASA insignia on its side sped by directly below the alien orbiting vessel. The International Space Station moved into view from the backside of the planet along a much lower orbit. The mile-long star ship dwarfed the space station as it passed by far below it to fade from view around the opposite side of the planet.

Admiral Starland was concerned as he looked at Marin and ordered, "Lieutenant, you better put the ship on stealth invisibility mode. Even with such primitive technology they could get lucky and detect us with a military tracking device."

"I'm already on it, Admiral," she replied.

The Admiral grinned and closed his eyes to begin a deep contemplation.

Hmm, beloved Ancient One, he pondered, *I wonder what havoc Sen Dar may cause next to amuse his twisted conscience, before we can finally permanently stop him?*

CHAPTER THIRTY-SEVEN

RETURN TO THE PARALLEL LEMURIA OF EARTH

"Well, where are we headed now?" asked Kalem, eagerly gazing at Master Ra Mu.

"We're going to another Lemuria, Captain, one that was never destroyed by polar shifts," replied Ra Mu with an encouraging smile. "It is located in a well-protected parallel dimension on this Earth planet that no one has access to – except the Adepts and their guests. Please take the ship up beside the mountain summit, and they will open the inter-dimensional doorway for us."

Mayleena and Etta, hovering beside her, were gazing with great curiosity at Master Ra Mu, as Kalem placed his hands into the two hand impressions to guide the ship.

The Scout ship flew upward along the right side of the mountain and hovered beside the summit far above High Seer Stralim and his people gathered around him on the upper plateau that overlooked the new lower plateau shoreline. A long, graceful wave coming in along the new shoreline crashed against the base of the one remaining golden pyramid resting on the emerald-green sand.

A flash of gold light appeared several hundred feet in front of Kalem's ship and expanded into a huge golden ball that spun open a spiraling sparkling energy doorway. In the distance was a turquoise ocean that reached to the horizon as it curved around an ancient-looking, tropical black sand cove. Further inland, a tall snowcapped mountain towered above a grass-covered plateau. A majestic waterfall was cascading several thousand feet down the mountainside to disappear behind the forest trees surrounding the backside of a huge clear domed city nestled near its base. The light around the ship's hull pulsed brighter and it darted through the vortex toward the domed city.

The ship continued its flight into the mysterious secret parallel dimension on Earth, headed away from the open vortex whirling in the atmosphere just beyond two jagged black rock peaks. They extended several thousand feet above the end of a beach cove. The vortex in the distance behind the ship spiraled closed and vanished, leaving a clear background sky between the peaks.

Master Lumiera was standing in the center of the field of grass on the wide plateau that overlooked the curved shoreline. Many thousands of grateful Lemurian and Atlantian people were crowded around him. With an expectant smile, he looked up, and the massive crowd followed his gaze to observe the approaching Galactic Alliance Scout ship.

Master Ra Mu was standing by Kalem's right side behind the ship's control console. Mayleena had her arm around Kalem's shoulder, and Etta was cheerfully hovering to their left side. They were looking at the view screen, observing the large mass of people gathered in the field around Master Lumiera.

"Look at all of them," remarked Ra Mu with a benevolent smile. "These people were spared destruction because they were ready." He sighed and added, "A little love and trust in The Ancient One's Sound and Light goes a really long way."

"I'm so pleased they all made it," said Mayleena smiling. "I would still like to know if Kalem and I would ever have time to be together."

Surprised by her remark, Kalem beamed at her.

"Enough time?" replied Ra Mu softly chuckling. "Young one, there is no time where we're headed, not as you two are thinking of it."

Kalem gave Mayleena an encouraging hug. She relaxed and playfully grinned up at him, but his smile faded again as he recalled the one ever-present danger.

"What about Sen Dar?" Kalem asked. "I would still like to get my hands around his evil neck."

Master Ra Mu watched him steadily, and then looked at Mayleena and Etta.

"We will deal with Sen Dar when the three of you have learned more about the mysteries of The Ancient One that lives in the sacred

326

place of the golden heart," he remarked. "Each of you will confront him soon enough. For now, I suggest you take us to the protected city so we may enjoy a few moments of eternity in this paradise."

The Scout ship flew past the black sand dunes high over the heads of Master Lumiera and the many thousands of people gathered on the grass-covered plateau. It continued past the stunted fir forest toward the domed city nestled at the base of the snowcapped mountain. Then it stopped directly above the dome that towered high over the three pyramids centered in the city. Several dozen Galactic Scout Interceptors and three huge Oceanan Crystal Spectrum ships had landed on individual circular landing pads that surrounded the base of the huge dome.

As Kalem's Scout ship descended out of view toward one of the landing pads between two of the giant Oceanan Spectrum ships, the image receded into the distance until Harry Faldwell's Atma reappeared coming out of the holographic light sphere. He floated back to his physical body still sitting on the coat with eyes closed and a cigar sticking out of the corner of the mouth. The body softly jerked as the sphere reentered it through the top of the head.

General Harry Faldwell blinked several times, shook his head to clear his vision, then stared at the scene of the mountain and domed city that was still clearly visible within the holographic sphere of light. His eyes widened as he realized that he had actually been there. Then it dawned upon him that he had experienced firsthand the entire record log leading up to his being on the beach at that very moment, just as the holographic sphere of light coming from the staff shut off. Ra Mu reached out and grabbed the staff as it started to fall over, and he held it at arm's length.

Amazed by it all, Harry's jaw dropped, and the cigar he had stuffed into the corner of his mouth was now hanging down, stuck to his dry lower lip. He grabbed it and swallowed hard. Kalem and Carine were still snuggled close together sitting on their coats to Harry's right side, gazing patiently at him when he looked in their direction and their eyes locked. A moment later, all three simultaneously got up to their feet without saying a word.

Harry gazed beyond Master Ra Mu over the black sand dunes and into the distance at the mysterious domed city nestled at the base of the snowcapped mountain. He looked in the opposite direction at the twin black rock peaks that jutted up above the end of the tropical cove and then back at Ra Mu as recognition lit across his face.

"Then the beach we're standing on right now is the same one I witnessed in the record log?" Harry inquired.

Ra Mu smiled, giving him an affirmative nod, and Harry was in a state of wonder.

"And the domed city in the distance is the same one?" he asked with greater wonder.

Ra Mu smiled back at him but did not answer. Harry swallowed hard again and looked to Captain Kalem.

"General, do you see the open sky between the twin peaks at the far end of the beach?" asked Kalem, and he pointed in their direction.

Harry glanced around, then looked back at Kalem and nodded.

"When activated by a Guardian Adept within the city," continued Kalem, "that space becomes a controlled inter-dimensional doorway between here and what you call the Bermuda Triangle area. Many unique openings like it on Earth in your parallel dimension connect to other parallel and higher dimensional realities that vibrate at different time rates. This is something I only recently discovered myself."

Harry's eyes widened with more realization.

"Right," he excitedly exclaimed, "you came through that vortex in your ship to stop the 747 and deliver the message."

"That's absolutely correct," replied Kalem, pleased.

"As you now know, General," added Carine, "the cave in the mountainside we traveled through to get here leads to Mt Shasta in the northern part of the state of California in your United States. Similar inter-dimensional parallel time doorways exist in the atmosphere above the volcanic caldera on the big island of Hawaii, in the Andes Mountains of Peru, and at many other locations on Earth. By simply raising your vibration you can perceive their existence, if you know where to look."

Harry girded up courage and looked at Ra Mu for more answers.

"General Faldwell, Sen Dar is now free on Earth in your parallel time," Master Ra Mu began more seriously. "His power is growing, he has the Emerald Doorway Crystal, and he desperately desires the other two mystic crystals of The Ancient One. Our hope is that you and your government will help us and the Guardian's Research Group stop Sen Dar before his lust for power ends in the destruction of Earth as it did on Maldec."

Harry thoughtfully chewed on the end of his cigar to ponder the situation, and then he began pacing back and forth.

A moment later, he looked at Ra Mu and replied, "After what I've seen, how can I refuse?"

With joyful sparkling eyes, Carine took a few steps toward Harry and proclaimed, "Now that you have chosen wisely, you should behold me as I really am."

She transformed into the beautiful Mayleena in front of his astonished eyes and extended her open hand, revealing the small curved webs at the base of each of her fingers.

"Mayleena!" gasped Harry, and he cleared his throat.

"I promise I won't bite," she replied, amused.

He stared at her amazed, still doubtful as he cautiously extended his hand. She grabbed it, firmly shook it, and then released her grip just as Harry heard Etta's jovial chattering in Dren as he approached their position. He flew over several black sand dunes headed toward the General and soon came to a stop in front of Harry's face, grinning from ear to ear with his tail glowing from the root to the tip with brilliant opalescent colors.

"Etta," gasped Harry in a state of greater wonder.

"Quibb, General Faldwell, Q ka semtant." ("Yes, General Faldwell, I do exist.") Etta exuberantly remarked with a nod.

"I heard what you said, Etta, in my head in perfect English, but how?" Harry excitedly blurted out.

"You will learn more about the Drens in time," Ra Mu stated with a jolly chuckle, "but I think you would agree they are really quite amazing beings."

Harry looked, blank-faced, at Ra Mu, then back at Etta as he forced a very nervous smile and took a step back.

"Then it's all true," he replied. "But... it's incredible. It's too damned incredible."

Etta extended his green hand and Harry reached out, and with some hesitancy, quickly shook it.

"Please excuse us, General. Mayleena and I have an old appointment to keep with each other," Kalem remarked cordially.

Mayleena smiled at Harry and bowed before him. Then she grabbed Kalem's hand and they walked over to their personal gravity transports and stepped upon them. The discs lit up enshrouded by a blue light and they hovered on them a few feet above the black sands. As they flew over the sand dunes toward the ocean, they swooped in and out around each other in a game of tag with Mayleena in the lead.

"Hey, wait a minute!" yelled out Harry. "How will I get back?"

Kalem and Mayleena could no longer hear him as they flew over the vibrant turquoise waves that curled to break on the black sand beach. Mayleena flew upward in an arc toward the clouds above the ocean, and Kalem darted after her. Then Mayleena made several swift loops and Kalem duplicated her maneuver. Laughing and playing like children, they darted up into the clouds.

Etta appeared a moment later, flying above the ocean near the clouds they had entered. He spun around, grinning back in the direction of Ra Mu and Harry, winked at them, then spun back around and darted up into the clouds in playful pursuit.

Back on the beach, Master Ra Mu chuckled. Then he gazed at Harry and noticed his growing concern.

"There is no need for worry or fear, General Faldwell. I will send you back in a much more swift, direct manner," he announced.

Ra Mu reached into his robe, pulled out a small clear crystal ball with a faceted ruby embedded in its center, and held it in his open palm.

"Please accept this record log of all that you experienced here today," he requested. "It will be needed to convince your President that you are sane when he asks where you've been."

He handed Harry the crystal sphere. Harry looked at it and then put it in his pants pocket. Then he realized the ramifications.

"Are you crazy?" he blurted out. "You think I'm gonna tell him?"

Master Ra Mu stared back at Harry patiently, while Harry desperately looked around. He soon calmed himself, lowered his eyes, and then gazed apologetically back up at Master Ra Mu.

"Ya' know, you're right. I'll have to and I will need proof."

Ra Mu nodded, "The device in your pocket is set to your frequency alone. After you arrive back in Washington, D.C. with your President, place the crystal on the floor in front of him and slowly say my name aloud three times. The crystal will display a holographic image of everything that has taken place. Now, General, please excuse me as well. I also have an old appointment to keep."

Ra Mu let go of his crystal staff and it once again stood upright in the black sand on its own. He raised his hands, and beams of thick blue light emanated from his palms and painlessly hit Harry's chest, then surrounded him in a blue aura.

"Now wait a damned minute," yelled Harry, "you can't just send me back..."

The last word he managed to say echoed and faded away as his body dissolved into his true spherical Atma encased in a blue energy bubble. The bubble instantly changed to gold light and darted over the beach. It continued past the top of the forest, beyond the domed city, up the mountainside, and above the transport tube, then into the cave opening in the side of the snowcapped mountain.

The golden sphere continued to fly within the mountain cavern down the length of the smooth tunnel to its end where it stopped in front of a blue energy field that was shielding a familiar flat gray rock wall. The golden bubble vanished around Harry's light sphere and his physical form materialized around him.

"...anyway, you damn well please," exclaimed Harry, completing the sentence he was yelling at Ra Mu before he was so unexpectedly dematerialized by him.

Then he realized he was once again in his good old familiar physical form. He looked down and patted his body all over to be sure he was actually all there and in one piece.

"Hmm, I guess he can," he added, grinning as he looked up.

He turned around and looked over at the energy shield wavering across the face of the flat rock wall and it spiraled open revealing a wide cavern opening. He walked over to the edge and peered out. The heavy snow that had been falling on the backside of Mt Shasta when he first started his journey had stopped, and there were only a few patches of melting snow left on the ground. The sun brightly shining through the forest trees was glittering off the patches of snow like fine diamonds in the crisp early morning air.

Six military helicopters were hovering overhead, and three tanks were positioning themselves, aiming their cannon turrets at the cavern opening, while two dozen soldiers carrying automatic weapons rapidly approached.

Harry looked behind himself down the long, lighted cavern tunnel and then back out at the two-dozen soldiers running toward the entrance. He took a deep breath and let it out, then grabbed a fresh cigar from his shirt and looked curiously at it.

"I should give these up," he remarked to himself with a grimace, and then he grinned, stuffed the cigar back into the corner of his mouth, and bit down.

He watched the approaching soldiers, reluctantly shaking his head, and took another deep breath.

"This is going to be interesting," he said under his breath.

He stepped through the opening holding a hand in front of his eyes to shield them from the bright sunlight.

The two-dozen soldiers quickly surrounded Harry, as the blue energy shield reappeared in front of the cavern opening behind him. Then the cavern entrance dwindled with the shield as it spiraled closed and vanished, leaving the rock wall in its place. The soldiers were stunned, but Harry paid no attention to them or the wall while he chewed thoughtfully on the end of the cigar. Then he walked at a quick pace past them and up to a landing US Air Force helicopter with the side-door sliding open, and a government agent wearing a suit jumped out of the helicopter to the ground.

"General Faldwell, what on God's Earth happened to you?" inquired the concerned agent. "You've been missing for two weeks."

"Two what?" replied Harry, disbelieving, and he looked away to ponder all that had recently happened to him.

He composed himself and looked back at the agent's questioning eyes. "Don't even ask," he commanded.

Harry reached in through the helicopter's door and grabbed a special red phone that was hung on the inside wall, and then put it to his ear.

"This is General Faldwell," he stated and then commanded, "Get me the President right now. Then get me Judith Cranston, my fiancée." He paused and then replied, "Yeah, that's right, the Senator." He lowered the phone with an annoyed roll of his eyes and quietly said to himself, "How am I gonna explain this to her?" Then he put the phone back up to his ear and ordered, "Then call that wacky scientist. You know... the nut on UFOs." He paused again and replied, "Yes, Griswald, that's him."

Harry took the crystal sphere out of his pocket, looked at it curiously, and then stuffed it back.

He hung up the phone and looked at the government agent standing patiently by his side.

"You have got to get me back to Washington, D.C. right now," he commanded.

The Agent nodded and helped Harry step up through the open helicopter door. Then he jumped inside and slammed the door closed. A moment later, the helicopter lifted off the ground and headed away from the soldiers, tanks, and military attack helicopters surrounding the area. It flew high over the forest treetops away from the secret doorway of Mt Shasta and gradually receded into the distant clear blue sky.

CHAPTER THIRTY-EIGHT

MASTER RA MU RETURNS HOME

*M*aster Ra Mu appeared serene while standing alone on the black sands of the protected Lemuria in the secret parallel dimension on Earth. He grabbed his crystal staff and looked out over the ocean waves. A faint halo of gold began to radiate around his body, and a loving smile slowly widened on his face. His eyes were moist as he turned his head to gaze beyond the mountain that loomed high above the domed city built at its base.

He pulled the crystal staff to his side and lifted his legs under himself in yoga fashion, but he did not fall. Instead, he was now levitating four feet in the air in a cross-legged position, and he flew swiftly away from the ocean over the forest treetops. He soon passed high above the mountain and disappeared in the distant sky.

The wind was gently blowing through his hair while he flew gracefully over beautiful rivers, glistening lakes, and waterfalls that adorned the countryside beyond the other side of the majestic snowcapped mountain. Then he passed over lush green valleys in the direction of a red rock plateau that glistened on the horizon from the setting sunlight.

He was gazing toward the heavens with a wondrous smile beaming on his face as he sped across the vast Lemurian landscape. Then he heard The Ancient One's wondrous humming Spirit Sound. He listened with complete serenity as he levitated down toward a secret rendezvous on the black sand beach cove. Once before, from this very same special cove, he had projected his true Atma sphere into the crest of a curling wave and transported himself to the parallel time dimension of present-day Earth. There he stealthily observed the 747-jet airliner take off from Miami International Airport in Florida.

Ra Mu continued his graceful levitation down to the secret pristine cove and stopped to hover four feet above the glistening black sand. A turquoise wave flowing in a long, lustrous curl crashed in a continuous smooth thunderous roll down the beach twenty feet beyond him. He unfolded his legs, landed gently on his feet, and held the crystal staff out at arm's length as the sun set on the horizon.

He looked high above the ocean, and a large area of the sky whirled open into a huge spiraling golden vortex filled with countless tiny blue stars. Celestial music emanated from the opening, as an unseen heavenly choir of the flawless voices of a thousand men and women started singing the oldest and most dynamic name in the universe for The Ancient One, known simply as... HU.

The enchanting voices were reverberating gently on many levels in perfect harmony mixed with the haunting melody of the unseen mystical flute, the pervasive low frequency humming like millions of bees, and long crashing ocean waves. The heavenly sounds gracefully wove in and out of each other like a magical color tapestry.

The Ancient One's ethereal city in the far, far higher dimension of its sacred realm became visible, stretching into the distance on the other side of the whirling vortex. The brilliant spherical light of The Ancient One appeared coming through the opening. The many thousands of teardrop shaped lights comprising its layers so brightly glistened they blotted out the sun beginning to set on the horizon.

Master Ra Mu raised his head high, sighed with pleasure, and then beamed a humble smile. The radiant light streaming from The Ancient One intensified, and a soft golden light surrounded Master Ra Mu's body. Then The Ancient One moved down closer and appeared to be now fifteen feet in diameter and an equal distance above Ra Mu's head. The lights glowing within the majestic sphere's layers pulsed gently, raining sparkling rainbow light particles down over Ra Mu's body and around him in a wide circle on the black sand.

Master Ra Mu, are you ready to journey home again for a moment in eternity? asked The Ancient One with a familiar benevolent voice.

Yes, Ancient One, more than ready, replied Master Ra Mu, smiling.

A beam of light suddenly projected from The Ancient One's white core center down to Ra Mu's forehead, turning his body and the Master

Crystal Staff into a bright oval gold light. The light glistened with silver light particles and slowly transformed into a much smaller radiant Atmasphere that appeared identical to The Ancient One. Master Ra Mu's smaller sphere then hovered up beside The Ancient One's huge sphere and passed right through the luminous outer light layer. It stopped a third of the way toward the white light core, and they flew together as one higher in the sky and back through the whirling vortex opening.

Their graceful flight continued through the vortex and gradually disappeared in the distance among millions of sparkling golden atoms that began to rain in a gentle whirlwind around them. Then the huge vortex spun closed and vanished with a roaring thunderous double... *ka-boom...* that echoed across the black sand beach.

The sun was just setting, and the few clouds passing over the horizon above the ocean lit up with an array of sunset colors that cast intriguing shadows across the cove. A large crashing wave along the beach grew gently louder, while an unseen celestial orchestra played a majestic, uplifting melody in The Ancient One's honor.

The graceful music expanded out from the crashing waves and grew in prominence, while exotic birds called out with sweet voices from the jungle behind the beach. The brilliant display of sunset colors arrayed through the fleecy clouds passing over the horizon intensified and receded swiftly toward night. The celestial music built to a crescendo and faded away into the predominating sound of another large, graceful turquoise wave as it curled and crashed in a continuous thunderous roll along the shoreline. Then everything diminished to total silence.

Overhead, the atmosphere swiftly darkened to night, and several bright twinkling stars appeared in a widening panorama. Then thousands of stars manifested with their entire majestic multicolored sparkling splendor. A few crickets chirped happily in the background, and a few frogs chimed in with their merry croaks. Gradually, hundreds of crickets and frogs joined in the chorus of their happy song celebrating the sublime celestial night sky. A meteor, or one might now assume it was something else, sped across the star-filled heavens.

The End
of
THE EMERALD DOORWAY

(Three Mystic Crystals)

Other Books
by
R. Scott Lemriel

The Seres Agenda

(Special 5ᵗʰ edition published April, 2019)
(Larger 6 X 9 size - new original cover)
(E-book techniques section - new hyperlinks)

Before they suddenly vanished long ago in galactic history, the mysterious eighteen to twenty-five-feet tall extraterrestrial human Seres race seeded humankind throughout the many galaxies. Then, they sponsored the creation of the entire Galactic Inter-dimensional Alliance of Free Worlds. Now, they have finally decided to return, and they will make their presence known by bringing about a permanent benevolent end to the experiment of evil on Earth.

Coming To Earth

Guardians of the Ancient One

The Parallel Time Trilogy (Book Two) expanding adventure unveils more about The Ancient One's mysterious Master Adepts and their involvement with Admiral Starland and the space fleet of the Galactic Inter-dimensional Alliance of Free Worlds. Witness the ever-deepening love affair between Captain Kalem and Mayleena, Etta's courageous antics, and their ongoing struggle to achieve self-mastery to be able to one day return to The Ancient One's far higher mystic realm of sublime Sound and Light. Along the way, they must somehow survive Sen Dar's unremitting efforts to destroy them and rule Earth.

Journey to the Center of the Universe

In The Parallel Time Trilogy (Book Three), we travel to the hidden world of Oceana with Master Opellum to behold the mystical marriage of Kalem and Mayleena, and to explore the wondrous Dren home world civilization with Etta. The grand adventure reveals how Master Ra Mu and several Guardian Adepts mystically merge with Kalem, Mayleena, and Etta to focus on the one struggle to stop Sen Dar's lust for power from destroying the Earth. Cleverly hidden behind world events today, our own coming adventure to survive or perish in the near future on Earth is curiously parallel to the unexpected trilogy story resolution revealed on the other side of…

Journey to the Center of the Universe

GLOSSARY OF CHARACTERS AND TERMS

CHARACTERS:

Admiral Starland – This Admiral of the Galactic Inter-dimensional Alliance of Free Worlds is Captain Kalem's father. He is trim and well built, appearing to be in his early fifties by Earth standards, with short brown hair swept back at the sides. The only hair, streaked white, is at his temples and sideburns. His high forehead, squared jaw, smooth round chin, and blue eyes make him appear wise and stately in his uniform. His slim gray-blue pants have an oval gold buckle belting them at the waist that is identical to the one worn by his son, Captain Kalem. The Galactic Alliance symbol of three blue stars set in triangular formation above the apex of a gold pyramid suspended above a silvery galaxy, is also embossed over the left chest area of his long-sleeved shirt. Three gold bands encircled each cuff and the neck collar of the shirt that is open in front with a V-shape, which gradually tapers to a point a few inches below the base of his neck.

Beel – This is the fake name Sen Dar concocts before the guards that capture him present him to High Seer Stralim on Atlantis. There he feigns having been tortured by Master Ra Mu on Lemuria and claims allies later rescued him. He further elaborates that he discovered a plot contrived by this benevolent Master teacher to take over the almost independent colony of Atlantis by force. He makes the fake story more convincing by his misuse of the stolen Transport Matrix crystal he carries.

Benock – He is the eldest and wisest, rotund, Dren that puts Etta through a secret test, and then counsels him about his importance to the Oceanan race, the Dren race, and the entire Galactic Alliance. He is secretly working with Master Opellum and the Adepts of The Ancient One.

Captain Gralik – Kalem and Etta discover this taller Yalgull Captain (enemy soldier) on planet Seltium (4) in the outlying regions beyond Yalgull space.

Captain Holshoon – He is not quite as tall as the Glonden Captain (enemy soldier). Etta witnesses the conversation between Gralik, Holshoon and Moonask on planet Seltium (4) before they discover his presence spying on them.

Cadet Kalem – This extraterrestrial Caucasian human male, sixteen years old, is the son of Admiral Starland, and a cadet in training at one of the Galactic Alliance of Free World's academies. The form-fitting bodysuit he wears has sleek shoes molded into the pant cuffs. He would slip his feet into the opening where his head and neck would later fit through, and then slip his feet into each molded shoe. Then he would pull stretchable material up over his torso, then over his shoulders, pop his head through the opening and put an arm through each sleeve. The top part of the body suit has no collar. It is open in a V-shape that comes down to a point several inches above his solar plexus. A single thin gold band encircles the cuff of each sleeve. Belted at the waist and clasped with an oval gold buckle, the garment is made from a dark blue-gray, silky cotton-type fabric. Embossed upon it, and on the left chest of the uniform, is the symbol for the Galactic Alliance: a gold, quartz-capped pyramid suspended above a silvery spiral galaxy with three blue stars in triangle formation set above the apex.

Cadet Moreau – He is an extraterrestrial Norbrian human male, sixteen years of age, with dark-brown skin in the hidden truth revealing adventure. He and his best friend Cadet Kalem attended the Academy together. At this age, he and Kalem are in training to one day become Scout Interceptor fighter pilots. As a Norbrian, he just naturally always looks out for Kalem's wellbeing in one way or another, especially when it comes to reminding him to be in class on time.

Captain Kalem Starland – He briefly appears in his youth within this episode of the hidden truth revealing trilogy, but as an adult, he is six-feet-tall, ruggedly handsome and courageous. This extraterrestrial human man in his late twenties, with blue eyes and short brown hair, is a renowned fighter pilot Captain in the space fleet of the Galactic Inter-dimensional Alliance of Free Worlds. He wears a single piece, formfitting body uniform made of a silvery-gray fabric. Two gold bands encircle the sleeves that widen slightly at the wrists. Three blue stars set in a triangular formation are embossed on the uniform's left chest area above the apex of a golden pyramid, positioned directly over the star nucleus of a silvery galaxy.

Carine – This is the fictitious cover name for Mayleena. She utilizes her naturally developed Oceanan defensive ability to disguise her appearance. She does this by telepathically sending the image of a Caucasian woman into the minds of anyone that would be shocked or terrified the first time by her true extraterrestrial appearance with pointed ears and blue skin.

Chief Scientist Dom – He is slightly shorter in stature than Opellum, and as Chief Scientist of the Oceanan race wears a white Oceanan scientist's robe. A thin oval gold buckle set with a large oval aquamarine jewel clasps the blue leather-like belt around his waist.

Commander Baroon – He is the disheveled and exhausted Glonden joint commander of the Glonden – Yalgull Alliance space fleet, who survives Sen Dar's laser gun wound. Bandaged and supported by two medical staff personnel, he contacts Admiral Starland after the battle is over to confess that he knows Sen Dar deceived all of them by using the crystal he wears to control them.

Commander Dal – This rugged looking Glonden enemy Commander aboard one of the fleet ships of the Glonden – Yalgull Alliance, is in his forties, with a scarred chin. He defiantly disbelieves Admiral Starland after his ship and all the enemy command ships lose all power from the effect of the Galactic Alliance Magnetic Blanket weapon. He finally realizes how deceived Yalgull Alliance people have been by Sen Dar, after Starland reveals his rescued wife is still alive and aboard his Galactic Alliance flagship.

Communications Officer Lieutenant Marin – She is the petite, young woman communications officer aboard Admiral Starland's Galactic Alliance Emerald Star flagship.

Commander Zarel – This is a commander of one of the Emerald Star heavy cruisers of the Galactic Alliance fleet under the command of Admiral Starland. He is a strongly built, handsome dark-skinned man in his fifties with full gray hair. Two gold bands surround his sleeve cuffs compared to Starland's three giving him the rank of Vice-Admiral – one level below Admiral Starland.

Dan – The rugged-faced and gray-haired United States Air Force pilot in his fifties with a southern accent is the senior pilot of what appears to be a commercial jet airliner headed to South America. Actually, on board are diplomats from around the world, General Harry Faldwell and Senator Judith Cranston. They are flying to a classified undisclosed location for worldwide peace talks.

Din – She is Etta's lovely female Dren wife, who has characteristic longer feminine eyelashes and a petite body. Her bulbous blue eyes are more feminine in expression. Her arms and legs, and her thinner long feminine fingers are similar to the five fingered hands and toes of a trim human female woman. She and Etta are more loving bonded to each other and their two Dren children than most human beings on planet Earth ever experience. Like Etta and all Drens, she uses her hands and fingers in expressive dexterous ways.

Elder Councilman Melnor – He is slightly bald, in his sixties, a little rotund, and one of High Seer Stralim's eleven council members. This Council is located in the capital city of Atla on the ancient Lemuria colony continent of Atlantis. Each council member wears a different colored long flowing robe.

Etta – This extraordinary benevolent and immediately endearing member of the extraterrestrial silica-based Dren race (not carbon-based like human beings) is very courageous. He is also telepathic with a photographic memory and has vocal cords. He is three-and-a-half- feet-long with smooth pale-green dry skin. Etta's large, bulbous, dark blue eyes are semispherical shaped and the short eyelashes at the top of his eyelids are short and masculine. They are long and feminine on his wife, Din, and all other Dren females. Etta's six-inch-long jaw squared off in front has two flared nostrils about an inch apart, positioned on the front of each side of his nose. His mouth is a smiling crease around his jaw, which gives the impression he is amused about something when his mouth is closed. His arms are slightly shorter than his hind legs, but both are strongly contoured. Like all Drens, his tail glows like crystal opal in sunlight when activated, giving him antigravity levitating and flying ability. He has a more loving bonded dedication to his wife Din and to their two Dren children than most human beings on Earth ever experience.

General Harry Faldwell – This strongly built, no-nonsense, four-star Air Force General in his mid-fifties is a member of the President's cabinet, one of his personal national security advisors, and the fiancé of Senator Judith Cranston.

342

Glag – He is one of Gorn's two tall guards. He is violet-skinned, very hairy, and has five finger-sized bones sticking upward from the center of his forehead that spread out like a fan similar to the spread five fingers of a human hand. He is one of Gorn's special military intimidation Lieutenants.

Gorn – He is the ruthless militaristic Supreme Ruler of the Lands of Seth on the planet Maldec. Sen Dar's negative influence upon him unexpectedly inspires him to use an experimental bomb against his two adversaries overseas that chain-reacts with all matter. Once the rocket is launched that carries this weapon, it cannot be turned off. Gorn orders its launch anyway, and the planet is blown apart from the core outward to become the asteroid belt that now circles in the orbit of a planet between Mars and Jupiter in our present-day solar system.

Gorn's Chief Scientist Glorin – The chief scientist looks away from the console by Gorn's sleek silver metal rocket being prepared for launch to worn Gorn his experimental rocket will not be ready for at least another day. Gorn ignores him to focus on the assistant scientist who then pleads with him not to order them to launch the rocket because once it is launched it cannot be shut down. Gorn ignores his urgent appeal and disintegrates him with the laser gun Sen Dar gave to him.

Guardian Protector – This term is used to designate the Master teacher who guards one of three powerful consciousness transforming crystal devices. They are: the green Transport Matrix crystal, the green Emerald Doorway crystal, and the Master Crystal Staff. The Ancient One gave them to the Master Adept teachers eons ago to train their students in the right use of love, wisdom, and freedom. When a Master teacher guarding them is about to depart a particular lifetime, he passes the crystal device on to a selected student who is ready to accept the guardianship responsibility.

Helmsman & Ship's Navigator Drelim – He is Admiral Starland's Emerald Star class flagship ship navigator and helmsman (pilot).

High Commander General Hontull – He is the same height as Supreme Emperor Garn, with the same length hair but it is jet-black. He is very muscular with a more rounded and rugged looking face than

Garn, and he wears the Yalgull military uniform of the High Commander. The belt around the waist of his sleek black trousers is a thin gold metallic-looking strap, clasped with a triangular emblem etched with the talons of an exotic bird. Fastened along the left side of his sheer long sleeved shirt are triangular gold buttons, and three gold stars are pined on the left side of his upper chest, indicating his high-ranking position. Attached to the belt at his side is a holstered polished silver laser weapon.

High Seer Stralim – He is the elected leader of Atlantis – the nearly independent Lemurian colony continent. This tall, trim, and stately looking man in his mid-fifties, wears a long flowing elegant robe that comes down directly above his ankles. Sheer fitting silken pants extend below the hem of the robe to his sandal-clad feet. The symbol of a radiant eye above a quartz-capped golden pyramid hangs from a gold chain worn around his neck.

Kalem Summerhill – Captain Kalem uses this fictitious Earth cover-name when he first meets General Harry Faldwell, so as not to shock him initially with his true human extraterrestrial origin.

Lagrar – He is one of Gorn's two tall guards, and he has the same five finger-sized bones sticking upward from the center of his forehead that spread out like a fan similar to the spread five fingers of a human hand. He is another one of Gorn's special military intimidation Lieutenants.

Large Male Bottlenose Dolphin – The tidal force of an undersea earth tremor knocks Mayleena unconscious. After she awakens with amnesia, this intelligent benevolent sea mammal telepathically communicates with her to reveal the way to go to reach the safety of land. Known as Yelfim by the people of Atlantis, they have saved human lives in trouble in the ocean for thousands of years.

Layliella – High Seer Stralim of Atlantis gives this adopted name to Mayleena when he finds her washed ashore by the capital city of Atla. When she revives, she sends to his mind the appearance of a young Caucasian woman with long blond hair. Captain Kalem, disguised as Lemurian Diplomat Aeron, first meets her picking flowers in a field near High Seer Stralim's council chambers.

Lemurian Diplomat Aeron – Before he arrives on Atlantis, Kalem is disguised by Master Ra Mu's use of the Master Crystal Staff to appear with a beard and diplomatic attire in order to take the place of the recently deceased Lemurian Diplomat Aeron. As the diplomat, he wears a blue silken slip-on robe that comes down just below his knees, matching pants underneath it, and well-made leather sandals. The top of the robe around his neck opens in a thin V-shaped gold collar with two narrow gold diplomatic bands embroidered around the edge and around the end of each long sleeve. An oval dark-blue lapis lazuli buckle clasps his green stained woven leather-like belt around his waist. An ancient gold hieroglyphic symbol embossed upon the buckle's surface signifies that Lemuria is the motherland of humanity on Earth.

Lieutenant Moonask – He is lesser ranked and the shortest of the two Glonden soldiers (enemy soldier), standing with Holshoon and the taller Yalgull Captain Gralik on Seltium (4) when they discover Etta spying on them while he is hiding behind a tree.

Lieutenant Moreau – This Norbrian in his late twenties from the planet Ulanim is Captain Kalem's best friend. He is clean-shaven with an oval-shaped face, strong jaw, dark-brown skin, brown eyes, and short curly brown hair. He wears the Lieutenant's uniform of the Galactic Inter-dimensional Alliance of Free worlds that looks identical to the one worn by Captain Kalem; except, a single gold band surrounds the cuff of each sleeve instead of two.

Master Lumiera – This Master Adept of The Ancient One is the guardian of the secret parallel dimension on Earth, where the continent of Lemuria never sinks beneath ocean waves because no polar shift takes place in this protected reality. He is a vibrant, healthy-looking elderly bald man, who wears a gold-colored silk robe tied with a matching sash at the waist and simple sandals. He emanates a subtle pastel gold light.

Master Nim – His teaching sanctuary located near an oasis pond, a rustic white domed red brick building, is not far from a long snowcapped mountain range on the planet Promintis. He is a trim, virile looking, and white-haired Asian man in his sixties, residing and teaching students on the planet Promintis. However, unlike most Asian men on Earth, his oval eyes are bright blue with penetrating black pupils set below bushy eyebrows, and a long beard with no mustache. A simple wraparound maroon colored robe flows down to six inches above his ankles. Nim's forehead is oval shaped with a subtle indentation that runs vertically down the center. His long white hair is evenly receded at the hairline above his forehead. Yet, it is still thick like fine white silk as it flows down behind his head between his shoulder blades. A faint pastel golden light radiating in an aura around his body is visible by observers that have developed spiritual sight.

Master Opellum – Being over six feet, Opellum is tall for an Oceanan male. He appears to be in his late forties according to Earth human comparisons. Strong of limb, his body is trim and precisely contoured. He is handsome in a most mature way beyond description, at least to his daughter's young perceptions. Like Mayleena, his nose is straight and slender. His jet-black hair flows gracefully straight back over the top of his pointed ears and down the back of his neck between his shoulder blades. Opellum's hair does not grow at the sides of his temples or directly above his ears. This makes his forehead appear to extend around the sides of his head, giving a powerful impression of silent strength and wisdom. He wears a very elegant blue, silken wraparound robe tied at his side by a smooth silken gold sash, and matching tight-fitting slip-on shoes.

Master Ra Mu – The six-foot tall man with black curly hair and a short-cropped beard, wearing a knee-length, maroon robe belted at the waist and simple sandals, grasps in his right hand a tall transparent crystal staff crested with a symbol similar to the ancient Egyptian Ankh – an oval with a hollow center atop a cross. As a very advanced spiritual Master teacher, he instructs and guides those individuals who want to return to their true nature as the Atma (pure eternal spherical energy being), whose destiny is to become a fully conscious trusted co-creator with the primordial omnipresent source behind and supporting all that exists. He is also one of the Master Adepts of the Ancient One and Captain Kalem's, Mayleena's, and Etta's personal mentor and friend.

Mayleena – She is a humanoid extraterrestrial from the planet Oceana hidden in a higher parallel dimension of the physical universe. She spent her young and teenage years under the ocean in a domed city also named Oceana after their home world. The adult Mayleena is an exceptionally beautiful woman, even among other Oceanan women. Her long, soft black hair is combed straight back over her head and behind her delicately pointed elf-like ears. It flows down to the middle of her

346

back. Like all Oceanans, she can breathe underwater or on land and she is telepathic, capable of sending the image of a blond Caucasian human woman into the minds of anyone that might capture her or see her as a threat when they first meet.

Mira – She is Commander Dal's pretty but haggard wife in her late twenties, with tears running down her pale cheeks when Admiral Starland has Lieutenant Marin escort her to his bridge so that her husband can realize she is still alive, and just how much Sen Dar deceived him and their people.

Montoc – The more simply designed slip-on garment without gold stripes worn by this Lemurian Colonial Transport pilot is similar to the slip-on garment Kalem wears disguised as Diplomat Aeron. A thin brown leather belt ties it snug around his waist. He flies Diplomat Aeron to the capital city of Atla on Atlantis.

Mr. Da Vep – This elderly man on the planet Kormaljis is dressed in simple farmer's clothing when the boy Sen Dar meets with him at the bottom of the clear elevator that rides a vertical rail up a cliff. It drops off passengers on the plateau near the cavern where hydroponics food is grown. He is very kind and supportive of the boy Sen Dar's need to explore and have adventure.

Nara – Nara is a much younger disciple of Master Nim than Sen Dar is on the planet Promintis. He is thirteen years of age when Master Nim announces to Sen Dar that Nara will be the next Guardian of The Ancient One's Transport Matrix crystal and half of its cosmic map – to Sen Dar's great angry surprise.

Pete – The trim and handsomely chiseled Air Force Lieutenant in his mid-forties, with dark curly hair and a mustache, is the co-pilot of what appears to be a commercial jet airliner headed to South America. On board are diplomats from around the world, General Harry Faldwell and Senator Judith Cranston. They are flying to a classified undisclosed location for worldwide peace talks.

Rumon – He is Admiral Starland's first born son, Kalem's older brother, who was killed when the Helix Beam weapon secretly deployed on the planet's surface by Yalgull spies destroyed his cutter-class, fast attack medium destroyer called…The Deep Star.

Sand Daringe – This nearly extinct, normally benign vegetarian creature lives on Earth in a close parallel dimension to us. The twenty-foot-high caterpillar like creature lives by the ocean shoreline and when arched fully above the fine volcanic black sands, it reveals that its body is comprised of stacked rounded sections extending from the smallest one at the tip of the tall, to the largest one that comprises its head. Row after row of long, sharp, white teeth recede into its large cavernous mouth. Its two eyes hang from the ends of long, arched antennae-like protrusions extended from the top of its head between two flared nostrils. The round white eyeballs, with penetrating blue pupils, rotate individually within their sockets to locate anyone that may have startled it while protecting its young. When frightened or startled, great spikes rise up along the ridge on the back of a mature Sand Daringe and it darts a long sticky tongue toward the source of the potential threat to wrap it around one of their legs, before it starts to drag their body toward its gaping mouth to destroy it.

Sen Dar – He is a diabolical, malevolent thirty-year-old slender man with high cheekbones, a long straight nose, and slightly wavy black hair that flows down to his shoulders. He usually wears a long black cape and a gray slip-on body uniform, belted at the waist with a gold buckle. Etched into the buckle, on the front of a thin gold metal band around his forehead, and on the right chest area of his body uniform is the symbol of a vertical sword superimposed over a red world. Two snakes are wound around and above the shaft of the handle with their heads pointed toward each other and their extended forked tongues touching. The tip of the blade below the red world points to the middle of an upside-down black obsidian pyramid with its inverted apex touching the top of the star nucleus of a silvery galaxy. He wears The Ancient One's Transport Matrix crystal; hung from a sturdy gold chain he stole from Master Nim's dead body after he killed him.

Senator Judith Cranston – This United States Senator is trim and very attractive in her mid-forties with long black hair. She stands her own ground on important issues with her fiancé General Harry Faldwell.

Supreme Emperor Garn – In his mid-forties, he is thin, six feet three inches tall with high cheekbones, and a long-pointed jaw. His long, slightly wavy brown hair falls down over his shoulders. Like all the Yalgull, he is humanoid but he has the faintest hint of a pastel-violet hue over his ivory-white skin. He wears a golden-brown robe laced with an iridescent light-blue material that slightly shimmers when he moves. Under his robe, he wears sheer matching pants and his feet are clad with highly polished black leather-like boots. A flexible thin shiny black metal belt, akin to obsidian, is around his waist.

Supreme Grand Grontiff Gloeen – The humanoid Glonden leader on planet Lodrea (3) is a six-foot tall obese bald man with long drooping jowls and thick lips. He wears a gaudy robe with a gold sash placed from the right shoulder down across the front to his left hip. A large gold metal sun is pinned to the sash on the right side of his chest.

The Ancient One – This living presence or source behind and supporting all that exists is from a dimension far above the void know to certain religions on Earth. This mighty primordial living presence looks like a brilliant golden ball or sphere of luminous being more spectacular than anything witnessed by people on planet Earth or on most worlds of the physical universe. To the Atma or Soul – the true individual, after proper training or preparation, The Ancient One appears as a fifteen-feet-in-diameter radiant sphere: comprised of self-effulgent teardrop shaped lights built in layers; from a radiant white light core; through the color spectrum to a shimmering violet outer layer; surrounded by a radiant golden aura.

The Boy Sen Dar – He is a Caucasian lad ten years of age, who wears simple country clothes. Right after a meteor storm destroys the surface of his planet, killing his parents and all but a dozen men and a dozen women, the medical staff of a passing Galactic Alliance deep space scientific exploration spaceship – Galactic Alliance Explorer (3) – rescues him from certain death. They discover him still alive but dehydrated, and with many skin abrasions and several burns. Before the catastrophe, he is a happy and healthy lad.

The Young Mayleena – Mayleena is an exceptionally beautiful young sixteen-year-old extraterrestrial humanoid girl, even among other young Oceanan females. At five-feet eight-inches, she has a remarkably slender waist and athletic legs. She received her straight nose from her father and her green eyes, radiant pools of enchantment, from her mother, who had died in an accident when she was very young. All Oceanan people that evolved on a planet in a slightly higher parallel dimension of the universe can breathe on land or under water. Her long, soft black hair is combed straight back over her head and behind her delicately pointed elf-like ears. It flows down to the middle of her back. Two long locks of hair from above her ears drop down the front of her chest over the tops of her mature breasts outlined through her single-piece, blue, silken robe. A wide violet sash wrapped around her waist ties it off at the side. The large sleeves flow down over her slender arms and open wide just past the elbows, where they end in inch-wide cuffs. Matching blue, silken slip-on shoes cover her feet.

Trebor – He is one of two benevolent leaders on the Planet Maldec. He is a six-foot tall male humanoid with a protruding forehead, ivory-white skin and pink oval eyes that talks with stilted awkward English to Admiral Starland when they meet on Maldec. His ears have a large round hole through each earlobe that extends below his jaw, and his head is completely bald: except for a thin strip of hair that runs along the top of his skull from his forehead to the back of his neck.

Two of High Seer Stralim's Councilman – Unlike Councilman Melnor, these two council members vote with the other eight councilmen to attack the motherland continent of Lemuria first before they are covertly attacked. Like the High Seer, the misuse by Sen Dar of The Ancient One's Transport Matrix crystal influences them, against their better judgment, to embark on this foolish plan.

Yulan – He is also one of the two benevolent leaders on the Planet Maldec. He is a well-built humanoid male with human body contours in every way: except, he has no hair, smooth snake-like skin patterns, and vertical snake-like pupils in his eyes. He speaks in his own language.

Yulan's Interpreter – To interpret what Yulan says, he speaks with poignant flawless English to Admiral Starland.

Zerod – This thin middle-aged man with sagging, bony shoulders and a scar across the top of his forehead, standing before Grand Grontiff Gloeen in his palace, is threatened by the corpulent leader to make an example of him so that the royal staff witnessing it will remain forever loyal.

TERMS:

Alabaster Gold Crowned & Quartz-tipped Pyramids – These mystical pyramids existed on ancient Lemuria, it's almost independent colony continent of Atlantis, and they exist now on other world systems that the people of Earth today, for the most part, do not know exist. They indefinitely extend the youthfulness and vitality of the physical bodies of human beings, animals, and plants. Master Ra Mu lives in a specially designed gold covered and quartz crowned pyramid inside a mountainous hillside in the countryside of Lemuria – before a polar shift destroys the entire continent.

Ancient Dren Scrolls – These are historical Dren records of events dating back more than half-a-million years. They describe the first meeting the Drens had with the Oceanan humanoid race and what happened.

Ancient Symbol for Lemuria – This oval, dark-blue lapis lazuli buckle, embossed with the symbol in gold on the surface, clasps the green stained woven leather-like belt worn around Captain Kalem's waist. This is part of a disguise he wears to portray Diplomat Aaron from Lemuria. It signifies that Lemuria is the motherland of humanity on Earth.

Ancient Symbol for Atlantis – Below High Seer Stralim's council chambers, the unadorned dark-blue granite tiles continue over the surface of the lower oval floor of the ballroom around the ten-feet-in-diameter golden symbol set in its center. This is the same Atlantian symbol; an Egyptian-looking eye suspended above a golden pyramid, that High Seer Stralim always wears on the gold chain around his neck.

Antigravity Wave-Vector Pods – Three semispherical antigravity wave-vector pods, built in a triangular pattern on the bottom of each Scout ship's hull, is the power source for their antigravity drives. When activated, they project a balanced antigravity field around the ship's hull. Each pod contains twelve quartz crystal spires pointing downward in different directions.

Atla – This is the capital city of the Lemuria colony continent of Atlantis near the coast. Two gold quartz tipped pyramids tower just above the tops of the deep valley of tropical forest trees. Many gold, spiral towers and blue-domed buildings laced throughout the jungle countryside comprise the capital city of Atla on Atlantis. Past the edge of the forest is the curve of the fine emerald-green volcanic sands of the Atlantis coastline.

Atlantis – This nearly independent colony continent two-thirds the size of the massive motherland was located halfway around planet Earth 100,000 years ago, before it was destroyed during a cyclic polar shift: except for a surviving 500 square-mile volcanic Atlantis Island. The continent landmasses of Lemuria and the colony continent of Atlantis, centered over the planet's equator on opposite side of the planet, extended far into the northern and southern hemispheres. During the twenty-four-hour catastrophe, planet Earth's poles flipped one-hundred-eighty-degrees overnight, sinking the continents into the ocean depths. New land masses simultaneously ascended above the churning oceans to dramatically form into the familiar shapes of the continents we live on today – including the continent of Antarctica, which swiftly rose up last in the new southern polar region.

Atlantis Elongated Oval Ballroom – Built partially down inside the hilltop a level below Stralim's council room chamber, this lavish elongated oval ballroom is much larger. A fifty-feet-long and thirty-feet-wide oval upper floor level, set with intricate flower pattern mosaics in dark-blue granite tiles, is followed by three oval one-foot-wide steps that lead to a forty-feet-wide lower oval floor. The unadorned dark-blue granite tiles continue over the surface of the lower oval floor and around the ten-feet-in-diameter golden Atlantis symbol set in its center. Tall blue lapis lazuli pillars laced with gold that support the oval ceiling surround the inner circumference of the walls. Tapered two-feet-long rods, extended at a slant upward from mountings in the lapis lazuli pillars, end in clear oval glass-like covered incandescent torches that brilliantly light the room. They highlight beautifully woven tapestries, hung on the walls between them that depict various historical nature scenes.

Atlantis Energy Discharge Weapon – This is a hand-held holstered gun shaped energy discharge weapon strapped to the sides of Atlantis guards. The handles sticking out of the holsters, made from a rectangular piece of hardwood, have smooth carved out finger impressions to grip it with a clenched fist.

Atlantis Island – This five-hundred-square-mile volcanic island survived the catastrophic sinking 100,000 years ago on Earth of the massive Lemuria continent and its large Atlantis colony continent. The remaining mountainous volcanic Atlantis Island, centered in the infamous Bermuda Triangle, eventually became the new colonizing power on Earth until it was destroyed through the misuse of science 35,000 years ago.

Arrow Tipped Air Guns – Gorn's guards on planet Maldec wear a viciously tipped metal arrow sticking out of an air gun in a leather holster strapped around their waists. Woven-cloth covered air tubes attached to the gun handles connect to small twin metal canisters strapped on their backs.

Blue Mazon Energy Fireball Weapon – This is a blue fireball energy projectile weapon used by the Galactic Inter-dimensional Alliance of Free Worlds starships and defensive Scout class ships like the one Kalem pilots.

Capital City of Marnanth – One of the Galactic Alliance teaching facility Academies, where Captain Kalem and Lieutenant Moreau were trained, is located within this domed city of Marnanth on planet Telemadia III. A huge clear crystal dome covers the building towers and sealed transport tubes that link the many metropolitan structures together. The city lights cast a dull glow on the night sky above, but not enough to obstruct the celestial beauty of outer space spread across the heavens.

Cavern of the Drens – The huge tube-shaped volcanic cavern under the ground near an extinct volcano on ancient Lemuria is self-luminous from phosphorescent minerals lining the cavern walls. This light casts a blue-violet illumination along the tunnel's entire length that stretches many miles into the distance. Higher up on a ledge extended out from the cavern wall is a small cave opening where the Drens Etta and Din have their home away from their home planet of Oceana located underground on the ancient continent of Lemuria.

Colonial Transport – This Lemuria designed aircraft, shaped like an eagle's body, has slanted curved wings and a horizontal tail with feathers painted on it. However, there is no rudder, propeller, or exhaust system. It is antigravity powered by a porcelain engine with no moving parts and has extended claws for landing gear. A clear curved cockpit window is located on the upper front end of the fuselage.

Although not designed for space travel, they have special antigravity porcelain engines with no moving parts and they do not pollute the environment.

Concave Energy Shield – This violet energy shield shaped like a dish antenna, when created by one of the functions of the Master Crystal Staff used by Master Ra Mu, wards off any extraterrestrial weapon attack and then it becomes an offensive weapon.

Converted Multiple Violet Fireball Weapon – Master Ra Mu projects from the Master Crystal Staff this violet concave shaped energy shield outside Kalem's ship. It first protects the ship from a red Mazon fireball weapon shot from Sen Dar's ship. Then it begins to whirl and transforms into a much larger violet fireball that darts toward the cloud cover. It divides into two-dozen smaller fireballs that spread out over a wide area just before they enter the clouds. The fireballs blaze through the air where Sen Dar's ship had just been, before it escaped inside a closing whirling energy vortex. They instantly rejoin into one much larger fireball that races toward the fading vortex and impacts it, creating a tremendous violet light explosion.

Deep Blue Time-link Tunnel – This is an inter-dimensional energy tunnel created by one of the functions of the Emerald Doorway Crystal of The Ancient One. A radiant emerald beam forms into a whirling inter-dimensional vortex that opens to reveal Earth's distant future on the other side. Sen Dar escapes in his ship through it to avoid certain destruction.

Deep Star Cutter Class Spaceships – This fast-attack destroyer class ship, shaped the same as one of the Emerald Star Galaxy Class Cruisers of the Galactic Alliance, is only half the size. Ten years before the end of the Sen Darion War, Admiral Starland's first-born son, Rumon, perishes when his Cutter-class, fast attack medium destroyer called The Deep Star explodes after taking heavy fire from a surprise attack. It blows up after receiving heavy damage from the firepower of the Helix-Projection Beam weapon hidden on the surface of a nearby planet, as well as from the firepower of five Yalgull Destroyer class vessels that had been hiding in the planet's thick cloud cover.

Diamond Tipped Gold Wire Headset – This thin gold wire headset with a faceted diamond-like crystal on each end fits into the ear holes on each side of Etta's head. When activated, they light up and it transmits whatever Etta sees or hears back to Captain Kalem's receiver aboard his ship, so that he can monitor what is taking place around Etta.

Dren Race – This highly evolved benevolent extraterrestrial race (silica based – not carbon based like human beings) look similar to Earth's light-green salamanders but with smooth dry skin, and they are much larger with distinct differences. They have longer noses, and expressive big bulbous dark blue eyes. From the tip of their thick tails to the end of their noses, they range in size from two-and-half-feet to over four-feet-in-length. When any of them blink, a transparent set of inner eyelids closes down over their eyes just before their outer eyelids. They are telepathic and can speak with vocal cords, have photographic memories, and can levitate or fly through the air with their natural ability – developed over millions of years – to defy gravity when their tails glow from the root to the tip like crystal opal in bright sunlight.

Emerald Star Galaxy Class Cruisers – These massive starships of the Galactic Inter-dimensional Alliance of Free worlds are surrounded by pale-blue antigravity luminosity and a subtle, very low frequency, oscillating humming sound. They have a wide rectangular launch bay positioned on the upper curved surface of the front of each end of the ship. A clear observation dome one hundred feet across is located just above and behind each launch bay. City-sized crystalline structures built next to the observation domes gradually increase in height from each end of the ship until they reach their height at the central hull area.

Faceted Ruby Centered Crystal Sphere Record Log – Master Ra Mu gives this clear crystal ball device with a faceted ruby embedded in its center to General Faldwell before he is returned to his own parallel dimension. The crystal displays a holographic image of everything he experienced before his return.

Foot-long Atlantian Stun Weapon – This non-lethal weapon is used by Atlantis guards to pacify unruly prisoners brought before the High Seer. If utilized, it will incapacitate the target for ten minutes.

Galactic Alliance Laser Gun – The sleek, smoothly polished, clear crystal laser gun of the Galactic Inter-dimensional Alliance of Free Worlds has octagon-shaped green and red crystals clearly visible running up the handle and down the length of the barrel through the transparent shell.

Galactic Alliance Explorer (3) – This is one of many scientist-staffed Galactic Inter-dimensional Alliance of Free Worlds deep space exploration spaceships. The large, wide oval spaceship's hull has the symbol of a silvery spiral galaxy, above which is suspended a quartz-capped gold pyramid with three blue stars set in triangular formation above the apex. The words GALACTIC ALLIANCE EXPLORER (3) inscribed in distinct blue is directly below it. The wide oval shape of the ship is seven hundred feet long and five hundred feet wide with a slightly curved bottom hull. A dozen clear semispherical observation domes positioned around the circumference of the upper half of the ship surround a complex of luminous crystal shaped bridge control towers. A thin, pale-blue glow surrounds the ship's exterior.

Galactic Inter-dimensional Alliance of Free Worlds – Even with their differences, the DNA (the double helix of life) is almost identical for humans, Oceanans, and many other human and humanoid species that comprise the larger part of the Galactic Inter-dimensional Alliance of Free Worlds. Hundreds of millions of world systems in 144 parallel dimensions comprise this vast organization of benevolent human, humanoid, and other advanced space-faring races before the next major higher astral plane dimension is reached. They are committed to a non-interference core agreement to preserve the autonomy of the freedom loving races on many worlds, within many parallel dimensions, to choose their own destiny. However, under the right conditions, they will intervene in order to stop tyrant races from dominating and destroying evolving world systems that are not yet part of the Galactic Alliance.

Galactic Alliance Scout Interceptor – This defensive, Galactic Inter-dimensional Alliance of Free Worlds sleek disc shaped, antigravity powered spaceship, is thirty-feet-in-diameter made from a silver-blue metal. Three semispherical-shaped pods in a triangular pattern protrude downward from the curved bottom hull. When the alien craft is in flight, a pale-blue light surrounds the entire hull.

Glonden Scout Class Interceptor – Although similar in design to their parent space battleships, the V-shape of the Yalgull Scout fighters sweep back more sharply for speed and maneuverability in space and in atmospheres, and they have only one clear oval cockpit window at the front apex of the ship.

Glonden Viper Class Starships – These are heavily armored V-shaped space battleships. They look like flying wings; except, the trailing legs or wing-sections fiercely sweep back in a V-shaped design. Surrounding the bridge control areas, built inside the top front of the apex of the V-shape, are three large convexly oval shaped observation windows that arch in a gradual curve around the front of the bridge, and a short way along each trailing wing section. Centered directly between the back of the trailing V-shaped wings is a launch bay that opens facing behind the ship. Enveloping the hull of the Yalgull starships is a thin pale-red antigravity light, unlike the characteristic blue glow of the Galactic Alliance ships.

Gorn's Propeller Driven Hovercraft – The twenty-feet-long rectangular hovercraft with smooth rounded edges is made of dark-blue metal. The back half has a large horizontal propeller with ten blades spinning inside a round pivoting frame that is open on the top and bottom for free airflow. In this way, the craft can hover or fly forward at several hundred miles per hour. The propeller is located behind a curved rectangular cockpit with a clear oval window. The wings that begin on each side of the hull below the cockpit gradually sweep back and curve upward behind the propeller to end in twin ailerons that extend to sharp points along each side of a tall narrow rudder.

Gravitic Suspension Transport Cars – After a double-ended transport car that looks similar to a double-terminated quartz crystal turns on, it hovers in front of the open end of a Gravitic Suspension Transport Tube and stops. Any passengers wishing to board it step from the loading dock down inside the car, and then strap themselves into one of the two sets of seats that face each other. A six-inch-wide semispherical moonstone-colored crystal control, set in the center of the flat-topped control monolith, activates when a hand passes over it. The transparent curved hatch of the transport car then swings down and locks with a…whoosh, sealing the car airtight. The car then levitates forward into the Gravitic Suspension Transport Tube and stops after it clears the tube's open end. The tube end swings down and closes with a quick… s-s-sip... to vacuum seal the tube. Instantly, the outer circumference of the tube illuminates with a radiant blue light along its entire length and the transport car levitates up inside the tube with a foot to spare between it and the transport tube's inner wall. Both pointed ends of the car light up, changing colors from blue, to green, and to red every few seconds, right before the car darts away at tremendous speed headed for the intended destination.

Gravitic Suspension Transport Tubes – These vacuum-sealed, antigravity, round transparent transport tubes are six feet wide and many miles long as they wind their way along the ground all over the city, throughout the countryside inside the ancient domed undersea city of Oceana, and along the bottom of Earth's ancient ocean. Gravitic Suspension Transport Cars travel inside them at tremendous speed.

Guardian Master Adepts of The Ancient One – The benevolent order of Master teacher guardians that are secretly stationed on Earth, on many other world systems, and in parallel and higher dimensional realities, have been in existence for ages beyond the imagination of humankind on Earth. They do not normally interfere with the freewill choice of the people on any planet unless there is an emergency that requires their direct intervention. When the people of a world system no longer have the freewill, they think they have to create a benevolent future, and they are walking on the brink of destruction, the Guardian Adepts act to prevent it.

Helix-Projection Beam Weapon – This powerful particle beam weapon projected from a hidden location on a planet's surface, without any resistance from the atmosphere, cuts through the molecules of the hull of a targeted spaceship to tear it in half in seconds.

Hidden Planet of Oceana – This emerald-green ocean-covered world, surrounded by light pink pastel clouds, has only two large equatorial islands protruding above the surface. It is located in a slightly higher parallel physical dimension of our Milky Way Galaxy. This is the home world of the Oceanans – the most advanced humanoid, pale-blue skinned race that is telepathic, and they can breathe on land or under water. They established huge domed city colonies at the bottom of their vast ocean covered world that are connected to each other and to the domed cities on the two islands by vacuum-sealed transport tubes. Only the very tall human Seres race, not mentioned in *The Parallel Time Trilogy* books, are more highly evolved. They are not revealed in this hidden past disclosing adventure but are introduced in the hidden truth revealing 5th edition of *The Seres Agenda* book with a newly designed original cover.

High Seer Stralim's Council Chambers – The oval palace built upon the tallest hill overlooking the flower laden jungle city is still twenty feet above the apexes of two nearby quartz-capped gold pyramids. The view through the dozen open, oval windows surrounding the interior of this forty-feet-long and twenty-feet-wide oval room reveal the capitol city of Atla on the Lemuria colony continent of Atlantis. Evenly dispersed in the jungle valley, and along the surrounding hills and ridge-tops are many palatial dwellings.

HU – This is the first sound that emanated from the source behind all life (Prime Creator) that created the entire multi-dimensional universe. It is what the individual Atma or Soul travels upon to return home to attain a co-creative status with Prime Creator or the source of the primordial omnipresent living force behind all life. This first sound is often perceived or heard to be like the celestial voices of an unseen heavenly choir comprised of a thousand male and female voices sending out, on whole round tones, the oldest and most dynamic life-transforming name in the universe simply known as… HU.

Kormaljisians – Sen Dar's extinct people came from this benevolent human civilization. They are unique among all the known races that existed or that exist in or outside of the Galactic Alliance planets because they built their technically advanced homes in the branches of giant trees. Enclosed walkways interconnected together their homes built between most of the giant forest trees in an ascending manner to over a mile above the ground. Their beautiful geodesic domed dwellings made of a silver reflective plastic-like material stronger than the toughest metal include skylights, observation platforms, swimming pools, and a fiber optic light source derived from a microscopic luminous mineral in their water. Like the Dren race, the people of this world polluted nothing in their environment by working in harmony with nature.

Largest Bottlenose Male Dolphin – This very intelligent male Dolphin communicates telepathically with Mayleena when she has amnesia on the bottom of ancient Earth's Ocean, to protect her and give her a safe direction to go to reach the safety of dry land.

Lemuria – This is the continental name of the motherland of human beings on Earth. Also known as MU, this uniquely evolved culture lasted for 100,000 years before it sank beneath the ocean waves, caused when the physical and gravitational poles of planet Earth flipped over 180 degrees during the course of one night. This very advanced civilization began after the previous cyclic polar shift took place. Although the tallest mountain ranges had risen little more than seven thousand feet, each landmass extended more than halfway into the northern and southern hemispheres, and vast oceans surrounded them. The original large colony continent of Atlantis was two-thirds the size of Lemuria centered over the equator but on the opposite side of the planet. It too sank beneath the ocean waves: except for a remaining five hundred square-mile volcanic Atlantis Island.

Magnetic Blanket – When activated, this special Galactic Alliance defensive weapon instantly projects beams of violent light from the front end of each of the Galactic Alliance star ships that converge in the center of the space between enemy vessels to form a transparent sphere of light. The beams then begin to pull the sphere of light back toward the Galactic ships, expanding and enlarging it, until it completely encases all the enemy ships within a gigantic transparent sphere of light that cuts off their power.

Master Crystal Staff Record Log – This slightly curved, thin rectangular, clear quartz crystal record log, three-inches-long and an-inch-wide, magnetically locks into the exact shaped impression cutout on the side of the Master Crystal Staff. When Master Ra Mu activates the staff, the oval opening in the Ankh symbol atop it projects a radiant red energy beam into the air that forms a three-feet-wide transparent sphere four-feet above the ground. Then realistic holographic recorded historical images take shape within it.

Master Guardian Adepts of The Ancient One Records – The blue marble pillars that support the arched entryway of a bridge and along the open arches of the inside walls and curved ceiling leading to Master Ra Mu's hidden sanctuary are intricately carved with the likenesses of many former Adepts of The Ancient One. Also etched into several of the columns are the clear images of Galactic Alliance Scout Class Interceptors. Before the majestic Lemuria civilization reached its zenith and sank beneath seething ocean waves 100,000 years ago, these were the records of the Masters Guardian Adepts of The Ancient One dating back many thousands of years.

Master Nim's Teaching Sanctuary – The rustic white domed red brick building is located on planet Promintis near an oasis pond, not far from a long snowcapped mountain range. Inside, six big square green silken pillows, carefully arranged in a circular pattern on a round rug upon the blue marble tiled floor, surround another larger blue silken pillow with gold tassels hanging from the tip of each corner. They are located in the exact center of the room on the ornate circular rug woven with arcane symbols around the edges. Master Nim teaches his students while sitting on the big pillow centered in the room.

Master Opellum's Crystal Wand Device – This special device utilized by Master Opellum displays recorded past events and it can transport or camouflage any being until he wishes to reveal them. To activate it, he holds this six-inch-long, octagon faceted blue-green crystal out a foot in front of his chest. It emits a pulsing and wavering blue-green light. Then swirling particles of the gold and silver light project from the crystal to form a holographic type recorded image or to unveil something stored in its memory.

Master Ra Mu's Hidden Golden Wisdom Temple – A roaring waterfall drops under the arched apex of the white stone bridge that connects two lush, tropical foliage covered hillsides two thirds of the way toward their summit. Master Ra Mu's sanctuary is located inside the left tall hill opposite the hillside with the stone stairs leading up to the bridge. A circle of twelve, round ten-feet-high and two-feet-wide deep-blue lapis lazuli pillars, streaked with gold veins, surround the room that does not appear to support anything. Miniature two-feet square, clear quartz crystal pyramids sit atop each pillar. The four walls, many feet across at their square base, slant inward as they rise past the tops of the pillars into the darkness beyond visual range, to converge far up inside the chamber.

Matter Chain-Reactor Bomb – The imminent explosion of this planet destroying experimental device is irreversible, once Gorn orders its launch in an equally experimental rocket from his tyrant run kingdom on planet Maldec. It chain reacts with all matter and destroys the entire planet Maldec by releasing the energy of the exploding and expanding matter from the core outward.

MU – This is the coastal capital city of the continent Lemuria before it is destroyed 100,000 years ago by the cyclic 180 degree overnight polar shift of the physical and magnetic poles of planet Earth.

Norbrians – This humanoid race is from the planet Ulanim. Captain Kalem's friend, Moreau is a Norbrian with an oval-shaped face, brown eyes, a strong jaw, short curly brown hair, and dark brown skin. He is trim and firmly built like Kalem. During their training at the Academy on planet Telemadia (3), Moreau was always reminding Kalem of one appointment to keep or another. After all, Norbrians are like that. They grow up early with an innate sense of the responsible and the sensible.

Oceana – This mostly water covered world in a slightly higher parallel dimension of our Milky Way Galaxy is the home world of the Oceanan humanoid race. Only two large island landmasses extend above the vast oceans. This is also the home world of the Dren race that evolved within and lives inside huge extinct volcanic lava tubes at the bottom of the planet Oceana oceans.

Oceanan Crystalline Based Science – The programmable crystalline-based science of the Oceanan race from a higher parallel dimension of the physical universe is beyond any other known science in the galaxy. Their pure laboratory grown crystal technology actually repairs Captain Kalem's mangled dead body and brings him back to life after two Oceanan men pluck his body from the bottom of the ocean near the secret undersea domed city of Oceana. This science also powers the most advanced inter-dimensional spacecraft of the Oceanans known as Crystal Spectrum Ships.

Oceanan Crystal Spectrum Ships – They are gigantic spherical spaceships with multiple triangular spires extending from their surfaces. The dozen differently colored luminous crystal spires protrude outward to fine points from all around the spherical cobalt-blue main body of each ship. The rounded pointed ends of three of the spires that protrude downward from the bottom half of the sphere support the landed craft. This amazing spaceship can travel through space hundreds of times beyond the speed of light, into higher parallel dimensions of finer physical reality far beyond worlds like Earth and other planets in our Milky Way galaxy, and to or from Oceana – the home world of the Oceanan people.

Oceanan Race – The Oceanan humanoid extraterrestrial race look much like beautiful blue-skinned elves with slightly pointed ears. Any human being from Earth suddenly exposed to them would fall in love with them at first sight, for they emit an aura of very powerful uplifting energies. They originally evolved on a mostly water-covered world in a hidden location within a higher physical parallel dimension of our Milky Way Galaxy, far away from planet Earth. Their home world is also far from the temporary residence they inhabit in a domed city they built on the ocean floor during the time of Lemuria and Atlantis. They call their world Oceana, and they gave the foster-city at the bottom of Earth's ancient ocean the same name. The Oceanans have small webs between the fingers on their hands and between their toes for the ease of swimming, and a second set of clear eyelids to see through while under water. Three unobtrusive tiny gill slits located on each side of their necks underneath the backs of their chins open and close for breathing while under water. There is also a common ancestry going back billions of years in galactic history between human beings on Earth and other human and humanoid races like the far more advanced Oceanans. Therefore, human beings on Earth can mate with Oceanan humanoid beings.

Personal Gravitic Transport Disc – The antigravity powered metallic transport disc is an inch-thick and two-feet in diameter. When activated, the disc hovers a foot above the ground surrounded by a luminous blue aura and a one-inch circumference of the disc's outer ring lowers to the surface like a step. After the rider steps upon the disk a gravitational field firmly anchors their shoes and legs to its smooth flat surface. The inner disc then rejoins the outer ring leaving no seam and the rider than directs it with their imagination to fly through the air. When the rider wishes to stop the flight, the disc lowers to a foot above the ground and the disc's outer ring lowers to the surface like a step. Once the person steps off the disc, the disc lowers to the ground and rejoins the one-inch outer circumference ring, and then molecularly rejoins with it, leaving no seam. The disc then shuts off.

Planet Dromkal (4) – Also called Yalgull Prime, this planet is the home world and location of Emperor Garn and the humanoid Yalgull space-faring race.

Planet Earth's Cyclic Polar Shifts – Every 100,000 years, the solar system of planets containing planet Earth passes through an area of space that causes Earth's physical and gravitational poles to flip overnight. This event sinks most of the existing continental landmasses and raises from the sea floor entirely new contents like those we live on today.

Planet Kormaljis – One of the Galactic Alliance science vessels discovers this previously unknown world on the outer rim of the seventh spiral arm of the galaxy, just after a meteor storm decimates its surface. The advanced human inhabitants, Sen Dar's people, lived on this planet they called Kormaljis. General Harry Faldwell reviews the history before the destruction to discover that several slightly smaller crystal-clear deep-turquoise-blue oceans surrounded vast continental landmasses, and small polar icecaps clearly visible over each end of the planet's poles appear just three to four months out of the year. If any other space faring explorers had visited Kormaljis before the planet's demise, they would find the massive mile-high trees to be quite beyond majestic and absolutely awe inspiring.

Planet Lodrea (3) – This world is as close to perfect as any world can get; except, of course, for the people that live on its surface, for this is the home world of the cold-hearted, space-faring, Glonden humanoid race. However, anyone from Earth would instantly notice how oxygen-rich and sweet the air is to breath, and how abundantly rich this world is with vast numbers of mammalian and exotic plant life. The gorgeous violet water of their oceans, or the crimson rock plateaus overlooking it, or the year-round tropical weather with little humidity would please anyone but the Glonden people. The several large continents on the planet are literally thick with fruit trees that need no tending. Lovely huge flowers grow everywhere. Some of them are ten to twenty-feet-tall like a small tree and covered with beautiful blue-green silken petals. The Glonden people pick these flowers to gather the sweet nectar from them to make a very strong alcoholic drink they call Snorage. The animal and colorful bird life, a food source, are so abundant that the grouchy Glonden scientists are not able to keep track of them all.

Planet Maldec – The map half that Sen Dar stole from his former Master mentions that a planet called Maldec, far away in a distant solar system under Galactic Alliance protection, has the other half of the map hidden somewhere on its surface. The planet is similar to Earth but with no moons, and with slightly thicker light-blue and faint pink-tinged clouds, blue oceans, and three continental landmasses. It circled the sun of our solar system between Mars and Jupiter before a single experimental matter-disintegrating bomb exploded the planet from the core outward. It is now the asteroid belt in our solar system that circles the sun between the planets Mars and Jupiter.

Planet Mentroff – Three moons with breathable atmospheres circle this planet in the Galactic Inter-dimensional Alliance of Free Worlds. Captain Kalem and his best friend, Lieutenant Moreau, begin their first tour of duty on Mentroff as officers in the Galactic Alliance after graduating from the Academy on Telemadia (3). It is only warm on Mentroff, if you call sixty degrees warm, three months out of the year.

Planet Promintis – There is a clear blue sky over this semi-desert world with a relatively comfortable climate. It is one of the secluded training planets for the Guardian Adepts of The Ancient One, where Master Nim is head spiritual instructor. His teaching sanctuary located near an oasis pond in a rustic white domed red brick building is not far from a long snowcapped mountain range.

Planet Santinaby (5) In the Constellation of Rendgunyam – This the planet where the Sen Darion War began, started by the surprise attack by Yalgull spaceships upon an unsuspecting Galactic Alliance squadron patrolling nearby space.

Planet Seltium (4) In the Quantran System – This planet is near the border of Yalgull space. Supposedly uninhabited, it actually hides a hidden cavern base for the Glonden – Yalgull Alliance forces under Sen Dar's hypnotic control. Kalem sends Etta stealthily into the base where he discovers that Sen Dar is in fact the hidden leader of the Glonden – Yalgull Alliance forces.

Planet Sirus (6) in the Comrane Solar System – Sirus is the sixth planet of the Comrane solar system, where the Galactic Alliance detected a number of gathering enemy base ships from the Glonden – Yalgull Alliance under Sen Dar's control, preparing for a counter-attack.

Planet Telemadia (3) – This planet is where Captain Kalem spent his youth in training for eventual entrance into the Galactic Inter-dimensional Alliance of Free Worlds. Two suns are in the skies of this world. A galactic panorama of multicolored nebula, stellar dust, and another entire galaxy looms huge in the night sky, viewed from this world, located near the outer upper edge of the center of the seventh spiral arm in our Milky Way Galaxy. Future Earth astronomers call it Andromeda, but the Galactic Alliance planetary member races call it Sefaris – the distant wonder.

Polished Silver Metal Rocket – The tyrant ruler Gorn launches this sleek thirty-foot tall, polished silver-blue metal rocket from his large cylindrical laboratory up through two opened rectangular silver metal doors that curve across the ceiling. The malfunctioning rocked carrying an experimental prototype bomb, which chain-reacts with all matter, detonates causing the planet to explode from the center outward. This creates the asteroid belt that circles our sun in the orbit of a planet, which Earth scientists can see and detect.

Rectangular Silver Metallic Device – Mayleena, disguised as the blonde-haired Caucasian woman calling herself Carine, activates this for General Faldwell's benefit at the backside of Mt Shasta. She touches the tips of three of the five flush-mounted crystal controls on its top with her forefinger, and the crystals pulse repetitively with light in order from blue, to green, and to red. This opens the invisible oval cavern tunnel leading inside the mysterious Mt Shasta. She also uses it to contact Captain Kalem aboard his Scout Class Interceptor spaceship in orbit around the planet. To do this, she touches the other two crystals on its top, one violet and the other gold, and in one quick pulse, a green laser beam darts from the end of the device up into the doughnut-shaped shaped cloud surrounding the Mt Shasta summit.

Red Mazon Fireball Weapon – This is a red fireball energy projectile weapon used by both the extraterrestrial Glonden and Yalgull, and by Sen Dar's personal customized Glonden Scout class interceptor.

Secret City of Oceana – The Oceanan race that originally evolved on a mostly water-covered world located in a higher physical parallel dimension from the dimension where planet Earth exists, gave this same name to their massive clear domed city built at the bottom of our planet's ancient ocean. For a time, this is their home away from home.

Sefaris – Galactic Alliance astronomers call it the Andromeda Galaxy, the nearest galactic neighbor to our Milky Way Galaxy. However, the benevolent extraterrestrial Galactic Alliance planetary member races call it Sefaris – the distant wonder.

Sen Dar's Customized Yalgull Interceptor – This weapon upgraded charcoal-colored, disc-shaped spaceship has a tapered edge along the front of the hull that curves out wide to each side and gradually curves back inward to the smaller curved back of the hull.

The gives the ship a slightly more fierce, sleek Stingray shark wing-like appearance than the standard Yalgull Scout Class Interceptor. Three pods protruding downward under the hull are like those on Kalem's ship, but a thin red antigravity glow enshrouds the hull when it is in flight. A vertical sword superimposed in front of a red world is emblazoned centered on the top hull. Two snakes are wound around the shaft up to the handle with their heads pointed toward each other and their forked tongues touching. The tip of the blade below the red world touches the middle of an upside-down black obsidian pyramid. Its inverted pyramid apex touches the top of the star nucleus of a silvery galaxy.

Silver Flamboshual Flask of Tincari Ale – This flask contains a highly potent and flavorful alcoholic beverage prized by the Glonden and Yalgull soldiers secretly stationed on planet Seltium (4) at Sen Dar's hidden Glonden – Yalgull Alliance cavern base.

Spirit Sound Access Code Words – The Ancient One's map reveals and explains how to envision the planet or place you wish to go to, and then by utilizing a specific command code word sound the Blue Matrix Crystal of The Ancient One will transport you to the destination in a matter of seconds. In this way, certain precise sound frequencies woven into the omnipresent Spirit sound that supports and sustains all life are accessible.

The Ancient One's Cosmic Parchment Map – If the student can master the right use of the Transport Matrix Crystal by learning to properly read and apply the instructions revealed in The Ancient One's cosmic map, training then begins with the other two mystic crystals. This eventually requires training from two Master Adept teachers because only half of this special map is under the guardianship of one chosen Master Adept at a time. Sen Dar acquires half of the original map and seeks the other half. He eventually discovers the other part of the map located in a secret cavern on the planet called Maldec in ancient Earth's solar system between the planets Mars and Jupiter. Placing the two map halves side by side, triggers them to mend themselves back together through an unknown mystical process. Then the locations of the other two mystic crystals of The Ancient One are revealed, along with the Guardian Adepts who wield them. In addition, also revealed are other ways to utilize the cosmic crystal devices.

The Ancient One's Gold Pyramid Channel Device – This mystical three-feet-tall, radiant translucent gold pyramid device channels two forms of The Ancient One's (Prime Creator's) spirit voice: sound and light. This device stops to hover above Ra Mu's head after he summons it through his crystal staff. The pyramid device divides itself into one large and a dozen smaller pyramid shaped devices. The large pyramid section remains in position hovering above Ra Mu's head, and the smaller sections spin, and then instantly blur away at incredible speed in every direction up into the darkening churning clouds. They arrive at other locations around the planet and Master Ra Mu's voice emanates from them to give instructions to the people about how to survive the coming destruction of the continents of Lemuria and Atlantis.

The Ancient One's Spirit Light – This is the Light anyone can experience, usually when the physical eyes are closed, after they discover how to connect with it. It is actually one of two primary experiential aspects of the omnipresent living power or Spirit presence of The Ancient One – what advanced benevolent extraterrestrials refer to as Prime Creator. This is the source of life within the individual. It supports them and all that exists. Beautiful uplifting and enlightening light of many high color vibrations often accompanies the experience of tuning in to it with the inner sight – what is known in certain esoteric circles as the proverbial third or inner eye of the Atma or Soul.

The Ancient One's Spirit Sound – This is the Sound anyone can experience, after how to connect with it is discovered. It is actually one of two primary experiential aspects of the omnipresent living power or Spirit presence of The Ancient One – what advanced benevolent extraterrestrials refer to as Prime Creator or the source of life within us that also sustains and supports all that exists. A deep humming sound and the consistent high single note of a flute faintly playing a hauntingly beautiful melody from far away often accompanies the experience of tuning in to it with the inner hearing – what is known in certain esoteric circles as the proverbial third or inner ear of the Atma or Soul. This is one manifestation of the primordial omnipresent first sound or word behind all creation simply known as HU – sounds like the name Hugh when an individual sends it out aloud using their vocal cords to connect with it. To connect with the primordial HU, send out the HU sound with vocal cords or send it out silently through the creative imagination. Unmistakable inner sounds from parallel and higher dimensional realities in faraway places will often accompany the adventuresome explorer that connects with the HU.

The Blue Transport Matrix Crystal – When an individual utilizes this crystal, for an instant, their body is suspended in the air, before it is turned into brilliantly luminous rainbow-colored molecules to vanish with a great…swish and…an echoing boom. It transports the wearer across any distance on any world or through space to any location they imagine. By collapsing time and space between the beginning location and the destination location, the wearer can instantly travel to a location on a planet or to a location on any other planet within in the vastness of the galaxies. The Transport Matrix Crystal can only connect two points within the same physical dimension of the universe and open a brief corridor between them. It has other functions, like mind control, but they require unique sound frequencies to trigger them into operation. Sen Dar discovers how to misuse one for the mind control of others. Great disciplined training is required to properly master its overall intended use.

The Dren City of Onn – This Dren habitat located inside a large extinct tube-shaped volcanic lava flow at the bottom of planet Oceana's Ocean, runs along the seabed toward the largest island. Inside it, a gigantic air-filled volcanic cavern many miles in length and a-half-mile-high glows with a mineral lining the rock walls that lights the countryside as if normal sunlight were the source. Luminous blue-green algae that covers the ground, like closely cropped grass, adds to the illumination. Well cultivated, palm-type fronds and flowers grow along many winding paths that lead from a two-hundred-feet-high waterfall cascading out of a cave opening down to an elongated oval blue-green lake. Four-feet-in-diameter dome shaped windows curve outward from the rock walls along both sides of the falling water. Large growths of every gem crystal known, and many more unknown by the rest of the Galactic Alliance citizens, cover the volcanic rock surfaces between the windows. Near the city's outer borders, the crystals are dozens-of-feet-high and over four-feet-wide. At a higher elevation, natural deep-water springs bubble-up to feed tributary pools that run off in small streams to empty into the lake. The far end of the lake drops down a wide cavernous opening.

The Emerald Doorway Matrix Crystal – This special crystal device of The Ancient One is capable of transporting a ship and anyone inside it across time and into parallel dimensions of the physical universe. It looks exactly the same size and shape as the Transport Matrix Crystal that Sen Dar stole from Master Nim on the planet Promintis – but it is green instead of blue.

The Galactic Council – This is the central benevolent governing council that dates back to its beginning 500,000 years ago from present time on Earth. The wisest spiritually advanced individuals representing many millions of advanced space-faring world systems comprise the governing council of the entire Galactic Inter-dimensional Alliance of Free Worlds.

The Glonden Race – They are humanoid with slightly raised foreheads. Otherwise, they are not too unlike those beings on many other worlds, especially those in the Galactic Inter-dimensional Alliance of Free Worlds. Their home world is one of the most stunning and ideal natural living environments in the galaxy and yet the Glonden people are contemptuous, self-righteous, arrogant, pompous, and self-indulgent people. They developed a sheer bullheaded determination to squash flat, the slightest sign of freedom and independence they might have stumbled across during their space-faring conquering campaigns, with the one exception of the Yalgull, their most feared imperial space-faring neighboring race. Sen Dar acquires the obedience of both races through his misuse of the Blue Transport Matrix Crystal to eventually create the Glonden – Yalgull Alliance. He compels them to go to war with the Galactic Inter-dimensional Alliance of Free Worlds.

The Imperial Glonden – Yalgull Alliance – The Glonden race is humanoid but they have not always been enemies of the Galactic Alliance. However, they have an Emperor who rules over many worlds. The Yalgull group of worlds are populated by more aggressive totalitarians with a ruthless leader that had to be kept in check by Galactic Alliance space patrols for many years before the Sen Darion War began. It is this group that first begins the conflict by attacking several Galactic Alliance outposts, killing thousands of its innocent civilian occupants. A discovery a short time later reveals that the two totalitarian world systems previously secretly joined forces under Sen Dar's control.

The Law of Love – The good and bad experiences that beings receive from the repercussions of the benevolent or malevolent use of their imaginations, is the way that each individual eventually learns self-Mastery, while living in the physical universe. This is also true up through the finer dimensions above the physical worlds. However, this is not so in the fifth dimension or the true realm of the Atma or Soul. From this glorious realm of joy, and into the yet much higher pure dimensions that eventually lead to the realm of The Ancient One or what many benevolent extraterrestrial races refer to as Prime Creator, there is only one law that rules supreme over all others. It simply states, "Love and do as you will."

The Master Crystal Staff – This is the most important of the three mystic crystals given to the Master Adepts of The Ancient One so far back in galactic history that no race but the Silent Mentors know when the event took place. This cosmic device is under the guardianship of Master Ra Mu – the Adept of The Ancient One entrusted to use it only for the benefit of all life. The round transparent pure quartz crystal staff is six-foot-tall, crested with a symbol similar to the ancient Earth Egyptian Ankh – an oval with a hollow center atop a cross.

The Mythological Atlantis Known Today – When people today debate its past location, it is understandable if they believe it may have been located somewhere in the area of the Mediterranean Sea, the Indian Ocean, or perhaps near Africa or Central America. They are likely basing their belief on a glimpse they had into a lifetime they once lived at some point along the past time-track of the most ancient Atlantis continent that was destroyed 100,000 years ago at the same time that the massive Lemuria motherland continent was destroyed. Only the five-hundred-square-mile island of Atlantis survived. It is important to realize, that the physical poles of the planet were in opposite positions back then, and those past continent locations cannot be pinpointed by placing them somewhere relative to present day continental landmasses with the poles positioned as they are today. To understand where this more recent Atlantis Island was located, the individual must travel down the past time track and witness it for themselves.

The Sen Darion War – This secretly inspired Galactic War, by Sen Dar's misuse of the mind control function of the Transport Matrix Crystal, gives him control over two advanced tyrant space-faring races. He makes them join forces, and then directs the first attack of the Yalgull forces on several civilian Galactic Alliance outposts. A later surprise attack kills Admiral Starland's elder-son, Rumon. Sen Dar's entire Imperial Glonden – Yalgull Alliance is defeated after ten years near the planet Santinaby (6) by Admiral Starland's use of the advanced Magnetic Blanket weapon. It cuts off power to the Glonden – Yalgull Alliance fleet ships. Sen Dar escapes capture before the battle ends.

The Three Mystic Crystals of The Ancient One – These three special tools were given to certain Master Adepts in ancient Galactic history, so they could properly train chosen students in the right use of love, wisdom, and power or charity. Special guardians protect them because the longer that anyone possesses a mystic crystal of The Ancient One, the greater is the increase of occult powers that awakens within them. Therefore, it is important to put the three crystals together in a special way – a method given to only a properly trained and prepared student. When this is done, the student goes through a mystical experience to become enlightened when they personally meet with The Ancient One or the source behind all that exists – located in the highest pure dimensional realm, very far beyond the lower worlds of creation. The student then becomes a God-conscious co-creator with the source behind all life, and then a Master Adept of The Ancient One in their own right.

The Quantran System – This is a star system located near the borders of the Yalgull dominated world territories. Planet Seltium (4) is located in this star system. This is where Sen Dar hid his secret base to prepare for a Glonden – Yalgull Alliance counter-attack against the Galactic Alliance.

Trans-light Speed – This very advanced extraterrestrial technology allows spaceships to leap by entire star systems in what are called multiple trans-light jumps. It is one of the byproducts experienced when using antigravity propulsion systems. Although one cannot calculate this in terms of speed, it means that a space ship utilizing this function can leap through naturally occurring vortexes or openings in space, normally invisible to human perception, that link parallel dimensions together. The ship then travels for a short time in the space of a parallel dimension before it pops out of another invisible opening back into its own parallel dimension. In this way, the occupants discover they travel a great distance across the galaxy in a short time.

True Atma or Soul Energy Spheres – This is the true self of all individual beings – what many benevolent extraterrestrial races refer to as the Atma or what the human inhabitants of planet Earth often refer to as the Soul. Like The Ancient One but much smaller in size, the Atma is made of spherical light energy that extends in ever widening concentric spherical levels. Each layer, from a white core through the spectrum to a violet exterior is comprised of many luminous teardrop-shaped lights. A subtle blue-violet hue softly radiating between the layers culminates in the blue-violet exterior layer, surrounded by a pale-golden aura.

Yalgull Scout Class Fighter – The Yalgull saucer shaped Scout class fighter has a trailing edge extending gracefully outward around both sides of the front of the hull that gradually slants slightly downward and then upward again as it curves around the back half of the ship. This gives it the overall appearance of a disc shaped ship with stingray shark curved wing-like hull extensions. Three semispherical pods, positioned in a triangular pattern on the bottom hull, are similar to Galactic Alliance Scout class fighters.

Yalgull Star Class Battle Cruisers – The Yalgull starships are more elongated oval shaped than Galactic Alliance starships but they curve similarly under the hull. The bridge control towers of these large Yalgull starships, which gradually increase in height toward the center of the upper middle section of the ships, have large rectangular observation windows centered along all four of their sides. However, the structures are not crystalline in appearance like those of the Galactic Alliance ships but conventional triangular, rectangular, and spherical shapes with many windows mostly concentrated in the central third of the upper deck. There are no clear semispherical observation domes on each end of these starships.

Yalgull Silver Handgun Weapons – These are sleek, silver energy weapons used by Yalgull guards that protect Emperor Garn of the Yalgull race in the command center of his home planet.

The Yalgull Race – Long ago in galactic history, the Yalgull humanoid race developed from the same DNA source as human beings. However, they evolved with the faintest hint of a violet hue that appears to emanate from their ivory-white skin. Sen Dar acquires the willing obedience of this race by misusing the Blue Transport Matrix Crystal. He eventually creates the Glonden – Yalgull Alliance and commands them to go to war with the Galactic Inter-dimensional Alliance of Free Worlds. This Sen Dar concludes is his destiny and necessary because the Yalgull are worse totalitarians than the Glonden he gained control over previously and less forgiving.

Under The Snorage – Huge lovely flowers grew everywhere on the Glonden planet Lodrea (3). Some of them are ten to twenty feet tall like a small tree and covered with beautiful blue-green silken petals. The Glonden people pick these flowers to gather the sweet nectar from them to make a very strong alcoholic drink called Snorage. If they are not busy dominating other weaker people by taking over their worlds in wild space-faring warfare campaigns, they are all often "Under the Snorage" as the old Glonden phrase goes. When that happens, they get up days later with huge hangovers.

Yelfim – On the Lemurian colony continent of Atlantis, High Seer Stralim tells the young woman washed ashore (Mayleena), who awakens with amnesia, that the Atlantians call the sea creature she inquired about that saved her life Yelfim. He also states they have been known to save human lives in trouble in the ocean for thousands of years – (known today as the large Bottlenose Dolphin). Mayleena's self-defense mechanism subconsciously projects in the minds of Stralim and his guards the image of a blond Caucasian women to disguise her true Oceanan features.

About the Author

Photo by: Jungle Jim (Behrens)

After over forty years of extensive experiential research, R. Scott Lemriel has finally put forth his second book, *The Emerald Doorway (Three Mystic Crystals)* – the first book of *The Parallel Time Trilogy*. The three-part episodic story is fictional but entirely based upon the author's direct experience exploring the past time track for the last four decades. His experiential research uncovered a vast depth of deliberately hidden truth regarding a significant aspect of the true history of planet Earth and our solar system, and the benevolent and malevolent extraterrestrial beings that have, in one way or another, directly influenced the condition of our world and the direction it is headed today. These journeys revealed a treasure far beyond any expectations. Written prior to *The Seres Agenda*, all three book manuscripts of the trilogy were created for the purpose of sharing the experiential benefits of this unique uplifting life transforming adventure with his current and future readers right here on planet Earth.

Lemriel was originally inspired to write *The Emerald Doorway (Three Mystic Crystals)* – experiential truth-based adventure and *The Seres Agenda* hidden truth revealing book he first published, to provide the inspiration and techniques for the readers to have their own direct experiences with awakening deliberately hidden truth. Many awareness-expanding events occurred during his childhood and throughout his adult lifetime that enabled him to bring these books to the public awareness. They involved a series of experiences mostly with benevolent UFO phenomena events, extraterrestrial technology and the kind spiritually advanced beings that wield it, journeys via out-of-body travel into the parallel and higher dimensional realities, as well as numerous excursions along the past time track. These adventures eventually revealed a hidden history of Earth and our solar system that subsequently helped to confirm the depth of suppressed truth he was uncovering in his own life. In addition, the music compositions and productions he developed throughout his life from his early twenties continue to kindle the fire which drives his ongoing explorations into knowing ever deeper hidden truth by direct experience – in contrast to believing or theorizing.

Today, his continuing journeys into the vast nature of the multi-dimensional universe and his unique uplifting music continue to serve as an inner channel of inspiration to further explore and awaken ever so much more about our true nature as knowing eternal beings.

Lemriel is genuinely passionate about sharing eye-opening enlightening experiences and unusual encounters he gratefully received while uncovering cleverly hidden truth. For the first time, he discloses how our planet is about to be unexpectedly, benevolently transformed in the near future instead of destroyed because of a recent off-world decision that was finally made concerning changing Earth's current destructive destiny. He takes the reader on their own personal journey to discover the reality of the existence of UFOs or advanced alien spacecraft, extraterrestrials both benevolent and malevolent who fly them, the nature of our true spherical energy form – what people on Earth call the Soul or the non-destructible energy form that people from other worlds call Atma, and the reality of the existence of parallel and higher dimensions. He further reveals to his readers what he discovered about a most important part of planet Earth's missing ancient history, and discloses how he experienced much about the depth of purposefully hidden truth from the guidance of masterful teachers the majority of human beings dwelling on earth today do not know existed at any time.

He gratefully acknowledges his mother for being the first person to read and experience the revealing depth of the transforming, truth-revealing pages that these books represent. She discovered, greatly surprised, much about her son she never knew or even imagined, because he kept silent about his uplifting life transforming experiences – until now.

Originally, from Salt Lake City, Utah, where Lemriel spent the first six years of his life, he devotes a lot of his time to writing about his continuing explorations into uncovering deliberately hidden truth. He does this through ongoing out-of-body journeys and direct experiential explorations into the UFO and extraterrestrial phenomena with the great majority of kind beings that live in our vast multi-dimensional universe. He has a passion for writing books and screenplays, musical compositions, and has an ongoing dedication to bring into reality very special feature film and episodic TV story projects. This, coupled with a series of awakening lifetime events, provide him with the rare opportunity to serve as a co-creative conduit of the uplifting life transforming, omnipresent living energy that supports and sustains all that exists.

The changing destiny for grand new life-transforming adventures to be experienced is now opening up in a very definite protected manner for human beings worldwide, including the book reading public.

For your experiential benefit, explore the free YouTube.com videos of the author's personal presentations he conducts at International UFO/Extraterrestrial hidden truth disclosure conferences held around the world. If you wish, watch several promotional videos about *The Seres Agenda* and *The Parallel Time Trilogy*, as well as listen to many radio-show interviews with Lemriel inside his unique uplifting, eye-opening website at: www.ParallelTime.com. You can explore various overviews of his feature film projects and listen to his feature film related music productions. Discover two uplifting recordings of his voice sending out the very special vibratory word... HU... (HU-U-U-U... that sounds like the name Hugh sent out on the outgoing breath), that can safely connect each individual to the pure source behind and supporting all that exists.

All four of his interconnected websites are located at:
www.ParallelTime.com
www.TotalSpectrumPublishing.com
www.TotalSpectrumProductions.com &
www.TotalSpectrumMedia.com

It is a wondrous adventure to experience the recovery or awakening of deliberately hidden truth on a grand cosmic multi-dimensional scale, and discover the much greater knowing of the vast love within it. The books, videos, radio interviews, music productions, and website links are also accessible through a search on Google by title, the author's official Washington, D.C. Library of Congress copyright pseudonym R. Scott Lemriel or his legal name R. Scott Rochek. Links to the websites are also on Facebook, LinkedIn, and Twitter.